To Magg

Shine so brightly that all the other stars in the sky wish they were you ♡

Love,

Tracey :)

PRAISE FOR
MOTORCYCLES MOOSE & MAGIC

More than a memoir – these pages are as exhilarating to tear through as an open road, filled with glorious sights, devastating wreckage, and outrageous characters – all set to a solid soundtrack and the comforting purr of a motorcycle engine. Felt like I was riding in the side car. A story about running away and finding home in your own skin.
Dan MacDonald, Radio Personality, AM 800 CKLW

You'll gasp. You'll laugh. You'll cry. You'll write in the margins and you'll share quotes with your friends. Motorcycles, Moose & Magic: The Ride to Self-Love is Tracey's gift to us, to love, to the truth that is the brilliant transformation of the self.
Vanessa Shields, Author of *thimbles* and *Look At Her*

In Motorcycles, Moose and Magic: The Ride To Self Love, Tracey Rogers shares her nearly half century life journey, a journey that is at times gut-wrenching, but mostly heart-soaring. She has compressed her decades of living, learning, failing, growing, and ever-evolving into a refreshing 12-step (day) program of self-reflection. A must read for everyone needing hope and direction in their personal journey to self love.
Joe McParland, Biz X Magazine

What an amazing journey of self-discovery, filled with so many "Awe" moments that read like a Spiritual GPS.
Conni Ma'iingan, Urban Ndn Connection

Motorcycles, Moose & Magic: The Ride to Self Love, lived and written by an inspiring and powerful woman who rose from trauma and addiction to overcome life's obstacles, fulfilling achievements through determination, healing, and positive choices to inspire others that your past does not define your future – happiness with peace is possible.
Lisa Valente, uPMedia

A story so real it will reach every emotion. From the highest of highs to the lowest of lows. You are brought through a rollercoaster of emotion. Tracey Rogers is as real as it gets. Inspiring is the one word that comes to mind when I think of her.
Brandon Bailey, Founder WASUN, and VP CAPUD

To lose yourself in the story of another is to find balance in a spinning bundle of thread. My curious, fearless, street smartish inner child followed Tracey, in and out of rabbit holes. With a mouth full of too much chocolate, with knees bloody and scraped from constantly tripping over my own feet; climbing trees to find the ground, I wrapped myself in a blankie of real living as I treaded the waves of a life lived the human way.
Teajai Travis, Artist

MOTORCYCLES MOOSE & MAGIC

THE RIDE TO SELF LOVE

MOTORCYCLES MOOSE & MAGIC

THE RIDE TO SELF LOVE

TRACEY ROGERS

Never has there been

a greater love story,

than the story of learning how

to fall in love with you.

White Feather Holistic Arts
1350 Ottawa Street
Windsor ON CANADA
www.WhiteFeatherArts.com

ISBN : 978-1-927591-22-2

Cover Design: Tracey Rogers

Book Design: Walkerville Publishing Inc.
walkerville.com

Printed in Canada

Mum
this book is for you.

My number one fan forever.

And for you, dear reader,
I invite you to load the Spotify music list:

MOTORCYCLES, MOOSE & MAGIC.

Allow the music that inspired me
on my journey, to inspire you as you read.

INTRODUCTION

DREAM ON

I'm bent over the handlebars of a Ninja crotch rocket, flying down the road, the scenery a blur. I feel powerful and free. I can taste it, I can smell it, it surges through my entire soul. This is the most incredible feeling I've ever had in my life. Then I wake up. I am 15 years old. I am not powerful. I am not free. I am not in control of my life.

This is my story about the power of dreams.

I have never forgotten that dream. I've craved the feelings it raged in me, and I've chased after it in all the wrong places. Feeling powerful always eluded me. Until I changed.

Power isn't about what you wield over someone else. True power, personal empowerment, is the level of ownership you take in your own life. It's the realization that you write your own story; you create your own magic, and you manifest the best life you can with the cards you've been dealt.

Personal power is about healing the things in your life that were traumatic or difficult, so that the triggers of that pain are no longer writing the story for you, no longer dictating your choices and creating more pain, more chaos, more trauma.

I can pinpoint the exact moment when I began coming into my personal power – when the last of my triggers were healed and personal empowerment became a reality in my life. Within a few weeks of that moment, I purchased my first motorcycle in November of 2017.

It wasn't an easy journey, nor a short one, but was it worth it? Hell, yes! I've been on a road that's taken me from being addicted, homeless, struggling with severe PTSD, depression, anxiety, and losing my mind to being successfully self-employed, happy, fulfilled, in a healthy relationship and loving life.

My story isn't just about recovery from alcohol and drugs because addiction was merely a symptom of a bigger problem – my deep self loathing. My journey was (and is) about learning to love myself and my story – the whole story, not just the parts that are shiny and pretty.

I've learned to embrace all parts of myself, and to have compassion for what I found within, at every stage of my life. I understand now how the horrible choices I made along my path became my coping mechanisms. I have taught myself how to have compassion for the girl and the woman who didn't have better tools. I have taken ownership of the healing of my past, of healing my triggers, and discovering the emotions that sat underneath all of my worst decisions. I've learned how to make better decisions from a place of healing – from a place of empowerment.

In September of 2019, I participated in the Women Riders World Relay – the largest motorcycle relay in history. I rode by myself for eight days on a meandering ride from Windsor, Ontario, Canada up to Thunder Bay, Ontario, Canada where I met up with a group of strong, courageous kick-ass women.

From Thunder Bay, I rode for three days as part of the relay. During that incredible time, I met dozens more amazing warriors on motorcycles. However, the motorcycle trip became much more than being a warrior in the WRWR – I found freedom in the ride. The time I spent by myself on my motorcycle became a golden opportunity for me to reflect on everything that had happened in my life. I reflected on what I'd overcome, and how incredibly awesome it was that I was able to do a journey like this on my own.

Each day on my trip is represented as a 'part' in my story. Within each part, I bring you back into my life – back to the places where I was broken, back to the places where I started to heal. Come take a bike ride with me and we'll take the adventure of a lifetime together. Every woman on the Women Riders World Relay has her own story, this is mine.

Though my thighs weren't hugging a crotch-rocket, they were wrapped around my beautiful 'Stella," a Honda VTX 1300T, flying down the road, the scenery a blur. I felt powerful and free. I could taste it, I could smell it. I could feel my power and my freedom surging through my entire soul. I was living the most incredible dream I'd ever had.

DAY 1 – SEPTEMBER 11TH, 2019

THE JOURNEY BEGINS

My bike was packed and ready to go. I was nervous and excited all at once. My tummy was full of butterflies, not of dread, but of joy. I was doing something that I knew in my bones was going to be amazing and life changing, something full of opportunity and risk. I'd been waiting months for this day to arrive.

This trip wasn't the same as going on a charity ride or taking a journey together for a week with my husband. This was all me – riding alone with no one to rescue me if something didn't go right. Previously, my longest solo journey was one full day. This journey I was beginning was drastically different! I would be doing eight days of solo riding, followed by three days of riding with the relay, and then the ride for one day with friends to get back to Windsor.

No matter what the weather, no matter how long the days would be, I was determined to make this journey happen, and make the best of every moment. I had been preparing in my mind for this trip for months. As soon as the routes for each day had been released, I plotted out my own trip up north, booking my rooms for each night, and considered what precious gear would go in my bags. I say precious because there isn't room for any kind of 'extra' on a bike – I could only pack what was absolutely necessary. Regardless of whether it got really cold or really wet or really hot, I had to be prepared for all weather and bring what was needed accordingly. Each t-shirt and long-sleeved shirt was chosen with great care. Every day's outfit would make a statement about me, my bike, and my attitude.

I was feeling brave and courageous, and my t-shirt for day one matched my determination. I was wearing my West Coast Trail t-shirt. That was a well-earned t-shirt. It had cost me blood, sweat and tears to find it and purchase it.

* * *

Back in 2015, close to Christmas, over supper one night, my friend Jess asked me if I wanted to 'do' the West Coast Trail with her and some friends the following summer. She knew I would be in British Columbia visiting my dad, and that's where the trail was. I had no idea what the West Coast Trail was! I said, "Sure, why not!" Why not, indeed.

It turned out that the WCT was rated as one of Canada's most difficult hiking trails (still is!), and it advised that novice hikers should not attempt to hike it. I was a novice hiker.

I found this information after dinner that night when I searched it on the internet. But, I didn't give the trail too much thought until a few weeks before the hike when it was time to collect my gear and pack my backpack.

Having no idea what I'd need for the trip, I took the advice of my friend Jess and some of her friends who were joining us for the hike. Jess had never done a trail quite like this either, and both of us could have packed better for it and been more prepared. Things like hiking poles, lighter weight gear and less of everything would have been awesome. But we learned quickly on the trail, and we'd never make those same mistakes again.

Our first day on the trail as six of us headed out, it was pouring rain. I was praying that the river we had to cross was too flooded, so we'd have to stop and go home. But no, passable it was, and cross it we did. Setting up camp in the never-ending rain, I felt exhausted and exhilarated at the same time. I couldn't believe I was doing this! It was still pouring rain on day two. I continued to pray that we wouldn't be able to get through the next river of water we needed to cross. But again, we crossed it. We were up to our hips in rushing waters that felt like they were going to barrel us over. I remember being terrified crossing the rivers. I only had one hiking stick to balance me, my gear was 45-pounds by this point due to all of the rain, the rocks were slippery like eels under my boots, and I thought if I fell, I'd get swept away in the rushing waters.

I trudged through water up to my knees at many points. I climbed ladders. I scurried under fallen trees. I adeptly balanced myself on logs as we crossed over large chasms. I cried. I bitched. I sang. I laughed. I hated it and I loved it all at the same time.

One of my favourite moments on the trip was quickly followed by a waking nightmare. We had just stopped at Chez Monique's. Picture this, because I never would have believed it if I hadn't seen it with my own eyes. We were out in the middle of nowhere. We'd taken a 6-hour shuttle ride down logging roads to reach this isolated place. There was no way in or out except by hiking, boating, being lifted by a helicopter or taking the 6-hour ride back.

The reason the West Coast Trail was originally re-discovered, was to help rescue stranded shipwreck survivors along the coast – otherwise it would have been a week's worth of impassable countryside. I say re-discovered, because the local First Nations people had created and used this trail for hundreds of years to travel between villages, long before Europeans had arrived. So, we were hiking that morning, day four, when I saw a campfire and a few large white tents up ahead. Someone exclaimed, "Chez Monique's!"

Out there, in about as inaccessible a spot as one could choose, a woman named Monique had set up a little restaurant with tents. For twenty-five dollars, you could buy a real hamburger – a real, bona fide, amazing, delicious hamburger! After four days of trail food, this was beyond a treat – it was a delicacy. I've had people say to me, "Twenty-five dollars?! That's crazy!" But was it? People will pay for 'unique' at restaurants. People will pay for the atmosphere, they'll pay for the service – this was a super unique opportunity on the trail! I had never been to a more unique establishment, set in a more awe-inspiring atmosphere, served by one of the most beautiful people I'd ever met – Monique. I chose the veggie burger, which was divine, and I also grabbed a bag of sour jube-jubes for a treat along the trail.

Monique has since transitioned from this world but let me share with you a bit about this one-of-a-kind woman. Over the years she had to fight for her right to stay on the land with her makeshift tents set up to help hikers along the trail. I am told the park respected her right to be there, but not necessarily the surrounding government. And how did she win that battle every time? Monique, according to an online hiking article, was a First Nations woman. The Ditidaht tribe owns the land. Their land, their decision. Much of the land rights story I could not verify, though I found bits and pieces about it on the internet since I met her in 2016. What I can tell you is that of all the people I encountered on the trail, including myself and our group, no one belonged there more than Monique. She was part of the trail, part of the spirit of the trail. Back in her series of tents, not only did she have food, but she had bins of donated items from hikers passing through that would get recycled and used by other hikers who would end up needing them. Any extra food, gear, clothing or anything else our crew had, we left there, knowing it would benefit other hikers. Monique had the ability to bring out the generosity in people.

I wanted to stay all day and chat with Monique, but we left after an hour-and-a-half of wonderful time spent with her. Our moments in heaven with Monique quickly shifted into something hellish. Forty-five minutes later, when an Air Force helicopter landed to pick up our friend and hiking companion who had fallen 30 feet onto rock, I hoped with all of my heart that Jess would say, "Let's go home now," but she didn't.

What I witnessed was traumatic. We had been attempting to cross over a river in a cable car that was set up for that purpose. Two people could fit in the car at once and the rest of the group would push or pull the cables. Crystal and I went across first, sent the car back over to the others. We were just starting to pull the next two across when Crystal got pulled by the cable and went tumbling off the platform we were standing on. As she screamed for help from the rocks below, in a panic, I hurriedly searched for the path down to the water's edge. When I arrived, others were wading across the river to help, including our most experienced first aid responder, who arrived at the scene at the same time as myself. Crystal was sprawled on the beach, which wasn't sand, but large, rigid rocks. I looked up in horror at the cable car platform she had fallen from – it was a good three stories or thirty feet above us.

Nearby hikers set off an epirb (an emergency beacon that called all emergency services in the surrounding area). Another person in our group ran back to the lighthouse to find a park ranger. I brushed sand off her face and I gently washed the blood that was flowing out of a large cut. Normally, I nearly faint at the sight of blood – I'd be the last person you'd want near you in an emergency – but due to the seriousness of what was happening, I kicked into high gear and did everything I was told to do by people who knew what to do.

While Crystal was inspected, one of the helpers from Chez Monique arrived with a sleeping bag to put over Crystal and asked if we needed anything else. It was relayed to us that Monique had offered for all of us to stay in her cabin that night if we needed. My heart was bursting with love and respect for that woman. Monique's purpose wasn't merely to offer $25 burgers. Her purpose was so much higher than a commercial undertaking. Halfway through the trail she was there to offer sanctuary, assistance, and hints and pointers for how to succeed at finishing the trail. Before there was a trail, the First Nations inhabitants would have been the only people in that area who could possibly find and help shipwrecked sailors. And here was Monique, still doing that, hundreds of years later. Her sleeping bag was laid over Crystal to help keep her warm while we waited for more help. It brought me warmth and comfort too.

Our team found no spinal injury, but Crystal was in excruciating pain, so we didn't move her an inch. The evac helicopter the Air Force sent was massive – all of us could have easily fit in it. We watched as it landed, the air, sand and noise rushed all around us as it settled onto the rocks. The emergency crew could find no sign of spinal injury either, but they took no chances, and gently shifted Crystal onto a spinal board.

One of our team was allowed to go on the helicopter with her for the ride to Victoria, British Columbia. Everyone else opted to walk back to the ranger's station and take a boat ride back to civilization and the hospital. Jess was determined to continue the hike – this was on her bucket list, and we only had a few days left to complete it. Since Jess was the only reason I was there, I allowed her to make that decision for us. There was nothing more we could do to help Crystal, and all signs pointed to her being extremely sore, but miraculously 'okay'. Inside I was screaming, "For the love of god, let's go home! Someone almost died!" But on the outside, I put on a brave look and said, "Ok, let's do this".

For those wondering, it did turn out that Crystal had no serious injuries. She received staples for her head gash and physio for her leg which luckily hadn't broken.

The morning after the accident, Jess and I set out at a grossly early hour. Our tent and gear were packed and ready to go by 5am. Neither of us had been in charge of the tidal charts, and we weren't confident about how to read them correctly. Tidal charts let you know what time the tides go in and out and at what time each day. Tides vary every day of the year. Some of our hike was down by the water, but it was also higher up in the woods, depending on what the tides were doing. Getting caught on the beach when the tide was rising could cause disasters. Crystal had been in charge of the tides for our group of six. She was the one who had paid closest attention during the tidal training with Parks Canada before our trek. But, Crystal was away and healing from her fall.

The night before, after the horrific accident, I had prayed to god to send help for Jess and I. I prayed for large strapping young men to help us across the water with the next cable cars, and through to the end of the hike. I'd take anything god could offer to help us complete the trail! Amazingly, right after finding an eagle feather and seeing two eagles staring right at us, the help I prayed for arrived. There was a group ahead of us on the trail. Screaming and whistling as loud as I could, the people up ahead stopped and one of them waited for us. It was Richard! We had talked with Richard and his family every day on our journey, including during the six-hour shuttle ride to the park. At camping areas each night and sometimes during the day on the hike, we would bump into them and share stories.

After telling him about the accident the day before, and how we were now a group of two instead of six, Richard didn't miss a beat – he calmly asked us if we'd like to travel with himself and his family. We agreed with joy to hike with them!

With Richard as our trusty guide, Jess and I finished the WCT. The whole time we were with Richard and his family, we were treated as family. It was a relief and a blessing to have finished the trail with them.

In total, we trudged through six days of rain. We experienced six days of aching muscles, six days of challenging terrain, six days of laughter and tears. I never would have done it if someone had told me how incredibly hard it would be. I was so glad I did it, though. It wasn't graceful. I could have complained less. My knees and I were a weak link. But I didn't give up, and I didn't give in. I finished it. In tears.

I had a history of not finishing things I started. It was because of Jess that I finished that trail – she inspired me to keep going. And without Richard and his family, I'm not sure how the final few days would have gone. I was ready to quit, but Jess kept moving us forward. The West Coast Trail was the physical embodiment of the healing journey I'd been on for the previous ten years.

During those ten years, the Universe had placed many key people in my path – like Jess, like Richard – who kept pushing me forward. At times, the path seemed impossible, impassable even, but a log would get tossed down by the heavens, and my healing would move forward. Something inside of me, or something inside of the Universe, was determined to help me finish a critical task – the task of learning to love myself.

* * *

The weather was beautiful, and sunny with blue skies. It was warm enough that I wouldn't need my leather jacket or my chaps - though for safety, wearing a leather jacket while riding was always recommended. I had mixed feelings about not riding with my jacket on in the heat. Part of me thought it was a ridiculously bad idea to just wear a t-shirt and jeans on my bike, but another part of me absolutely loved the feeling of the wind over my whole body engaged in the freedom of no constrictive leather.

One of the mottos in my healed life was No Fear. And I lived that – I didn't just speak it. I had been terrified for too long. When I looked back on those times, I recognized that I always kept moving forward. This momentum was always inside of me. There was something healing about hopping on my motorcycle without a jacket on, and letting the Universe know that I wasn't afraid of the risk. I was also aware that taking risks stemmed from my time spent in hell. I lost my fear of death during the worst of my experiences. I almost became friends with it.

I opted for my leather vest. It wasn't a full jacket, but it was enough to protect my chest, keep me cool, and satiate my No Fear motto. The vest was sparsely decorated with a few patches I accumulated in my motorcycle career – a Port Dover Friday the 13th patch, a Hogs for Hospice patch, a memorial patch for my friend's brother, Tyler Knight, a Run to the North Wall (an event to honour veterans) patch, and right in the middle of the back of my vest were the patches I took pride in the most: my Canadian Motorcycle Cruisers (CMC) Madison patch and the Women Riders World Relay patch.

I could wear the WRWR patch because I had participated in the Ripple Relays back in June, a few months before. The WRWR had both a main relay (around the world) and Ripple Relays. The ripples were to allow people to ride closer to home and bring the relay into many of the smaller communities and cities throughout each province. The main relay plowed across the country as quickly as it could over a ten-day stretch.

In June, I had ridden up to Tobermory to meet Kelly, a friend from my club. We rode back through Sarnia to Windsor for a ripple relay. That had been my longest solo ride to date – that one day ride up to Tobermory. I was super proud of myself for doing that. Not because women don't do solo rides but because I hadn't ever done a solo ride. It made me think about how far I'd come with my self-confidence and my ability to do what I wanted to do without comparing myself to others.

Years ago, I gave up comparing my journey to the journey of other women. If I had been comparing, I would have felt small and unaccomplished beside Kelly. Kelly rode by herself up to Terrace Bay to collect the WRWR Canada Coin (the baton for the Ripple Relay), and then stayed with the relay for just under two weeks to make sure that the coin got to Quebec. Her trip was an amazing adventure, and something for her to be proud of.

My one-day trip to Tobermory was a fantastic experience, and it was something for me to be proud of, especially since I was only in my second season of riding. My journey and your journey are not the same, nor are they comparable because we started at different places.

My husband wished me a safe journey and kissed me good-bye. As I rolled out of the driveway, I turned my Blue Tooth ear buds on. The first song on my playlist was AC/DC's Back in Black. As the music began to play, a deep self reflection was triggered, and would continue for the rest of my journey. As songs blasted or whispered in my ears, they made direct connections with stories in my past. AC/DC's Back in Black was an anthem for me in my rebuilt life, but it also triggered a memory about things when they were already falling apart.

* * *

I was 18 years-old and in a limo with five of my friends headed to see AC/DC. It was my first big stadium concert ever. We were flying down the 401 highway, high as kites on acid and drinking our faces off in the back of the black stretch limo. The highway ride was a riot! We laughed, feeling like Kings and Queens riding in luxury! Bottles littered the back of the limo – vodka, whiskey, beer, and god only knew what else.

Monty, our driver, stone cold sober, opened the door and the harsh light from outside shone in; a light that my LSD-blitzed mind couldn't handle. I wanted to yank the door away from him and close it. I looked at my friends and asked, "Do we really want to go? It's more fun in the limo!" We all agreed it was a riot in the limo but had paid a lot of money for this concert experience. Into the stadium we went – leaving Monty to deal with the disaster in the vehicle.

The concert was horrible. Not because AC/DC was horrible, but because we had such bad seats in the stadium. I don't know if they've changed it since then, but we were in the top seats near the roof, and the echo was so bad we couldn't even make out what songs were playing. It wasn't the drugs, it was the stadium. We managed to have fun anyway and smoked a hell of a lot of joints while trying to decipher what song was being performed. Angus Young was a madman on stage, and we didn't need the music to be entertained by his actions and antics.

Afterwards, we stumbled back to our limo which Monty had parked right at the stadium exit for us. He opened the door to reveal a spotless interior. I felt horrible.

Oh, poor Monty! As we thanked him and apologized, he explained he was happy to clean up, he had nothing better to do for three hours while he waited for us. The party didn't stop. We kept drinking, we kept toking, and we were pumped up from the show. Eventually Monty had us all back in London, safe and sound. I had a blast that night!

I had no understanding of the personal responsibility I had taken on only a few months before when I turned eighteen. I had begun to feel responsible for my own life, my own choices, and my decisions at age eighteen. I had known that at that age adulthood would begin. Though our parents can hold a certain level of responsibility for us until we hit adulthood, no matter how ill-fitted we are to begin being responsible for our own choices at eighteen, the fact remains that we are – even the law says so. That night's choices set the stage for what was to come – acid, pot, hash, alcohol, and a never-ending party.

* * *

Why do I consider Back in Black to be an anthem for my rebuilt life? My life had been a train wreck for years. I spent more than a decade trying to fix it. Thirteen years after the blackest black part of my life, I am fully back, confident, wearing black, and riding my motorcycle. I too let loose, from a noose. That noose had been mental health issues deeply entangled with addiction. I write deeply entangled because the mental health issues disappeared at the same time as my active addiction. My addictions were coping mechanisms for my mental struggles that I had no tools to handle. This wasn't a case of which came first, the chicken or the egg. I know which came first – the mental health issues. Those issues snowballed into catastrophes when my addictions snowballed into worse addictions. There was a direct correlation between my mental health, my addiction, and my self hatred.

* * *

I didn't realize until just after rolling out the driveway, AC/DC blaring in my ears, that September 11th was the anniversary of the day I decided to start making changes in my life. On September 11th, thirteen years prior, I had walked away from everything I knew, everything that felt comfortable – even in its dysfunction – and declared, "There's got to be a different way! I can't do this anymore." I knew for sure what I didn't want, but I had no idea what I did want. Knowing what I didn't want would get me one step closer to what would make me happy, but I had to be willing to walk (or run) away.

It made me smile when I realized my epic bike ride was starting on my anniversary. It made me smile from ear-to-ear, in my heart and right down to my toes. Thirteen years it took to get to this momentous place. I was a disaster the day I began changing my life – look at me now! Loving life. I sent a thank you to the Universe.

* * *

I'd been on the road for a while. It was such a beautiful drive, and it was getting more enjoyable once I passed Leamington because that was where the heavy traffic ended. On the other side of Leamington was Lake Erie and tonnes of open majestic road. Farmhouses dotted the landscape as well as huge ancient trees, corn fields, and wineries. Eagles were often present for the attentive eye.

I decided I would not take any major highways, but instead take small back-road-style highways on my solo journey. I found nothing interesting about riding my bike down Highway 401 or any vehicle for that matter. It was flat, uneventful, and boring regarding anything exciting to look at. Also, it allowed for much higher speed limits, which for me, resulted in higher blood pressure.

Maybe not all riders found this particular highway stressful, but I did. I chose to drive according to my own comfort. I wouldn't go on larger highways unless I had a pressing reason to. Had I chosen to take the fastest route to Thunder Bay, I could have completed my journey in two very long days or three more manageable days. My choice was to take the backroads and take my sweet time. I would arrive in Thunder Bay on day eight of my overall ride. I decided against taking the route through the United States. I wasn't taking the most direct Canadian route either. I chose the 'I'm-on-my-own-road-trip-and-I'm-in-no-rush-to-get-there' route.

I decided my first stop would be to visit my brother Bob in Port Dover because I hadn't seen him or his partner since Christmas, and it was kinda sorta on the way. Highway 3, a more rural highway, would take me a good portion of the way there.

I had my tunes on. Adventure of a Lifetime by Coldplay was playing in my ears as I came up to the amber light in Shedden. I made a spur-of-the-moment decision to turn left instead of continuing to Port Dover. This turn took me onto Union Road which was the way to the farmhouse I lived in from age eight to fifteen. I'm not sure what compelled me to turn left there, I'd driven by it on the 401 a million times.

As I was cruising towards the farm, I remembered all the times I had ridden my bicycle down the road. How my older sister Michelle and I would hop on our bikes and ride to the variety store in Shedden to spend all or most of our allowance money on candy and chocolate. Black balls, Gobstoppers, sour gum, chocolate chunks, licorice, Nerds, and whatever other candy was currently in season, we'd jammed into our bags and into our cheeks. Our bicycle ride had been about 5km each way to the variety store, but it had been a great way to kill a few hours on the farm.

I also felt a sadness flowing in – nearly nothing in the neighbourhood was the same as it was during my childhood. I felt relief when I looked closely, I could see markers – things that had been left untouched. I saw a farmhouse or a building that hadn't changed, but so much else had. The little white church which had stood for years at the corner of Union Road and our road, Road 3, was no longer there. The gravel was gone from our road, and it was now paved. For my motorcycle's sake,

I was grateful for this upgrade. A bit down the road I spotted McNiven's place. Jack McNiven had been a partner in my Dad's business – an accountant's partnership. Jack was no more a farmer than my father was.

Almost right across the road from them was the Beharrell farm. Jan and Ralph had owned that farm and still did. During my youth, I would play with their son Brad sometimes, but not too often. Brad was always working on the farm, ploughing, harvesting or working with the cattle. Brad had only been a year older than me, but to my child's eyes, his life resembled that of an adult more than a kid.

I didn't recall ever riding bicycles with him. I did have some memories of us playing in the barns – either his or ours. Brad had been a master at making super cool hay bale forts. In his own barn, he had made a kick ass hay fort that was quite large, so large, we could walk right into it. One memory that always stuck with me was when I went into his fort one day and he pulled out some hay to reveal a secret hidey-hole. In it was a little metal box. In this box were trinkets and small toys – a ten-year-old boy's treasure trove worth hiding. That treasure box was one of the few things that showed me he did have things a child would have.

I rode my motorcycle past their farm. Just across the way on the right was our old farmhouse. My intention was to maybe stop and take a picture from the road. Our house had a huge laneway, probably 150 meters long, and it kept the farm semi-private from the world. I didn't plan to pull into the driveway, but as I approached, I saw a man with a weed wacker standing near a truck, who then began tending to the lawn at the end of the laneway. Fate was offering its hand to me. I pulled into the driveway, shut off my bike, and after a few pleasantries, he told me that his daughter owned the place. Explaining that I had grown up in this house, he graciously invited me down the lane for a tour.

The first thing I noticed, with sadness, was that all the beautiful old sugar maple trees were gone. It was like a piece of my childhood had been cut away, erased.

I remembered when my Dad had gotten it in his head that he wanted to make maple syrup. I had no idea where he got the equipment, but he had found old taps and old buckets. Every Spring we'd tap each tree down the long driveway and around the house. I had loathed having to collect the sap in huge paint buckets – they were heavy, and we didn't have a cart for moving them. Each tin pail that had been attached to a tree would have to get emptied into the paint bucket twice a day then hauled up behind the house to where Dad had hung a huge pot, almost like a witch's cauldron, that he'd attached to a tree with a heavy steel chain.

Under the massive pot was a blackened old oil barrel that had the top cut out, and a square on the side cut out that was used for inserting wood and keeping a red-hot fire going. Sap had been poured in, and over a period of weeks, it would boil down to a thick syrup. After weeks of exhausting work, we'd had our own maple syrup! As a kid who had been raised in a city for the first eight years of her life, I had found making maple syrup fascinating and amazing – though exhausting! It was incredible that our maple syrup hadn't come from the grocery store, it had come from our own trees!

Many things were different now. The property wasn't just missing maple trees. The lawn was reduced and more farmland created. Two rickety old sheds along with a massive barn and silo – all gone. We had played for hours and hours in that barn – running along the thick wooden beams, playing hide and seek, sliding down the hay shoot. Where they had stood was now farmland. When I was a child, my Dad had made a skating rink every year on the lawn between the house and the sheds; even the lawn had been reduced by half. There was nowhere to put a skating rink now.

I was shocked to see the huge oak front doors with red stained glass and a half moon glass above them were entirely gone. What madman had replaced the doors? When I was a kid, they were 120 years-old, and the glass was the original glass with warps, bubbles and all. They had been a showpiece to anyone who had visited the farm.

I asked Dan, the man who was showing me around, what happened to the doors. He said he wasn't sure who had taken them out, but he had found them in the new metal garage/shed that was now on the property. He told me he was considering reinstalling them. All I could think in my head was, "Oh, for the love of everything that's holy, please do!" I noticed that I was taking it very personally that such a beautiful piece of my childhood home had been removed.

Something I did like about the home improvements was that they were installing a huge, wrap-around porch – it added something beautiful and charming to the house. I visualized how much more character the original oak doors would lend to the porch too. Maybe when the porch was complete, Dan would realize that the doors needed to go back in!

As we stepped inside the house, I was astonished to see that the kitchen counter and the cupboards were the exact same ones my parents had installed back in 1980. My amazement wasn't lost on Dan when I told him how the kitchen hadn't changed at all. I opened the cupboard where my sister Sarah had almost split herself in half when she had been swinging the door between her feet while sitting on the counter. She had slipped and landed right on the open cupboard door.

Dan laughed and said he had just fixed that cupboard because it didn't hang right, as if something had fallen on it and dislodged the hinge. Can you imagine if my sister's fall was the reason it hadn't been hanging properly for the past 37 years!? I believed it was. The thought gave me comfort that parts of my family were still very much attached to this house.

The laundry room was virtually the same. The family room had different floors. The living room looked almost identical to how it was in my childhood – right down to the beautiful wood flooring and fireplace. I didn't ask to go upstairs as I knew bedrooms were a place of privacy. There was no need to see my old bedroom. It still had massive bay windows that I could see from the outside of the house, and in my heart, I will remember it as if nothing changed. I imagined it still had the rose-coloured wallpaper and beige shag carpet. That it was my room. My safe space. My retreat.

We did stop at the bottom of the staircase which I was happy to see still had its original oak. Dad had done a lot of work to restore it properly and make it safe. It was beautiful then and still was. In the small foyer at the foot of the steps should also have been the old oak front doors. I closed my eyes and pictured the red stained glass. I could hear the laughter of children – Michelle and I – as we flew down the stairs in sleeping bags, crashing into the wall and oak doors. Tears welled in my eyes as I stood in the old house. I quickly wiped my eyes before Dan noticed.

* * *

I miss the simplicity of childhood sometimes. I miss not worrying about money and bills. I miss having not a care in the world. I miss playing with my sisters every day. Family is so very important, and yet, somehow, it gets put on the back burner too often. I love my family. And I miss riding the tractor and cutting the lawn and feeding the cows and collecting eggs from the barn and being bored out of my tree on rainy days.

None of us will be alive forever, but when we go half a year or even a year without seeing each other, we tend to act like nothing has changed when we finally meet. But things do change. And walking through this house reminded me that some things change very slowly or hardly at all, while other things, POOF, one day they are just gone, like they never existed. This location, this house, this farmland was physical proof of my childhood – and to come back as an adult and sweep through the land and indoor spaces, memories were triggered. And loss and joy were measured both by what remained and what was gone.

* * *

After taking a tour of some more of the outside property, it was time to go. I took enough of this man's time, and I wanted to stop and see Brad Beharrell, (my neighbour when I was a kid) if he was home. According to Dan, Brad owned all the farmland now and had also taken over his aunt's farm just down the road. Thanking my host, I hopped on my motorcycle and slowly drove down the gravel drive leaving a trail of dust behind me. I didn't look back.

Slowing the motorcycle down, I took a quick peek to my right where our creek still ran, and our forest still stood – perhaps not as dense as it once had been, but it was still there. In my heart, the forest will forever belong to me and my sisters.

As a child, I loved that forest. I spent endless hours there. I would light little fires in the ravine and pretend I was out in the wild, surviving on what I could hunt, fish and forage – although I didn't hunt, fish, or forage because Mum packed me a lunch.

I remember one day I had planted a flag I made in a tree and declared the land 'Terabithia'; a make-believe kingdom I had read about in a book. There were many times I'd hunt with my father in the forest. He'd be carrying the shotgun. I'd be carrying the 22 rifle. He'd try to catch game while I'd try to scare it away before he could shoot it.

As I pulled up in front of Brad's house, I could hear a child laughing from inside, and another came peeking out from the garage. This beautiful little girl stood looking at me, curious as to who this stranger was that had ridden up on a motorcycle. After a few moments, Brad appeared.

"Hi Brad! Remember me? Tracey Rogers!" I said.

Brad smiled, said hello and that of course he remembered me. We stood out front and caught up with each other. He knew a bit about my life because his mom and dad had come to my Mum's funeral a few years previous. I had been so happy to see Jan and Ralph there. They hadn't spoken to my Mum in years, and yet they had the decency to remember an old friend at her funeral. Ralph and Jan always had great character and solid morals. I was happy to hear about Brad's young family and his marriage.

Somewhere in our conversation, we got talking about family ancestry and I mentioned Scotland. Brad then mentioned that his family, the MacIntosh's, extended back to Moy Hall in Scotland. What?! I stopped him right there! My god! I was so excited when he said that! My business in Windsor, White Feather Holistic Arts, stood between the roads Moy and Hall. They had gotten those names because back in the 1700s, at the end of the roads down by the river was Moy Hall, a trading post named after the original Moy Hall in Scotland.

Apparently, the business owner of the hall had been one of the sons from that estate in Scotland. My husband and I had just gone to Scotland in 2018, and we had made a special point of seeing Moy Hall. I felt such a strong connection to this place in my heart, my soul, and my spirit. My Mum had traced our family ancestry, person-by-person, back to the late 1300s in Scotland, and I just knew in my soul that we had a connection to Moy Hall. I tried my best to explain some of this to Brad.

I had no idea if Brad would understand what I was about to say, but I said it anyways. I told him that I believed that we carried karma from our ancestors; that if my great-great-great-great grandfather did his great-great-great-great grandfather a favour, that this would carry good karma forward to us, their ancestors.

Brad seemed to understand because his reply was, "And if my great-great-great-great- grandfather screwed your great great-great-great-grandfather over in some way, we'd have bad or difficult karma now, as their ancestors?" Right! Exactly! We enjoyed the far-reaching ancestral and karmic relations.

My spirituality and my understanding of the Universe was an important part of my healed self. It brought meaning to a world that otherwise seemed chaotic and random. It brought me peace in my heart to have beliefs about how things were ordered. I doubt I would have gotten to where I was that day, on my healing path, without having created a strong relationship with the divine Universe.

I believed our family karma was good – Brad's and mine – because Brad's family had been a saving grace to ours. My father was an accountant by trade but he lived on and needed to work the farm. When my Dad had no clue what he was doing on the farm, he would talk to Ralph, and Ralph would rescue him.

When Brad and I talked about that, I told him, "God bless your father for helping mine. He must have been sick of hearing from us."

"Nope. Your Dad was an endless source of laughter for us. We got a kick out of the things he would get up to on the farm!" Brad replied.

That made me smile from ear-to-ear. Ralph had never seemed like he begrudged helping my Dad get out of his farming messes. I have nothing but fond memories of Ralph, Jan and Brad. And somewhere back there in history, perhaps at Moy Hall, some awesome karma must have been passed along between Jan's family and my own because Ralph and Jan had been angels here on earth sent to help my sorry, city-slicker family.

As I was saddling up on my bike, Brad's daughter handed me a daisy. I leaned over and explained to her that white daisies were my favourite flower! It was true, I wasn't just saying that. Daisies always had and always would be my favourite flower. I loved their simplicity. In my eyes, they were the perfect flower.

I tucked the daisy into my luggage so that it would stay preserved for the rest of the day. I waved to Brad and his daughter as I drove down the driveway, choking back the tears the daisy had pushed up. They were tears of happiness.

I've learned that the world changes when you change the way you look at the world. Once upon a time, that gift would have been cute, but it wouldn't have caused tears. The gift wasn't just the flower. The gift was also in the gesture of the beautiful little girl wanting to give a gift to a new friend. The gift was also in a happy memory.

* * *

I remembered a day during my healing journey that was particularly horrible. When I say horrible, I mean I was depressed and sad; I missed my family and I felt like I wanted to give up. I had turned on my computer to check whatever social media I had signed myself up on. While the computer was booting up, I'd said out loud, "God, please give me something, anything, to hold onto here. I'm not sure how much longer I can do this."

The site had loaded. I had logged on. From a total stranger, there on my page had been an image of a huge yellow smiley face with arms offering me a daisy. I'd felt like god had given me a daisy! I had asked for something, anything, and voila, there it was, the gift (albeit digital!) of my favourite flower. It was what I had needed to carry on that day. My tears had been replaced with a smile. My heart had been filled with gratitude. Ever since that day, the face of god looked like a yellow smiley face in my mind. So when Brad's daughter handed me a daisy, all I could feel and see was god giving me my favourite flower.

SCHOOL DAYS

Back on the road, I wasn't using my GPS. Instead, I was relying on my memories of riding school buses and traveling with my Dad in his truck to navigate. Without having to think twice about how to get there, I found myself in front of my old public school – Southwold. Since I was taking this trip down memory lane, I figured I might as well do a full sweep and stop at the elementary school too! I hadn't seen it in years. It looked virtually the same, except a large fence had been erected to keep the children away from the highway.

After parking my bike in front, I went in the entrance I knew would be closest to the office. Dressed in my motorcycle boots, elastic bands keeping my hair back in a ponytail, I looked like I had just gotten off a bike and I knew it. Immediately, I went to the front desk so that no one would think I was trying to sneak in. Asking if anyone was there to show an old student around, I was told the vice principal would arrive in a few minutes to give me a tour. She called me an 'alumna'. Wow! An alumna! I hadn't thought of it that way, but she was right.

While waiting, I peered down the hallways. They looked the same, only smaller. I could remember exactly where my grade three class had been, way down at the end – I could see it from where I stood. We moved in February of my third-grade year. Mrs. Manager had been my first teacher at Southwold.

I can recall it being a frustrating year for me. I had gotten exceptionally high marks in all my classes at my old school in London, and my parents hadn't brought my report cards to my new school for the teachers to gauge where I was in my studies. I recall Mrs. Manager asking me "Which reader are you reading, which level?"

I was eight. I had no idea! All I could tell her was the name of the books. She had no idea what they were when I told her, so she put me into the middle reading group. I had been bored out of my tree for the rest of the school year. I wasn't an average reader – I had been reading books meant for students in upper primary grades, and even some beyond that. It wasn't until grade six that my academic accomplishments had begun to reach their full potential again.

A young, smiling woman approached me in the hallway. She was not what I expected at all. My vice principal had been a short, stout little man by the name of Mr. Axel who was of the generation that believed students should get the strap if a situation was severe enough. I had a hard time picturing this woman with a strap. She would be my tour guide.

The first room she showed me was just behind us which would have been the old library but was now a primary gym. As a child who had read hundreds of books and loved nothing but receiving books for Christmas and birthdays, it made me sad to see the library replaced by a gym. She assured me that the library had been moved to another part of the school. I assumed it must be much larger now.

We moved along to the main gym where I had spent endless hours practising with and playing games with the volleyball and basketball teams. It looked almost the same. The big Cougar emblem still hung on the wall. It took me deeper back into my days of blue and gold.

When we found the library, I was sad to see that it was in what used to be a few classrooms. Not only was it not larger than the old library, it was noticeably smaller. Were kids not reading books anymore? My bookbag had always been full of treasures from the library, taking as many out as the librarian would allow me to, and devouring all of them! The fact that my old elementary school library was replaced by a gym was very symbolic regarding my own current shift away from libraries. Over the years, my interests fell far more into the realm of experiencing things, doing things, and much less in the realm of reading about things. Somewhere along the way I had stopped reading things for knowledge and pleasure. It was an interesting discovery to make in the library from my youth.

The new library was in the same classroom that my grade seven class had been. Mr. Monteith had been my teacher. That year, I had been in the enriched class for gifted students. I had been told by my teacher that my IQ was 142. I don't believe they were supposed to tell me, but I had been proud of myself when I heard that. My grades the previous year had been straight As (except in art and cursive). I had been in the band and on all the sports teams. I had won the speech contest for my entire grade. Life had been awesome!

The enriched grade seven class had a total of eight students. We'd been put in with a grade eight class as a split. Once a week, the eight of us had been able to leave our regular class and do enriched studies with Mrs. Snowsell, who taught the enriched studies. I had been in my glory! I had been a member of a group of kids who were extremely bright and had the opportunity to be challenged intellectually.

I loved that we'd worked on matrices and things that were out of my comfort zone. I loved that we'd done extra projects and extracurricular work that went beyond spelling, math, science and geography. Something that stood out in my memories was a project we'd done that year. We had been allowed to do a project on absolutely any topic we'd wanted. I had liked this unique opportunity to have the ability to choose any topic I wanted. I had chosen to do my project on 'Human Attraction'.

At the time, there had been nothing particularly profound about that project to me, but looking back on it as an adult, it occurred to me that everything about it was profound! I'd spent the greater portion of my life not understanding exactly what it was that I'd been attracted to. Certainly not recognizing that most often what I'd been attracted to was disaster, and situations that would bring me down, not up. I had been attracted to anything that could reinforce my self loathing. If it involved self sabotage, you could count me in.

Ironically, it would be the events that started to snowball in grade seven that would trigger my attraction to self-destruction and chaos. At the time of working on that project, I had healthy self-esteem and a healthy outlook on life. I was certain I was never going to do drugs. I aspired to be an English teacher and had been carrying that dream in my heart since grade two. I had loved school. I had loved sports. I had loved music and being in the band. I had loved reading. I had loved being my Dad's little helper on the farm. All the elements of my life were shining. Life was awesome, as I mentioned.

What I could never have predicted was the bomb that was about to drop; the destruction of which would change everything.

CUE EXPLOSION. In the middle of grade seven, I had come home from a friend's house after a weekend sleepover. (It still feels like it was yesterday.) As soon as I had charged in the front door, things were different. Usually when I'd charge in the front door, boisterously letting everyone know I was home, there'd be some type of acknowledgment. But not that day. Silence had greeted me like wind out of my sails.

The look on my sister Michelle's face when she popped in the room had been sadness. Had someone died while I was gone? Anxiety had quickly crept up through my belly into my chest. I'd known when something wasn't right, and something wasn't right. Everyone was supposed to have greeted me at the door and been happy to see me. They should have been there asking about my weekend. But that hadn't happened. A dark cloud had descended over my happiness, filling me with dread, right there in the middle of our kitchen.

Michelle had followed me down to the cellar when I was asked to go put some wood in the furnace.

"I think Mom and Dad are getting a divorce," she'd said with as much gentleness as an older sister who was perpetually annoyed with her younger sister could. "Dad didn't come home on the weekend. He was with another woman."

What? I had felt like a Mack truck had plowed into my stomach. Part of me had wanted to cry, but I didn't know why. Part of me had wanted to go yell at my father. I had felt anger growing inside of me, starting down in my toes and creeping up through my legs and my torso, until it reached my skull creating a deafening scream. An inside scream I had not released. My sister's words had been impossible to my ears. My parents had never fought. There had been no visible or outward indications that anything between them was wrong.

I hadn't understood, but I'd tried to look like I did. I was 12 years old. I was old enough to handle grown-up stuff, I'd told myself. So, I'd played the role and acted like a grown-up. I'd nodded my head to my sister. That had been enough for that moment. But after that, I'd just been completely confused. And I hadn't wanted to talk about it. So what? My parents were getting divorced. I can deal with this I'd said to my jumbled insides. I am smart. I am mature. I'd heard the words echo in my head. Everyone had told me so. So, I'd acted mature, and I didn't let anyone know how confused and scared I had been.

Before that poignant moment in time, I didn't remember pushing my emotions down like I'd done that evening. I don't recall any memories where I'd been hurt and hadn't cried about it. To the best of my recollection that event had been the first time I'd kept my feelings inside. I'd made the choice to act that way because I did not understand the new feelings I'd had.

If I got benched in a basketball game or after falling and skinning my knee or if my sister made fun of me – I could identify having these emotional hurts. But my family breaking up? I hadn't had the words for what I was feeling because I'd never felt anything like how I'd been feeling. I'd felt afraid but couldn't put my finger on what I was afraid of. I'd just known that something wasn't right, that things weren't good, and I absolutely had not wanted to talk about any of it.

The following months created memories that I'd never be happy to recall. I remember my mother desperately trying to get my father to fall back in love with her. I remember her drinking more than usual. I remember phone calls between my mother and my father's girlfriend (Yvonne), when my mother would call her horrible names – words I had never heard before, except when they'd been whispered in the schoolyard between giggles. I have memories of my mother, drunk, trying to trick my father into the bedroom with her – she wanted to prove she could be 'a good wife'. I remember witnessing screaming, yelling and silence. All of this was my introduction to the 'real world.'

My mom gradually grew to accept her new reality and moved us all back to London, Ontario, not far from where we had lived before we'd moved to the farm. Back I went to the school I had left in grade three – Westmount Public School. But nothing had been the same.

I hadn't wanted to be friends with my old best friend. I had no interest in being known as a 'browner'. I had wanted to be cool. But I'd also been aware that I didn't 'fit in' from the moment I returned. I hadn't known how to be anything other than who I was becoming, and I hadn't recognized that person either.

I didn't see it then, but I could see it now – there'd been a great big, angry chip on my shoulder. And I'd missed my Dad, horribly. I had been Daddy's girl for years – I had bonded wonderfully with my father after about age six, and considerably less so with my mother. Dad and I had done everything together – he'd driven me to all my games, to band practice. I'd helped him every moment I could on the farm, always by his side. We'd been a team and I'd been desperately missing my teammate.

When I'd visited him every other weekend on the farm, nothing had been the same there either. He had a new team, and I wasn't a part of it. In the spring of that same year (I was still 12 years old), another major bomb dropped on my life. Its impact set off a chain reaction of wreckage even bigger than my parents' divorce.

In London, I'd been in my neighbour Dennis' backyard telling jokes to him and one of his male friends. Dennis had been close to retirement age; his friend Don was a co-worker at Ford, and twenty-years his junior. Before my parents divorced, I'd tell jokes with my Dad and his friends for hours. Dad could never remember jokes, so I had been the one to remember them for him. As soon as he and his friends had a beer or two, Dad would laugh and ask me to tell his friends some jokes. I'd go on for hours; Dad and his friends laughing, me grinning from ear to ear, happy to be the center of attention. Dennis wasn't one of my Dad's friends, nor was Don. It never dawned on me that it wasn't a safe space for a twelve-year-old girl. Telling jokes in Dennis's backyard reminded me of the feeling of home. It reminded me of my Dad.

Don had given me some of his beer that afternoon while the three of us were telling jokes. As Don and I were leaving the backyard at supper time, he'd asked me to meet him later that evening for a beer behind the townhouses. I'd known his intentions were not good, but I went anyway.

I remembered him kissing me roughly and how surprised I'd been by his rough whiskers. I had only ever kissed one boy, and he'd been my own age. Being kissed by this man with beer on his breath had been something entirely different. I had not felt comfortable. I had instantly regretted going to see him, but I'd found myself walking across the road with him and heading out back by the woods. He'd tried to get me to give him oral sex, but I had no idea what I was doing or what he was doing, so he ended up jacking off into my mouth.

I had no words for this experience, for my confusion, for my shame, for my self-loathing. I had no way of understanding what had happened. I'd just known it was bad. That I was bad. If my parents found out, I'd be in trouble. His actions had silenced my voice.

The chip on my shoulder grew bigger, and I'd started to build the wall that would keep me from showing my true self for years. I couldn't let anyone see me, not the real me. The real me was a bad person.

I'd moved back to the farm to live with my dad when grade seven was over. That had been within six months of having moved to London with Mum. Mum had been devastated by my choice to move. She couldn't understand why I was breaking up the family. She loved me. How could I do this? But I did it. I'd wanted out of London. I'd wanted to be away from Don. I'd wanted my father back. I'd wanted things to be the way they used to be, with or without my Mum and sisters.

* * *

I didn't get along well with my stepmom, and I blamed her for it. I look back on it now, from a healed place, and I recognize that it wasn't anyone's fault. She didn't know how to navigate being a stepmom and I didn't know how to navigate being a stepchild – neither of us had done anything like that before. Neither of us did or said the right things. Both of us said some harmful, hurtful things when we were angry or disappointed.

There were also times when we each made efforts to make things better, but they never got better, they only got worse. I found out years later that her and my Dad believed that I had made every effort to break up their relationship. I honestly don't recall having that thought in my mind – I do recall wishing I could be friends with my Dad again. I recall wishing we could spend more one-on-one time together. But I don't recall wanting to break up their relationship. I just wanted my friendship back with my Dad.

I'm sure on some subconscious level I had been trying to destroy their relationship. I had no self-awareness at that time in my life. I was angry. It was a difficult situation for everyone. And this new relationship and new family drove a wedge between my father and I.

* * *

When things had been falling apart in the house with my Dad and Yvonne, they'd been even worse back in London. Don, the 42-year-old man who had molested me once already, had approached me again during one of my weekends with Mum. It had only been a few months since the first encounter, and he'd progressed to having sex with me. I'd been thirteen at this point because I remember he'd asked me if I'd had my period yet. I'd told him yes I had gotten it on my 13th birthday. He'd let me know that he'd had a vasectomy so I couldn't get pregnant. I hadn't even known what that meant; I had to look it up when I went home. That particular encounter had occurred outdoors near the same area where the first assault had taken place. After that, there had been a few encounters in his home when it was empty of other people.

There had been parts of the abuse that felt physically good – I'd experienced my own sexual arousal. This had caused more feelings of shame, guilt and personal responsibility for the abuse that was happening to me. The belief I'd had that I was bad had deeply rooted. As I'd felt worse and worse about myself, I'd acted out more and more. I'd been arguing with both of my parents. I'd been talking back, and the main message I'd been receiving from everyone around me was: "You're a bad person."

My marks were falling. I'd had to drop out of the band because I'd been told to choose between sports or music. I'd had a bad attitude on my sports teams and my coaches had noted this. Everything had been going wrong. My whole world had been whipped upside down, and I had no idea how to navigate it. Where had the straight-A kid who'd loved to help out gone? Where had the girl who'd loved being a 'part of' everything, who'd tell jokes, who'd loved to ride her bike disappeared to? I had not been able to find her. I had not cried. I had not expressed my pain. I had buried it all deeply inside, and grew angrier and angrier, feeling more ashamed and more guilty. And I'd hated the person I was becoming.

During the times I'd spent with Don, I'd learned that he had been raised in the residential school system. When I'd asked him about it, he'd refused to say more. Even at my young age, I'd known that attending a residential school had been bad – that his childhood must have been horrible.

At age thirteen-and-a-half, in the spring or early summer of the following year, I'd begun to understand that things had to stop between myself and Don. Up to that time, there had been four or five incidents of abuse. One night, I'd been playing hide-and-seek with neighbourhood kids. A kid had told me Don was looking for me and he had a knife. My heart had pounded in fear. I knew he had a mean streak – he'd been physically abusing his stepson for years, and everyone in the neighbourhood knew it.

I'd managed to avoid him the last few visits to my Mum's. I'd known the abuse wasn't right. I'd known it had to stop. I'd known it was wrong. I'd told my friend that Don had tried to kiss me. Shocked, she'd told me that I had to tell my mother. We'd told her together. Mum went into mama-bear mode; angry, protective, wanting to hurt someone. Immediately she called the cops. When the cops had shown up to interview me, my Mum had sat right beside me.

I vividly remember wishing that she'd just leave the room or that the cops would ask her to leave so they could interview me alone, but that hadn't happened. There had been no way in hell I'd tell the whole story of what had been happening to the police with my mom in the room. I'd just said that he had kissed me and grabbed my ass the previous year, and that he had been stalking me recently, trying to get me to hang out with him. It hadn't been a complete lie – but it hadn't been close to the whole truth either.

* * *

The abuse by Don was the very first domino to fall triggering my downward spiral into darkness. I'd be lying if I said it doesn't make me sad to look back on this time. What if it had never happened? What direction would my life have taken? Would it have been the same – filled with self-hatred and addiction – or would I have stayed on my course, loving learning, sports and music? I never stay long in the land of What If because it can't coexist with What Is.

Reality is What Is. I can't go back and change the past, but I can change the way I look at it. Every single thing I have overcome in my life has taught me a way to assist another person with overcoming the same thing(s). I didn't become a fighter, persistent and unwilling to ever give up because things were easy. Difficult moments shaped me. What happened when I was twelve and thirteen shaped me. The truth I've discovered is that the deeper the pain inflicted, the deeper the forgiveness that has to be reached. If I'm looking for the blessings hidden in the darkness – the silver lining – this discovery about pain and its relationship with forgiveness is a major blessing.

If I could go back and change my history, would I? Absolutely not. Because I wouldn't be the me who is writing this book, having this adventure, living this life. I like me. I like my life. Everything has value, especially pain, if we put it in perspective.

Never regret your past. You don't have to love it. You don't even have to like it. Learn from it. Grow from it. Find knowledge and understanding in it. Deepen your ability to forgive – not just others – but most importantly, yourself. Turn your pain into your greatest teacher. Shape your pain into the thing that makes you amazing. Drag your skeletons out of the closet, dress them up, and dance with them. These are some of the ways I used my past life choices to shift my soul, spirit, mind and body into the woman I am today. They are integral parts of my journey that I'm sharing with you.

Understanding where I've been and what happened to me is important if I want to fully understand where things went wrong, and how they were able to right themselves again. My self-destruction didn't happen in a vacuum. There were critical moments that birthed my self-hatred. That self-hatred was the foundation for my addictions and my destructive life choices. In owning those adult decisions and bad choices, I also acknowledge and have compassion for the little girl who got hurt and learned a profoundly unhealthy set of coping mechanisms in order to survive.

* * *

Motorcycle beneath me, I left the school satisfied with my visit and happy with the trip back into the past, seeing the old classrooms and finding out what changed. (What was fascinating, however, was that while I was visiting these places, none of the dark memories about my past were in my mind; it was only in writing that I resurrected what happened.).

My headphones were singing Stressed Out by Twenty One Pilots. Every time I listened to the lyrics of this song, it made me think of the joys of childhood as compared to the responsibilities of adulthood. My adult life had been stressful for a long time – full of student debt, addiction, jobs I couldn't stand, depression; a whole big heap of unhappiness and negativity. But I discovered something – there was a way out.

I chose to walk the difficult path that the Universe lit up for me. It wasn't what I wanted to do, but I eventually got to a spot where doing the same thing(s) just wasn't an option anymore. The craziness got too crazy. The pain started bubbling at the surface, refusing to stay hidden inside any longer. I finally got to the place I just couldn't stand it any longer. I just couldn't stand myself any longer. I just couldn't keep the rage inside any longer. I couldn't keep pretending I was ok. In that moment I shouted to the heavens: "I give. Please help me!" A chorus of angels sang and the Universe smiled. That was the day my Tower card fell – the day I walked out and closed the door on the life I'd known.

* * *

There's a card in Tarot called The Tower. People often cringe when they see it come up in a reading. The Tower card represents a time when things will fall apart and crumble to the ground so that we can rebuild on a firmer foundation. For some, it can represent losing a job, ending a marriage or destroying some other significant aspect of their lives. For others, it can represent losing everything. When I'm doing a reading for someone and this card falls, I like to remind them that although it will be difficult to go through the falling apart that is happening or about to happen, things are always better on the other side of The Tower – as long as they don't build on the same ground again. "You'll wish it happened sooner," I tell them. No pain, no gain. That's one of the Tower card mottos.

The Tower Card
Rider-Waite Tarot deck

* * *

My tummy was grumbling as I bopped to the tunes while I was riding my bike. I was still in St.Thomas but getting close to Port Stanley. I only had a grapefruit for breakfast. It was time to stop to eat. To my right, I saw a sign for the Sunset Café. Perfect! I pulled over and into the parking lot. As I opened the doors, I saw a 'Help Wanted' sign. I stood for some time in the entrance to observe the café. Yes indeed, help was wanted here!

There was only one woman serving the entire restaurant, working the cash register, and seating the folks like me who were hungry. After waiting for a while then finally getting a seat, I sat down and opened my phone to message my husband. He wanted to know that I had made it to my next stop so that he wouldn't worry while I was on the road.

Sitting there waiting for my food, a song came on the radio that I couldn't believe wasn't on my playlist on my phone! Dobie Gray's Drift Away. When I first discovered this song years ago, I had loved it immediately. Then, it had been a song that sat comfortably in my heart and my soul for no particular reason. At the very beginning of my healing journey in September of 2006, it became something more.

Things had gotten bad, dreadfully bad. It had only been a few weeks since I had walked away from my crumbled Tower when the song had come on during an outdoor concert. As I listened to it, a whisper in my heart had said, "Yes, drift away. Far away Tracey. You need to be away from this place...from the familiar...from the old story." But I had no idea where I was supposed to go. I had no money, no job and I wasn't in any condition to get a job. I was not well – my spirit had been broken by a prolonged psychotic episode.

During those first few weeks away from my old life, I had drifted into the no-man's-land between psychosis and PTSD. My psychosis had included dark conspiracies, imagined terrors and tales from the abyss - the abyss of addiction. I can look back on it from a healed place and see how my psychosis had been rooted in reality, things that had actually happened that were too much for me to bear, but they slipped into the unreal, and that had taken its toll on me. Prolonged terror can cause PTSD, even if the terror is imagined – and especially if the terror is connected to an unstable reality. My reality had been more than unstable. I had been drowning in chemical drugs, heavy pot use, and making dangerous, stressful choices. The temporary psychotic episode I had experienced had been planted in a garden perfectly fertilized for turning the temporary into a long drawn out nightmare.

Swaying there, alone, at the concert, I had an epiphany that my brain could not attach any action to. Because of the way I had been living, I had no tools to know how to stop the choices I had been making. And so, my terrors had taken control of my ability to heal. Yet, the words of the song had worked some sort of karmic magic that would keep me connected to the idea of 'drifting away'. Hearing that message had brought a feeling of peace. It had felt right; like there could be a solution to my problems. Part of me had been ready to drift away, all I had needed was somewhere to drift to and a way to get there.

CRYSTAL CLEAR

My sandwich arrived and I hungrily ate it as I spoke to my husband on the phone. I mentioned that I wanted to find a dollar store so I could grab a notebook to journal in about my motorcycle adventure. When I got off the phone, the lady beside me apologetically mentioned that, though she wasn't trying to eavesdrop, she overheard I was looking for a dollar store and directed me to one close by.

Heading back onto the road, after stopping to find a journal-worthy notebook, I set my heading again towards Port Dover. The day was still young and there was lots of time before my brother would be home from work to let me in the house. As I neared the turn off for Port Burwell, I decided to stop and see Rhonda, a friend who also owned a holistic shop.

Parking my motorcycle beside three others, I entered her store. I was joyously greeted by crystal skulls, rocks, oracle cards, pendulums, books and all things Reiki and New Age. It felt like home. It was very much like my store, White Feather Holistic Arts in Windsor, only different. Rhonda's store reflected her healing journey, mine reflected my path. But right down to riding motorcycles, Reiki and crystals, Rhonda and I were on a similar road in life.

After browsing around the store for a bit, I went outside to find Rhonda eating lunch with a few of her motorcycle friends on a picnic table between two buildings. There were people, like me, who loved their bike and loved to ride on adventures, and then there were people for whom bikes were a way of life, which I believed was the category these women fit into.

Once upon a time in my life, I would have felt uncomfortable about the fact that I knew I didn't fit in at a table surrounded by women like them, but that time had passed. I didn't need to fit in everywhere. I no longer craved belonging in my life. I belonged. I belonged here on Earth. I belonged with my close friends. I belonged in my own business. I belonged in my community. The unhealed version of me had felt like I hadn't fit in anywhere; the healed me realized that I didn't have to fit in everywhere, but I definitely fit in somewhere.

The key was to find my space, my tribe, and claim it. Learning how to do this didn't happen overnight; it happened as my self-esteem and my ability to validate myself grew. It happened as I really got to know myself – the real me, not the me who needed to 'fit in'. That journey to healthy self-esteem had started in 2006, and it was a journey that continued to this very day.

My path of self-loathing had started at age twelve, and there had been a whole hell of a lot of internal programming that had to be rewired for me to even contemplate self-love since then. You see, at age twelve, I had felt responsible for what had happened between myself and that 42-year-old man. As my relationship with my father had quickly deteriorated, I had felt like he didn't love me anymore, and so I felt unlovable. My choices had become that of someone who didn't love herself. I had started to steal, to experiment with alcohol, smoking, drugs, and I had become promiscuous.

All my choices had reflected how I felt about myself and then, living through these choices, they'd made me feel even worse. I had led myself into a downward spiral of bad choices and low self-esteem. One day, I had woken up and found myself living a life of bad choice after bad choice. I had begun feeling worse and worse about myself. Hating myself had appeared to be the only sane decision I could make by the time I hit my 30s.

And then a miracle had happened at age 33 (2006), when I left; a thought crossed my mind that there was a different way. Contemplating that this different choice existed had been the first chance I had given to myself – would I listen to the call to healing? Or would I ignore it and continue in the insanity of self-hatred and bad choices?

It didn't matter when I had said 'yes' to a new way of living, it had mattered that, at some point, I had become willing to try something new, something different – to make different choices. It hadn't mattered how far down into the abyss I'd fallen. Something had stirred within me and it had awakened the awareness that I could be different.

That had been the day my Tower crumbled. That had been the very first day that I said 'yes' to a new way of living. I had no idea what this new me/life would be. I had no idea how I would get to a place that was different from what my reality had been for so long. But I had known I had to find a way to get there, and I wasn't going to find it by staying in the same place in the same dysfunction making the same self-sabotaging choices.

Much like The Fool card in the Tarot deck, I had my hobo stick slung over my shoulder, ready for a new adventure, and the adventure was called, 'Anything but This'. And that's the day I left my old life behind. I walked out the door, closing it behind me. In Tarot, the Tower card has a castle on fire with a person leaping or falling out the window. The way I visualize my exit from my Tower is more like this... a half crazed woman with a bag slung over her shoulder, walking out the door of her house, and as she gets ten steps away from it, the house explodes into oblivion behind her – the fire and smoke a beautiful backdrop to her next chapter.

* * *

I had a lovely lunch with Rhonda and her friends while they regaled me with a few stories about things going on in the motorcycle world. After lunch, Rhonda and I went into her store and I went upstairs with her to check out all her new crystal skulls.

I'm a huge fan of crystal skulls – I wasn't always. Once upon a time they reminded me of death. When I first opened my shop and started selling crystals, people were asking for crystal skulls, and I would say, "Nope, I don't like them! They remind me of death." And that would be the end of it.

The Fool Card
Rider- Waite Tarot Deck

However, I was asked by enough people to get them that eventually I decided to get one. I ordered a nice little amethyst skull, it arrived, and I decided to work with it for a few minutes. I created a crystal grid by putting different crystals around it in a symmetrical shape with the skull in the middle. Then I sat down to meditate. Closing my eyes, my hands on my lap, I allowed my mind to clear and my thoughts to drift away as I exhaled. As empty space formed in my mind a thought dropped in out of nowhere, "Hi. I'm Fred the Head. I'm not about death. I'm all about knowledge. The skull is the casing for the brain – the holder of knowledge. I too am a holder of knowledge. I have knowledge to give you, and I also hold a key that will unlock knowledge within you."

I laughed at the name! Of course, his name was Fred the Head – how better to get into my world than to have a sense of humour and make light of the experience? From that day on, I had a wonderful relationship with crystal skulls, not to mention a personal collection that continues to grow.

Rhonda has an incredible multitude of crystal skulls. Every time I visit, I make sure to head upstairs and say hello to them. Normally, I leave with a handful, but not on this day – I was on a twelve-day motorcycle adventure and there wasn't room for a single skull on my bike except my own! Giving her a hug, I let Rhonda know I'd be back when I could, and I heard the bell on the door tinkle as I left.

I hopped on my bike, circling down by the lake so that I could get a good view of it before riding out. I breathed in the moment. Man, it felt good to be riding my motorcycle with no set schedule and go wherever my heart wanted to go. Off I rumbled down the road with my GPS showing me the way to my brother's house, in Port Dover.

WE ARE FAMILY

An hour later I rolled into the driveway at my brother's house. Rain was threatening and I was anxious to get my gear off the bike, so I unloaded while I waited for Bob and Sandy to get home from work. Bob is my long-lost brother whom I met when I was eighteen. At the time my parents divorced, my Mum had let me know that my father had a son from his first marriage who he hadn't seen since the boy was five. When he was an adult, Bob Jr. sought my father out. He had introduced himself to Dad, and we all eventually were able to meet him.

I had a new brother, and he was all grown up and he was awesome! Bob was into adventure games and he had a degree in philosophy. He was a questioner and a thinker, and he was way outside of the box! Though he looked exactly like my Dad, his personality and interests were the opposite.

When the opportunity strikes, I try to spend a bit of time with him. I try to get to know this guy whom I love very much as a brother, but whom I didn't grow up with. I don't yet know his life experience, his feelings about different things. He's a brother I didn't meet until I was eighteen. And he's a person who reminds me that I have things to be grateful for. As a child, I had twelve awesome years with my Dad. Those years with my dad helped create the person I am today – they were character building years, years that formed my morals, years that cultivated my sense of humour, my personality, my strength.

Years later (after I turned eighteen), after I had destroyed my life, I had a place with my dad that I could return to – to the kid I had been who was courageous, brave, confident, smart and so much more – I could return to that place and start again. My dad was a very integral part of forming that kid version of myself. I am grateful for that. But I have no idea what parts of Bob's childhood were difficult or easy. I have no idea what (or who) helped form him into the incredibly awesome guy he is today. I'm always trying to find out more and grateful for when I succeed.

Not even ten minutes into my wait, Sandy and Bob hopped out of their car and greeted me on the porch where I was waiting with my motorcycle luggage to go inside. Once in the house, we talked about what we'd been up to, how my day on the bike had gone, and how Bob and Sandy's jobs were going. For an evening, I got a very narrow glimpse into their lives, and I gleaned every bit of information I could from their household items, from their words as I tried to get to know my brother just a little bit more. Deep inside, I continued to yearn to know him better.

After supper, I was laughing at a portrait painting in their living room. The painting was of a woman and man. Someone attached a pair of joke glasses with a nose and big eyebrows to the man in the painting. As I laughed, Sandy came in and told me that when she came home to find that on her painting one day that was when she knew that Bob was the one – he had a sense of humour to match her own. I didn't know if this had happened early in their relationship or years into it. What I did know was that I was grateful to get that tidbit of information – that little peek – into who they were.

The end of my journal entry for that evening read:

"Thoroughly enjoyed my time here tonight with Bob and Sandy! Some good laughs, nice company. I love my family. Thank you, Universe. Good night."

* * *

That's how I feel every time I get together with family – I feel love in my heart and I'm grateful to spend time with them. Every single member, no matter how good or how strained our relationship is, is important to me. I no longer struggle with the fact that our relationships aren't what they 'could' be – they are what they are, and I will make the best of each relationship. I don't care what happened when I (we) grew up. I don't care that I didn't know how to navigate the divorce of my parents; neither did my parents, neither did my sisters. We all stumbled through it. We all did the best we could at the time, and I feel it's accurate to say that most of us could have done better. I could carry resentments in my heart forever and tell myself a story about why I was such a mess for a great many years, but that story would only be as true as I allowed it to be. I am blessed.

As much as I thought for years that my family was part of the problem, the truth is that my family was not part of the problem. I look at other families and I am grateful for what I have experienced with mine. My parents loved me. I have a gaggle of siblings who are all awesome, beautiful people spread across Canada. I had to grow up, really grow up, before I could fully understand how amazing my family is and how blessed I am to have each of them in my life.

Family is hard, I believe, for almost everyone. We each face our own challenges within our unique family units. Once I began on my healing path, I began to recognize my family members as my greatest teachers. These lessons are more difficult to recognize for some than for others. For some, the healing path ends in divorcing an entire family – parents, siblings, everyone. For some, the healing path ends in forgiveness and love.

I do know one thing, the path is best walked when it ends in some level of acceptance because we can't change our families. We can leave them. We can choose to stay with or near them. But we can't change them. Acceptance is the option that brings peace. Acceptance does not mean condoning bad behaviour, it means coming to the realization that family members are who they are – struggling against that, trying to fix or change them is an effort in futility. Sometimes even after acceptance, the choice can still be to walk away.

How did I learn to move into acceptance? It's all about paying attention to the conversation going on in my head. If I'm thinking, 'she needs to ______', 'they'd be happier if they______', 'I wish he could______', and thoughts that show I am wishing or hoping or wanting something different, I'm struggling against what is. People are who they are. Very few people, if any, change because someone else told them it would be good for them to change.

Instead of struggling against the current (fighting against who people are, and wishing they'd change), I choose to flow with it. I can't change people into what I think the best version of them would be, I can only change the way I react to people. I can change how I respond to them, and I can create boundaries in my relationships with them. If I want my family members in my life, I have to practice a level of acceptance. If I cannot move into the energy of acceptance, then I need to step away. Trying to change people is as effective as herding cats. There have been times when I wasn't able to move into the acceptance space, and I made the choice to be away from my family and family events. This was part of the process of learning how to make healthy choices regarding my family.

The Serenity Prayer isn't just for alcoholics and addicts, it's for everyone. Here it is with my own two cents included:

God grant me the serenity to accept the things I cannot change – every single thing, person event, except myself

The courage to change the things I can – me and my responses to events and people

And the wisdom to know the difference – self awareness

I repeat this prayer to myself often. It's a loaded gift to keep my mind on track. If I find myself desiring to be more accepting of difficult people in my life, whom I love, I start catching my efforts to change them, and begin to put that same energy into changing how I react to them.

A great quote by Ram Dass always sums this life lesson up nicely for me, "If you think you are enlightened, go spend a week with your family." I feel there is always room for personal growth, no matter how far along we are on our journey, and for me, family helps me to grow. Seeing Bob that day, filled my heart.

DAY 2 – SEPTEMBER 12TH, 2019

THANK YOU

Having loaded up my bike the next morning, I locked the door to Bob's house behind me. It was a much cooler day so I put my chaps and leather coat on. My first destination was to visit a motorcycle shop I found online. I wanted to see if I could find a t-shirt. After typing 'Brass Pole Motorcycle Accessories' into my GPS and following the directions, I found myself at someone's house. I climbed up to the porch and was welcomed inside by a pretty lady in her 60s with blond hair and a welcoming smile. I was instantly surrounded by bike stuff – keychains, t-shirts, leather belts, jeans, patches, pins, cup holders, and a million different things a biker may want when traveling through town.

After introducing myself to Trish, the pretty smiling lady, she asked me where I was headed, and I explained that I was ultimately riding up to Thunder Bay to ride with the WRWR for three days.

"No way, you're kidding! I'm doing some of the relay too!" she exclaimed.

We laughed as we excitedly told each other which parts of the relay we were doing.

"Wow, what a small world!" we commented at the same time. Small world indeed. I was only on day two of my trip, and I'd already met another rider in the relay.

I milled about amongst her trinkets and beautiful things and purchased a few pins for myself and Ron. I found myself a sheepskin seat cover to help make my 12-day ride more comfortable. I also bought a cup holder (which I never ended up using!). Trish's husband helped me attach the seat cover onto my bike but warned that I might want to take it off because it looked like it was going to rain.

"Nah, that's ok, I'll be fine!" I told him as I rolled carefully down the gravel lane to the road. Day two, here I come! I thought to myself as I rumbled away.

My destination was Gravenhurst, a beautiful little town in Muskoka. For years I had called this area my happy place, visiting a cottage here in the summers, but when I walked out the door of my life in 2006, I left that happy place behind. I no longer had a claim on it, and I have since discovered new happy places. New happy places for the new me.

British Columbia is a happy place. Bruce Peninsula is a happy place. Cuba is a happy place. I have so many happy places and it's because I'm happy now. I take happiness with me everywhere I go. Having spent years in deep depression, finding only glimpses of happiness when I came up north or being on certain drugs, there was little to be happy about. But every day now I wake up grateful that this is my experience. I am grateful that, like The Fool, I set out on a journey to find and create this new world that thrives on happiness.

Not long after I left the store, it started to drizzle. Carefully, I pulled into a parking lot. I ran around to my lower side saddlebag and I got my Frogg Toggs out. Frogg Toggs are pants and a jacket to wear in the rainy weather. These things would keep me dry in a hurricane, which my husband attested to a few years back having been unfortunate enough to ride during a hurricane. Throwing them on over my chaps and leather coat, I set back out on the road hoping for some drier weather.

Within less than an hour, blue skies appeared ahead of me and I was able to pop into a small diner to eat and dry off. I had no idea where I was. Instead of driving from memory down a well-known highway like I did the day before, I was now following my GPS. I turned off highways and toll roads on my GPS, so that I would only be led down smaller highways and backroads. I didn't see any signs indicating where exactly I was – and I was totally okay with that!

While I was at the diner, a few people came and asked me where I was going. This happened a lot. Anyone who has ever owned a bike or who owns a bike or who wished they owned a bike, would come up and talk to me about their bike or why they sold their bike or how much they'd love to get a bike. I loved it. This trip was no different than any other in that regard. Any time I stopped for more than gas, a conversation would ensue with some wonderful stranger who wanted to talk motorcycles with me. Happy to oblige, I would show off my bike and talk about her.

Perhaps I haven't mentioned this yet, but I love my bike. I'm like a kid every time I get on my motorcycle. I feel happy, excited, cool. It's like I'm 9-years-old again riding my red Raleigh bicycle, standing on the banana seat, flying down Dunsmoore Road. I am more than happy to talk about my bike at every single stop. I ate a quick meal then headed out once again.

The rest of the day was incredible and gorgeous. My view was filled with trees with leaves of all different colours. The leaves were just starting to change. The GPS was leading me down some incredible roadways. Oh, there were some lovely hills, especially up around Airport Road somewhere past Orangeville. While enjoying the hills and the trees and the beautiful blue skies, a song came on my headphones, one that carried a wonderful set of memories for me. It was Natasha Bedingfield's, Unwritten.

***

I vividly remember the very first time I heard the song. It had been in October of 2006 at a women's emergency shelter in Toronto, Ontario. The Fool had set out on her journey and the shelter had been one of my earliest stops. Walking away from everything had not been a smooth transition. I had tried to stay with the familiar in the London area, but it hadn't worked out. First had been my sister's, then a short stop at the hospital, then a few weeks at the Oneida Family Healing Lodge. My fears had persisted, the old story had persisted, and the shaky foundation upon which I had built my former Tower had continued to shift beneath my feet. So, I up and left it – all of it. I had ditched my ID, my name, my past, and I had tried desperately to ditch my fears and phobias into the mix. I had found myself in Toronto.

It had not been easy to restart with no name, no past, no proof of existence. I can't say I had been mentally well at the time, but I was better than I'd been the year before I left . Psychosis – temporary or not – had been a horrible experience, and it left gaping wounds. That had been the place I was starting over from.

During my first three weeks in Toronto, before I found the emergency shelter, I had been off drugs for the first time in years – not just pot, mushrooms, ecstasy, coke, and whatever else – but prescription drugs as well. I had not taken any anti-anxiety meds, any antidepressants – nothing. I'm certain that had made my situation worse, not better – but it was temporarily worse because things got better, much better.

I want to express the emotions I had at that time, but it's almost impossible to connect with that 'me' anymore. I know that my mind hadn't been functioning well, my body had been detoxing from drugs, my spirit had been shattered. I had been terrified every moment of every day – looking over my shoulder constantly. I had ducked around corners. I had hid in buildings. I had escaped non-existent horrors that my psychosis had been telling me were real.

Prayers had forever been muttered under my breath. Somehow food had always come to me though I hadn't been hungry most of the time. I would discover drop-in centres in Toronto here and there, and at each stop they had offered day-old sandwiches, coffee, hot chocolate, and a warm place to sit for an afternoon. I had found clothing that had been donated. I had found places to shower and laundry facilities. Anything I had with me, which wasn't much, I had carted around in a few plastic shopping bags. The weird epiphany had been this: being in Toronto, homeless, cold, afraid, lonely, and out of my mind with psychosis had been better than what I'd walked away from. I had my freedom.

I also had a new-found relationship with god. When I say 'god', know that I use the term loosely. My idea of god might be different than yours; my god doesn't fit into a book or any particular set of beliefs. Back at that time in Toronto, I was trying to establish what god was to me – who god was.

I'd felt god's presence not long after walking away from my life. It had been such a profound moment for me that it changed everything I believed. I had gone from being a virtual atheist to knowing that there was something larger than me. This 'something larger' I had named god for lack of a better word. The feelings that had come from this new-found presence had been comfort, safety, trust, and more than anything – Love. Love with a capital L. I will talk more about that event later. It's one of the most personal and profound events of my entire life.

That very first time I had become aware of god's presence, I had felt Love – more Love than I had ever felt from any person, any experience, any drug, any anything. I had felt a deep Unconditional-ness. Even though I'd messed up my entire life and everything that had meant something to me, I had felt that I was just as loveable in god's eyes as the day I had shown up on Earth – naked, innocent and precious. Along with that feeling of Love had come a feeling that everything was going to be ok. I hadn't been able to put into words why or how it was going to be ok; I had just known that it was going to be. That was the beginning of my divine relationship with god (the Universe).

Once I had known there was a god, then I had known everything was going to be fine. That's how sure I was that I had felt god's presence, and that's what gave me the courage to step forward as The Fool with my hobo stick on my shoulder, no clue what I was doing but ready to try something new, ready to do things differently. God and I had set out for a walk-about.

After three weeks of not having anywhere to sleep at night, I had gotten up the courage to venture into an emergency shelter for women that I had heard about. It had been the beginning of November. My detox off prescription drugs was almost done – I was feeling the best I had since leaving my old life behind. When I had showed up on the steps of the big red brick building, I had seen women carrying bags, just like me. I had seen vacant eyes. I had seen hopeful eyes. I had seen angry eyes. I had seen crazy eyes. My own eyes, if any woman had looked into them, had been a mixture of all of those emotions.

When the doors had opened, I got in line and was ushered to the side to do an intake since I'd never been to the shelter before. A young intern, still in university, had interviewed me. She had been full of compassion; I could tell that all she had wanted to do was help. That interview had been the most humbling experience of my life. Going to the emergency shelter had been one huge helping of humble pie, and frankly, it had been exactly what I'd needed. My spirit had needed breaking in all the right places.

The young intern had asked if I wanted to apply for transitional housing. She had explained that it was housing I could go to and live in for up to two years if I was accepted. Of course, there would be strict rules for living there, but it would be a big step up from a temporary bed at an emergency shelter. I had said yes without hesitation. After we'd finished my application, she had pointed across the hall to where I could find hot food. My tummy rumbled as I followed her pointing finger.

Inside a large room, there had been hall tables with chairs, and women were filtering in and out of the room. On one of the tables, music played from a small black AM/FM radio not far from a big pot of hot soup, a bowl of buns, a pile of spoons, and a plate of butter. Setting my bags of things down on a chair, I had scooped myself a full bowl of soup, put extra amounts of butter on a bun, and I went back to take my seat so I could indulge in the hot food. Never, ever in my life had I enjoyed a bowl of soup as much as I had enjoyed that one.

I had been eating my soup, watching women come and go, trying not to stare at anyone, and enjoying the hell out of the music streaming from the radio. That was something else I had promised myself I'd never take for granted again – music! Oh, how I had always loved music! And until the fall of 2006, I had never struggled with access to it. Finishing my bowl of soup, a song I'd never heard before began to play – Unwritten, by Natasha Bedingfield. My ears had perked up, tuned in, and the song imprinted on my mind.

As I listened to the song, I had felt a soul-connected confirmation that I was going to write a book about my life. I already knew that writing a book was a goal, but in that moment, I had felt the reality of it happening in my gut. It was like god had been singing to me about the book I would write.

I'll be honest, I had misunderstood my intuition and I had thought that me writing a book had been imminent. I hadn't understood that I still had to live my book. I hadn't understood that the important message in the song hadn't been the act of writing of a book as much as it had been a call to live a life to the fullest – to live a life worth writing a book about! My understanding at that time had been perfect for that moment. I had needed to believe in something. My whole life had been packed into a couple of shopping bags. I had been about to sleep in a bed for the first time in three weeks. If my psyche had been giving me a hope to cling to – like writing a book – so be it. I had needed something and a book was as good as anything.

From that song on, I had journaled every moment, every song, every thought, every regret, every rambling – I had put it all down on paper. I had journalled my thoughts about god, my thoughts about my past, my thoughts about memories from my life. And I'll tell you what, my journal had become a poor woman's psychologist!

By listening to myself, I could hear what I had needed to hear. By writing things out, I had written what I needed to read. By thinking I was going to write a book, I had motivated myself to write all the time, about anything, everything and nothing. Instead of sitting around feeling sorry for myself about being homeless, I had felt excited! I had things to write, important thoughts to convey. I had written about my growing gratitude, about my spiritual realizations, about god, the Universe, and everything. I had a place to begin to put my story.

* * *

I recommend writing to everyone who is on their healing journey. Write often. Journal about your day, scribble your thoughts, write a poem about your anger – anything and everything counts. It doesn't matter what you write, just write. There is so much value wrapped up in a pen and paper, and I have personally watched hundreds, possibly thousands of people, heal through writing. It's one more tool for our toolbox.

My spiritual awakening and understanding started to form through my writing based on the experiences I'd had. I wrote about my intuition – though I didn't have the word for it at the time. Never before in my life had I listened to my gut. I'm sure my intuition had tried warning me or helping me before – but I hadn't had the ears to hear it with. But my relationship with my intuition had begun to show itself. Awareness and cultivation of my intuition became a major part of my healing journey. I can consider the reasons why before I left my life on that fateful day in 2006, I did not have a strong relationship with intuition.

Maybe it was because of the drugs I'd taken. Maybe it was because of the depression I had experienced for a decade. Maybe it was because I was not where I was supposed to be – I'd been in the wrong place for years. It was potentially for all of these reasons that I had not been aware of my intuition. All I knew was that once I left and I discovered god and writing, my sense of knowing had awakened for the first time. I was starting to know things without knowing why I knew them.

Ever known something without knowing how you know? Like when you're in a room of five hundred people and you can feel someone looking at you? You turn around and twenty rows back, there is someone you know actually looking right at you? Or when you get the thought that says, 'Call Susan', and when you call her, it is the perfect time to call her because she really needed you right then. That kind of knowing had started to happen right before my Tower had crumbled. In fact, it's what led me out the door.

* * *

That first night at the emergency shelter in Toronto, I remember I had crawled into my bed, exhausted beyond belief. I'd been assigned a room number and bed number I considered lucky, so I knew I had been exactly where I was supposed to be. Tears had streamed down my face as I lay staring at the bunk above me. I had been awake for hours, so happy to be laying in clean sheets in a warm bed inside a building.

I thanked god over and over again for giving me a bowl of soup and a bed to sleep in. I had never been grateful for food before my homeless experience. I had never been grateful for anything before the experiences I had after setting out on the road as The Fool. I couldn't think of a time when I ever had such a true feeling of gratitude before that night. Oh, I may have said thank you, and I may have thought I was grateful, but that night as I had felt grateful from my head to my toes, I realized I had never felt that kind of grateful. It had been a good feeling. To appreciate the tiniest things had felt awesome.

I had felt like a child experiencing new emotions for the first time. I had felt a strange combination of feelings. I had been ashamed but then humbled for being in the shelter in the first place. I had been full of gratitude for the simplest of comforts. I had been terrified because I hadn't known what was going to happen in my life after I left. Yet, I had also been excited about that same unknown future – I had trusted that it would be good. I still hadn't learned to like myself. Indeed, I had been busy beating myself up inside my head and in my journal for having destroyed my entire life. But at the same time, I had felt loved by god, despite having no idea why god would love such a pitiful creature like me. But god did love me. And I had felt it. Powerfully.

* * *

Continuing ever northwards, I cruised down the highway on my bike, my feet were propped up in the pegs. The sun was shining. I'd been riding for a while. My body needed to stretch out, and the pegs were the best I could do at the time. My music had continued to sing in my ears, a number of songs had passed since Unwritten. I shifted my butt, wiggled around, and settled into the song Bittersweet Symphony, by the Verve, written by Mick Jagger and Keith Richards. My memories flashed back again to Toronto in 2006.

After only one week in the emergency shelter, I had been admitted into transitional housing. I had been walking down some street in the heart of downtown Toronto and Bittersweet Symphony had blared through an outside set of speakers from one of the stores. I had stopped. I had started singing and dancing my own little dance. People had walked around me, ignoring my moment. The song had filled my soul, and for a moment I had forgotten about everything that was happening in my life. I had been just another person lost in the sea of people.

At the time, my interpretation of the song had been a far cry from the real meaning. Listening to the lyrics, when the singer says, "I'm a million different people from one day to the next", I had focused on the fact that I'd already given myself five different names since I'd walked away from my life. The rest of the song lyrics hadn't caught my attention. The meaning had been lost on me. I'd since discovered that the song was about being trapped in being who you were. Like it was beyond your control to change, to be anything other than who you were due to circumstances beyond your control. It was interesting to me that I'd never caught the meaning of the whole song, but rather only the one line. That was ok. At that time, I probably would have believed that I was trapped by my past choices, and that would have been a bad thing. I didn't think that anymore. Since I rediscovered myself, I know that nothing will ever change the core of who I am - not even years of addiction and self hatred.

Many times in my life, I had felt that what was happening was out of my control. I had felt like a victim of fate and circumstance. I know better now. No matter what hand we are dealt, every single hand can be a winner, it simply depends on how you play. No, we aren't all coming from the same place, and no two people are given the same set of circumstances or opportunities – the starting line is different for every single person.

I do believe, however, that we always have a choice – to make the best of our situation or to make the worst of it. The unhealed me made the worst of my situations (whether it was me driving my choices or not). I wallowed in my inability to move past or around circumstances.

In Toronto, homeless and in transitional housing, I had started believing that I could create my life in whatever way I wanted it to be. I had absolutely nothing but a bag of clothes and some toiletries, and I had firmly believed that I would be successful and wealthy one day. It had been amazing that I'd set out with nothing – not a dime to my name, no ID – and somehow within two weeks, I had a place to call home, I was well fed, and I had been given opportunities to start my life over. If that had been possible and happening, anything and everything could also be possible. I had believed that god was part of the equation – I knew I was getting help from somewhere out there in the Universe, and if god had done this much already, in such a short time, what else could god do?! I had to start somewhere on my road to success. My starting line had been homeless and hopeful.

* * *

In Tarot, there is a card called The Magician. Only after the Fool sets out on his journey can the Magician come to life. The Magician recognizes that we (fools or otherwise!) create our own story. The Magician chooses to believe that life is filled with awesomeness or that the world is a horrible place out to get us. In the illustration on the The Magician card, all four suits are shown – the pentacles, the cups, the swords and the wands which are essentially representations of life tools. The Magician is given every tool he needs to create a wonderful life. Will he choose to use his inner skills and decide his own course or will he sit back and wait to see what the Universe will deliver?

The Magician Card
Rider- Waite Tarot Deck

When I had been homeless in Toronto, I had clearly decided that I was going to have an amazing life! I had never heard of books like The Secret or teachings about the Law of Attraction. I would find out a few years later when I had heard about these ways of thinking, that in Toronto, homeless and penniless, I had discovered the beginnings of these enlightening spiritual paths on my own. I had known that I needed to be the Magician. I had known that I needed to believe in my own magic, my own capabilities, and that abundance and success were within my grasp. Every part of my soul had believed I was going to write a book, and every part of my soul had believed my life was going to be fantastical.

One set of my journal writings in the late fall of 2006 while I was in transitional housing had been about my relationship with god. I had been trying to figure out why being homeless was a blessing for me. Buddha had started on his path of enlightenment by giving away all his possessions. I had known this because I had studied religions and mythologies for years as an atheist – I was fascinated by all of it, even though I believed none of it. Without being encumbered by material things, Buddha had been able to ponder real things – existential things – like a blade of grass, for example.

Maybe I had been like Buddha at that time in my life? I had walked away from all my possessions – I left with nothing. I had no money, no material items. Yet even though I had walked away with nothing, merely two months later, I was alive; fed, clothed and housed.

What choices had I been making then? I had chosen writing as one of the ways to create and build my relationship with god. Had I really met god, like a singular guy with a big white beard up in the clouds throwing lightning bolts at me? Or had it been more like an omnipotent energy that was the inclusion of all things that had enveloped me? Or was it the realization of a combined consciousness – the split personalities of god – 7 billion of them – god as an aspect in every single person on earth? What parts of the different religions had been 'true'? Hinduism? Islam? Christianity? Japanese animism? The Medicine Wheel? The Greek and Roman pantheon of gods and goddesses? Paganism? Atheism? Science? New Age? Buddhism?

I had been writing in my journal about the deep pondering I had been doing about god because I hadn't had a single other thing in the world to do. I had the time and energy to think, to wonder, to consider, to discover. The blessings of being homeless, jobless, identity-less had absolutely included a shift in my relationship with time and in my relationship with myself. It had been a life-changing blessing to not have to consider my own safety and sanity in relation to the things I had left. It had been a blessing to clean my body of drugs and alcohol. It had afforded me a clarity I hadn't felt in decades.

Beyond these new life experiences I had been writing about, I had also been trying to work through the mess of my past. Why things had happened and what I was to learn from them. I had the time and energy to consider and begin reflection on how I had felt about what had happened, what I had understood or not during and after those events. I had been trying desperately to reach a place of true forgiveness in my heart for everyone involved in my past.

Imagining that my experience at that time had been similar to the Buddha's was a thought that had made me smile. I had known perfectly well that I wasn't the Buddha. I had known perfectly well that I was only drawing a comparison, but I had enjoyed drawing that comparison. Maybe god/the Universe had been the guide leading me on a journey to full self-discovery. Maybe by the time we completed the journey, I would be able to understand myself deeply. Maybe I would become enlightened, like the Buddha, and understand the meaning of Life. These had all been possibilities.

It makes me smile remembering that I had those thoughts and contemplations – that I wrote them down too! Seriously! My entire life had effectively been in shambles at that point. I had been half out of my mind, but at the same time, very much in my mind. I had been aware of my surroundings, aware of my circumstances, aware that I had been terrified, aware that the choice I had made to leave was crazy – but necessary. I had few people to talk to.

At the point when I had left, I had no idea what I was going to do or where I was going to go. I had to leave and that was it. And in the middle of all of that, I had been romanticizing my life, making comparisons between myself and the Buddha, dreaming of writing a book, and trusting that all of it was possible. Call me crazy. You wouldn't be the first.

GOING TO CALIFORNIA

The roads twisted and turned, my motorcycle gliding over them. I was guided down tunnels of colour where nothing could be seen but trees with leaves in colour spectrums only nature could create. Drives like this were the dream – visually beautiful, twisty, turny, and fun to ride on a bike. I wasn't a speed demon, I didn't go flying down the roads, rather I enjoyed them at a leisurely pace. For me, the joy wasn't in seeing how quickly I could take the turns, it was knowing that I could take them at whatever pace I liked. Just like life. I wasn't racing against anyone else. I wasn't even racing against myself, I was moving forward and doing my damnedest to enjoy the trip along the way.

Hotel California, by the Eagles gently strummed its way into my ears. Riding the curves, hiding amongst the trees on the beautiful lane, I was taken to another time, another place. I had my own Hotel California – the LA Adventurers Hotel in Inglewood, California. I had taken a six day bus ride to get from London, Ontario, Canada, to downtown LA, (which was also the scariest neighbourhood I'd ever been in, to date).

After being in transitional housing in Toronto for six weeks or so, I knew I had to leave. At first it had been one song – Born in the USA, by Bruce Springstein that had triggered my itch to leave. When I had heard it, my gut said, "Yes! Go to the US!" But how on earth would I get there? Where would I go? And then some songs had played about California – Santa Monica by Theory of a Deadman, Dani California, by The Red Hot Chili Peppers, and numerous songs by the Beach Boys. Every time my three-dollar

FM Walkman had played a song about California, my gut was saying, "Yes! Go! Go! Go!" The longer I had stayed put, the more my destiny pulled at my soul. I had no idea what was waiting for me there, I just knew I had to go. California had been where I was supposed to drift away to.

It hadn't mattered why I was going. Truth be told, I would have been ok with leaving even if my destination had simply been to die by the ocean. Three weeks without a bed, three weeks with no shelter on the streets of Toronto had brought me to a place of acceptance about death. I had shifted into a survival mode that made the possibility of death less scary...at times relieving. And it had also been like a part of me died when I left my name and my identity behind. That version of me had already been dead for some time. The reborn version of myself, the one with a new relationship with god, the one who found the courage to leave hadn't been attached to living yet.

There was a part of me that had still been terrified of the life I had run away from. It had been hunting me. My phobias and fears had not subsided in any way – and anytime something triggered my phobias, my PTSD would get triggered, and I would be filled with anxiety and panic. All it would take to trigger me had been a guy riding by on a motorcycle or a white van with no windows or someone looking directly at me while they dialed a number on their cell phone. By the way certain things had triggered me, it seemed that I hadn't been quite far enough away from my recent past to clear the psychosis it had caused. I had felt an intuition telling me that going to a whole other country (USA) could offer me the possibility of moving out of those fears and into the new life I had been trying to create. Maybe it had been the thought of a whole new group of people to know or a whole new land to love or a whole new me to get to know? I just knew, like I knew god was with me, like I knew I had to leave my old life that I had to leave Canada.

One day, in my comfortable warm room at transitional housing, I had packed a couple of bags and left without anyone noticing I was leaving. I had headed down to the railroad tracks in hopes of finding a good spot to hop on a train. I had figured that if there was a way to get into the United States without anyone knowing I had left the country, pulling a 'Boxcar Willy' from the trainyard could be my (free) ticket.

Wandering along the tracks that first afternoon while trying to locate a good place to hop on a train, I had found a piece of ID – a driver's license. The name on the license said Julie Nolke and she was from the Calgary area. Julie's ID had said she was 16 years old. I had been thirty-four. The photo on the ID had shown a girl with blue eyes. I had (have) brown eyes. Her hair was much darker than my mousy brown hair had been. I had found her ID in a weird place – there were a couple of cheap old lawn chairs and a milk crate or two serving as a table near the tracks. Strewn about had been some cheesy porn mags, used needles and discarded garbage and junk. Laying in the junk, I had found a wallet that had been emptied of everything except the ID and a student card. I had left the student card and taken the driver's license. I had felt like it had been left there for me, for a reason. All my ID had been destroyed or thrown out – I hadn't used my real name in months.

For seven days, I had stayed in a temporary shelter that I made. It consisted of two old-style discarded front doors with glass panel windows and a few other boards propped up here and there. It had resembled a coffin made of doors. I had been able to stretch out in the shelter and keep out of the chilly wind. At that point, it had been late December. I had been frozen to the bone. I had brought extra layers of clothing and extra blankets with me, along with granola bars and water, but that was barely enough. My feet had been cold. Then the cold crept into my bones.

I had watched every train that came into the train yard looking for an opportunity to hop on one. I had been able to tell that others had done the same thing from this spot because I found little clues – old boxes, chairs, anything tall enough that one could use to climb onto a train. Hours had turned into days, and I knew I couldn't stay out there forever. The cold had been unbearable.

I remember I had cried and asked god for my Mum. I had really wanted my Mum. I remember I had been praying to Santa too because it was December and telling him the only thing I wanted for Christmas was to see my Mum. I had been missing her. I hadn't seen her since the end of September. I had known she had no idea if I was dead or alive. I had been feeling like a little girl who was sick and feeling horrible and all she wanted was her mommy. I had cried in my little shelter while waiting for a train to leave a car door open so I could hop on. I had still been certain I was supposed to go to California. But I had been so cold. I had felt a deep need for my Mum. I had started to get frustrated with god. Why had I felt in my gut that I was supposed to leave the temporary housing? Why had I been led to the empty, cold train yard?

It hadn't happened. I had run out of food. I had run out of the desire to hop on a train. I had bundled up my things and walked for hours until I landed at the Bay Street Greyhound bus station. I had enough money in my pocket to buy a bus ticket to London if I could get charged the student fare. I had pleaded with the man behind the glass at the station who insisted that I needed a student card (oh why hadn't I taken the student card too?). I had shown him my ID, stating that I was sixteen. I told him I had obviously still been in school, who isn't in school at sixteen?!

"Please, it's Christmas? I just need to get home," I had begged him. Those had been the magic words. Ticket in my hand, I had waited impatiently for the bus to arrive. I would go home to see my Mum.

What would I say to her? How would I explain the last two and a half months? I had no idea what I would say or how I would say it. The bus station had been warm and so was the bus. My toes had hurt – they had been cold for a full week. Climbing off the bus in London, I still had enough money to take a city bus to Mum's neighbourhood. With my bag of clothes and blankets on my shoulder, I had stepped up the stairs onto the porch of the house. At about 5:30 on December 22nd, three days before Christmas, I had made it. I had rung the doorbell. Mum had opened the door and recognized me immediately, even with my bleached blonde much shorter hair, hiding under a winter toque. Gasping, she'd taken me into her arms.

"Oh honey, I thought you were dead!" she'd said, and gathered me off the porch into her townhome. I hadn't been surprised that she thought I was dead. A part of me had wanted everyone to think I was dead, so that they would just leave me alone.

Mum hadn't rushed to ask me where I'd been or what I'd gotten up to. Instead, she'd helped me get out of boots, out of my coat, and asked me if I needed something to eat. I had been starving. Mum was always practical, a first-things-first woman – get me some food, a drink, and then we would talk. In this case, the talking had been about the few months I'd been missing. I was grateful for this way of hers because I hadn't wanted to talk about everything and she respected what I was willing to share. I had been overwhelmed by the experience of being back home in London.

"I'd love something to eat Mum, I'm a bit hungry," I had told her.

Within a few minutes, a ham and cheese sandwich had appeared in front of me as well a glass of Diet Coke. A look of motherly satisfaction crossed her face, as I had polished it off in just minutes. After refusing a few offerings of more food, I had asked Mum for a cigarette. She'd passed her pack to me; I lit one up. I'm pretty sure that was the best ham and cheese sandwich ever. The best cigarette ever. It had felt wonderful to just be there, in her presence, feeling her love radiate out towards me through smiles, sandwiches and soft looks of concern. While homeless in Toronto, no one really knew me...how could they care about me? God had loved me since I'd been gone, but Mum was the first person I'd felt it from in a long time. No matter how much I fucked up my life, I knew that Mum and god loved me.

"Mum, I'm going to the United States but you can't tell anyone. I'm never coming back here. I need to get away, Mum. I need to feel safe again," I had announced. My mom and I had let the words hover in the room with the cigarette smoke. I had known I could trust her but I knew it would still be difficult for her to hear me tell her I had to leave.

It had been extremely important to me that she not tell anyone what my plans were. A year earlier, I'd had a full-blown psychotic episode that had landed me in the hospital for five weeks. Everyone in my family had been certain they knew exactly what I needed, exactly what was best for me, and any time I suggested something different, I had been met with arguments and threats of returning me to the hospital. I had known if members of my family knew my plans, they'd try to stop me or involve people who could stop me. It hadn't been up to my family to make choices for me anymore. No one could.

I hadn't cared if my plan to go to California sounded crazy. I hadn't cared if everyone in my family, including my Mum, thought I should be back on my medication. My gut had told me that the course I had promised myself to take was the right one for me. I had just needed my Mum to grant me this one wish of secrecy so I could make my plans happen.

Mum had looked confused and understanding at the same time. I could see the wheels turning inside her mind and I had known she was weighing the pros and cons of not telling anyone in the family. I had known I was asking a lot of her. It took time, but she had eventually agreed to go along with my request.

At some point during the conversation I had slipped my socks off to inspect my fiery, sore feet. Mum had gasped as she saw my toes and exclaimed that I had chilblains!

"What are chilblains?" I'd asked.

She explained that chilblains were similar to frostbite but not as severe. My big toenails had been solid black – bruised from wearing boots a size too small. I was going to lose them. My toes had been all red and itchy. Mum had assured me that they should heal, it just might take a little time.

Laying in an old bed of mine that night upstairs had felt like a slice of heaven. The blankets were familiar – they smelled like home, they felt like home. The bed had been lumpy in all the same places it had always been lumpy. I hadn't felt entirely safe there because if I had been looking for me, my Mum's would have been the first place I'd have looked. But I hadn't felt in danger there either because I'd been lost for months and no one had a clue where I was.

I had thought I might be able to hang out there for a week or two, spend some time with my Mum, and figure out a way to get into the States. I had laid awake for hours, smelling the sheets, cuddling the old wool blanket that had once been my Granny's, and thanking god that I was there, that Mum was there.

The following morning Mum had taken me into the basement where all my things (from when I left my life) had been stored after being dropped off. Amazing! There were piles of clothes, boxes and bags of books, a tonne of cds, a few household items, a few sentimental items, and some family crystal. My previous life had been piled into a big heap of dusty containers. Four months before, it would have looked pitiful to me. But then? It had been a treasure chest compared to the one bag of items I had brought back with me from Toronto.

That Christmas had been the most wonderful Christmas I could remember to date. We'd set up a small little plastic tree and some decorations. It hadn't been much but that was totally fine. Mum hadn't bought me anything because she knew I was leaving the country soon. It hadn't been about gifts. I hadn't bought her anything because I was afraid to leave the house unless it was absolutely necessary.

Christmas day my Mum had gone to my sister Sarah's. My Mum had kept it a secret that I was back at her house. That was an important gift. The following day, Mum and I had our own Christmas, sipping red wine and smoking like chimneys. Mum had a small stocking for me stuffed with coloured markers and pencils. No present had ever seemed so wonderful! I would take these with me to the US. I had started drawing since becoming The Fool. Mum had known about my drawings – I'd shown her some. That day, she'd prepared a Christmas dinner complete with turkey and all the trimmings – bacon, stuffing, mashed potatoes and even brussel sprouts which I had always detested!

Everything I had asked Santa for that year had been delivered. I had asked to see my Mum for Christmas, and there we were, having dinner together, drinking wine and doing our best to pretend everything was ok. Nothing had been ok. My life had fallen apart at the seams. I wasn't well. All that was left of my life had been piled into boxes and bags. And yet, I had been hopeful. My gut had told me that everything was going to be ok – and I had faith in this feeling.

I had spent the next few days organizing my things, visiting pawn shops, music stores that resold cds and used book shops. My collection of cds and books had brought in quite a bit of money at the pawn and music shops. I had been a bit of a collector of books. I owned quite a few antique books that hadn't lost their value. When it was all said and done, I had somewhere around $1,700.

The most painful thing to sell, in fact, the only painful thing to sell, had been an antique Bible. My brother Bob had held that aside for me at the City Lights Bookstore years ago because he knew I collected old books. It was beautiful. Filled with etchings illustrated by Dore, it had gold leaf writing and hand painted maps. The Bible hadn't been worth that much, maybe a few hundred dollars, but since I had recently formed a relationship with god, it saddened me to have to part with it.

The reality of my situation was that I couldn't take any of these things with me. I knew I could only bring some clothes. Everything else would have just weighed me down. I had made the choice to leave everything and everyone that ever mattered in my life. I had done it so that I could create a new life for myself, somewhere that I felt safe. I had no intention of ever coming back to Canada. Canada wasn't even an option in my mind at this point. I had been so engulfed in fear, whether it was real or imagined hadn't mattered. All I had known was that it was time to leave.

With a pocket full of money, I had researched online what a teenager needed to do to get across the United States border. A passport hadn't been required in January of 2007, although it was recommended. I could use my driver's license – well, Julie's driver's licence – and a note written by her parents, to get across the border. I had created the letter I'd need with a story about attending a wedding in California. After that, I'd researched other ways I could get across the border. Nothing had looked simple. I could have either tried my luck at the border in British Columbia or I could have tried to sneak across the border in the middle of a provincial park in Alberta that crossed into a US park. At the bus station, I had purchased a bus ticket to Calgary, Alberta. My departure had been in two weeks' time on January 11th. That meant I had two more weeks to be with my Mum.

During those two weeks together, I had been able to tell my Mum about a lot of what had happened since she last saw me. I hadn't told her the hardest parts, the parts that would have brought her to tears. I'd made it sound pretty good, like I'd gotten help quickly. She didn't need to hear about the three weeks I'd spent on the streets, terrified and hungry, running for my life from psychosis triggers. Instead, I'd told her about the emergency shelter and then transitional housing, about the women I'd met there and what it was like. I'd been sure to share the story about how I'd participated in a Guinness Book of World Records event in Toronto – one that involved the Rockettes and dancing!

That day in November had been so much fun as me and a woman named Kay from the shelter had headed down to the Hummingbird Centre to be part of the world's largest dance line ever – with the Rockettes at the centre of it all! I had been homeless and dancing with the Rockettes! God was amazing and so were the miracles. After the dance, we had all been given a free ticket to The Rockettes Christmas Spectacular in December and I had attended that too. The free $75 seat had felt like a gift straight from Heaven. The evening of the event, I'd worn the best clothes I'd been able to find through donation centers and transitional housing. I'd felt like a princess, a child of god, being treated to a royal event. Imagine that, eh? Being homeless, having nothing, getting into the Guinness Book of World Records, and attending a fancy show with the Rockettes – for free! Anything was possible – I had been living that statement. Special happenings like these had helped me feel loved, feel special. There may not have been people making me feel that way at that time, but the Universe sure was going out of its way to help me feel Loved.

Mum had been fascinated by my stories, and I'm sure, in her mind, she'd questioned if they were true or not. They were. The only thing I'd told my Mum about that wasn't true was how I had believed I was being hunted. It's not that I'd been intentionally lying to my Mum, it's that I'd believed it to be real at the time. I'd believed it so much that I'd been ready to give up my entire life, to run away from it. Truth was, I'd been haunted, not hunted.

On January 11th, 2007, my Mum had waved to me from the platform as I waved from inside the bus. She had packed many sandwiches and drinks for me. Mum had expected to see me back sooner than she did – not because I said I'd be back, but because she hadn't had any faith in my plan to move to the US. It had broken my heart to leave. I just couldn't stay there anymore – not just in her house, not just in the city of London or in shelters in Toronto. I knew I couldn't live in shelters. And I hadn't felt safe to live the life I had been familiar with. My gut had been right. It had been time to move to the United States. Something better was waiting for me in California. I could feel it.

Mum had taught me a lot in those few weeks we spent together. From our shared experience, I'd witnessed Love without conditions in its purest form. Mum had thought what I was doing was crazy. The things I had said concerned her. She hadn't understood my newfound belief in 'god'. Certain I'd be back sooner rather than later from the US, she'd still done everything she could to help me make my trip a success. Mum had supported me during all my lowest moments, and years later, she would be my biggest fan when I got my shit together. For years I had judged my Mum, finding it difficult to extend my Love. But she hadn't judged me. She'd always supported me and Loved me through the worst of it. Mum has always been one of my greatest teachers. Though I knew she hadn't agreed with my choice to leave, she did every kind thing she could to help me prepare to go. That had been a major support and what had helped me step on that bus and continue my Fool's adventure.

Across the country I'd rode, sleeping a total of maybe eight hours over the five days it took to get to Calgary. I had been wide awake, pulsing with adrenaline. Something that helped immensely with my nervousness as I rode forward on my adventure into the complete unknown was that a complete stranger on the bus, a kind soul, had given me a big chunk of hash to smoke while we rode across Canada. None of my drug friends had given me much more than a few joints but this guy had handed me half an ounce, and only asked that I'd return to him what I didn't use when we got to Calgary. Angels come in strange guises. Drugs aren't always about getting high. Sometimes drugs are about just getting by and coping.

In Calgary, I had a decision to make: travel south and sneak across the border in the middle of a massive park in the snow or take my chances at the border to Washington State on the bus. I opted for the bus. The idea of trying to find my way through a park in the middle of winter had looked like the potential for an unpleasant death. I had purchased a bus ticket to Los Angeles at the Calgary bus station. The ticket to Los Angeles had cost almost as much as my ticket across most of Canada. I'd resented the price, but I continued on.

I had stayed overnight at a hostel in Vancouver before the day I'd cross into Washington. That morning, I'd put on the youngest looking outfit I could find, complete with a cute little pink winter toque, adorable purple puffy jacket, tight jeans, lip gloss, and a colourful t-shirt that said something sweet and sixteen-sounding. The ID I had said I was sixteen, I knew I needed to look the part. After boarding the bus, I'd prayed to all of the heavens – god, goddess, angels, St. Jude (the patron Saint of lost causes, who was, by this time, a favourite of mine), and any other saint, god, or deity who might be able to help me – that I'd make it across the border without hassle.

It hadn't been long before we arrived at the border, and every passenger was told to get off the bus and get out their ID. I had two choices regarding the border guard I'd show my ID to – a young male who looked like he was close to my own age or an old male who looked ready to retire. I went with the old guy. When it was my turn, I had produced the letter from my parents, my driver's license, and I answered his questions.

He had almost caught me. While looking at his computer he had asked, "When was the last time you took a plane?"

I answered, "I haven't". Because I had never been on a plane in my entire life. But that was Tracey's life, not Julie's, I'd naturally answered for.

He corrected himself, and said, "No, I know you didn't today, Julie, but when was the last time you traveled on a plane?"

Oh, my dear lord, are you serious? I had thought. I had to think quickly. I'd found the ID in December in Toronto. The wallet had looked tattered and weathered, so it had been there for a while.

"In September, for a school trip to Toronto," I'd told him.

"Yes, thank you," he'd said. And that had been it. Without showing my emotions, I'd gone back onto the bus with all the others.

As the bus rolled across the United States border, I had started to cry. The knot in my stomach had relaxed. I'm free!! The words had clamoured in me like a celebratory concert. I couldn't believe it had happened. No one would ever be able to find me because Tracey Rogers hadn't crossed the border, Julie Nolke did. A wave of relief had washed over my entire being. That very moment had been a key step in my upcoming healing. I had needed to feel safe. And to do that, I had needed to feel like I had disappeared from danger or nothing, absolutely nothing, was going to get better. I had successfully shifted into the new life as Julie Nolke – away from my past, literally and figuratively.

Wherever and whoever you are Julie, I am sorry that someone stole your wallet in September of 2006 or that you lost it. From the bottom of my heart, thank you for whatever hassle that caused you. For the first time in over a year, I hadn't been afraid that my life was in danger. Your identification granted me safe passage away from this danger. Thank you, Julie. You're an angel.

The rest of the bus ride had been easy. My favourite part was traveling between Portland and Seattle. The folks on the bus for that stretch had been wild and fun! A few of them had alcohol with them, and they were sharing. Bottles had quietly been passed around and stories had been loudly shared. Every person three rows in front of me and three rows behind me had done time in jail for something or another – most of their charges were for petty crimes. I'd learned about this through the open storytelling that was shared on the bus.

The Elastic Band Bandit (as I'd jokingly named him) had done a few days for stealing a package of elastic bands. Somehow, he'd taken that event and made a wild, hilarity-filled story out of it which all of us enjoyed thoroughly. Others had tried to compete with their jailhouse tales, but no one came close to his. In my journal, I had been faithfully recording my entire journey, and I'd dubbed the group 'Felon's Alley'. I had decided that spending some time in jail gave a person character because of all the people I'd met on the bus over those seven days, the 'Felon's Alley' folks had been the most interesting and entertaining.

I believe it was in Portland that Angelo had gotten on the bus and sat beside me – the bus was almost full. He was about 6 foot 6 and all muscle. A good-looking African American man, I had felt safe sitting beside him, sharing Bible passages and testimony of god. His words were gentle and his conviction strong. The entire ride to Los Angeles, we'd talked and shared our thoughts about god – even though they differed greatly. Angelo had been all Bible. I had been all open-mind and possibility.

When we arrived at the LA terminal, I'd quickly looked for a hotel on some boards they had for advertising. I'd found one, the LA Adventurers Hotel, that also had hostel services. Perfect! I'd scribbled the address and phone number down. Angelo had wanted to help me get to where I was going, he said he knew the neighbourhood like the back of his hand – he'd lived here all his life. Once out on the street, however, I'd known something was wrong because he kept getting confused and saying things like, "Oh, that didn't used to be here."

He'd tried to take me to a bar he knew and it wasn't there anymore. Carrying his cardboard box, and helping me with one of my two huge bags, we'd stumbled around the scariest neighbourhood I'd ever been in. The bus had let out at 9pm; it had been dark. Addicts and sellers were scattered on the street. Storefronts had iron bars on them and security guards in the doorways. Acting as casually as I could with Angelo, I'd prayed for god to get me out of there. After trying unsuccessfully to get us into a very scary looking 'hotel', I'd told Angelo I was going to try to get down to the LA Adventurers Hotel. Angelo got impatient and angry with me. We'd argued for a few moments, but eventually he dropped my second bag and wished me well. Finding a payphone, I'd called the hotel and spoke to someone to find out which bus I should take to get there. Standing at the bus stop wondering if I'd been at the right one, a guy who looked homeless tried to help me. I gave him a sweater because he'd looked cold.

I found out later that Angelo had most likely just gotten out of prison. When a person gets out of prison, they'd be given a cardboard box full of personal belongings and a bus ticket. Angelo had been carrying a cardboard box. It hadn't mattered to me where he'd come from. As far as I had been concerned, he was straight from Heaven. No one had even looked at me sideways when I walked through that dangerous part of town with him by my side or even after he'd left me at the bus stop.

Half an hour later, I stood in front of the LA Adventurers Hotel in Inglewood, California. I'd made it! After a bit of sweet talking with the front desk person, I'd managed to get myself into the hotel without the proper identification. I'd booked myself into a dorm room which cost ten dollars a night. Little did I know, I had just checked myself into Hotel California…"you can check out any time you like, but you can never leave."

* * *

With my motorcycle purring beneath me, I was deeply woven into my memories. I remembered how it felt to get to LA that night. I had been elated and rather impressed with myself. It reminded me of completing a quest while playing Dungeons and Dragons in my younger years – I had just completed the quest of getting to California! The pull to achieve this quest had first surfaced back in early October of 2006 and on January 17th, 2007, I'd checked into a hotel in California. Not bad for someone who had been half out of her mind, penniless, and without a single piece of legal ID. In my mind's eye, I stood in the lobby of the Hotel California in my past while maneuvering my way towards Gravenhurst in the present. The past pulled me in deeper.

After dropping off my bags in the LA Adventurers hostel dorm room, having a shower, and freshening up, I'd made my way to the hotel bar where I was delighted to hear they had $1 beers. After my second beer, a rumpled looking man in a rumpled looking suit slid over to the seat beside me and introduced himself as Chris, the manager of the hotel. He'd inquired about where I was from and what I was doing in LA. I gave him the same story I had given everyone – I was from Toronto, Canada, and I was getting as far away from my ex as possible.

When he found out that I had just spent six days on a Greyhound bus, Chris insisted that I should have more comfortable accommodations than a bunk in the dorm room. Explaining that his room had two separate bedrooms with a locking door in between, he'd promised I could have a sleep, by myself, in the second bed. Not entirely trusting him or his offer, I let the conversation continue as we chatted at the bar. I was determined to have a few beers; it had been a long week, it had been an even longer year.

Handing me a one-dollar bill, Chris had pointed me towards a jukebox and told me to pick some music out. Wow! Cool! A jukebox! I love jukeboxes – magical music machines that invite you to pick your own story for the few minutes that a song plays. Now that we live in the land of MP3s and personal music lists, a jukebox could have outgrown its novelty, its magic. But not for me. Perhaps the magic is only lost on youth. It certainly isn't lost on those of us who start to dance inside every time we see a jukebox and excitedly flip the solid pages to reveal more and more songs to choose from. That had been me at the bar – dancing on the inside, excitedly flipping through magical musical stories to play.

I had been delighted to find Prince on the list, along with lots of other music I enjoyed. Prince was so perfectly purple and magic for that moment – that moment – the 'I've landed in the United States with a new name, and I'm free' moment. (My favourite colour is purple, and one of my all-time favourite musicians is Prince.) As I sat on my barstool, drinking my beer, 'Let's Go Crazy' had me twirling, spinning and dancing inside my head. Yes, let's go crazy! Let's celebrate crazy! Let's stop saying it like it's a bad thing! That was how I had felt inside and no one in the bar had any idea that I was separated by a million miles of magic and purple in that moment – feeling the power of the music as it played out the perfect moments of that incredible first evening of the kind of freedom I'd been needing.

Sometime after midnight, probably close to 2am, Chris and I had made our way to his room. He wasn't lying, he had two rooms with a door in between. I can't recall if the door really did lock, but it never did get locked. Both rooms had been a complete disaster – like a 15-year-old boy had been living there for months unsupervised. Clothes had been strewn everywhere, empty food boxes, bags, and ties hung on the dresser and over chairs. This mess had been Chris's living space. I didn't trust this guy as far as I could pick him up and throw him, and that wasn't far; he was a tall, overweight man. But I'd needed someone on my side, even if he was a snake. I had $700 to my name and I had no plan. Until I had a plan, I wasn't willing to refuse offers of help, even if I didn't fully trust them. I had no idea when and how god was going to help me, I'd just trusted that he would, and it would likely be through an unexpected source.

After getting myself tucked into bed, Chris had promptly made a move on me and tried to kiss me. Sitting straight up in bed, I told him I was going back to the dorm.

"No, no, don't do that, I'm sorry. You can stay here, I promise to leave you be," he'd said. And he did. That night.

Chris had wanted me to stay in his extra room. And I had agreed on the condition that he not pursue me in any way. Up to that point, he'd seemed harmless. He had been drunk when I met him at the bar the night before, and by 11 am the next day, he'd been drunk again. Drunks with an agenda I could usually handle. Stone-cold sober people with an agenda – that was never easy. I had moved all his mess into his room, and I cleared some space for myself and my things in the room I was in.

Across the road, I'd found a dollar store that had some art supplies in it, and I got myself some paper and pens, in addition to the ones I had brought with me from Mum. I had been delighted to buy a pack of Marlboros – I always loved American cigarettes. The musty sweet taste of Texas filled my mouth, my lungs. Why Texas? I have no idea, I've never been there. But that's how I'd imagined Texas tasted, musty and sweet, like a Marlboro.

By the pool at the hotel, there was another jukebox. Chris had offered to turn off the payment part of it so that I could listen to music by the pool all day, every day. Perfect! Bringing my art stuff down, I sat in the sun. Every day I met new people from around the world who were staying at the hotel for a day or two.

Since I had arrived, I had felt relieved. I had felt like an entire year in hell had lifted off my shoulders. I wasn't afraid. In fact, for the first time in over a year, I hadn't been afraid of anything at all. I felt like god was with me. I knew Tracey had disappeared on the other side of the border, back in Canada. I still had no idea why I'd been guided to LA, but I was excited to be there. Anything could happen there. A book could get written. A new identity could be created. A peaceful life could begin. Absolutely anything was possible.

I hadn't been conscious of the toll that the previous year had taken on me. The previous year? More like the previous four years. There hadn't been any part of me that was ready to look at the seriousness of my addictions or the damage my choices had done to my spirit. I had been unaware of how exhausted my body was – adrenaline had kept me going for weeks. As soon as I had crossed the border, I had released all the fears that had been chasing me. My demons were standing back with the border guards in Canada.

At lunch, Chris had offered to take me out; I was happy to accept a free meal. When we stepped out front of the hotel, there was a limo waiting. Maybe not as nice or in as good shape as the one I had taken to AC/DC years before, but a limo, nonetheless. After we'd climbed in, I was laughing and smiling as I played with the stereo to get some cool tunes blasting. Windows down, I could not believe the awesomeness of the moment! I had run away from my life and had virtually nothing, but on my very first day in LA, I was riding in a limo! I had felt like I owned the world. If I was riding in a limo on day one, what on earth did the Universe have in store for me for the rest of my days in the United States? Whatever it was, it must be awesome, I'd thought to myself.

Chris smiled, drink in hand, as we made our way to his lunch spot – the Buggy Whip. Inside the restaurant, everyone had known him, and everyone was curious about who I was. I explained that I had come to California with no idea of what I was going to do. Chris bought me a steak, and I enjoyed a wonderful meal.

Chris' motives had been obvious from the first moment of our time together. He'd wanted sex and I really didn't want to give him that. There was absolutely nothing attractive about Chris to me, no matter how hard I tried to find something. He was a jerk to his staff, he was perpetually drunk, he stunk of stale alcohol, and he smoked more than I did. I'd felt trapped though. I'd known I didn't have a lot of money, and I had no idea what on earth I was going to do about that fact. I hadn't had a plan.

Afraid of catching an STD from this guy, I'd finally agreed to have sex but he'd have to wear a condom. As my luck would have it, in his drunkenness he could not maintain a hard-on and wear a condom at the same time. Because of this, we never had sex. Thank you, god. (Seriously. Big thank you on that one.) My willingness to attempt sex with a condom had been enough to keep him hopeful and keep him interested.

As time went on, I'd started to get to know some of the staff and some of the regulars at the hotel. The glamour of the limo faded quickly as weeks passed. I was getting a picture of a hotel manager who slept with anything he could and took advantage of women who had no place to go and were willing to shack up for a bit.

I explained to him one day that I'd wanted some ID, in case I ever needed it. He'd known me as Julie, but I didn't use that ID with anyone because it was obvious that I wasn't 16-years- old. In his room, he'd opened a dresser drawer and inside was a small mountain of IDs. He told me to look through and pick something that worked. Holy crap! What a goldmine! I didn't want to know where these had all come from, but he'd said they were left at the hotel at various times by people who had stayed. Ever been in a situation where you wonder, even just for a moment, if the person you are sitting beside is a serial killer? It had crossed my mind briefly. I doubted he'd be capable of that. As a hotel manager he had access to all sorts of stuff that got left or lost at the hotel and obviously he'd been willing to hang onto loose IDs, in case one of his girls needed it. And there I was, one of his girls, needing an ID.

Out of the pile of IDs, I'd found one that I could use: Mary Auker from Australia. She had long brown hair, sort of like mine, except mine was much shorter and dyed blonde. She was a bit older than me. Any work visa she would have had would have expired, and she'd probably be back in Australia based on the out of date ID I was looking at. It would work in a pinch. And sometimes, I could get in a pinch.

During our time together, Chris had taken me to San Diego for a few days. We'd gone to the zoo, to the Hard Rock Café. I remember there'd been a lot of alcohol consumption. I don't remember much else, except that we'd taken a train there. Oh, and I also remember that San Diego was where he got his one and only blow job from me. I hope it was worth it to him. At the time, I'd been able to justify it to myself. I wasn't proud of it. I'd felt like a prostitute. But I'd chalked it up to a not-so-bad choice. I'd been afraid of the future. I had no idea what was coming, and I'd needed a few people in my corner, even if it cost me my self respect.

The truth was, I'd felt like a prostitute for the final few years of my old life – this was pretty tame compared to what I'd left. Moments like this one with Chris though, made little digs at my self esteem. I think my self esteem had lifted a smidge since leaving my old life. Feeling Loved by god had been helping. I'd been told for years by people in my life how loved I was, but I hadn't felt it. The Love I'd started to feel at that time was so much more intense, so much more real. It didn't have any conditions on it, not one. The Divine saw me, it saw me and Chris, it saw me and my past, and it still had its arms wrapped around me, telling me I was Loved.

One day in the hotel, I'd met a man named Peter. He'd called himself a Kiwi from New Zealand. Noticing my strange relationship with Chris, he'd straight up asked me about it one day. I'd told him the situation and was honest about it. Peter offered to let me sleep on the couch in his room that had a separate room he slept in. Laughing, he'd said he had no intention of being a dirty old man like Chris, he'd just wanted to help me out of the situation for a few weeks if he could. And that's exactly what had happened – I moved into his room and Peter never once made a move on me – he was a total gentleman. Angels come in many forms – a big, good looking guy named Angelo, a high school kid from Calgary named Julie, and Peter from New Zealand. Earth angels.

Peter had driven me and one of the other women at the hotel up to Santa Barbara one sunny Sunday. What a beautiful drive it had been, up the #1 Highway along the ocean. I'd seen dolphins that day. Life was such a miracle! That was what California was supposed to be like – ocean, sunshine, dolphins, surfers and beaches full of people in colourful bathing suits. Before my trip to LA, I'd never seen the ocean. I vividly remember bawling my eyes out on the Greyhound bus ride when I'd seen it for the first time. The mountains too – seeing them had been a first as well. The day trip with Peter had been the best opportunity to get out of the city and see California. It was beautiful.

The ocean. I was being called to it. Every day there was a shuttle that left the hotel and went down to Santa Monica, and later it would go back to the hotel. Since I'd seen the ocean properly, I knew I had to go back and check it out. One morning, shortly after my drive with Peter, I'd hopped on the shuttle and rode through LA to get to the ocean. After making sure I knew where I was supposed to get picked up later in the day, I'd hopped off and smiled into another adventure – Santa Monica.

Very quickly, I'd found myself at the pier – the shuttle dropped me off just a block or two from it. At the very beginning of the pier was a man playing a keyboard. A bubble machine pumped out a never-ending stream of rainbow bubbles that danced in the ocean air while he sang Elton John songs. I had started to cry. Tears had streamed down my face as I watched the bubbles soar, pop, dance, and do what bubbles do. I had finally made it! I had known for months that I was supposed to come to Santa Monica and here I was!

Looking nothing like Elton John, playing his keyboard in his tacky Hawaiian shirt with a little pot belly poking out, with his worn-out flip flops, an unshaven face, the man with the bubbles began to sing Your Song, by Elton John. Surrounded by beautiful bubbles, I'd wept in the sunshine, feeling like god was singing this song to me. I take that back. God was singing to me that day, at that moment. And there were other moments like that in my life where I knew the song was being sung just for me. There on the Santa Monica Pier for the first time in my life, after struggling to get there for the past seven months, that was one of those moments where god took the time to sing me a song. I'd sat down. I'd listened. And I'd let god sing me a few more songs. Who knew god liked Hawaiian shirts?

Imagining that god was singing love songs to me had been one of the earliest steps I'd taken in learning how to love myself. I hadn't loved myself. But I was really beginning to believe that god loved me, or the Universe, or whatever you call it. Looking back on how I started to love myself, this first step, of accepting god's love for me, was a big one. I'll tell you why. God sees everything. God knew all of my foibles, my mistakes, my most glorious disasters. God was there in the middle of the night when I was drunk or high, selling my soul and body to a complete stranger in exchange for feeling wanted, by anyone, by someone. When I'd accepted god's love for me, it had opened the door to me forgiving myself one day when I'd be ready to do so. If god loved me, knowing all of the worst stuff, the hardest stuff... then I could love me one day too. Try it sometime. Listen to a beautiful love song and imagine god, an angel or the Universe singing it to you. It creates a lovely, snuggly, warm feeling inside. The truth is, I'm pretty certain that if the Universe did have a singing voice, it would do exactly that all day long – sing us love songs, remind us of who we really are, and tell us stories about how and when and why it fell in love with us.

My visits to Santa Monica had marked the beginning of the end for Hotel California. The changeover from that place hadn't happened overnight, however. First, I'd discover Venice Beach and it's cast of characters. But stepping onto the Santa Monica Pier sparked the change. I knew there was something else, something more than the Hotel California in Inglewood. I knew there was something beautiful waiting for me, I just had to figure out how to get there and stay.

* * *

I don't regret my time at Hotel California. It had value on my journey to self understanding. As I became more self aware, I was able to reflect back on that time and see it for what it was. I was using Chris for a cheap place to live, and he was using me in hopes of getting some action. Both of us had substance abuse problems. Chris was a mirror for where I was at that time in my life while also being a warning sign. His lifestyle, his abuse of alcohol, his unhappiness were all warnings from the Universe that if I made similar choices, my outcome would be similar.

I easily could have stayed at the hotel without moving into his room but I didn't trust myself yet, and I didn't trust the Universe to have my back. I can look back at that entire chapter in my life – The Hotel California Chapter – and forgive myself for not knowing better, forgive myself for thinking I had to manipulate the situation in order to feel safe, forgive myself for not seeing myself in the mirror of Chris' alcohol consumption. I can now love the me who was still entirely unaware of herself and fumbling through mistakes.

A LITTLE FURTHER NORTH

As I got closer to Gravenhurst, the roads I was riding on became more and more obscure. It was almost impossible to get to Gravenhurst without taking highway 11 at some point, almost. The roads I was being directed down were breathtaking, but as the scenery became increasingly stunning, the roads were less and less maintained. I was avoiding potholes and bumps and felt pretty certain that my next turn would dump me on a gravel road. I finally changed the settings on my GPS, allowing it to guide me back to highway 11. Turning my tunes back up, I coasted through the trees, welcomed the picturesque rocks and breathed in the stillness of Nature's beauty.

Around 4pm, I rolled up to my Airbnb in Gravenhurst. It was close to the bay. I had a lovely bedroom to myself, just what I needed. After unpacking my bike and all my accessories, I freshened up and decided to go to a park just down the road that appeared to be on the water. Hopping off my bike at the park, there were two older gentlemen coming back from the short walk to the water. They started talking to me about my bike and asking about my trip. After explaining the WRWR briefly, one of them started telling me about his motorcycle. Like I said, people love to talk about motorcycles with anyone they see riding one. As we were parting ways, I asked if they knew a good place to go for dinner. They said that Boston Pizza was right on the water and I'd love it.

As they got in their car, I walked the short distance to the rocks that overlooked the Bay. It was beautiful. Absolutely gorgeous. Sitting down on the rocks, I breathed Muskoka in. I loved this. I loved it here. I'd never actually spent any real time in Gravenhurst, I was always near it. It's the kind of place I could happily live with incredible surroundings and amazing hiking trails.

After taking a moment to get a few selfies, put a post up on Facebook, and scribble a few notes in my journal, I headed to Boston Pizza. As they said, it was right on the water. I asked to sit on the outdoor patio. Perusing the menu, I felt a tap on my shoulder. It was one of the men I had just met half an hour before. His name was Tony. He invited me to join him at their table. I happily agreed and sat down with him and the other man, Bob. I discovered that one of them had retired from the Peel Regional Police and the other had retired from the Ontario Provincial Police. Upon further discussion, I discovered the Peel officer had been a narcotics officer. I laughed when they told me!

"You know, not that many years ago I definitely wouldn't have sat for dinner with the likes of you two!" I joked. But I was serious too!

Over supper they shared interesting stories about busts, about criminals, about people who had rehabilitated, the whole gamut. Being eight-and-a-half-years clean and sober myself, I appreciated the stories.

Dinner with Tony and Bob was fantastic. I have always enjoyed meeting new people and hearing new stories. My heart was full and so was my belly. Something I've noticed in my travels is this – people who travel alone, maybe even more so if you're a woman, will get approached a lot more often by strangers. And I don't mean getting hit on, I just mean, people will invite you to their table or strike up a conversation if you're alone.

When I traveled to the US, I experienced this all the time, and it was the same back in Canada. When I travel alone, I meet a lot more people. I guess it's because we look occupied and busy if we are with someone...but alone, a person is approachable. Some might even think you're lonely and want to alleviate that. I like it. Two of my favourite things about traveling alone are the alone time (the being alone part I really do enjoy!) and being approached by strangers and meeting new, wonderful people.

Bob and Tony wished me a good night and we all went our separate ways – me on my motorcycle back to the Airbnb, them back to Orangeville. The day was just perfect – I was held in beautiful sunshine, wrapped up in colourful trees, swayed down winding, curving backroads, and enjoyed dinner with two brothers-in-law who entertained me with policing stories. Life doesn't get much better than this.

For years I viewed authority figures in a negative light – not when I was a child, but after the loss of my innocence. The older I got, the less respect I had for people in authority. The deeper my addiction to drugs, the deeper my disdain for folks like Bob and Tony. Sitting there having dinner with them gave me a wonderful opportunity to understand how much they cared about the people they locked up over the years. Bob's favourite story was about a man who rehabilitated while he was in prison. He smiled from ear to ear as he told me about how the man changed his life and helped so many people when he got out. In my life, there were lots of Tonys and Bobs who cared while putting on the stern face of authority. Being so self involved during my addiction, I failed to understand or appreciate folks who did their best to move me in a different direction.

I have a very good friend, Mandy, who is a retired cop. This woman tirelessly helps folks who are having a rough time. She goes out of her way to give a hand up to people who are trying to change their life. During her years as a police officer, she was the one who would go back to the house where a domestic dispute had occurred. She'd return with donated beds for the kids and clothes for the mom. I know that my disdain for authority figures over the years is connected to my addiction and to my abuse as a youth. I'm grateful that I've worked through that trigger so that I can appreciate the Bobs, Tonys and Mandys out there who just want to make the world a safer place.

Back at the Airbnb, I jotted a few notes into my journal. After calling my husband and telling him about my day, I signed off for the night. Sleep overtook me quickly.

DAY 3 – SEPTEMBER 13TH, 2019

WILD WORLD

I was up bright and early the next morning yet again! I couldn't sleep until sunrise, let alone past sunrise. Each morning I was excited about where I was going next. My planned route would be rolling through my head the moment I awoke. No matter how hard I tried to sleep more than four or five hours, I just couldn't.

On my third day, I was set to make it to North Bay where my high school friend Amanda was waiting for me. Google Maps showed me that if I was willing to take Highway 11, my ride would be around 1 hour and 45 minutes. On the other hand, taking the backroads I was looking at a four hour or more drive. The backroads it was! The whole point of my trip was to take my time and see as much of the area as possible. I'd driven up Highway 11 before; it wasn't how I wanted to travel. I wanted a scenic drive. I wanted new memories. Rain was threatening later in the day, so I knew I had to get on the road at a decent time if I wanted to avoid it.

Having driven out of Gravenhurst and heading up the highway towards Parry Sound, a song I've always loved came on. The song was Feeling Stronger Everyday, by Chicago. Since leaving my life in 2006, this song has taken on meaning for me that didn't exist before. My life was so much better than it would have ever the potential to be if I hadn't changed things drastically. And I don't just mean the final few years of my addiction – I mean the whole thing. I can't look back and say, "Oh well, I made some bad mistakes near the end." No, the whole damn thing was a disaster right from the start. Right from the day I turned eighteen and started taking responsibility for my life and decisions. I'd been making poor choices for a long time. That's not to say that I don't have some awesome memories from those years, because I do. But I was never going to find true happiness on that path.

Depression set in early in my adult life and it clung to me like a vampire, sucking the life out of me for over a decade. By the time I finally found an antidepressant that worked I was already thirty years old, and I was neck deep in addiction to other drugs.

Getting out of that abyss wasn't going to happen in the same environment – it required change, massive change. Something I tell clients when the Tower card comes up in the future part of their reading is that there are two ways to deal with the impending doom of the Tower card.

We can listen to our intuition and leave the job we hate or leave the marriage that we're not happy in or do the thing we know we should do but we may not have the courage to do so before the Tower starts burning down. We can walk out the front door and avoid the catastrophe or we can avoid doing the thing we know we should do (out of fear or any other emotion), wait for the Tower to catch fire and barely make it out alive as we jump out of the second story window while the building is burning to the ground.

When the building is burning, however, that's when people get fired, disasters happen in marriages or life crumbles in some way or another. Me and my Tower? I'd had numerous warning signals from the Universe. The last signal had been in the fall of 2004. It was a loud-and-clear red flag signal from the Universe that said, "get out while you still can!" I didn't. I was too high and too deep in my own dysfunction to get out while the getting was good. So, as it goes with the Tower card, it proceeded to burn to the ground – with me inside. And I'm ok with that. Because I had to leave, one way or another. It took a disaster for me to leave – a disaster I created – and I'm ok with that too. I feel stronger every day, and I've been feeling this strength (in different bursts and states) since the day I walked away from the ashes of my Tower in 2006. Being a part of my burning Tower was the best thing that happened to me. It might not take the burn for everyone to make a massive life change but for me, it did.

When I had lived in California in 2007, I first started to feel that way – like the disaster I'd lived through had some level of blessing hidden inside of it. It would be years before I'd work through all my emotions about what I'd left behind – the aftermath of the disaster I had made of my life. But that was ok. Love was patient. And step one was relieving some of the terror I'd been feeling, so that I could be able to start working toward healing the past, coming to terms with it and beginning to see things differently.

I hadn't ended up staying in Santa Monica because I fell in love with Venice Beach. Still staying at the hotel back in Inglewood, I had been taking a shuttle every day out to the ocean. On my second visit, I'd wandered down to Venice Beach and was mesmerised with what I discovered there – artists all lined up along the boardwalk selling and doing everything imaginable. People roller skating, riding bicycles, smoking pot, skateboarding; performers miming, people singing, artists painting; foot-long hotdogs, colourful sarongs – it had been culture, madness and magic. It had been everything my broken heart needed.

Venice Beach had been technicolour. I had left such a darkness behind me, and this, this was bright, and sunshine, and hope. I remember I'd go onto the sand and draw a huge peace sign, and then sit beside it and pray to god for world peace. Little had I realized that world peace came one person at a time. I had needed to find peace within myself. Praying for peace had been a good start. Just that intention had been enough to start energy in motion and get events moving in the right direction – toward peace in my own life.

I'd made friends in Venice right away. Don was the first person I'd met. I'd been sitting in the sandy grass near the boardwalk watching people go by, and he offered me a hit off a joint. Hell yes, please and thank you! Don had a bicycle with him and told me he was in the process of opening a small bike shop on the boardwalk. We'd quickly become friends. Don took me to my first drum circle in Venice. Every Saturday and Sunday, drummers started showing up before sundown, and by the time the sun was setting, seventy-five or a hundred people would be jamming out on drums, dancing, swaying, praying to the sun, smoking joints, and capturing a moment of peace and happiness in the sand. It had been pure magic. It was there that I'd fallen in love with drum circles.

I remember the first circle we went to. It had been like entering a new country, experiencing a new culture. Flowing skirts with bright floral patterns, dreadlocked hair, long flowing golden hair, afros, cool hats that looked like they dropped right out of 1969, bell-bottomed jeans, faded swim trunks – a cacophony of bohemian clothes and hairstyles had surrounded me like armor. Some folks had drums with them, more didn't. Don had a drum – an African-style djembe. Showing me how to play with my fingers for the tones on the edge of the drum, and with my full hand bouncing off the centre of the drum for deeper bass, he had passed his drum to me and allowed me to play with the group.

My sense of rhythm had been atrocious, and I'd laughed at my attempts to keep up with the group. Eventually, I fell into the back bass beat as it had been simple to keep rhythm and it was more my speed. Drumming had created a trance state for me – it was like the world fell away. There had been nothing but me and my drum. I had been so focused on staying in beat with the larger group that my busy mind stopped thinking, stopped analyzing, and was just experiencing. I hadn't known it then, but that had been a type of spontaneous meditation. Drums and drumming would become one of my healers.

After heading out to the beach for a few weeks in a row, Don and I had become romantically involved. Don was a super sweet guy with a heart of gold. Good looking too. Drifting away from Inglewood, I had stayed a few nights at Don's little one-room apartment. It had been right around that time that I started to desire to move to Venice. Moving in with Don, however, had not been an option.

This was exactly the time in my life when I began to observe 'manifesting.' I hadn't known yet that it was called manifesting, I hadn't had a word for it, but I'd started to notice it happening. I'd called it Magic. I figured it was god working Magic for me. One morning I'd been sitting at Don's bike shop with him on the boardwalk. Beautiful people – bizarre, wonderful beach people – had been milling around, walking by, riding bikes. The sun was shining.

"I need to find a job here on Venice Beach," I'd commented to Don. Approximately three minutes later, we both watched as the shopkeeper two doors down from him –

about ten feet away – put a sign up saying 'Help Wanted'. Wandering over, I spoke to him and within minutes, I'd had a job. I would start that day.

A week later, or maybe two, I had said to another friend, "I need to find a place to live here. I really need to move to Venice." I couldn't keep bussing in every day from the hotel. Later that day, Al, one of the beach artists, had sauntered up in his black beret with his Tommy Chong beard and pothead drawl, saying, "Hey man. Do you know anyone who wants to buy a van, man?" After speaking to him for a few minutes, I'd asked if it was something I could live in, and he assured me I could. I'd asked if I could rent it instead. He said he'd go ask his old lady. By the end of the day, I had my answer – I had a van to live in that I could rent. Inside, there was a bed, shelves for my clothing, and a small sink. I'd be able to park this on the street and have someone move it for me once a week for the street cleaners. Voila, I was living in Venice Beach!

I'd loved that van! I remember how happy I had been the day I moved in. It had been my own space – the first personal space I'd had since walking away from my life. I sat down on the bed and smiled from ear to ear, pleased with myself for having found a home for all my belongings. Al had parked it outside of a place called Ace's Garage. It was written on the cement bricks in very faded paint. It obviously wasn't Ace's Garage anymore, but it once had been. That brought me a feeling of pure joy and magic! A very good friend of mine used to call me Ace. I missed her. It was like she was there, telling me that everything was going to be ok – I was home at Ace's Garage.

Shortly after I had moved to Venice, I commented to a friend that I needed a bicycle. It was a long walk to get food and things in Venice. I had wanted a simple cruiser bike. One with rounded handlebars, a big cushy seat, and when you pushed the pedals backwards, you got the brakes. Simple. The next day, I was having tea and a morning joint with Don, when Bear, one of our beach homeless friends, carried a cruiser bike with the front wheel detached but intact to the garbage can and propped it there as if it were junk. I asked Bear if he was ditching it and if there was anything wrong with it other than the tire. He said he found it with a flat front tire, and yes, he was throwing it out. I gave him a few dollars and said, "Thank you!" as I took hold of the bike.

Don helped me carry it twenty feet to his bike shop. Ten minutes later, Don had inserted a new inner tube and snapped the wheel back on. Then he'd asked me to try and ride it. It worked perfectly! Oh my gosh! A bike! It had been the simple cruiser with rounded handlebars, a cushy seat and the brakes that worked when I pushed the pedals backwards – just as I had wished! I asked Don how much for the repair. He said, "Two dollars for the inner tube is what that just cost me, so two dollars!" I could manage that no problem!

I had wanted to move to Venice because the place brought me happiness. I smiled and laughed when I was there. The Universe answered my requests quickly with a job, a place to sleep and a bicycle. That was the basics of manifesting – request and receive. The Universe honed-in on what was bringing me joy and brought more of it. I hadn't understood the science of it yet. I'd never heard of the Law of Attraction or read books like The Secret. But what I observed was that my happiness and gratitude combined seemed to be able to bring in more of whatever it was that was making me happy. It was Magic!

At that time, I hadn't begun to learn or understand Tarot, yet my experiences in California were essentially shifting me through the Major Arcana cards at record speed. The High Priestess accesses the subconscious mind, the hidden world of intuition, the realm of the sacred. My intuition had brought me here California, and even though my first stop was anything but enlightened, it had been a necessary stop in my travels to get to the next step – Venice Beach. And it was there, on the beach, that I had begun to create my new reality, my new world.

As I did that, I stepped out of the High Priestess energy and into the role of The Empress – a magnificent, curvaceous woman, pregnant with life, pregnant with ideas, pregnant with abundance and creation. The beach had shifted me into that role for a short while as I found myself immersed in an awe-inspiring natural setting, creating and manifesting without a thought or even an understanding of what that was – employment, a living space, transportation, friends, music, laughter and freedom came at me

The High Priestess
& The Empress Cards.
Rider-Waite Tarot deck

like feathers in the sand. My soul had been full of ideas, full of magic, full of appreciation and gratitude, and all of that was bursting forth from me into a brand new world – one of my own creation. I had begun to live according to a newness in self-awareness that the place I was in mirrored; from the warmth to the ocean to the people. I chose to surround myself with things and people that brought me joy, safety, and spiritual enlightenment. My choices were affecting my ability to change deeply in ways that I couldn't have changed before. The places, the people, the things I'd surrounded myself with previously hadn't been able to ignite this kind of change within. I wasn't consciously doing things differently yet, but I had changed. I was starting to see the rainbow instead of the rain. I was starting to expect good things instead of expecting the worst. I was seeing all that I had instead of all I was lacking. My whole life, I had seen the world from a negative perspective, and it was finally flipping around where I could see it correctly.

Laying in my van the first few nights in Venice, I'd been awestruck at how I had managed to get from London, Ontario to Venice Beach! Gratitude oozed out of every pore in my body. Just three or four months previous, I had been homeless in Toronto, gripped in terror. But that had all changed. I had a job that supported my lifestyle, and I was living in Venice Beach, right by the ocean – one of the most expensive places to live in America. How was all of this even possible? I had chalked it all up to god. I said, 'thank you' an awful lot. It hadn't dawned on me yet that my new choices were an essential part of the equation for my happiness. The person who had made horrible, destructive choices had been starting to make a few good ones.

There was a brief incident that happened one day in Venice Beach that remains at the forefront of my mind. It had been a moment that gave me an incredible feeling of hope. One of the ladies who had worked on the beach as a psychic came up to me out of the blue, held my elbow for a moment, and she said, "All your dreams are going to come true within seven years." I had tried to ask for more information, but she'd waved me off and kept walking. Seven years, I'd thought to myself. I could do seven years.

As soon as I had fully moved into Venice Beach, I broke up with Don. I'm not proud or happy to say this. I remember why I'd broken up with him, why I hadn't been attracted to him. We'd had sex and it hadn't been great sex. It had been awkward. That doesn't mean he was the reason it had been awkward. He had been the first guy I'd slept with since my ex.

No sex had been great sex for me. Sex had always included a whole bunch of faking for me. Faking everything. It had been that way since I was 15-years-old. I had gotten good at having great faked sex. Why had I needed it to be great faked sex? I hadn't had a clue, and I wouldn't understand it until 2016 or thereabouts. My sexuality, my self-esteem, and my notions of self-worth had been so messed up by this time in my life. It was turning out that I'd felt more loved when sex had been wild and crazy, even if my pleasure was all faked. And because I had unhealthy personal awareness around sex and relationships, I had let this fantastic guy go. Don would have been a perfect guy to be with. He was stable, he was responsible, he was kind, he was cute, creative and fun. He was everything that would have been good for me. And that's why I hadn't been attracted to him. It had been a clear-cut choice in self-sabotage. What I thought I had needed was a boyfriend who would reinforce my belief that I was a bad person. A boyfriend who would be nothing but trouble.

And I found him. His name was Rob. Rob was from England originally, and I'd fallen for his accent. Up to that point in my life, I'd never fallen for anyone who had been as hard-core alcoholic as he was. With him at my side, I'd started walking down that exact same path. Not long after getting involved with Rob, I'd lost my $10/hour awesome job. I'd started selling my artwork on the beach, sitting by Rob and Art every day.

My heart lights up when I think about Arthur (Art). He was a hell of a lot of fun and he had a heart of gold. I have no idea what his backstory was. What I knew was that he was homeless and lived on Venice Beach. He was also an artist; one of the better selling artists on the beach too. He had been famous for making a series of artworks that had 'Funky' in the title – the most popular piece had been Funky Pussy. He'd painted that piece over and over and it always sold. It consisted of a cat posing while giving the finger. He'd painted a Funky Buddha, a Funky Goddess, and Funky all sorts of things. People loved it!

Art was hilarious and was a fabulous storyteller. He was the kind of guy who had a crowd in stitches laughing as he told a tale about making a sandwich. Kindness had radiated from his being. I recall applying for a job selling t-shirts on the pier later that spring, and I'd needed a reference. Art had been the only person I knew who had a cell phone, and he'd offered to be my work reference. Answering the phone when it rang, "Art's Beach Gallery", we'd all burst out into laughter after the call. Art's Beach Gallery indeed! We had all been selling our artwork on the boardwalk from vendor's squares – 10 by 10 squares on the pavement. As a beach artist, I'd found myself drinking from about noon on. I'd laughed and I'd had fun, and sometimes I'd gotten drunk. There were times when I'd get sad and I'd miss my old life.

One day on the boardwalk after drinks, I got to reminiscing and I'd told Rob a story.

"It was back when I was in Toronto. The grocery store I worked at had a Christmas party for staff. We were all given tickets for a whole bunch of prizes that had been donated by vendors. My name was drawn early and I won a cookie house! You know, a gingerbread house! I was so happy because I'd never had a gingerbread house as a child. All night I went on and on about my cookie house. I was plastered walking home with my friend Darren, and I dropped my cookie house. It broke all over the sidewalk. I was so sad," I paused as a realization had struck me. "You know, I owned a real cookie house less than a year before everything blew up. It looked just like a gingerbread house.I smashed that gingerbread house too. I got drunk and I destroyed it. I broke everything that meant anything to me. My cookie house is in a million pieces."

As I'd revealed the story, it had revealed a lesson to me. It had hit me like a tonne of bricks. I'd been avoiding thoughts about my old life as much as possible. But being in the US, being in the sunshine, drinking alcohol, laughing again...my anxiety had begun to subside, and my past had started to creep in. It had been nearly nine months since the day I'd walked out of my house to that day in May of 2007 sitting in the Venice Beach sand telling that story for me to realize what I'd lost. That was the very first time I'd felt remorse about what I'd done when things blew up.

What happened next was that my drinking increased. I was no longer in the effects of my madness. I couldn't avoid the truth of my life by being scared of it anymore because I hadn't felt scared. California had done its job and it had done it well. I had felt safe in California. I had laughed wholeheartedly in California. I had connected with god and the Universe in California. And when I was ready for it, when I was ready to start looking at my life, the Universe had served it up to me one very small piece at a time. My heart began to break and I had started to feel it breaking.

I'd been terrified when I left – I just wanted out alive. There had been no room for a broken heart. I had been terrified since November, 2005, when I had my full blown breakdown. After telling that story to Rob, I'd asked him to leave so I could be alone on the beach and sob. I'd cried my busted heart out. But it hadn't resulted in a healthy reaction or a healing release. No. I'd started to blame myself for destroying my gingerbread house, for leaving the destruction. And I drank. A lot. My self-loathing hadn't gone away, it had dug deeper and deeper within and burrowed into me no matter how far I'd go to try to escape it.

That April I had been invited to someone's apartment in Venice – it was one of the hippy chicks, as we'd called their group. The occasion was Easter. Everyone had brought something to add to the meal – there was no set meal plan. There was fast food, there was cooked food, there were munchies. There was pie. There was pot galore. Someone had even brought chocolate – what's Easter without chocolate? Upon arriving, I'd noticed that there wasn't alcohol, so I went and got a few 24s of beer to share.

I can still feel the feeling in my soul that I'd felt on that occasion. I had been so overcome with gratitude that I'd left the apartment to go stand on the street and have a good cry. That had been my first holiday celebration in California. But I had also felt what wasn't there. I was missing my sisters. I was missing my Mum. They were the people I'd missed the most. By this time, it had been six months since I'd seen my sisters Sarah and Michelle. It had been four months since seeing my Mum. It hadn't been that I didn't love other members of my family – my awesome sister Breanna, my brother Ryan, Bob, my Dad, Yvonne – it was just that I'd had a history of going long periods of time without seeing them. I had called Mum when I arrived in L.A. to let her know I'd gotten there safely, but otherwise, I'd not called anyone else in Canada. The entire time I was in the US, Michelle, Sarah and my Mum were the ones I'd missed so much it hurt. My emotions had been raw that evening – a mixture of gratitude and longing.

I was grateful for that Easter meal with what I'd felt was my 'Venice family.' None of us had families to celebrate with. We were a ragtag bunch of Venice artists, musicians, hippies, beach bums, and drop-outs from life who were all still very human and needed to fill our hearts with the comfort of a family meal. All of us had remembered the feeling of home and we'd gathered to tap into that need for togetherness.

TEQUILA

The ride between Gravenhurst and North Bay was turning out to be spectacular. The further north I went, the more beautiful the ride was becoming. How was I feeling? I was feeling awesome! I was in control of my life and having an amazing trip. My bike was running beautifully. Did it get any better?

Yes! I believe it does. The Universe once told me, "The best is yet to come." Those words were spoken to me early in my recovery by someone who had been clean and sober for a number of years. I'd believed those words with all my heart, and I still believe them to this day. Even though my life has become amazing, I still know the best is yet to come. I look forward to experiencing how each today will be even better than the day before. Life has not disappointed me since I first heard those words; it's only gotten better and better. Have I mentioned yet that beliefs matter? Beliefs have power. If I believe something will get better, it will. If I believe something will suck, it will. Because of the choices I've made and the abilities I've chosen to enhance on my spiritual journey (like my intuition, my tarot readings, my reiki, and my openness for example), I have taught myself how essential it is to believe. To believe in myself and to trust that I can make the best decisions for myself that will result in positivity. I've learned to choose my beliefs wisely because I've made enough unwise choices that I no longer need to exist in them. I choose empowering, unlimited beliefs. What do I mean by unlimited? A limiting belief is something like, "If I can get $20,000 somehow, I know my dream of a business will come true!" This belief is limited – the only way the business can open is if I find $20,000 first. An unlimited belief would be, "I know my dream of opening my own business will come true!" My world is full of possibilities. Possibilities that I believe I can achieve.

Riding along, smiling, reminiscing about days on the beach, and remarking to myself how wonderful the day was turning out to be, a song came on that filled my soul with laughter and a memory that will follow me into eternity - Thirty Days in the Hole, by Humble Pie.

***

I'd been living on Venice Beach for three months or so. The weather was fantastic so living in a vehicle was easy. It was Cinco De Mayo, May 5th – a day celebrated by Mexicans, Latinos, Californians, and me! Venice Beach was alive with a party that day. I hadn't heard of Cinco De Mayo until earlier that week, but in California, it was a big deal and a big party. Marky Mark – a nickname we'd used for one of the locals who lived in a condo on the beach – was serving up margaritas for everyone, myself included. I was a beer or cooler drinker, but I was never one to turn down a margarita. The sun shone, the music played, and from start to finish I drank. In fact, everyone did.

Later, I was invited with Rob to the apartment of one of the members of Peace Frog, a local Doors cover band. Food had been served up and so had more margaritas.

I drank. I had fun. I laughed. I cherished the moments as I was still grateful for being able to laugh again with ease. I hadn't had a good, deep, belly laugh yet, the kind of laugh that puts you in tears, but I had been laughing again and it was wonderful.

After the house party, we headed to the Bistro on the beach. This was where we had drinks most nights, watched Peace Frog play once a week, and pretended life was perfect. Everyone I'd hung out with had a story. I hadn't been entirely sure that my boyfriend Rob was legally in the country, even if he had been once upon a time. I believed that Lance had the same condition as Andre the Giant or something similar, and from my understanding, he wasn't expected to have a long life – his health was always a concern. Lance was super cool. He had a deep voice, he always thought before he spoke, and when he did speak, it was slow and patient. He had long sideburns, a scraggly beard and hair halfway down his back. He rode the sweetest bike – this black bike with red flame decals on it and big ape-hanger handlebars to match. Lance looked so Venice when he rode his bike around the boardwalk.

Don was around sometimes. His bicycle shop hadn't worked out, and there was still a bit of a wedge between him and I, but we would talk sometimes. Dave with his loose, mousy curls was around my age and had wanted to be a full-time artist. He was gifted and talented. Dave was a drifter but he wasn't sure where he was drifting to. Spike was homeless, but he did his best to not appear so. Spike was a good guy and Don's closest friend on the beach. When I hurt Don, I'd angered Spike. I had a tonne more friends on the beach – Dave the ex bouncer, girls from the sarong shop, people whose names escape me now. We'd been a community with relationships spanning from brief hellos to acquaintances to pals to partners.

Lance had rode up to the bistro on his lowrider bike. Begging him to take it for a spin through my margarita-laced drawl, he'd laughed and let me take a drunken ride down the deserted boardwalk. I rode to the weight-lifters area then turned around and came back. When I was almost back to the Bistro, a cop car passed me on the boardwalk. Technically, I wasn't supposed to ride a bike on the boardwalk, but since it was evening and empty, the cops hadn't seemed to care that I was there as they drove by. And they wouldn't have stopped...except...sigh ...except, I'd started singing quite loudly, "Fuck you L.A.P.D.! Fuck you, L.A.P.D!"

I was hammered. And this little song? This was the song that I'd quietly sing to my friends during the day when we saw cops coming along the beach. When I sang it, folks would put away their joints, their open alcohol and anything else illegal.

The brake lights of the cop car went on. I was pulled over right in front of the Bistro. They'd asked me to get off the bicycle, which I did, but then one cop tried to pull me up onto the hood of the car. I wouldn't let him without a fight. I'd made my body go limp. I vaguely recall reciting parts of Psalms 23 out loud as the cops had dragged me to the front of the car.

A lot of what followed remains very fuzzy. Apparently, Rob almost had me out of my predicament until I had told one of the cops to fuck off while I kicked him from the backseat of the cruiser. In my purse, they'd found a small amount of marijuana. I was driven to a police station. Once inside, I'd been put on a bench and handcuffed to a guy beside me. As they'd checked me in, I discovered I was charged with possession of marijuana and a DUI on a bicycle. I had thought to myself – no big deal, these were only misdemeanors. But as I'd listened, they were also charging me with two counts of assaulting a police officer. These were felony charges. Holy shit. Nothing had ever sobered me up so quickly than being charged with a felony in a country I didn't belong in. I had never been charged with a crime in my adult life before my stay in California. Normally it would have bothered me more but I was being charged under a false name. The real me 'Tracey Rogers' had still never been charged with a crime. But I'd quickly realized that even being charged with a felony using a false identity – this could lead to Tracey Rogers being charged with everything. That exact scenario was the kind of thing that could send me home to Canada, after first doing time in the United States.

I was put in a cell with around twenty other women. There were bunks. My cellmates were Latina and African American women. I'm not going to lie and say I wasn't aware of that fact – I was. I'd been the only Caucasian woman there, and I'd felt self conscious. Because it had been Cinco De Mayo which happened to fall on a weekend, I figured that almost everyone in the cell was there because of incidents involving alcohol or drugs. I'd heard someone talking about a domestic violence charge, and something about crack. I hadn't known for sure. I hadn't spoken to a single person myself.

I had been absolutely terrified out of my mind. I'd never been in jail before. I hadn't associated myself with ever being a part of that environment. I'd told myself a story about being better than that, being better than 'them' – people in jail. But I hadn't been. I hadn't been able to see it at the time, but I'd very much been a part of a community that included those who'd been in jail. (Remember the bus ride up with the travelers who'd all been to jail?) I'd been participating in actions that could have easily led the way into a jail cell. When I'd gotten on the bike, I'd been drunk. I'd known it wasn't safe or lawful. The fact that I'd been intoxicated was a factor in what I'd sang out to the cops. At the time of making those decisions, however, consequences had been nowhere on my mind.

I'd crawled onto a bunk and faced the wall. The only time I'd changed my position was to eat meals or to use the toilet to urinate. That had been a most unpleasant experience. There had been no toilet seat, just a stainless steel toilet. There were no walls and no privacy. It had been me, a toilet and twenty other women. We'd all been in varying states of sobering up. Meals consisted of two pieces of bread with a slice of processed cheese (which constituted a sandwich, according to the LAPD), a red delicious apple and a small container of orange drink. Three times a day for four days, I'd been served that meal. Not once had we been offered a toothbrush, a bar of soap, a facecloth, or anything else that would have affected our hygiene. I don't think I'd slept at all during those four days. Adrenaline had kept me awake, the same way it had as I fled headlong from Canada.

Just before this had all happened, earlier in the week, I had read and cut out my horoscope from one of the LA newspapers. I had even put it in my journal. It had said: *Festivities are going to carry right on through the weekend for you.* I had been excited about that prediction and I couldn't wait to see what the weekend held for me. On the following Tuesday morning as I was being taken in a van to a courtroom, I'd cursed the gods for that horoscope – for its blatant trickery!

I had been appointed a court lawyer of some sort. He spent less than two minutes asking me for a few details – details I can't even remember now. I had to remain standing and plead something – I can't even remember what I plead to be completely honest. I did what I was told to do. I had no awareness of my appearance at the time – I must have been a sight after four days in jail without so much as a toothbrush. Then after a few muffled comments by a judge, the prosecution and my lawyer, I'd been released on my own recognizance. What?! Seriously?! For four days I had envisioned myself sitting in prison for a few years. I had played over in my mind how I'd survive. The entire court process, from me meeting my lawyer to me being released took under five minutes. The entire thing happened in a blur. I had no time to feel anything, I had no time to wonder anything. Ba-da-bing, ba-da-boom, I handed in my Get out of Jail Free card, avoided a trip back to the start at Go, and I got ready to roll the dice again.

Somehow, without any ID, no social security number, no permanent address, no phone number, I'd been set free. I had no idea if I had a criminal record or not.

When I'd been released from the jail, a police officer sitting behind a booth and plexiglass gave me some of my possessions back. My boots hadn't been in the pile so I'd asked her for them. She said they'd been kept as evidence because I'd kicked the police officer while wearing them. She asked me if Mary Auker was my real name. I said that it was. She said she had received a weird phone call from someone the night before, claiming to be a boyfriend, who was obviously very drunk, and he was looking for a Canadian girl who had been arrested at the Bistro. He said that her name was Tracey Moniker. She'd spelled it out for me. Keeping a straight face, I'd said, no, that it hadn't been me he was babbling about. I didn't even have a boyfriend, I'd told her.

It had been Rob who called. He'd known my real name because I had told him. Standing there at the police station, having the cop ask me if my real name was Tracey, I'd quickly realized I couldn't tell people I wasn't using my real name. I had to keep my true identity hidden. I'd been relieved that the cop hadn't pushed further on the subject. She'd given me the rest of my things and I had left. I hadn't given Rob my full real name, and that had probably been what helped me stay on my toes with the lie about it. I'd told him my name was Tracey. I'm guessing the Moniker came from 'Auker', the last name I was using. Incidentally, I'd looked up the meaning of the word moniker a few days later and laughed when I read that it meant 'nickname' or 'not a real name'. Tracey Moniker. Yep, that had been me.

I made my way back to Venice Beach via a twenty-minute ride from a very nice person who'd been picking up their spouse at the jail. My mind had already left jail behind. I wasn't focusing on what had just happened, I was already focused on what I'd do when I got back to Venice. I was starting to ponder if I'd stay or if it was time to move on. Dropping me at my RV, I'd said good-bye to the generous lady and her husband. Once inside, I'd used some water to wash up a bit. My hair was so frazzled from being bleached that you couldn't tell it hadn't been washed in days.

One of my natural ways of handling stressful or difficult situations has always been to use humour. Trying to picture how I'd reappear to my friends after the drunken disgrace of Cinco De Mayo, I'd dug out a bright orange LA County Jail t-shirt I had bought a few weeks prior that had the local ZIP code for the prisoner number on the back. The truth was that I'd been embarrassed and ashamed of my behaviour. That event was, hands down, the worst drunken stupor in memory. Never in my drinking career had I been arrested. Little snippets of alcohol drenched memory would flash in my mind – me trying to recite Psalms 23 while being dragged by two police officers. Me shouting and yelling and kicking. None of these were pleasant memories. Using humour to re-emerge in Venice was the only way I'd known how to handle the situation. I'd made a complete ass of myself and I could face my friends by doing something funny when I saw them. After putting my orange t-shirt on, I'd gone down to the Bistro, knowing that by that time, at 8pm, everyone would be there. It had been time to make an appearance, no matter how embarrassed I was to show my face again. My funny shirt would soften things with cheeky comedy.

As soon as I'd rounded the corner in front of the gate to the Bistro and casually sauntered up to the bar, I heard "Julie!" yelled out. Rob and some of my friends had rushed up to me. Everyone had been laughing, and they were amazed that I hadn't been shipped back to Canada. Cajoling me and mocking my Friday night antics, my friends had hugged me and bought me beers. It felt awesome to be welcomed back with open arms instead of being scorned. I hadn't been sure how everyone would react. Gratitude had been surging through me ever since the moment the judge had let me walk away, and by the time I was drinking beers in the Bistro, I had been overwhelmed with gratitude again. I knew I'd been given a pass by god but it was a warning shot. Being surrounded by friends, even if they were laughing about my drunken disgrace, had been exactly what I'd needed after four days of being in jail with my imagination in high-gear wondering how long I'd spend in prison and what tactics I would use to survive there.

The entire thing – the Cinco De Mayo Fiasco as I'd called it – caused such a range of pure emotions. It had gone from feelings of freedom while riding the bike alone on the boardwalk to feelings of love for my California life to a harsh wake-up with cop lights in my face then yelling and screaming and confusion in my drunkenness. Sobering fear came on strong as I'd been checked into the jail which then turned to terror as I'd stared at the wall in jail for four days, hoping no one would try to talk to me or beat the shit out of me. All the while I'd been imagining a nightmare stay in the US prison system. Court had been a bustle of confusion followed by amazement with the blur in which my freedom was revealed. I'd been elated at the outcome. Feeling relieved was followed by feelings of shame as I'd prepared myself to face my friends at the Bistro. At the end of that ordeal, I had been embraced by warm feelings of connection, humour, laughter, and acceptance by my rag-tag crew of friends. I'd survived one of the most disgraceful moments of my life.

I'd known that my partying had to stop. My court appointed lawyer had said something about AA, and not because it had been mandated. The judge hadn't ordered AA. My court appointed lawyer, only knowing me for five minutes total, knew I'd needed help to get sober and cared enough to say so. Getting arrested and held in jail for four nights had been serious whether I'd been charged or not. I wasn't a criminal, a felon, a person who got so drunk or high she'd get locked in jail, was I? If I wanted to stay in the US, and not get sent back to Canada, I had to smarten up, and fly straight. I'd been semi-aware of what I'd done and what I would have to do, but at that moment, with my friends laughing with me, buying me drinks, and celebrating my safe return, I turned to the tricky comfort of a buzz. I'd needed it.

In the days following, I'd written about my experience getting drunk, arrested, held in jail, standing before a judge, and getting released in my journal. As I'd unloaded what happened, I'd begun to realize that maybe my drinking was getting out of hand. I wasn't at a place yet where I was willing to look my drinking problem straight in the eyes. The denial I'd been in for years about my drug use, and now my alcohol use, still wanted to cloak the problem. I had been grateful that I had been set free. I revisited Felon's Alley through my writing. I wrote about those folks on the Greyhound bus who all had done jail time. When I'd met them, I had thought that it gave them character. Now that I'd been there myself, my opinion on that hadn't changed. Anything that adds to our wisdom, our experience, our understanding, gives us more character, not to mention, giving us a hell of story to share.

I'd gained some insights having been in jail. There were a few things of value I'd learned. First, I'd realized that jail was nothing like it was on TV. The jail I'd been in was in the police station. There was no television, no soap, no toothbrush, no comb, no nothing. There was no slop on a tin plate – just a paper bag with a processed cheese sandwich, an apple and an orange drink. There was no shouting, no yelling, no fighting. There were twenty people crammed into a small space, every one of them wishing they had behaved differently the night before.

Secondly, I'd seen first-hand that the jail I was in was full of people of colour. I was the only white woman in the group of twenty I'd been bunked with. I'd been aware of that fact even in my terrified, sobering-up state. What did that mean in the larger picture of jails in the US? Was it much different in the jails in Canada? Would my experience in a Canadian jail have been different? Many thoughts had surfaced in my mind about the incarceration system, and would continue to grow in my mind over time.

Having the shit scared out of me wasn't a bad thing either. Being terrified that I would spend two years in prison helped. Being terrified that I would get my ass kicked in jail helped. Being terrified of being sent back to Canada helped. Why? Because I needed to be scared straight. I needed to start walking on a different path, a more sober path, even if the only reason I was doing it had nothing to do with a change of heart, and more to do with fear.

The Buddha teaches that to understand something, you must experience it. All experiences have value, even going to jail. I am able to see the blessings from those experiences now. I am able to understand others who experience the same thing. I am able to understand how impersonal the US justice system is. I am able to understand that jail isn't a 'free ride' full of perks – it sucks, big time. I understand the fear of being arrested. I understand the fear of being sentenced. Having those experiences isn't something I consciously sought out, but in spiritual reflection, my soul probably did.

There had been a photographer creating photos for an art show on the beach a few weeks before my stint in jail. He'd asked if I'd pose for a picture. When I said yes, he'd opened one of the beach condo black iron gates and had me stand behind it as if I was about to walk out of the condo. A short time after, the photographer had his art show on the Boardwalk. The picture of me coming out from behind the black iron gate could have been a photo of me walking out of a prison cell – the image had been of me behind bars. How had god known?

I'm glad I smile every time I hear that song - Thirty Days in the Hole by Humble Pie. I'm happy that it never made it into the bad memories file – it's attached to a good story, one I'm grateful for. It's great that I can look back at myself and have a good laugh while at the same time appreciate the seriousness of what happened.

TAKE IT EASY

On my motorcycle ride, I came up over the north side of Lake Nipissing. I was leaning into the wind so it wouldn't knock me over. I was driving down a road I had never driven on before. The new road brought new visuals. The wind was whipping over the lake, sending spray into the air. Lake Nipissing looked dark and foreboding. With all of the waves and wind, it looked like she could swallow a boat whole, spitting out splinters of wood afterwards onto her rocky beaches. I loved visiting places for the first time. I loved new experiences. This bike trip was no exception – so many experiences were new, so many places were new. I'd never done anything like this trip before, and my heart was full of wonder and adventure.

While I kept myself balanced in the wind, Avicii came on my headphones. I turned up the volume as he started to sing, Wake Me Up. I'm not sure we can ever pinpoint the exact moment we start to spiritually awaken. It's possible that it's because it's more of a collection of moments that begin to illuminate the things we need to work on. For me, awakening begins with realizations that unfold through lived experiences. Perhaps beginning to realize that what I was taught in institutions may not have been entirely correct was a part of my awakening.

When there is a shift in my thinking and how I process events in the world – this too is all part of awakening. Awakening includes the realization that I haven't been self-aware. For me, that is probably the most important part of it. We can be run by our emotions, whether we realize it or not. Our emotions affect our choices. Things that happened to me when I was younger affected my decisions when I was older. Trauma lives in many sizes, and all sizes affect our self-awareness and our abilities to make decisions. And it doesn't have to be big traumas that create big reactions.

How you react as an adult when a man yells at you, can be directly related to how you reacted when your father yelled at you when you were a child. If it scared you as a child, it could scare you as an adult. There is a deep memory emotion attached to this experience be it fear, anger, etc.. Or, if a man yells at you as an adult, and you are connected and aware of that deep memory emotion attached to it, you can choose a different reaction. In fact, you can choose to respond not react. If you have an awareness of the emotions you felt when your father yelled at you as a child, you can respond to the yelling you may experience as an adult, instead of reacting to it out of the deep memory emotion (which may have been fear, anger, etc.). That's an example of self-awareness. My emotions had been running a program in the background for years. This program motivated the decisions I made, the relationships I formed, the reactions, the responses – my entire being. It took years to dismantle it.

I look at my breakdown at the end of 2005 as being a series of moments which fostered my awakening process. I certainly hadn't been awake at the time. I was out of my mind in the middle of a temporary psychotic episode but that was the moment that I cracked open and the light started to shine in. To see the light that had always been shining around me, I needed to stand in a blacker shade of dark. It's almost like seeing a match flame in the light – it's difficult to discern the light's edges. But if you light that same match in the darkness, the flame is easy to see, its edges crisp and sharp. In order to change almost everything I had ever believed about myself and how the world works because I am a true Leo, very stubborn in my opinions and thinking, my reality had to crack to make room for something new. My breakdown was a blessing in that regard.

During that breakdown I had started to get glimmers of insight that my lifestyle was not healthy. I had taken zero responsibility (actions) for it at the time, but realizing that my life hadn't been healthy kick-started a wake-up call. Out of that insight came the courage to walk out of my life on September 11th, 2006. I had known deep inside me that something had to change. I had thought that the people around me had to change – that if I took certain people out of my life, everything would be better. I didn't get it yet and that was okay. That certain people would and could be out of my life was a small part of the bigger equation I'd been starting to add up, so I wasn't entirely wrong in that thinking. Even though I hadn't been awake yet in the fall of 2006, the Universe was pushing me in that direction. The internal alarms had been going off. Maybe I had been hitting the snooze button repeatedly, but soon the alarms would have me wide awake.

It was in Arizona in 2007 – right after California – that I would begin the process of my true awakening. I hadn't always been into holistic healing or crystals and Reiki.

These practices I had picked up down there. Not long after the Cinco De Mayo Fiasco, I'd found myself being led to Arizona.

LEAVING CALIFORNIA

After the Cinco De Mayo Fiasco, I'd known it was time to leave California. Venice Beach had offered me a place to decompress, to learn how to smile again, to begin letting go of my fears. But instead of continuing to move my life forward, it had started moving me backwards because I'd been drinking and partying. The party had to end. I'd wanted to get sober and I knew I couldn't do it in Venice Beach.

The week I'd ended up leaving, I was doing artwork on the beach and I'd sold a picture of a phoenix I'd drawn. Then someone had asked me to draw a phoenix for a tattoo they'd wanted to get. In that one week, I'd ended up drawing and selling four art pieces of phoenixes. I'd stumbled upon a discarded tent. My intuition had said to pick it up, so I did. With no idea of where I needed to go to get sober, I'd spread out a map of the United States in front of me. I said out loud, "Ok god, where to next?"

As I spoke the words, a song had come on the radio that I'd never heard before, Get Your Kicks on Route 66, by Nat King Cole. Route 66 you said, eh, god? I'd looked at the map to where I was in Venice Beach. I'd been at the end of the line for Route 66! It ended on the Santa Monica pier where I'd been working every day selling t-shirts. Following Route 66 across the map, I noticed that it went close to Phoenix, Arizona. Oh! Phoenix! At that moment, I'd known I was supposed to go to Phoenix because I'd drawn four of them in that same week! This had to be where the Universe wanted me to go! My gut was saying, "Yes, Phoenix!" I'd just found a tent so I thought I could find a camp in Phoenix and stay there. I'd believed in all the signs around me and felt the strong intuitive pull in my gut guiding me to Phoenix.

While I was walking back to the beach after picking up my last pay at the pier, I'd found a little baggy with white powder in it on the street. I'd looked around wondering if I was on candid camera or being set up by cops but no one seemed to be looking at me. I'd picked it up and put it in my pocket. After I got back to the boat I was staying on with Rob, I'd dipped my finger in the bag of powder to taste and see if it was... could it be? It was! It was cocaine! I'd always loved coke and I had a secret fantasy to do coke on a boat. I'd loved boats, always had. I'd found them sexy. Coke was sexy to me too. I'd always loved sex on cocaine, so putting them together was like putting chocolate in my peanut butter – a perfect combination.

I showed Rob what I'd found. He laughed out loud and we turned the tunes up. That night turned out to be the best quality time I'd spend with Rob, and not just because of the sex – although that was fun too. It had been our best night together because it was the one and only time I'd seen the real Rob. Something had happened when he did coke that night – his walls had come down. Mine had too. And we'd talked for hours about our childhood and our families and our failed relationships. I'd gotten a glimpse into who Rob was. And I knew it was the real Rob because he wasn't bragging about all of his supposed accomplishments (which is what he usually did), he was reminiscing about his failures, his struggles, his hopes and dreams. What he shared with me showed vulnerability and imperfection. Rob received the same from me – stories he hadn't heard, vulnerabilities I had never shown. It was a precious night. Drug use isn't always nightmarish and dream shattering. Some very profound moments in my life were induced through pot, alcohol, cocaine, mushrooms, ecstasy or LSD. One of the most difficult things I've ever had to do is write a book with none of them to assist me in the creative process.

The cocaine I'd found in Santa Monica had been a gift from god. That night, I'd seen the real Rob and he'd seen the real Tracey. It would be the last time we'd see each other. It would be the last time I'd ever do cocaine and it was beautiful. God really does work in mysterious ways.

Off I went a few days later on the Greyhound bus to Phoenix. I knew nothing about Phoenix or Arizona, for that matter, except it had desert, and snakes and spiders. The images I'd conjured in my head looked a lot like the setting in a Coyote and Roadrunner episode. When I arrived, the temperature had been nearly 120 degrees. I quickly discovered there was no camping in Phoenix – a massive city with millions of people.

Hopping on a city bus to get to a hostel, I had my suitcase and a duffel bag. In the suitcase and duffel bag was everything I owned including the tent I'd found. I was wearing a string strap tank top, faded blue jeans and a straw cowboy hat. I thought I looked pretty damn Arizona! Only one other guy got on the bus. He'd asked me, "Where you going with all that gear?" I told him I wanted to camp, but that I'd realized there was no camping in Phoenix. Laughing, he'd told me about a great place to camp up near Payson in the Tonto National Forest. In the National Forest in the US, there were lots of free camping areas where there weren't really any campsites, but you could stay for free and pitch a tent for two weeks max. He drew me a map that included a good camp spot where there was an old mill and a stream. If I camped back a ways, out of sight from the rangers, I'd probably get away with being in that one spot for weeks and weeks. Drawing the map out on a napkin for me, he assured me I'd find it without a problem. Smiling a big smile, I shook his hand and thanked him for his help. Such had been another example of a positive coincidence – meeting a man on the bus who guided me directly to a free place to camp and live.

I had to get off that bus and get on another one to get back to the Greyhound station to find out how to get to Payson. Unfortunately, there were no buses to Payson, but I was told there might be a shuttle from the airport. I'd gone to the airport and found a shuttle ride for $80 but it didn't leave for another sixteen hours. I'd only had $300 to my name; $80 was a pricey ticket. While I'd waited for the shuttle, I'd decided to try my luck with hitch hiking. I'd put a sign on my suitcase that said, "Need a lift to Payson, God Bless." I'd known it was a dangerous move, but I'd felt protected on the journey. I'd felt like god was watching over me every step of the way. Angels had kept stepping in and making sure I was safe. At the airport, one of the employees buffed up his halo and stepped in. He told me he lived in Payson and he'd be driving there after his shift – he'd be happy to give me a lift.

I'd felt safe. He worked at the airport. Other people knew he'd offered to give me a lift and they'd seen me leave with him. What had immediately amazed me about the ride out of Phoenix was the landscape. It was spectacular, and it got more and more beautiful as we headed up into the mountains. The landscape had looked nothing like a Coyote cartoon. It reminded me of Muskoka, my happy place in Ontario. It was all rocks and pine trees. There'd been minor differences, but the closer we got to Payson, the more it looked like Muskoka. Inside, I'd been bursting with joy and happiness. I couldn't believe that god had gotten me to this place. I never would have chosen Arizona on my own. Snakes, spiders, scorpions and desert – these things were part of Arizona, yes! It would not have been my first choice – but four phoenixes and angels from god (including the man who drove me to Payson – I'd been totally safe) were hard to argue with.

Using the map on the napkin, the man from the airport took me right to the road I'd shown him and dropped me off. We'd waved goodbye and I expressed thanks for his help. Having camped throughout my childhood and many times as an adult, I was very comfortable setting up my little camp area and my tent. Luckily, everything I'd needed to set the tent up was included in the tent bag and everything worked except the zip-up door. In lieu of a working zipper, I used a safety pin I had with my things. I wasn't alone at the Mill site. There was a beat up old green RV there as well. I'd set up as far away from it as possible in order to maintain some privacy. Included in my things were a steel pot for cooking, camping utensils and a camp mug. I'd been lugging these items around since before I'd left Canada – just in case I had decided to cross the border through a shared Canada-US park. I'd surveyed my campsite and smiled. This certainly was an adventure!

Many would have thought me crazy to be out in the woods by myself with no vehicle, little money, and no plan of what to do next. But I'd trusted the process. I'd trusted a god that I felt had led me to this exact spot through a series of 'coincidences'– four phoenixes, a tent and a song. Thank you, Nat King Cole and Route 66. Thank you, folks who wanted my drawings of phoenixes. Thank you, The Celestine Prophecy. I'd follow the synchronicities – inside as my intuition grew and outside as my relationship with god enhanced.

I had been camping out in the Tonto National Forest. I'd been happy to do that for as long as my adventure called me to. While camping, I had two interesting encounters. One was with a man, maybe in his 30s, who had started to talk to me near my campsite. Upon finding out that I had actually been living in the park, he'd offered me a job stirring meth 'up in the hills' for his buddy. The second interesting encounter, or series of encounters, had been with the Mormons.

I had met a man named Glen while camping. Glen drove the beat up, dark green RV that looked like it was right out of 1955 or possibly right out of a junkyard. In it, he'd toted around his pug dogs and every earthly possession he'd owned. Alcohol was no friend of Glen's or perhaps, too much of a friend. Glen and I became chums due to the lack of any other people in the area – he was camping and so was I – that had been our connection. He was an alcoholic, which he admitted to me. I hadn't admitted that I was too – not to Glen or myself. Not at that point.

One Sunday, he'd asked me if I would like to join him in town to go to church – he knew a guy who ran a sermon out of his house, and who would host a dinner afterwards. Mmmmm! A home cooked meal! I had barely remembered what one of those was like, but I'd remembered enough to know I'd love one. I agreed to join him.

Glen and I set about hitching into town. Eventually we'd found a lift into town and we'd marched up and down the road searching for his preacher-friend's house. We'd searched. And searched. And sweated. And hunted. And hiked. And we had not found his house. After about 45 minutes of the nonsense, I'd said, "You know what? We walked by this church a dozen times this morning. I came to town to go to church. I'm going to this church!" As I'd said it, I'd pointed to a church. Glen had no interest in joining me as I marched off toward The Church of Latter-Day Saints.

Once inside, I found myself surrounded by very well-dressed folks, everyone was in their Sunday best.What a sight I must have been with my bleached blonde hair, faded jeans and spaghetti strap tank top. Surprisingly, no one snubbed their nose at me or looked away. In fact, everyone had smiled and said good morning. It'd felt genuine, this welcome I was receiving. Noticing a pamphlet on a nearby table, I saw the name 'Joseph Smith' and I instantly remembered who the Latter-Day Saints were – they were Mormons. How did I know that? I'd invited them into my apartment years before, curious about what they were teaching and preaching as they went door to door. I'd always been fascinated with religion and mythology, especially during my atheist years. Standing there in the church, I'd looked up at the ceiling, and to god I said, "You've got to be kidding! You know what, I'll stay for your Sunday worship, but that's it." I had walked in. I had nothing better to do, and by this time in my life, I had a great love for god, even if mine was packaged quite a bit differently.

Sitting near the back of the church, ready to make a quiet exit if I'd needed to, I was happy to learn that it was Fast Sunday. What I'd witnessed was people getting up to give their testimony of God, Jesus Christ and Joseph Smith. Not knowing that perhaps there were rules or etiquette for participating, I'd gathered the courage to walk up the aisle and speak into the microphone at the front of the church. I'd wanted to praise god. I'd wanted to share it with these people who obviously loved god too. My courage to speak was rooted in my bursting desire to share the incredible journey I was on, to share the Love I'd felt from god.

I'd told the congregation my story about changing from my atheist beliefs to knowing that there was a god, and that god loved me. With pure joy in my heart, I'd explained that I felt guided on my entire journey to California, and then to Arizona. God had led the way. Gushing with emotion and honesty, I'd given my personal testimony to the power of god, and shared my belief that miracles could happen. The more I'd opened up, been vulnerable and shared my story, the more I'd felt my connection to god deepening. I'd felt electric as I shared, and the energy expanded into the room.

As I'd looked into the crowd of people in attendance, I'd seen nothing but huge smiles, and eyes that said, "Yes, I know exactly what you are saying!" Happy with myself and smiling, I'd returned to my seat near the back. I'd felt accepted. I'd felt welcomed. I'd felt connected to a new group of people. Truth be told, I'd been ecstatic to have found people who loved god as much as I did. I knew they believed something different than me, but that hadn't mattered. The god I believed in spoke to people in whatever voice, with whatever name, and whatever story they needed to hear.

After church I'd been invited to a dozen or more homes for lunch, but I kept turning everyone down. I didn't want to impose on anyone. At some point, I finally gave a woman a 'yes' so that I could stop saying 'no thank you' (a co-dependent trait I'd work on later in my life). I don't remember her name because I never saw her again, but I'd gone home with her and her husband, and we'd had a lovely hot Sunday lunch together. Afterwards, I got a ride back to the Tonto National Forest. I'd written in my journal about my experience.

At that time, I had still journaled every detail of every day of my life, just as I had since becoming homeless in Toronto. I had been determined to keep working on the book I'd felt compelled to write. I had needed to remember everything that was happening and how I'd felt so I wrote as much as I could. What I can remember of that day's journaling is that I'd been confused about what god wanted of me. God knew I didn't believe Joseph Smith's story, the roots of Mormonism. Why had god delivered me to the doorstep of that church, of all churches? Why not a United Church or a non-denominational church? After writing, I'd told Glen about my day with the Mormons. Apparently, he had found his friend's house, and he too had a belly full of hot food. God was good.

After church, I'd been asked if I would return the following Sunday. I'd said, "Oh no, I'm not religious at all, and church isn't really my style," which had been entirely true. But that week, every single person I'd met was a Mormon. When hitchhiking in for groceries, a Mormon had picked me up; his Mormon Bible right up on the dash of his truck, as he'd exclaimed that he'd never picked up a hitchhiker before. Mormons had introduced themselves to me at the campground. Everywhere I went, there had been Mormons!

The guy who had offered me a job stirring meth came back to the campground to ask if I'd wanted the job. I'd been faced with a decision: go back to the Mormon church or stir meth. At that point in my life, I'd certainly been no expert on making good decisions, far from it. But I'd seen the answer staring me in my face and it wasn't the face of meth. Even though I hadn't been at a place in my life where I was aware that drugs had destroyed my life, I'd been wise enough to know that meth had destroyed every life it ever touched.

The following Sunday, I went back to church. I was introduced to the missionary sisters and had been invited to study with them during the upcoming weeks. I hadn't felt like I had a choice regarding learning more about the Mormon faith and participating in the community. God had given me a choice – it was meth or Mormons. Meth had scared the hell out of me. Mormons had seemed genuinely nice.

I had no idea where the Mormon thing was going. I didn't want to be dishonest about my feelings towards their beliefs – I hadn't believed in Joseph Smith's story. What I had believed was that god worked in very mysterious ways, and that god could reach people through a million different avenues and a million different religions. I'd been unsure about the outcome of this new journey until I had my third lesson with the sisters, whom I was growing to love. During the lesson, they'd started talking about the Word of Wisdom. As they'd explained that the Word of Wisdom declared that Mormons could not drink alcohol, smoke cigarettes, drink coffee or do drugs, I'd stared wide-eyed at them – all of the hairs on my arms stood on end as I was instantly covered in goosebumps.

I'd quietly said, "We need to set my baptism." Every eye in the room had turned and looked right at me. Our hosts, originally from New Zealand, the missionary sisters, another family, and a few other folks attempting to be converted – all of them had stared at me.

"Why now?" asked one of the sisters, with genuine curiosity.

I explained that before I'd left California, I had received a message from god. I had been working on the pier in Santa Monica selling t-shirts. The day had been very quiet. Sitting in a beat-up, old lawn chair, threads hanging from the underside, I'd entered a very meditative state without attempting to – it had just happened. I'd been watching the waves rolling in and rolling out...rolling in and rolling out...the rhythm and beauty had caused the meditation. I'd felt more relaxed than I had ever felt in my life. Clear as a bell, I'd heard the following words, "Tracey, you need to quit drinking, smoking, doing drugs and drinking coffee." Instantly, I had jolted out of my relaxed state. I'd responded out loud: "God, this is what I heard –Tracey, you need to quit drinking, smoking, doing drugs and drinking coffee." I'd repeated back the exact words. "If this is what you want me to do, please show me a clear sign," I'd said, and just as I'd said it, a huge blue-gray bird landed within five feet of me on a pole on the pier, and just stared at me.

Looking back at it dumbfounded, I'd noticed two seals playing in the water behind the exotic bird. I loved nature and always have. The bird, the seals – they'd been a sign. (To this day, I have no idea what kind of bird I had seen on the pier, but it was huge.) I'd had my sign and I'd had my directions. That message had been for Arizona. I couldn't have quit those things in California. California had been one big party, and though I had tried to stop the party, I had failed. There'd been too many friends and too many opportunities to make bad choices. I'd needed a new start. Again.

The Mormons in the room had stared at me with smiles on their faces. I had no idea if they'd believed my story or not, though it seemed likely that they did. It had been a true story.

A true story that had changed my life. I'd never forget the message. It had been an awakening moment. I had misunderstood the message slightly, however. In California and into Arizona, I'd thought the message was that I need to quit those things for now. One step at a time, but for a limited time. Stop your addictions for right now. I'd figured I could do that with a little help.

And the help had been staring me in the face literally and figuratively. The Word of Wisdom offered the same message. I still hadn't believed in Joseph Smith's story, but at that moment I sure as hell had believed that I was exactly where I was supposed to be. My past had included miserable failures quitting alcohol, pot, and cigarettes – only coffee had been an easy quit. But god had led me directly to a new way to quit. The Latter-Day Saints and their religion had been the way.

I had my baptism on July 27th, 2007 (7-2-7-2-7). I hadn't chosen that date, but I'd felt like it was another little gift from god – especially when I'd looked at the numerology of the date. The numbers were lucky. The baptism had consisted of me in a white jumpsuit getting into a dunk tank with the priest in the church. (The Church of Latter-Day Saints do full immersion baptisms.) I hadn't told the priest/congregation, but a few months earlier, I had baptised myself.

Before I left Canada, I'd baptized myself. I had been afraid for my life and I didn't want to die unbaptized (in case the Christians were right). I'd self-baptised myself while on the Oneida Reserve. No one had been there except me and god. I was using rainwater that was in a brass dish on a beat up table outside. On the ground at my feet had been a chain of huge rusted links – probably used to pull something behind a tractor or a truck. As I made the sign of the cross on my forehead while announcing my love for god and proclaiming a changed life, I'd felt that massive chain unwrap from around my feet like I was being set free. Something unattached itself from my soul in that moment. Like a heavy ball and chain was released. Like a punishment disappeared. Like.... sin washed clean away. In that moment, declaring to god that I was determined to change, it felt like the weight of my entire past was lifted. Something happened there on the Oneida Reserve and it was profound.

In 2007 with the Mormons, I'd felt it again – a release, only it had been even stronger. In their eyes, I'd been committing to bring Jesus into my heart, to renounce my sinful ways, and to take the teachings of Joseph Smith as my testimony. But for me, I'd brought god into my heart, and my commitment was to promising to live a new kind of life, a good life. As I'd come out of the water post-dunk, standing with the priest, my body still immersed in the pool, I'd bawled my eyes out with joy and happiness. Right then and there I'd prayed to feel forgiveness for others and to be forgiven myself, in the eyes of god. In my old life, a scene like this would have been hilarious to me. I'd been an atheist. Baptism had been for people who needed a crutch, I'd believed. Baptism had been for fools. But living through that moment myself, there had been nothing funny about it.

God works in very mysterious ways, and I really do believe that god, the Universe, Love, Higher Power, however you want to say it, can reach us through a million different names, voices or belief systems, including science. I don't see these as separate systems; I see them as an interwoven larger system that includes heaven, reincarnation, nirvana, enlightenment, karma, higher consciousness and the Creator. At the center of it all is the Universal Heartbeat.

At that exact moment in my life, when I had been running from myself for so long, feeling deep regret for many things in my past, and I'd realized it was time to quit drugs, alcohol and smoking, I knew in my heart that the baptismal pool was exactly where I was supposed to be – to stop running and start changing by making positive choices. I'd felt connected to God's will. God bless Joseph Smith and the Latter-Day Saints.

I'd begun by taking the path of attending church every Sunday, taking bible study classes, and hanging out with the missionaries. I'd even moved into town with a saint – Saint Bertha. I'd called her a saint because she was (and is!) truly one of the kindest people I'd ever met. She wasn't a weak woman – she was incredibly strong and will remain that way. Bertha was in her mid 80s when I'd met her, and she'd just remarried after having been widowed. Her basement had an apartment and she offered it to me while I got on my feet.

I did my best to do the house cleaning each week, but house cleaning had never been my strong suit. The missionary sisters had connected me with a woman who needed a babysitter, and so, I'd gotten the job. After not too long, I'd moved from Saint Bertha's to Roger's house. Roger was a baptized Mormon who was as much a Mormon as I was. Roger had gotten baptized in his youth when he was hot for a Mormon girl – he'd thought baptism would give him a better chance with her. Now and again he'd gone to church. The missionaries always took time to talk with him and he would philosophize for hours with them. Roger was a grumpy old man with a heart of gold. He'd been angry with the sheriff, critical of the mayor, fed up with some of the townsfolk, and he'd been a supporter of anyone who loved their dog.

Roger was an artist. I too was a budding artist. Roger was a thinker. I too was a thinker. Roger was a rebel. I too was a rebel. Roger and I had a friendship made in heaven. I'd been grateful to move into the little 1950s trailer he had behind his house. Painting it all light blue with dark blue trim inside, I'd made it feel cozy. I'd had access to the entire house, including the washroom, the office, the TV room, and the kitchen, but I had my own space in the trailer. That shift into the trailer had been a meaningful one. It had felt like home.

Roger had gone to AA meetings for years, but he wasn't an alcoholic – he'd liked to observe the social aspect of the meetings. This had been interesting to me. I think how we choose to define alcoholic affects our willingness and ability to wear the label. For most of my life, I'd envisioned someone who drank day and night, got angry and had black outs as an 'alcoholic'. The reality was much simpler as I've come to believe. If alcohol affects my life negatively, it is a problem. I had never been a black out drunk. I had never been an all-day or everyday drinker (well, maybe in California), but drinking alcohol sure had caused problems in my life. I had no idea whether alcohol had ever caused problems in Roger's life or not. He never let me into the places where he was hurt. I know he had regretted some things from his past that he had hinted at. I had regretted some things from my past too.

I view my time in Arizona as the time that The Emperor walked into my life. In Tarot, he is an authority figure. He represents institutions, doctrine, structure and stability. He is a father figure. It's not that I had become The Emperor, I certainly hadn't been strong enough to be a fatherly figure in anyone's life or even to speak from a place of authority. I had been seeking answers. I had needed structure, rules, guidelines. And I had found them in the Church, in Roger, and in many of my church brothers and sisters. The Latter Day Saints had offered my weary and tired spirit a new way of life, a new way of being. I'd received structured guidance which I very much needed at that time.

That first Christmas in Arizona had been something special. For probably the first time in my life, it wasn't about what I was going to receive, it was about what I was going to give. One of my Christmas plans was to ride around with the missionary sisters and a group of families and children to carol at people's doorsteps. The missionary sisters had chosen the homes of people who probably weren't going to see a lot of family that year or weren't going to see any children.

With a few truckloads of Mormons, I'd created a wonderful memory of breaking the speed limit so that we could get to as many homes as possible, zipping all around the

The Emperor Card
Rider-Waite Tarot deck

Payson area, and putting wonderful people into tears as we'd sang on their doorsteps. My heart had been so full that night. There was no snow, no snowmen, no eggnog – none of the things that I had been used to – but did it ever feel like Christmas! More than Christmas had ever felt like Christmas. Joy was overflowing from my spirit. I'd felt like I was in the middle of a Hallmark Christmas special.

It hadn't ended there. I had also decided to give Roger a Christmas to remember. He didn't have a lot of family. Due to events years ago, he'd been estranged from his daughter. I could tell that Roger didn't do much on Christmas. I hadn't had a lot of money, so my giving wasn't about buying a whole bunch of expensive things, but about the thoughtfulness of the gift. I'd gone to some yard sales and a thrift store, and I'd found some Christmas decorations to put up around the house. When the missionary sisters found out that I was trying to create a Christmas for Roger, someone had shown up on our porch with a Christmas tree. Some decorations were donated, and within a very short time, Roger's home had looked like Christmas had arrived.

I'd gifted him a drill and dremel set that year, and the following year, I'd made him a photo book with some of my favourite photos taken during my time with him. Christmas morning, I gave Roger a stocking filled with small treasures. I'm happy to say, I'd felt proud when I saw Roger, a grown man, cry upon receiving the gifts and the celebration. You know you're making progress on your healing journey when it ceases to be all about you, and you focus on how good it feels to give. The first Christmas had been slightly more than a year since I'd left my life, and when I look back, I can see now how large the steps I'd been taking really were. It was truly amazing how much my life changed simply by removing drugs and alcohol. Life hadn't been just about me anymore, it had been about the wonderful people surrounding me. Time took on a new shape as I'd been able to fill it differently without having alcohol and drugs affecting my choices. Clarity of mind and soul had begun to show incredible benefits. It was like I'd been able to feel more and therefore to give more – both tangible and intangible giving.

I'd noticed something one day. Roger's initials were the same as my father's – Bob Rogers – except reversed (RB). Bertha's initials were identical to my Dad's, and so were Beverley's – another amazing woman in the church who'd treated me like a daughter. It made me feel like I had family, even though my family was a million miles away. It was like the Universe was keeping me surrounded by people so special even their names were like my biological family.

I'd been invited to family dinners and the church itself became another kind of home for me. The LDS refer to each other as brother and sister. I hadn't felt safe to ever return to Canada, but I'd felt enveloped by this incredible group of people in Arizona who were taking me in like I was a long-lost daughter or a sister. I'd needed that, desperately. I'd needed places that felt like home. I'd needed people who'd help me feel needed and wanted.

My entire being, my self image, my understanding of self had been splattered during the events of 2005 and 2006. I had been riddled with feelings of guilt, feelings of shame, feelings of failure. The message that Jesus taught about forgiveness was something I'd needed to hear at the time I was in Arizona. And I'd been feeling emotions without the aid of alcohol, pot or cigarettes. For the first time since I was 15 years old, I'd been feeling everything because my body and mind wasn't being shadowed by my addictions to those things. But I hadn't had tools for coping with all the emotions I was feeling. God became a positive crutch and it helped immensely. I'd felt loved by god the moment we'd connected. I didn't understand why, but I knew that god loved me. I knew I'd been forgiven by god for the choices I'd made until recently. I'd needed to learn how to forgive myself.

Roger had been going on about the book The Celestine Prophecy in the late fall of 2007. I'd read the book while I'd been in California. Someone had said, "Here, you need to read this," and they'd handed it to me. The book was a teaching about coincidences, and how when one awakens, one can see more and more coincidences, otherwise known as synchronicities, and one should start paying attention to them. You know, synchronicities, like hearing a message during a meditation that you need to quit smoking, drinking, doing drugs and drinking coffee, and then running into a group of people who preach that you can't smoke, drink, do drugs or drink coffee – that kind of coincidence.

Well, Roger had been looking for a copy of the book, so we'd headed down to a local bookstore to find it. Inside the store, I'd instantly fallen in love – crystals were everywhere, used books were piled high on shelves and the floor, and oddities that I was attracted to but couldn't explain why, were scattered about. After rustling around in the store for a while, I'd noticed a flyer on the bulletin board for an upcoming meditation. Lynn, the owner of the shop, had explained that she was leading it and that I should attend. It would be held at the Center for Spiritual Awareness – a non-denominational spiritual center. I knew I was supposed to go to that meditation. My gut said yes.

And so it was that The Celestine Prophecy, a book about coincidences and synchronicities, had led me to the bookstore which had led me to the meditation which had led me to everything that would heal my life. The folks at the Centre for Spiritual Awareness taught meditation, but they'd offered so much more. There were folks there into shamanism, something called Reiki, and they spoke about Ekhart Tolle and Marianne Williamson. They'd shared books by Wayne Dyer and Louise Hay, taught classes and workshops about forgiveness, acceptance, self love, self compassion, and communication. I'd even found a teacher for A Course in Miracles. It had been a paradise hidden in the mountains of Arizona where everything I'd needed to get over my fears, my phobias, my PTSD, my shame, my guilt – everything I'd needed to get over myself, was gathered in one space nestled in the hills. God had led me there. Coincidences lined up like stones on my path to awakening.

My life of spending every Sunday at both the Church of Latter-Day Saints and the Center had begun. Within the church, I had been given rules, a family, safety and security, and a structure which I had very much needed in my life. At the centre, I had been given the tools to learn how to forgive, how to heal, how to accept, how to calm down, how to cope with my PTSD and anxiety, how to meditate, how to center, how to become self aware, how to leave my past behind – essentially, how to transform myself into a higher potential version of myself.

It's not that I had been a bad person (although I'd believed I was at the time I'd first arrived), it had been that my choices were not bringing me any happiness, and they weren't bringing the people around me happiness either. It's hard to learn how to make new choices if you have the same baggage and the same emotional triggers that run your life from a subconscious place. It's like you naturally make choices that are not good because you don't know any other way. You haven't learned that there can be different choices to make. And you haven't had any practice in making better choices. Awareness is key. Self-awareness. That is, being aware that the baggage and the triggers exist, and being open to the tools (books, spirituality, people, places, etc.) that can help you free yourself from the belief that the baggage and triggers are running your show. Through a very strange combination of Mormonism and New Age Spirituality, I'd embraced the tools to change and I'd started to heal.

Looking back on this time in my life, I see my experiences with both the Latter Day Saints and the folks from the Center for Spiritual Awareness as being reflective of the Hierophant card from Tarot. The Hierophant represents established religion, conventional teachings, a time of spiritual wisdom, conforming, and staying within tradition. When this card comes up, we are drawn to follow the teachings of a spiritual leader or teacher. I had a number of spiritual and religious teachers in Payson, and I listened intently to all of them. I journaled for hours after bible classes, after group meditations, after Sunday morning teachings, and Sunday afternoon talks. The church was full of teachers who had been studying Jesus and the bible their entire lives. The Spiritual Center was rife with wise and knowledgeable seekers who had been on their paths for decades. The Universe had dropped me smack dab in the middle of great wisdom, and all I had to do was show up, listen, and the rest would fall into place. My ears were open, my heart was expanding, my mind was processing, and my soul was ready. I was a teachable student surrounded by teachers.

* * *

North Bay was coming up ahead of me. Working with my phone GPS, I maneuvered my motorcycle through the streets of town. I was surprised that it took a full ten minutes to get to Amanda's house – I hadn't thought North Bay was that big.

Amanda and I became friends in high school. Though we'd never had a falling out, our friendship shifted in grade eleven and we slowly drifted apart. It wasn't until five or six years ago that we reconnected. I'm so grateful for that! My friendship with Amanda had been wonderful in my teens. She was a thoughtful, funny, kind friend. That hadn't changed about her as an adult. I consider Amanda one of my best friends – our friendship picked up right where it left off when we reunited a number of years ago.

The Hierophant Card
Rider-Waite Tarot deck

Rolling up slowly in her driveway, I heard a dog barking as I turned off my motorcycle. Amanda appeared in the front window. Coming outside and offering me big, squishy hugs and an excited hello, Amanda guided me to a gate leading to the backyard where I could keep my motorcycle safely. After getting my bike under a bike cover in her backyard, I happily went inside and plunked myself down on the sofa. Maverick, Amanda's super friendly standard poodle, was dancing around me excitedly, so happy to meet me. Amanda had a bowl of piping hot home-made chili made for me which I ate heartily. After the delicious food, we talked about how my ride up had been.

DAY 4 – SEPTEMBER 14TH, 2019

FIFTEEN

I'd known Amanda since high school. We'd met when I was in grade ten and she was in grade eleven. We'd taken an English class together. I was tame back then as I'd just moved back to London from my Dad's farm. The worst thing I'd done in grade nine was forge my Dad's signature so I could skip out of school to go see Rick Hansen when he came through St. Thomas. I'd had my first drunk ever at the end of grade nine when I was exempted from all my exams due to good grades. As soon as grade nine had finished, I'd moved from the farm back to my Mum's in London. It wasn't a far move – my Dad's farm was only twenty minutes outside of London, and he worked in London as an accountant.

I'd tried smoking pot for the first time that summer. I'd smoked oil (a sticky, black product that is made by processing pot – done by someone who knows what they are doing) with a neighbourhood friend, and I'd drank a few times, but not frequently. Sometime after my fifteenth birthday, I'd had consensual sex for the first time. I'd never consider my 'first' to be Don. What happened wasn't consensual. I had been a child.

Amanda had been my first friend at my new high school back in London. Right away we'd hit it off. She had a friend Tina who I also made friends with quickly. Amanda and I dated two brothers – Jay and Tom. I was head over heels for Jay. He dealt acid. I had tried it once or twice before meeting him, so I hadn't been put off by his dealing. In fact, I was thrilled to have it at my disposal, should I want it. Amanda hadn't been into acid the way I was. I absolutely loved it once I got over the weirdness of it.

Acid isn't like pot or alcohol. With pot and alcohol you have a similar perception to your sober self, except perhaps a bit slower to react, and your inhibitions often go out the window, not to mention laughter seems to come more easily. Acid is a psychedelic drug. Vision changes, thought patterns change, they say new parts of the brain open up that you normally don't have access to. You see the world from an angle you've never seen it from before. For myself, dropping acid also brought a desire to be with a very close-knit, small group of friends. Being on acid near people I did not know well brought feelings of paranoia and made me feel self conscious of my actions. And laughter...oh, acid always brought buckets full of gut wrenching laughter for me, about almost nothing. Acid literally took me to a different place, a different world. Looking back on it, I can see why I was attracted to it. It removed me from the trauma and hurt I wasn't ready to look at yet.

What I'd enjoyed about it was how I could create my own little world for eight hours during a high. My mind had opened in ways that it had never opened before. I looked at things from different angles I had not seen before. A lot of my thoughts had been nonsensical, but there were also a few brief moments of brilliance. The brilliance had been difficult to maintain because at some point I would go off on a tangent, and the next thing I knew I'd be talking to my carpet while it danced to Pink Floyd. I'd fallen in love with their album The Wall.

The acid combined with the music had created a place for me to hide. I'd been holding secrets inside of me that were killing me. I completely understood the lyrics to the album, and I'd felt like the main character, building walls around himself, not letting anyone in, traumatized by life. By age fifteen, I'd been angry as hell. I was hurting so badly with no outlet for what I was feeling inside – I didn't have the words for it. Everything was trapped inside my belly. Deep shame had been planted at ages twelve and thirteen. It had blossomed into self destruction, self loathing and anger.

We weren't bad kids, Amanda, Tina and I. We'd gotten up to a couple things our parents wouldn't have been happy about, but we weren't hooligans, and we weren't breaking the rules constantly, just sometimes. We were tame enough that we signed up with a group to do Air Band that year, and we were going to do Salt n Pepa's Push It, for our song. Every day after school we'd head to the gym mezzanine and practice our lip synch and dance moves.

Then something happened one day in the gym. I'd started talking to my gym teacher. I'd said something I'd been needing to say for a long time to someone, anyone. It had been weighing on my mind as an untold secret for a few years and it needed to be unloaded, even if unloading it was painful or backfired on me. I'd told her about Don. I'd never told an adult before. It had only been over the past summer when we'd been drinking that I had told two friends my own age about Don. Instead of reacting the way I thought she would, my teacher comforted me. I had partly expected that maybe she would be horrified by my actions with Don. I was afraid I'd feel more shame not less. But she'd told me it wasn't my fault. Out of that moment, a series of events would unfold that would take me years to unravel. Telling her had backfired, but not the way I'd expected.

I'd started talking to my teacher a lot – at lunch, before school. My friends had noticed. My Mum hadn't been paying attention to me at home – she was busy trying to rebuild her life. My relationship with my father was horrible and we weren't communicating. But an adult had been paying attention to me, listening to me and understanding my problems. That adult was my gym teacher. I'm not 100% sure if my actions had been misinterpreted or if grooming had been part of her intentions – but the teacher thought I was gay and that my sexuality was one of the things I'd been struggling with. She'd suggested that I was gay. I had never thought that nor had I ever been attracted to girls. I'd loved boys.

However, in her revelation that I was gay, I'd somehow seen an opportunity – an opportunity for more attention from her. It hadn't been a conscious need; I had zero self awareness. But I'm certain that something inside me was motivated to get more attention from her. I'd played into the role and allowed her to think that I was gay and in short time I believed it myself. Clearly, my confusion had been real. And so had all the pain inside that I hadn't known what to do with. It snowballed into a suicide attempt on April 15th when I was still only fifteen.

Even then I knew I hadn't wanted to die. I'd wanted my father to pay attention to me. I'd wanted him to know how much I was hurting. I'd wanted him to know that I had only moved out because Yvonne and I got along so poorly. I'd wanted him to know that the crumbling of our relationship was devastating to me. Leaving the farm earlier that year hadn't just been a physical move. It had signalled the loss of my hero-Dad, my best friend, and the start of a twenty-year wall between us that would just get higher and higher. My suicide attempt was my last attempt to fix things before I mortared in the rest of the bricks in our wall.

Amanda had been there that day at school after I'd taken the pills at home, and walked to the school before they'd affected me. As soon as she'd talked to me, she knew something was wrong. She'd asked me some questions, and I'd very groggily answered and told her what I'd done. She'd been the one who told my gym teacher that I had taken pills and needed help. Next thing I knew I was in the office with the VP and the teacher, begging them not to call my Mum, but to call my Dad. My Mum had been called anyway because my Dad said he was busy and couldn't come to the school to get me. My Mum went into full blown crisis mode. Mum had the ability to shut down her emotions in crisis mode and do what needed to be done. She'd come to the school. She'd hugged me. She'd held me and told me she loved me. And then she set her mind to what had to be done. My memory of the conversation in the VP's office is very fuzzy. I had taken a lot of pills. They asked me what kind of pills I'd taken. I had barely been conscious to answer them, but I mumbled about Tylenol with codeine and some prescription pills from the medicine cabinet at home. I had no idea what I'd taken. All I knew was that I had taken somewhere between thirty and fifty pills. And I remember what song I had played over and over that morning before I took the pills – Fade to Black, by Metallica. In my opinion, music does not lead to or cause suicide, instead, it gives us a soundtrack for the emotions we have no words for.

The fact that my father hadn't come caused a great deal of pain for me. My call for help from him hadn't been heard. That event was the final straw in the breaking point of my relationship with my father, and it would last for twenty years. I didn't need attention from my Mum that I was aware of – we hadn't been close over the years, I'd been close with my Dad. Mum was always there when I needed her, especially in a crisis. Dad had been the one who was traditionally there to congratulate me, to make me feel good about my accomplishments, to spend quality time with me. But neither of them had much time when I was fifteen, things had shifted – Dad was busy building a new life, and so was Mum. I'd been a confused, broken child and it seemed like no matter what I did, I hadn't been able to get the attention I'd needed from my parents. I'd had to spend the weekend in the hospital on suicide watch. Getting counselling became mandatory – I no longer had a choice. My parents weren't asking me if I wanted counselling, the hospital was telling me it was a required condition of my release.

After my suicide attempt, my gym teacher and I had become closer. I still wasn't in counselling as Mum was attempting to find someone for me. I had been writing poetry – not for my teacher at first. But it became that. I had written some poems about my boyfriend Jay, who had dumped me, and when I'd shown them to her she thought they were about her. I'd written some with her in mind. (I've since been shown copies of those poems – as an adult. What the poems reflected was a 15-year-old kid who trusted the woman implicitly. A 15-year-old kid who was really messed up. A girl who was crying out for help. A kid who had already been sexually abused, and as a result had messed up ideas around sex and love.)

One day during school, the teacher had asked if I would take a ride to Springbank Park with her at lunch. I'd agreed. During the conversation, while we'd sat in the car, she told me she was attracted to me, but couldn't be with me. I knew what she meant when she said this. She'd held my hand, which felt terribly uncomfortable, not fun and exciting like when a young boy would hold my hand. I remember hardly saying a word the entire time; I'd had no idea what to say. The situation I'd found myself in was grown up – but I was just a teenager. I hadn't felt grown up. Something within me had known that my actions for her attention had spiraled into something beyond what my life experience was ready for. But I'd not known what to do. I'd said nothing. I'd done nothing. I'd told no one.

Five weeks after my suicide attempt, my teacher had asked me to go to her house after school. I had known what was going to happen. I went anyway. Once at her house, she asked me to start calling her by her first name, Kaiya. That was the first thing she did. It was very awkward calling her Kaiya, it felt wrong coming out of my mouth. You don't call teachers by their first name. But then something else happened that made me using her first name seem like a blip. Kaiya had kissed me. It had made me feel uncomfortable. It had been weird. It had been weird in the same kind of way as when Don had first kissed me...yet somehow different. It hadn't been like getting a kiss from a boy my own age. When I'd kiss boys my age, there'd been excitement and I'd felt comfortable. With Don and Kaiya, I'd felt out of my comfort zone. I hadn't known if I was doing the right things. I'd felt like a child. Instead of creating butterflies of excitement in my belly, I'd felt rocks in my stomach and an anvil on my chest, weighing me down. And things just got weirder. Kaiya had walked me over to her couch and started making out with me. Within a few moments, she was on top of me, straddling my leg, grinding herself up and down on it. Mere moments later she orgasmed – I knew what that was – and I was shocked at how quickly it had all happened. It was like months of pent up anticipation climaxed in a weird, uncomfortable scene in her living room. I did not process that day in my mind or heart at that time. I'd shut it out and boxed it in. It would be years before I would ever look back at that day and try to make sense of it.

Within a month of that happening, I'd started hanging out with a new crowd at school – the party crowd or as we'd named them, 'rockers'. Everyone in the group had worn jean jackets, leather jackets or lumber jackets. On Fridays and Saturdays, our crew had roamed around looking for a place to party. My professional drinking career had just begun. I had found my tribe. What better way to shut things out and box them in than by drinking as often as possible?

My interactions with Kaiya had become 'normal' after a while. During the week, she'd sneak me into her house. She'd had a girlfriend of ten years, so we were sneaking around from everyone – my Mum, her girlfriend, my friends, students from school, other teachers. Often, she'd pick me up while I was already on my way to her house. I'd had to put the seat all the way down and lay back so no one could see me in the car.

It had been an affectionate relationship. I'd thought I was in love. She loved me, which she told me all the time. I said it back. But the relationship had also been obsessive. It had become like an addiction – for both of us. We'd each tried to pull away from it at numerous times, but we hadn't succeeded in our attempts. She had known it was wrong to be with a student, and in addition to that, she had been having an affair with me because she'd already lived with a partner. There has never been a doubt in my mind that she was having a moral battle within herself, daily, and moment by moment.

I had started counseling with a counsellor my Mum found outside of the school system, and not long into the sessions, I told the counsellor about my relationship with Kaiya. Before telling her, I'd made it clear I didn't want anyone to find out about it. She didn't agree with the relationship. She'd said it was harmful for me. My counselor had not reported the relationship to anyone; not the school board, not my parents. She thought keeping what I told her in confidence was most important – I'd trusted her. It had been a difficult decision for her to make, and I remember her telling me just that. She shared with me that it was a struggle to know what to do in my specific, unique situation. The relationship was causing a moral dilemma for more than just Kaiya and I.

Kaiya's girlfriend had caught us at the house one day as we were doing the dishes together – something so domestic. About a month later their relationship ended. It hadn't ended well. I have a horrific memory of her girlfriend coming to the house late one night after they'd broken up. Storming into the bedroom, finding the two of us there, she'd ripped the covers off the bed, and called me and Kaiya awful names. Her heart had been broken. She'd been furious. I remember I'd rolled over and covered my naked body, literally unable to face the situation. I can still feel her anger, and my confusion and shame. After that, I'd found myself in a committed relationship with Kaiya.

I don't even recall there being a discussion about it. It was like, when her partner left, she assumed we were an exclusive item, a partnership. I hadn't been happy about it. Having an affair had been easier for me, it lacked commitment. An affair had allowed the relationship to not enter the realm of the substantial, the real – it was something I could still end easily at any time in my mind. I had still been interested in and attracted to boys. In fact, right around that time I had started having affairs of my own with guys my age on a regular basis.

My entire life had been filled with lies. I'd been lying to Kaiya about the boys I'd been with. I'd been lying to my counselor about the same thing – I didn't talk about all the boys, only some of them. I'd been lying to my Mum about everything. I'd been lying to my friends at school about where I was spending my time. I'd been lying to every adult in my life about the amount of drinking I was doing. And, while all of this was going on, I was being counseled about what had happened with Don, and about my resentments towards my Dad. On the one hand, the counselor had been trying to fix my damaged self esteem from the horrible events that started when I was twelve; while on the other, I'd been digging myself further and further into self hatred by lying to everyone. I'd also been drenching my reality in alcohol and secrets.

A teacher from a different high school had come to Kaiya's house early one Saturday morning. As she'd walked across the back porch, she'd seen us both in t-shirts and underwear – our pajamas. Kaiya informed me later that that teacher had recently come out of the closet and was dating another teacher from my school. She'd been coming to visit Kaiya who she considered to be a friend, and the only person her and her girlfriend knew in the gay community. We'd been found out, and the result was that Kaiya revealed our relationship to all of her closest friends. After a while, her friends had accepted the situation. Not all of them had accepted it right away. They'd been concerned about my age and that I was her student. But, slowly, I had been welcomed into the adult gay community.

I can remember exactly what was going through my mind part way through my sixteenth year. I remember thinking: "How long do I have to stay in this relationship before I can leave?" The thing was that I hadn't felt like I could leave. Kaiya had given up a girlfriend of ten years for me. She had bought me diamond earrings and other gifts. She'd risked her career for me. I'd rationalized an answer for myself. I'd decided that we should be together for somewhere between five and ten years before I left. I'd thought I was being so mature. It seemed like everyone in our relationship circle had thought I was so mature. I hadn't been mature at all. I had just experienced things that were way too adult when I was way too young. My life had been so messed up. I'd been putting up a front pretending that everything was awesome. Not a single person in my life had been getting the full truth about me, not even me. I'd lied to myself every day. I'd lied to everyone and myself because it was the only way I could survive the choices I'd made.

In grade twelve, I'd taken a course called Sexuality and Self Esteem. It was a course given by the Health department which was also a part of the Physical Education

Department. I'd excelled in that class. I'd known all the right answers. I'd been able to share my childhood experiences openly. I'd even talked about being molested by Don and how it had hurt my self esteem. Having been in counselling for more than a year, I had come to terms with the abuse from age twelve, and I had a much deeper understanding of it. My teacher had decided I should talk to the grade nine students about sexuality and self esteem. I'd jumped at the opportunity. I knew this would only deepen the work that my counsellor and I were doing together – it would help lift any remaining feelings of shame about the abuse by Don. Many of the grade nine classes were Kaiya's gym classes. She'd sit and listen to me talking to the kids about sexuality and self esteem. I'd shared my story about being molested to them too, and I also talked about my drug and alcohol use. Not one kid ever made fun of me or called me names. In fact, a few kids had confided in me about their own abuse, and I'd helped steer them toward the school counseling department to get help. Doing this work helped me to feel good about myself. It uplifted my self esteem. I was helping.

On my healing journey, I've wondered if Kaiya had received insight while listening to me give those talks. Did she have any awareness that what was happening between her and I had the potential to cause the same kinds of problems? I know I certainly didn't. The answers regarding what was wrong and how to change had been staring me in the face and yet I hadn't seen them. I'd been teaching students about the thing that had hurt me in my past while at the present time a different version of it was happening. My relationship with Kaiya had been wrong but I hadn't been able to see it. Honestly, I'd thought everything was going well. I'd really believed that I had my shit together. I really did.

You know, I'd only ever received one award for achievement in high school and it was for what I'd done in that class. I'd gotten the highest mark in Sexuality and Self Esteem. It's a sobering reminder that we can know stuff in our head, as I'd known that it was wrong to be taken advantage of sexually by an adult, but I'd not been able to see that it was happening with Kaiya. I knew how to talk about it, but I hadn't known how to stop it for myself. My own sexuality and self esteem had been explosively damaged.

The signs had been everywhere, but I was a forest and couldn't see my own trees, as the saying goes. I'd been promiscuous. I'd been cheating on Kaiya. One group of people thought I was straight, the other group thought I was gay. I'd been skipping school. I'd been ingesting a hell of a lot of alcohol every weekend. I'd been making bad choices after bad choices. I'd hated myself. All I'd done was tell lies and that made me feel horrible about myself.

The relationship with Kaiya continued for two-and-a-half years in total, from age 15 to 18. I ended the relationship just after my eighteenth birthday. By the time I'd hit eighteen, I'd been drinking heavily. I'd made horrible choices and I'd hated myself for it. The stage had been set for the next phase in my life.

* * *

It's difficult for me to look back on that time between the teacher and I. It took me over twenty-seven years to finally open that closet and take the skeletons out for a dance. I'm overcome with emotion when I think about it, and yet expressing those emotions is one of the hardest things in the world for me to do. Drugs and alcohol do an amazing job of numbing our feelings – it's incredible the depth of pain we can completely ignore if we just add enough tequila and roll enough joints. Sobering up, unfortunately, doesn't mean that we'll be in touch with our emotions or even that we'll be able to access them right away. Far from it. I'm ten years into sobriety and I still struggle to connect with what I'm feeling, even though the feelings are very present. I have physical reactions when I reflect on that time with Kaiya. My breathing gets short, pain grows in my chest, my stomach does somersaults.

For years I'd been able to talk about Don and what happened there, but the teacher? No. What was it that made it so painful? There was love there. I loved her. And she loved me. Granted, it was a messed-up kind of love, but even after I'd recognized that something was unhealthy, inappropriate, and downright wrong, it didn't stop my heart from feeling what it felt. I felt sick when, as an adult, I realized there was a parental aspect to the relationship – a mothering element that I needed fulfilled because I hadn't received it elsewhere in my life. That understanding made me want to scream or vomit or curl up and stop feeling what I was feeling.

She had been sexually attracted to me. I had been emotionally attracted to the attention she'd given me – she was a female adult and I'd needed that attention. But it had been more than that too. Based on some of the things she'd said to me, she'd also been attracted to my neediness; to the fact that I'd needed rescuing. How does sex factor into that? No matter how I try to put this piece of the puzzle together and make sense of it, I can't. I'm left feeling sad, anxious, and confused. I can't imagine any sane adult knowing me when I was fifteen: screwed up and suicidal and looking at me and thinking 'a sexual relationship is what she needs...that will fix her'. But it happened. My chest feels like there's an elephant sitting on it – the pressure pushing down is intense. I will continue to connect with my emotions about this time in my life. I choose to walk into my triggers, not away from them... it's how the healing happens.

* * *

My visit to North Bay was heavenly. Amanda was in the process of getting a new puppy and I was able to spend a day with them. Oh my gosh, talk about adorable, fun and funny, my heart was just brimming with joy – not just for Nala, the pup, but for Amanda, her daughter McKenzie, for their poodle Maverick. The whole house was full of love and I was happy to be immersed in it. Pets have an amazing way of healing us. I have two cats myself – Peace and Serenity – and they offer me so much healing simply by being themselves. Every time Serenity rolls on her back and looks at me, I burst out laughing with love. Every time Peace (affectionately known as Little Buddy), stands up on his hind legs trying to reach the doorknob to be let outside, my heart bursts with joy. Laying on the couch, one of them or both, will inevitably come onto my lap seeking ear scratches and snuggles.

When I go outside for my birding photography, I get the same feelings – love and joy – simply by interacting with nature. There is a complete peace and joy I feel when animals, wild or domestic, are around me. Not everyone experiences this with animals, but a great many of us do. I personally recommend making a deeper connection with an animal as part of your healing journey. When I was first getting sober, I wasn't able to love anything or anyone unconditionally – until I got Serenity. And when I opened up my closet and let Kaiya's skeleton out to dance, that's when I got Little Buddy. He made me smile ear to ear during a time that was emotionally taxing for me.

Every time I pick up my camera and go into nature, I feel calm. My busy mind stops chattering and I focus on what I'm photographing while the little birds bring me joy and the powerful birds – the eagles and owls – bring me courage. I stand in awe of their majesty. My ability to love unconditionally blossomed when I got my cats. Being in nature as a witness to all its majestic and magical expressions through plants and animals has been an essential part of my healing journey. There are many ways to put into practice what I've learned as I've healed over the years, and animals and nature are amazing teachers.

Amanda and I spent time talking about her life, where she was happy, where she was unhappy. We talked about her hopes and dreams for her career. Both of us spent time with her daughter McKenzie, talking to her about school, her feelings, cute puppies, and life. I've always been able to share openly with Amanda. She's always accepted me, no matter where I was at. I found out recently that she'd known about Kaiya. She had figured it out based on some things I had said, and when she'd noticed a scribble on my school binder. I found out another best friend had known when I was seventeen. But no one had said anything to me. They hadn't known what to say. I didn't feel a sense of relief that they'd known. When I found out, I'd felt anxiety and tightness in my stomach. I'd lied to them back then. But I forgave myself for that quickly, realizing that feelings of guilt were part of my anxiety. I think none of us had known what to do, what to say about it, and they'd trusted me, on some level, to make my own decisions. Perhaps they'd only believed that staying out of it was the best thing they could do.

Included in my self love journey is my ability to forgive the younger versions of myself that didn't know any better at the time. I have compassion for the kid who was in way over her head. I am able to look back on all of that now and see a kid who was really messed up, looking for an adult, any adult, to pay attention to her, to give her time. I can see a kid who desperately needed to not just hear the words "I love you", but needed to feel loved. That kid graduated to an adult age eighteen and at the exact same time she freed herself from that unhealthy relationship. It wasn't a good starting place for personal responsibility, but the decision to leave had been fabulous – necessary and freeing. The choice to bury it and refuse to look at it, though? That decision would wreak havoc in my life for years to come.

I spent a total of two nights at Amanda's and then it was time for me to be on my way. I had to keep on schedule. My next stop was in Sault Ste. Marie! I'd never stopped there before except I think I'd driven through it on the Greyhound bus ride in 2007 that I'd taken across Canada. I was entering unexplored territory. I love new adventures!

DAY 5 – SEPTEMBER 15TH, 2019

GRATEFULLY ALIVE

I saddled up my bike, put all my luggage back on, and shockingly I still didn't have to use any of my special heated gear I purchased for this trip. The weather was phenomenal – Mother Nature certainly was being kind to me. I wore my chaps, a few layers of clothing, and my leather coat and vest. I was snug as a bug. Amanda and McKenzie both waved good-bye to me as I pulled away, and they took pictures and videos on their phones.

I had a 436km day in front of me with Sault Ste Marie my destination goal. The plan was to go through Sudbury, Espanola, Blind River and Bruce Mines before arriving at my final destination. The ride down Highway 17 was gorgeous. Riding my bike, tunes turned on, a flock of sand cranes flying over my head, I didn't stop smiling. I'm a bit of a birder, and we only get to see sandhill cranes for a short while during migration in my neck of the woods. I looked up the crane as a totem animal later that day. The crane signals a time when we discover a lost part of the self and can even recover it – amazing! There is a secrecy and sense of protection involved with crane totem. If we maintain focus, we can remain creative. Crane is associated with good fortune, luck, happiness and a long life.

What a perfect animal medicine message to receive while on my WRWR trip. When I was at the Oneida Family Healing Lodge in 2006, I had first started paying attention to animal signs/totems. There had been a hawk sitting in a nearby tree most times that I went out back of the lodge for a smoke. He'd sat looking at me. All my life, I had frequently seen red-tailed hawks. That particular hawk at the lodge had stared at me like it was watching over me. Protecting me. That hawk was the reason I got interested in paying attention to animal medicine.

When I'd mentioned to someone at the lodge about the hawk, they'd explained to me that the hawk had a message for me, and that I should listen for it. In addition to the hawk experience while at the lodge, I had another unique and interesting thing happen.

I was in the kitchen sitting at the table and chatting with a group of women who were in town for a funeral. I'd been doodling – something I'd started doing again after not doing it for years. My doodles had been shapes – squares, circles, oblongs – all connected with lines that I thickened with ink. I'd start with one shape and work my way out. I'd gotten up from the table to get a coffee and when I came back, I saw my doodle. I was looking at it upside-down and it looked like a hummingbird.

I held it up for the other women to see, "What do you see in this picture?" I'd asked.

They all said they saw the same thing – a hummingbird. Wow! I hadn't meant to draw a hummingbird at all and yet there it was. I took it as a sign from god that I was supposed to draw, and more specifically, I was supposed to draw animals. That's how it began, my drawing. At first, my art was very simple. Using black ink, I had no idea what animal would appear when I began drawing but an animal emerged. As time progressed, I started to draw animals on purpose, giving the picture an outside shape and then drawing more animals inside of it, along with my form of doodling. I called it 'totem art' because each picture carried certain healing energies with it. Eventually, I added red ink, then finally all colours.

This is the earliest piece of art I have.
This would have been drawn in the fall of 2006.

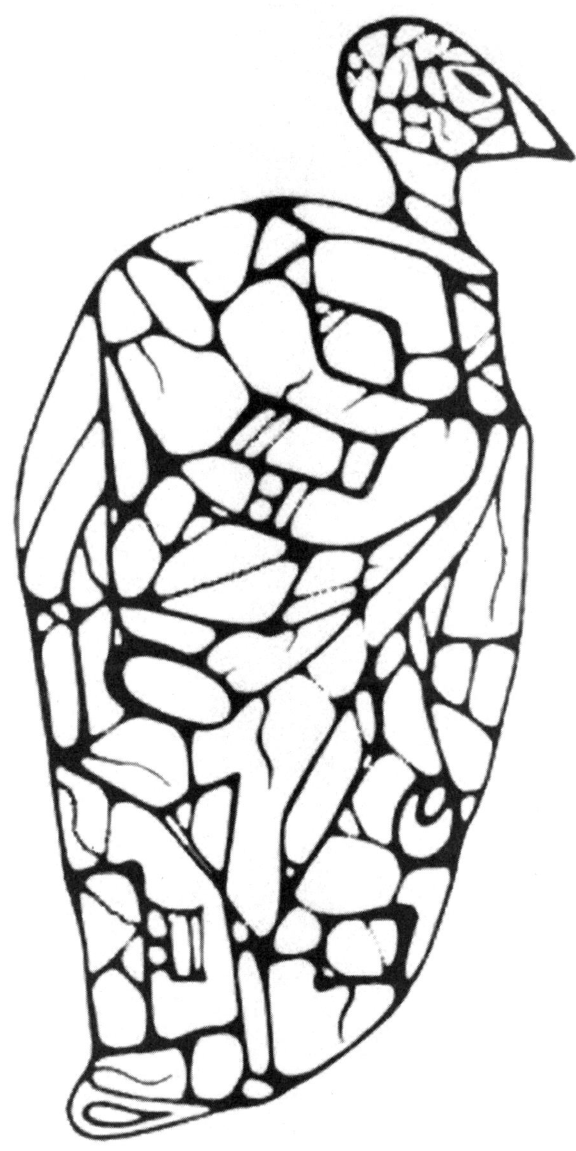

This is a picture I drew while still at my Mom's before leaving Canada in the first few weeks of 2007. I titled it then, "Beware the Vultures".

Ascension, 2007

Cranes still flying overhead, a song came on my headphones, a song that hadn't always been on my playlist but had been put back on about six months before my trip began: Terrapin Station, by the Grateful Dead.

Years ago, I believe I was in my very late teens, the Grateful Dead came to Hamilton, Ontario – it was their last Canadian show before Jerry Garcia passed. I hadn't been a Grateful Dead fan, in fact, I had complained any time anyone played their albums. However, I'd had some friends who were big time fans and I got coaxed into going to a concert. Eleven of us went in total. We'd rented a motel room nearby the concert venue. We'd spent the day drinking, getting high and eventually dropping acid before the show. We had to take two cabs to all get to the arena. I'd been in the first cab, so I'd arrived at the venue with the first bunch. I remember waiting for the second cab of my friends to arrive. It had sped up to the corner, slammed on its brakes, the door flew open, and my friend Freddy's head popped out just in time to spew vomit all over the pavement. He'd gotten out and off we all went into the crowd.

Tigerlily, 2007

Who is Freddy, you may ask? His real name is Paul, but a funny moment in shop class back in school had earned him the nickname Freddy. I have a warm place in my memory bank for Paul – he was a part of my life as a friend for a good many years. A lot of my memories involve partying with Paul, but not all of them. There are many parallels between my life, some of my struggles and his; the paths we took look different, but we arrived at a similar place – our authentic selves.

At the stadium, I'd been amazed by a whole community created by the Dead Heads (fans of the Grateful Dead) that had popped up outside. I'd never seen anything like it before or since. I remember seeing a cop walking around with a huge yellow smiley face buttoned onto his uniform. There were people cooking food; people selling tye dye t-shirts, and others selling home-made goods – nothing had been commercialized. There were no food trucks. No professionally made swag. Hippies and their modern counterparts had drifted through the crowds. It had been Shakedown Street and it was as much a part of the concert experience as the music itself. Shakedown Street was an album produced by the Grateful Dead, but it was also what Dead Heads (Grateful Dead fans) called the gatherings that would happen before a show – like the gathering I had attended there in Hamilton.

Even though Shakedown Street had been magical and marvelous, I'd still expected to not be amazed by the music since I wasn't a fan. But I'd been happily surprised; the music was, in fact, amazing. Perhaps one needed to see them live to get it, I don't know. Or maybe the light show, the acid and the pot had helped. Whatever the combination had been, it turned out to be the best concert experience of my life, and I've seen a tonne of concerts. I hadn't been familiar with any of their songs – the Dead wasn't known for top 40s hits, but that hadn't mattered. When they did a show, they'd do a different song list every single performance. You'd never know what song you might see performed for the first time in years.

During the show, they'd played a song that captured me from the very start – the song was Terrapin Station. I had gawked at the stage, listened to the lyrics and felt the rhythm. It had been spell binding. The song kept building and then it would drop, then it would build higher, then it would drop, then it would build even higher, and it hit crescendos that I've never forgotten. "Inspiration move me brightly," – those words were forever etched into my memory exactly the way they sounded as they were sung live. I had felt those words in my heart, living, ready to take action, ready to be inspired! Many times I have put this song on to feel inspired. And it works. Every. Single. Time.

So there I was riding my bike, a flock of cranes had just flown over my head, and Terrapin Station came on the radio. Before the crescendo hit, it dawned on me, "Oh my god, I could use this bike trip as the frame for my book! Inspiration! Move me Brightly!" The inspired a-ha moment filled my body with electricity. Yes! The crescendo released an inspired message – a frame for the book. The Book. The one I'd been wanting to write for thirteen years. The Book that had existed as a dream that kept me going when I was half out of my mind with no place to sleep on the streets of Toronto. The Book that had been the carrot dangling in my face as I'd entered a new country with only $700 in my pocket. The Book that had been the promise always lurking in the background that said, "Everything will be ok one day Tracey, we promise." And I'd believed it. I'd clung to it like a child to her blankie. The Book. Oh my god. The Book!

Tears streamed down my face soaking my mask, the wind quickly blew away any tears that didn't soak up. Nothing had ever felt more right than the idea of using my bike trip as the frame for The Book. It was back in 2006 that I had first realized I knew I was going to write a book. At no point between then and that inspired moment on my bike had it ever been far from my mind.

The Book – you notice it's capitalized, like that's the name. That's what I've called it for all these years as I've tried to write it. It's taken on a life of its own with that name. Never once had it turned out the way I wanted it to all the times I'd started to write it. And I'd started it many times with some versions having many, many pages. Then I'd start editing and I'd toss it aside in frustration. I couldn't find my voice. It couldn't express what my story needed me to express. At this point, I can pinpoint exactly what the problem was with my previous attempts. I hadn't healed enough. I hadn't let go of things that desperately needed letting go of. I hadn't been able to see the trees of my forest, to keep up that metaphor. But riding my beautiful Stella along forested roads with trees so lush and alive I couldn't help but reflect. I was finally able to figure out how to bring my story to life in book form. It needed a story within a story and this bike ride, this was the story.

They say authors should write a book that they would want to read. I had tried desperately to do that. But until this very version, I'd never wanted to read it. In writing this book, I've taken full ownership for everything I've done in my adult life – and that's the key for me. Taking full ownership, full responsibility, full reflection and acceptance; these are keys to my healing, and the keys to my self-empowerment.

Yes, there is truth to a part of me that had given up on The Book. After so many failed attempts to write it over the years, I'd come to accept that I didn't need to write a book. I'd decided it had just been a carrot that the Universe dangled in front of me to keep me going. I was self-employed, my business was going wonderfully, I was in a healthy relationship with my best friend. All was well. My life had turned out to be incredible, so it felt like it didn't matter if I wrote about it or not, right? Well, no matter how many times I'd tried to tell myself to forget about it, something would happen that would motivate me to try again and again.

I'd had a breast cancer scare and the first thing through my mind, the only regret that came up was the voice in my head that said: "Oh! No! I haven't written the book yet! I can't die!" True story! It happened a few times when I'd had scares of one kind or another. I kept realizing that my only regret was that I hadn't written The Book. I don't know how to say it better than to say it like this – The Book is a part of me. I'd been lugging a dream around in my heart that was so vibrant, so real, that I just knew it was going to happen. Timing had played with my ability to write though.

At first, the idea that I could write a book had motivated me to start writing at all. It had kept me writing during difficult times that I needed the act of writing for my healing. Journaling was a perfect example of writing that helped me to heal. But simply believing that a book was in me gave me hope that one day my life would be ok because The Book was part of that 'ok' picture. I'd had a wonderful adventure in the United States and I tried to write then, but it was an unhealed place that I was writing from. I'd been full of anger, full of so much hurt and brokenness. I had lacked the ability to see the big picture. So I lacked the ability to write about it.

As I was opening my business, I'd thought, "Wonderful, this will give me the time I need to write The Book." Even my business wasn't simply about a business, it was about creating a space in which creativity would flow and The Book could be born. At times, The Book felt like a plague that wouldn't go away, that wouldn't leave me alone. I know why now.

The time arrived. The stars aligned, as they say. The 'why' of me writing The Book is about me being able to write it from the right place for me to like it. I arrived at a place in my life where to tell my story means I have a story I'd want to read myself. The Universe wasn't going to let this dream disappear because the only way I would ever finish The damn Book was if I had let go of everything that needed to be let go of. If I could love myself enough to forgive everything from my past, and find a way to express my experience in a way that made me smile then I had arrived or to put it another way, then I had awakened. I had to be able to write from a place of personal empowerment – that means owning my entire story, letting go of the parts that would hurt or anger others, and accepting that I could choose what parts to include without needing validation about my choices. This, to me, was proof of my healing. That's the place where The Book needed to come from for me to love it. I had to love myself. Riding my motorcycle in the middle of my epic solo trip, I was certain that this was the healed place that I'd been trying to write from. I had never been stronger in my entire life. Inspiration move me brightly.

SOMEBODY THAT I USED TO KNOW

We are going to pretend that a song came on while I was driving my bike. We're going to treat it like a piece of inserted magic, a piece of inserted memory that cannot be totally ignored in the telling of my story. The singer's voice is smooth and sweet. It cuts into my soul like a knife through warm butter. The singer? Adele. The song? Hello. I've loved Adele's music, but I've rarely been able to relate to her heart breaks, break-ups, and midnight longings – not anymore.

In this song, she sang about California, and she sang about a relationship from her youth that needed reflection, that wanted forgiveness. I've had one of those relationships. But up to this point, I've written this book without saying a word about it. I realize I can't do this; it's not fair to you, reader. As you read my story, you may feel as though something, or someone is missing. You may think, "Um, it feels like someone important was here in your adult years, your broken years...where is this person? Who is it?" Your intuition would be correct. We will call him my Ex or the Ex – it's a fair title. Why on earth would I write an entire book without mentioning a significant relationship that started in my late teens and ended on September 11th, 2006? There are a few reasons, all of them good.

It was a love that once meant the world to me, and I cannot do it justice by looking back on it with the eyes and the knowledge I now have. When we break up with people, we can remember how bad things were at the end, the horrible things that were said and done. We can forget why we fell in love in the first place.

By telling the story of 'us', I would be revealing more than my own private life. I would be revealing someone else's. No matter how angry or hurt both of us were when we broke up, I cannot justify going into the details of how it all went wrong. Once upon a time, before Recovery, I would have been happy to yell the entire story from the rooftops – my words full of venom and anger. But all of that venom, anger, and, yes, fear, left me long ago. I am able to remember who we were when I was nineteen and full of love.

This is what's important to the story, to my story, regarding the Ex. It's something that I hope helps you on your own journey. When it's all said and done, after a significant relationship ends that we now view as having been entirely unhealthy and not good for either party, what really matters isn't what they did or didn't do. What matters is why we tolerated it. Why we participated in it for so long. Regardless of who was right and who was wrong – every single day, when we wake up as an adult in an adult relationship, we make the choice to stay or leave. Leaving may be scary for numerous reasons, but it's still one of our choices. For fifteen years, he woke up every single day and decided to stay. For fifteen years, I woke up every single day and decided to stay. And at first when I left, I wanted to point the finger and blame and throw it all back on him. I wanted to call out the things that he had done wrong. Then I grew a bit. I was able to look at myself and call out the things that I had done wrong. And then I grew a bit more. I found compassion for both of us. We were young and we made the best choices we could at the time with the tools and the knowledge we had. And if it wasn't healthy, it was because neither of us knew what healthy looked like.

Ultimately, what mattered to me in the end was being able to answer the question: why did I stay, when after looking back I knew how unhealthy it was? The answer was simple. I wanted to be loved... I needed to be loved. And every time he said I love you, I felt like I had a smidgen of value in this world. That I love you made me feel like I mattered. So I kept making the choice to stay in the same patterns and lifestyle choices that also tore down any self esteem and positive self image I had.

My self esteem bottomed out during those years. I have absolutely no one to blame but myself for that. For him, the answer is the same – he has no one to blame but himself. We were two adults. Making adult decisions. Both of us woke up every day for fifteen years and chose to stay. That's what I look at on my healing journey.

I look at the self esteem issues I had that kept me making that same choice for fifteen years. I look at my own codependency. I look at my own addiction. I look at my own sexual intimacy issues. I look at my own fears. I look at my own self sabotage. I look at my own lack of self confidence. I look at me, at what I can fix, and what I can change. There's no point in looking at him. There's nothing I can change there.

I'd love to be able to say I've forgiven everything that happened, that I don't have a single bitter bone left in my body regarding the Ex, but it would be a lie. I've come leagues from where I once was with this. I've grown immensely. I know that I loved him so much that I was unable to leave when it was a good time to leave. I know that I hurt him, and I've forgiven myself for my part in what went wrong. I know that he hurt me, and I've forgiven him for his part in what went wrong. Of all the people I've ever known, he has been one of my greatest teachers in the major karmic areas of my life – self esteem, addiction, codependency, self validation and more. If he's still an atheist, he might see it as a wasted fifteen years. As a spiritualist, I see it as fifteen years in one of hundreds of lifetimes that we've danced this same dance to numerous songs.

I feel it's important to walk away from relationships that at first leave us feeling bitter or angry or hurt, and at some point, when some healing has happened, be able to find the hidden blessings, the gifts that our exes gave us. Often when I ask people to look for those silver linings, they laugh or give a resentful look telling me nothing good came of it. "But did you grow in any way because of it?" I ask. Or I suggest that "perhaps you are more independent because of what happened?" Oh yes. There are many questions I ask. Perhaps you understand the importance of self compassion more now? Did you learn to pay attention to red flags? Did you realize the importance of following your own intuition and trusting yourself more? Do you have more self confidence now? Have you realized how to say "no" when you mean no, instead of being coaxed into a "yes"? Have you realized the importance of staying true to your own goals and dreams, even when in a relationship? I ask these questions because these are questions I asked myself, and the answers helped me discover the hidden blessings in the most difficult relationship of my life.

I walked away from the Ex with a basket full of blessings although at the time I didn't even know I had the basket, and that there were already little gifts in it. There are many things I feel grateful about even from a relationship that I hang in the "unhealthy" column. Gratitude heals.

Thank you for giving me the space to include a song that wasn't on my playlist, and for allowing me to include some thoughts on an important topic without including the details. I appreciate you understanding why some private things are better left private. And as for you? Once you're out, what your ex did or didn't do, doesn't really matter as much answering the question: Why did you tolerate it? Whatever the answer is, have compassion for that place; heal that place. Make healing that place your number one priority. Send that place within yourself all your love and compassion. That's what matters.

BRING ME TO LIFE

It hadn't dawned on me during my bike trip. That is, it was while writing the book and getting to this section that I'd realized what the date was when I'd had the epiphany to use my bike trip as the framework for the story. Looking back in my journal, I found proof of the date: September 15th. That same day, the day that I'd felt inspired to write The Book was my thirteenth anniversary of the day I had met god and had my original inspiration to write a book in the first place.

Flashback to September 15th, 2006. I had spent four days wandering around Rodney, Ontario, wondering what the hell had happened in my life. Wondering why things had gone so wrong? Who was to blame? What was to blame? I had played the questions in my head over and over. I knew I had made some horrible choices. My breakdown and the terror that followed hadn't happened in a vacuum – they'd happened in the storm of drug use and poor decisions.

At 11pm, I'd found myself sitting down on the front step of the United Church. It was well lit and I'd needed a place to rest. The rolling dialogue in my head hadn't stopped, it was still going strong. I'd been physically, mentally and emotionally exhausted. My whole life had blown up and everything that had once been my everything was nothing. I'd been scared of the future, haunted by the past, and I had no clue what was happening, where I was going, or what I planned to do.

Keep in mind, I had been an atheist at the time. Out of nowhere, while I was alone on the front steps of that church, I had an epiphany. It came in the form of a plea to god. I'd begged a god I didn't even believe in, to forgive me, to forgive all of us. I'd explained that we aren't bad, we'd just made bad choices. I'd even offered my own life, if it would somehow bring peace.

What happened next, changed my life forever.

Quiet as can be, but clear as a bell, I'd heard a voice clearly in my head. It said: "I Am." It was not my voice. It was not my ego. But I'd heard it – a clear "I Am." I had never in my life heard voices in my head like that – and I'd done a lot of drugs and had a hell of a breakdown, but during all of that, I'd never heard a single voice. As I'd heard the words "I Am", I'd felt a warmth wrap around me like a blanket. I'd felt the warmth of Love. I'd felt wrapped up in a wonderful blanket of warm Love. It had been similar to the feeling I'd felt when I did ecstasy. Except a hundred times stronger. The rushing, all-at-once of it I'd felt through my whole body. I'd felt like something outside of me was holding me in the most loving, tender embrace I'd ever experienced in my life. I'd felt loved. I couldn't remember ever feeling that loved. A comparison could perhaps have been being held as an infant by a mother for the first time...if that feeling could resurface as an adult. I've never attained the same feeling since – not quite.

As I'd heard "I Am" in my head and felt its power in and around my body, in one instantaneous moment, I'd been transformed from being atheist to knowing there was something bigger than me, something I would call 'god.'

A feeling of joy, pure, unadulterated joy, had swept over my entire being. In that moment, I'd gone from feeling distressed and distraught to feeling pure ecstasy in the true meaning of the word. I'd sought that feeling all of my life. I had taken so many drugs in search of that feeling. My whole body had been engulfed in bliss. That feeling lasted for an entire twenty-four hours. It was the most incredible high I'd ever had in my life. Since that miraculous moment on the stairs of that beloved church, I'd come close to feeling that version of ecstasy, very close, but never quite the same as that night on September 15th, 2006. And no drugs were involved in the creation of that feeling!

I had been stunned on the steps of the church. I had said for years, "I don't believe in god, but if he was standing right in front of me, I'd shake his hand." And there I'd been, shaking hands with god. I had so many questions flooding my mind at that moment; the very first being, "Does this mean the Christians are right?" because I'd been standing on the steps of the United Church. I'd laughed at my question. What I'd walked away from that experience with was this – a new-found belief in something bigger than myself, and a peaceful knowing that everything was going to be ok. There was a god, and apparently, god was on my team.

Because I'd heard the voice saying "I Am" right after I'd begged for forgiveness and offered myself as a sacrifice, I'd made two assumptions during the bliss of my ecstatic state. The first was that forgiveness was huge. It was god huge. It was a key to life – a key for my own life. The second assumption was that I might die. I'd offered my own life as a sacrifice, so it followed that the possibility of my dying was heightened. I wasn't sure how or why, I'd just felt the possibility of it. But it didn't matter if I did or not. I didn't care. I wasn't afraid of it. There was a god and that brought me peace. Everything would be ok whether I died or I lived.

If there was a single moment that had the most positive impact in my life, that was it. Everything had changed. Everything. I was no longer in charge, god was. And frankly, I'd needed anyone but me to be in charge. I'd needed someone to tell me what to do, where to go, how to fix my life. I hadn't trusted me – I'd just blown up my life.

While I'd stood on the steps talking to god that night, I had a realization: I was going to write a book. I'd felt inspired. It was beyond the idea that I would write a book, it was like the knowledge that I would write a book had just dropped into my understanding. It was as if my destiny had always been to write a book, and on that day, September 15th, 2006, I'd been awakened to that destiny.

And as I walked away from the church that night, out of the blue yet compelled, I'd started singing the chorus to Alive, by Pearl Jam, but I changed it slightly. I'd been on the highest natural high, and I was singing my heart out, *"Oh, oh oh, I, I, I, I, I'm still alive, and I'm doing fine god, thank you for being my friend, for watching my ass god, right til the very end."* I'd danced down the street, my arms outstretched above my head, my body spinning to the music in my head and the words pouring out my mouth. Alive! I had walked away from everything I once knew and loved and it didn't matter. I'd felt alive for the first time in my life. And I was going to write a book about it all.

Every time Alive plays on the radio, I'm back feeling that moment, shaking hands with god, ecstasy flowing through my being, a huge smile blossoming across my face. I am reminded that everything is going to be ok. And you know what? It is. All is well.

DARK TIMES

I stopped in Sudbury for gas. I'd already been to the Big Nickel, a must-see tourist attraction (it's a literal Big Nickel. Very big!), a few weeks previously on a motorcycle ride with Todd, Kelly and Ron. I suspected I'd be seeing the nickel again during the WRWR ride. I was getting excited about joining the WRWR. It wasn't long now! Just six days until I would join the largest motorcycle relay in history!

After stretching my legs and arms, twisting my hips, bending over, flexing my hands, I was ready to get back on the bike. I'd been calling her Stella lately. I wasn't sure if the name was going to stick, but it was the only one that had stuck so far. I'd purchased this beauty in June earlier in the year. Stella is a 2009 Honda VTX 1300T. She's a deep wine colour that sparkles in the sun. The previous owner babied her and she looked brand new when I purchased her. I wish I could still say the same. She's not quite looking off the lot anymore, but she still looks spectacular. I love her shape and lines. She's sleek, she's sexy. Bikes need chrome for me to be a fan, and she has chrome! One day I'd like to fix up a classic Mustang, just so I can have a car with chrome again.

I hit Espanola next. As I cruised through, I noted that a few weeks prior had been my first time visiting. But I wasn't stopping today. I exited the little town and was in uncharted territory. I was entering new lands. I'm one of those 'been there, done that, got the t-shirt' kind of people. For me, that often means visiting a place once is enough. I'm no longer the kind of person who goes back to the same vacation spot year after year. I want to see places and things I've never seen before, even if it's in the same country, I prefer new locations. While I'm in these new places, I try to get a t-shirt or a jacket or a piece of clothing that has the name of the town / city on it. A few t-shirts came back from this trip, but not one from Espanola. (There's only so much room on my bike!)

I'd picked up my love for adventure during my travels to the US. At that time, I had no idea where I was going or how long I'd be staying. I had been unwilling to commit to anything more than the few days in front of me. My time in California had been perfect. Then right around the same time as the Cinco De Mayo Fiasco, Venice Beach had lost its sparkle. At first, I'd loved the guy with his alto saxophone, skateboarding every day on the beach; the throngs of colourful artists, the music, the madness. But then it became... ordinary. It hadn't felt like home to me, and the thrill of seeing it all for the first time was gone. The colours had dulled. It had been easy to let it go when I left. My soul had been longing to leave, to see something new, experience something different. I hadn't grown up traveling and experiencing new places, but I had always longed for it. There's an entire world out there and I only have so many years to see it. I feel adventures calling me, so I don't want to go to the same place over and over.

I turned up the music when the next song came on – Paradise, by Coldplay. I love this song. Every time I hear it, I'm reminded of how I used to feel about life – it reminds me of a different version of me.

Depression was something I was haunted by for a solid decade. It started when I'd moved to Toronto for my fourth year of university. I was twenty-two at the time. Around the same time the depression started, I'd dropped out of school – and I'm not 100% sure which came first – the chicken or the egg. I also don't know for sure what had triggered the depression. I do know I had less access to pot at that time. I do know that dropping out of university was the end of my lifelong dream to be a teacher. I do know that it was difficult for me to make friends. I'd spent an awful lot of time alone.

I was desperate to figure out what was at the root of my depression. I tried self analyzing. A part of me knew there were unresolved issues around the relationship with Kaiya, but I wasn't self aware enough to get to the root of my sadness. I remember calling my old counselor, the one who knew about Kaiya, and I'd told her I thought I needed to have a meeting with her and Kaiya. My counsellor made the call, and Kaiya agreed to meet in London. I had really been hoping that meeting with Kaiya and the counselor would help me put my finger on what was causing my depression. I hadn't known exactly what I would say to her, hadn't planned to ask any specific questions, I just knew I had to talk with Kaiya about what had happened between us. As an adult having moved beyond our relationship, I knew it hadn't been right. I'd known it wasn't right at the time, but I wasn't able to change it, to understand it, to navigate out of it because I was a very wounded child. It's very possible that it was this wounded child who somehow found a voice to tell me to have the meeting.

The entire event was disappointing. Kaiya was there with her counselor and me with mine. The word awkward doesn't begin to encompass how I felt being in the same room as Kaiya. Any time I'd bumped into her in public since our being together, I'd avoided her like the plague – I would turn the other way, avoid eye contact, and do everything I could to not have to say hello. At that meeting, for the first time, I'd let Kaiya know that I believed our relationship had been inappropriate and that it hadn't been good for me. I didn't have the right words or the understanding at the time to fully grasp why it hadn't been good for me, I just knew that the way it made me feel when I so much as thought about the relationship, left me wanting to run away from myself and my thoughts. Years later I would be able to see it with much more clarity, but until that point it had been the kind of thing that would make me want to smoke a joint or have a few drinks, just to push it all back into its dark corner.

The most Kaiya was able to do was admit that it was against the law, but she hadn't seemed to feel she had done anything wrong beyond breaking the law. She had been unable to see how it was an unhealthy thing for me. I told her that I had never believed I was gay – that I had gone along with it because it was easier than telling her the things that were really bothering me. What had really been bothering me at the time was a sexual experience I had, shortly after turning 15, that made me feel bad about myself. I had been ashamed and I'd needed an adult in a counselor role, not a sexual relationship. Kaiya failed to take responsibility for any level of wrong she'd done, for the damage she'd added to my life, other than legally. This frustrated me. I knew she had started being a guidance counselor at school since we'd parted, and she'd had to take courses to do that, to help kids with their issues. How on earth was she helping kids with their issues, if she was failing to see how incredibly wrong it was for an adult to be with a fifteen year old suicidal student? I didn't say that though.

Words failed me that day. My inability to put words to emotions and feelings wasted that opportunity we'd had together, for me to find some sort of resolution to what was going on inside of me. Beyond the problem of lacking words, I still wasn't able to see how exactly it had damaged me, I just knew it wasn't healthy, what I felt inside of me anytime I thought about that relationship for even a moment. I'd left the meeting feeling completely unsatisfied that anything had been accomplished. I'd been no closer to figuring out why I was so depressed. I had no idea if it was Kaiya or something else.

At that time in Toronto, I'd discovered ecstasy. I'd been working at a grocery store and I met a young woman named Carrie who went to raves. She invited me to join her. I had no idea what a rave was so she'd explained it as best she could. It wouldn't be until I went to one that I understood what it was. A most basic description is that a rave is a large gathering of people in a big space, like a warehouse, dancing to a specific kind of dance music. It's impossible to put the feeling of being at a rave into words, but I'll try. Standing outside the warehouse where the rave was held, the entire neighbourhood shook with bass beats. Over and over, bass, bass, bass, bass pumped out of the building. The whole building trembled. As I stepped inside, the lights were low, smoke machines made the air hazy. It was difficult to see more than five feet ahead of me.. Young people dressed in all sorts of crazy outfits, wandered by, danced by, laughed by, swirled and twirled by. There was movement everywhere around me.

Up on a stage, a DJ with headphones, spun records and smiled at young girls trying to talk with him. On the dance floor, people swayed to the music with their eyes closed or jumped up and down as they twisted and turned glow sticks. There were lots of folks groping each other – all to the beat of the thumping music. Everyone was doing their own thing. No one cared what anyone else was doing but in a way that was easy, acceptable, fun. Within seconds of being in this wild environment, I'd felt my body wanting to move, to dance.

Carrie asked me if I'd wanted some ecstasy. I said no and asked if we could find some acid instead. Acid was familiar to me; I had no idea what ecstasy was. I'd found acid for five bucks and danced high as a kite for eight hours. I hadn't worried about anyone around me – I danced as if no one was watching. And you know why? Because at a rave no one was. Everyone was having their own experience. At some points, I'd stopped dancing so I could stand in front of someone dancing with glow sticks and allow them to put on a light show for me. I'd had a fantastic time. It was the first time I'd had fun in Toronto.

Over the next few months, I went to a bunch of raves with Carrie and her friends. I never quite felt like I'd fit in with that group, but I'd tried, and it was nice to have someone I considered a friend in Toronto. I'd enjoyed the dancing. I'd enjoyed the friendship. It was a reprieve from the depression I was experiencing. Raves didn't cost a terrible amount of money, but it was more than a movie cost – I recall paying around twenty-five dollars to enter. At one of them, we hadn't been able to find any drugs except ecstasy. I'd since found out that ecstasy released all the serotonin (the chemical that makes us feel happy) in the body at once. I decided I'd try it. Trying drugs was never something that made me nervous, it felt more like a social experiment to me. Ecstasy had made me feel amazing, awesome, wonderful, ecstatic, sensual – like every person

I saw was my best friend on the planet. I'd wanted to stroke my own arm, my neck, my face...touching my skin had felt phenomenal. Everything was perfect, that's how it had made me feel. And I'd loved it.

Money had been tight, so I didn't do much ecstasy due to the cost. Good ecstasy cost around twenty to twenty five dollars. I did some though, and I'd loved the high every time. I'd also made another good friend, Darren. Darren was gay, so he was a safe male friend, there would be no sexual tension between us. He'd made me laugh. He'd helped ease some of my depression. He was a creative, soulful person. We'd have long, heartfelt talks that helped me feel connected. Darren understood the depression I'd been experiencing as he wasn't a stranger to it himself. Darren was a godsend and he'd helped me survive a difficult time in my life. (Darren and I are still in touch, even though we live across the country from each other. I miss Darren. He's part of my heart.)

I lived in Toronto for just under two and a half years. During that time, I'd dropped out of school, I'd made a lifelong friend (Darren), and I'd discovered a drug that would become a problem for me – ecstasy. When I returned to London two years later, I'd expected the depression to go away, but it didn't. I got jobs I'd hated and had to start paying off student loans for a university degree I hadn't completed. That phase of my life was overshadowed by the dark depression that began in Toronto. It hadn't left. I'd smoked a lot of pot because it kept me feeling level. When I couldn't find pot, my moods worsened. I'd played a lot of computer games – they killed huge chunks of time and they distracted me from the depression. I had an addiction to playing video games. I'd played Everquest, one of the forerunner games to World of Warcraft. In the game, every character I'd met was a real person playing from their home. Characters could hook up to defeat monsters, and create online communities. We'd created a whole new world together, separate from the real world many, like me, had been avoiding.

I'd had my first mental health scares while I'd been deep into playing video games – scares that went beyond depression. A few times, I'd gone to the hospital for paranoia assessments because I'd been experiencing it enough to be concerned. I hadn't been honest with the doctors about the drugs I was doing. Never once had I been honest about how much pot I smoked. I wasn't up front about the fact that my ecstasy intake had increased quite a bit, and that I'd dabbled in cocaine once in a while, took mushrooms and whatever other drugs came my way. I could no longer call myself just a pothead – well, I could, but I wasn't being honest. None of my trips to the hospital had resulted in any kind of medical assistance or admittance to the hospital. The doctors had taken notes and sent me on my way. It hadn't dawned on me that drugs could be part of the reason I was having some delusional experiences.

I had left Toronto at age 24. Insert three more years of frustrating depression and heavy pot use. During that time I spent very little time analyzing why I was depressed, and more time just wishing it would stop. At the time, I thought the pot was helping me to manage the depression. In retrospect, I realize it was stopping me from feeling my emotions and taking a look at what things were causing the problem. In fact, it may have been a big part of the problem – pot. At the time, I would have argued the opposite. Even though I knew then that pot was a depressant, I didn't think it was a depressant for me.

Frustrated with the depression, and wondering if I was denying my sexuality (maybe Kaiya had been right, maybe I was gay) at age 27, I experimented in a relationship with a female friend. I had been fed up and ready to try anything to get to the root of my depression. Every day I was in tears, and I'd had no idea why. Any prescription drugs I had tried through doctors, I hated. All of them had horrible side effects. Pot had been my only relief. My line of thinking had been that maybe I was gay, but I was so far in the closet that I just couldn't see it. My friend knew that I was just exploring – I'd been up front and honest about the entire thing – with her and anyone else affected by this exploration. We'd spent a month getting to know each other, after which, we spent one night together. She was beautiful with chestnut hair down her back, big brown doe eyes, a sparkling personality – she was a perfectly and wonderfully attractive woman. But the feelings I felt weren't the same as when I was attracted to a guy. I can appreciate a beautiful woman, and beautiful curves, without having any desire to be intimate with her. The sexual impulse is missing. When the night was over, I'd been no closer to understanding why I was depressed. It hadn't been anything special for me.

Anyone who has suffered from long term depression will probably agree that it's beyond frustrating to endure. There's a part of you that knows what it feels like to feel normal because you've experienced it before – normal is when you don't cry all day long for no apparent reason. Normal is when you don't snap like a twig when someone says some small little thing that appears to have no connection to anything. Normal is when you feel like you have some semblance of control over your emotions. There are times when you get a glimpse of relief from it, but the feeling never lasts. And for no reason you can put your finger on, you can't find the energy to get out of bed in the morning; you find no pleasure in the company of friends and family; every moment is a struggle.

As people tell you to cheer up, go for a walk, drink some water, go watch a movie – you fight the urge to punch them in the throat. If it were that fucking easy, you'd be doing that. And you don't punch them in the throat because you know they love you and they're only trying to help. You're just fed up...frustrated and tired. Please god, you beg, just make it stop. That had been how it was for me.

At age thirty, another three years after my experimentation with a woman, it finally happened – the depression stopped. I was prescribed Celexa by a doctor, an SSRI, that worked in putting an end to my depression. Because it worked, I'd known that my chemical issue causing the depression had been in relation to my body's ability to release serotonin. The only bad side effect had been complete impotence. It was a fair trade in my mind and one I was willing to handle without even thinking twice about it.

I remember how I'd felt after about two weeks on Celexa – liberated. I remember I'd started writing for the first time in eons. I remember I'd walk down the street smiling for no reason. I'd felt like I finally had my life back. Oh my god, I'd had my life back! I had begun to feel invigorated with the belief that everything was going to be awesome! I'd started to know it.

Unfortunately, at the same time I'd been increasing my ecstasy consumption. At first I had just taken it at raves in Toronto. But once back in London, I started doing it now and again. In the five years leading up to me finding Celexa, my use of it had slowly increased. By the time I started on my anti-depressants, I'd been taking ecstasy almost every weekend. And I hadn't been taking it only on Friday or Saturday nights. I'd been taking it Friday, Saturday and Sunday. I'd been getting virtually no sleep on the weekends, and then working at a dead end job for the other five days of the week. During the week, I'd smoke pot as often as possible. My spiral of addiction had begun to swirl more quickly with every day that passed...my addiction intake was no longer just pot and video games...but ecstasy was now a problem. I had entered my body into an addiction warzone. Celexa and ecstasy are like opposing drugs – one regulates serotonin release, while the other releases it all at once. I was clueless to the risks I was taking, and the damage I could be causing.

RENEGADE

My GPS was leading the way through northern Ontario. Since I knew I'd be writing my book when I got home, I started to think about the pivotal moments in my life. What life experiences would I include, what wouldn't I include in The Book? A song came on that took me back to a wonderful memory... a horrible memory... a necessary memory. One of the things that just had to happen for my journey to wellness to keep progressing. The song was Goodbye Stranger, by Supertramp.

The song had been perfect for my exit from Arizona. It even had my Arizona name in the song – everyone there knew me as Mary Jane – Goodbye Mary, Goodbye Jane. It was also like the goodbye song between myself (Mary), and my good friend Jane. My time in Arizona had been amazing. In 2008, every Saturday for six months, I had taken Reiki classes with Annelle, my teacher. I had hung out with the search and rescue Jeep guys, and gone buzzing around in the mountains, building roads, winching over gullies, and having a generally awesome time. I had been part of a writer's group in Payson. My artwork had been developing nicely. I had supported myself through odd jobs. Each Saturday, I'd been a part of a Non-Violent Communication study group, and I was learning how to communicate differently. I had attended meditations and spiritual workshops. I had started working with crystals. I had even spent time with a shaman one weekend.

So many books were changing my life – most of all, You Can Heal Your Life by Louise Hay, A New Earth by Eckhart Tolle, and A Course in Miracles by Helen Schucman. My trailer walls had been covered in little yellow sticky notes – each one with a hand-written, loving affirmation on it. I am worthy of love. I am creative. I am loved. I am intelligent. And on, and on. I'd posted up hundreds of them, all doing small work to reprogram my twenty-five years of negative self talk and self loathing. I'd stayed deeply involved with the Church of Latter-Day Saints, with bible classes, study groups, Family Home Evenings, charity events, the choir, and hanging out with the missionary sisters. The year 2008 had been a pivotal year for healing and learning for me.

The church beliefs had demanded chastity and this was one area that I had not been 100% successful. I gave myself some grace with that. I was doing way better than I'd ever had – mentally, spiritually, physically. I'd only had two partners while I was in Arizona from July 2007 to February of 2009, and both of them were people I'd cared deeply for. The failure came in the fact that I hadn't been honest with the church about it. The Latter-Day Saints were strict about sex, and that strictness could create feelings of shame and guilt. For me, these feelings had ignited. I'd still had feelings of shame around sex in general. Sex and shame had been woven tightly together for me, reaching a long way back in my history.

From a healed place of perspective, I'd say it went back to Don. It had definitely been a part of my relationship with the teacher – the whole relationship had been clouded in shame-filled secrets. Shame and humiliation were ongoing experiences in my life. The church would have been horrified to hear my whole sexual past. Shame, shame, shame! Sex and shame. "I'm a bad person" had not stopped looping in my mind.

In addition to not following the rules strictly around chastity, I had also fallen off the wagon a few times with the Word of Wisdom. I drank at least twice when I had been a Mormon. At one point in 2008, I'd smoked some pot. Not smoking cigarettes had been a big challenge, but I did pretty damn well with it. Compared to my old life back in Canada, I'd done amazingly well. I'd taken huge steps forward.

In late August of 2008, I'd started feeling the hair standing up on the back of my neck. It had been caused by my intuition around fear. I'd told my friend Jane, "Something's going to happen. I don't know what, but I don't feel safe here anymore." I had broken my rule – I had let my friends Jane and Annelle know that Mary Jane wasn't my real name. I had also told the LDS church local leader about the fears I'd had in Canada. Both of those were major no-nos, but at the time I'd revealed these truths, I'd felt safe.

What I told the church leader was what I'd genuinely believed and feared – I was afraid that people were looking for me – bad people. Within weeks of that talk, my intuition had started tingling and telling me it was time to go. Part of me wanted to flee Arizona and hide somewhere else, but another part of me refused to run away. I'd known something was coming and it was time for me to face it. I was tired of running from my demons, so I'd mentally braced myself for their arrival.

In November, I'd been walking to go clean a house (that was one of the ways I'd supported my existence) when three vehicles pulled up. Plain-clothes officers hopped out and surrounded me on the sidewalk. They'd asked me where I was going, what I was doing. Then one of them asked me if I was Glenda somebody or another from California. I'd told them no. They asked if I'd had any tattoos. Again, I told them no. Knowing they didn't have a warrant for any of this questioning, nor did they have any reason to arrest me, they politely asked if they could look at my back – they were tattoo hunting. I'd allowed them to see my back. This was humiliating.

In my head, I already knew exactly what was going on... someone had told the local authorities that I wasn't who I said I was, and that I was likely running from the law. I wasn't running from the law. I'd been upfront with people about my experience in California – the Cinco De Mayo Fiasco wasn't a secret. That hadn't been why I was running in the US. I was running because I'd been afraid to go back home to Canada. I'd thought I'd made that clear when I broke my rule and shared that bit into my past. But apparently, that part of my story hadn't meant anything. None of it stopped the fact that I'd been terrified to go back to Canada since I'd left.

The officers asked me if I'd come down to the station with them. They weren't arresting me – but they wanted to know if I would submit to having my prints taken. I'd submitted. I'd had nothing to hide. Taking my prints meant I would probably get sent back to California to face the music there. That was music I'd been willing to face; it didn't scare me, although it didn't sound like a lot of fun either. After taking my prints, they began to run them through their program to find out in which state I'd been a wanted fugitive. In my head, I'd been thinking, "Oh you're the most crack team of investigators ever! You've caught the Cinco De Mayo Drunk!"

But they began drilling me with other questions, asking me my real name, where I was really from. They seemed to know I wasn't really Mary Jane Seymore. I'd told them I was from Toronto – technically, it was the last city I'd lived in, in Canada. I gave them my real name, Tracey Rogers, my real birthdate, and my correct social insurance number. After running my info through a few more systems, they'd called me a liar and asked for my real name and social insurance number.

"That is my real name and number, sirs," I'd said. They'd been looking for a criminal record or a warrant and they hadn't found one – that's why they didn't believe the real information I'd given them. Not only did I not have a criminal record or any warrants in Canada, I didn't have a driver's license. There was no way for them to link me back to Canada.

My heart had fallen in my feet. Tracey Rogers was no longer in hiding. She was wide out in the open, exposed. I'd felt like a deer during hunting season with a big red target on my chest. After an hour of asking me questions, they'd told me my prints were clear and I was free to go. What? There was no way my prints were clear. I knew that the arrest in California had to have shown up when they ran my prints because I'd been arrested, printed, and plead to charges in court. But they'd told me they were clear. This had made me feel even more exposed. Why were they lying to me? I'd given them my real name, they'd asked me multiple times to give them my real name – and I did. But they had no way of verifying if Tracey Rogers was who I really was – my prints hadn't revealed any information according to them, although I'd known for sure they'd came up in California as Mary Auker. I never understood why they hadn't asked me straight up – "Are you Mary Auker?" I had no idea whether they'd accepted that my name was Tracey Rogers after that or not.

That had been the beginning of the end. My intuition had known something was going to happen. Going to the sheriff's office to get printed was that something. I'd found out the sheriff's department had been watching me for a few months – right about the time the hair had started standing up on the back of my neck. People had been watching me. No wonder I hadn't felt safe. That triggered paranoia. At that point, everyone knew my real name was Tracey Rogers – my closest friends all found out about what had happened with the sheriff's office, but I'd continued to go by Mary Jane (Seymore) because it was how they knew me, and it was easier.

My mental health deteriorated quickly after that. The terror was back in full force. I hadn't felt this scared since the day I'd crossed the US border in January of 2007 and disappeared. In early December of 2008, I'd ended up in a mental health facility for a week. Someone in my Payson family had suggested I do so. I took that time to try to get my composure back. Using my spiritual skills, praying and meditating, I'd tried to find my centre. But the truth was that I never found my center in Payson again. After the day that the sheriff's department had surrounded me on the street, I'd started drinking and smoking cigarettes and pot to curb the stress I'd been feeling. I'd needed it to help quiet my PTSD which had been triggered when I realized I'd been being watched.

At that time, however, the pot just made my triggers worse. While all of this was going on, the LDS Church had been trying to recruit me for a role in the women's Relief Society – as the secretary or something. I can remember looking at the men in the church and not trusting a single one of them. I'd suspected that the man I had gone to for help had been the one who went to the sheriff. I'd felt betrayed. I had been doing my best to follow the teachings of the church while at the same time keeping myself safe. But someone had exposed me and taken away any feelings of safety I had created. I'd been right back at square one – trust no one.

DON'T KNOW WHEN I'LL BE BACK AGAIN

Christmas of 2008 holds many good memories. I'd become friends with Jane and her family. We'd spent an awful lot of time together. We'd go for long walks, do chores together, participate in church events, attend choir, talk for hours, bake, laugh, and do arts and crafts together. We'd even made Christmas wreaths together. Such fun! I had never made a Christmas wreath in my life. Jane had a good idea – she suggested I put a peace sign in the middle of mine – it was perfect! I was invited to spend Christmas morning with her and her family. Roger was going to spend his with friends near Phoenix. That morning, I was treated just like the rest of the family – her children and grandchildren. I was presented with a stocking and given lots of wonderful presents. It had reminded me of Christmases with my own family in a painful yet heartwarming way.

At that time, it had been over two years since I'd seen my family. There was a place inside of me that constantly ached for them. I missed all my siblings, my Mum, my Dad... everyone. But I'd said I'd never go back to Canada, and I was still stuck in that self-made promise. The PTSD hadn't gone away – it lurked in the background, always. Just the thought of going back to Canada brough feelings of terror and panic. The panic had returned because of the incident with the Payson Sheriff's department.

I was ever so grateful for that Christmas with Jane and her family. They truly had been family to me that year, and I had been welcomed into their household. Jane is one of the kindest women I have ever met – it poured from her being. She was always thinking of ways to help people, and she'd follow through and help them. Jane had been one of the few Latter-Day Saints I could talk about my spiritual beliefs with openly – she knew I didn't fit into the traditional LDS mould, and she hadn't tried to change that about me. She hadn't seen it as a flaw. Jane had allowed me to be me and I'd needed that. That Christmas, I knew things in Payson were almost over. The terror the incident with the sheriff's office had triggered wasn't going away. I knew that. I'd known it since August when my intuition had told me to get out of Payson.

In early February 2009, to try and deal with my returned mental health issues, I'd smoked some pot with a friend. I don't know what kind of strain it was, but it did not have the same effect that pot typically had on me. My tolerance had been down, way down. In the past, smoking a big fatty of the best stuff available had never been a problem for me because I'd toked all day, every day. But this stuff had fucked me up badly. I had hardly smoked any of it and I'd been severely affected. I've often wondered if it might have been laced with PCP. I'd had a nightmare high. Someone had to call an ambulance. Within minutes, fire trucks, police cars, EMS, and the sheriff's department had appeared, and I'd been taken to the hospital.

In the hospital, I'd feel nothing but pure terror – I'd been afraid of every nurse and doctor. They'd checked my vitals after hooking me up to machines. I have no idea how long I'd been there. Though it had probably only been a few hours until I'd calmed down, I'd felt like I was back in the nightmare of my psychosis. The tests were done and I was calming down. Thinking it was time for me to get up and go, a sheriff came into my hospital room and arrested me on charges related to me being high on pot – he charged me with possession of pot. I hadn't owned any of the pot I'd smoked that day nor had it been on my person. I'm not sure how possession works in the US, but in Canada, I was pretty sure you had to have pot on you to get a possession charge, regardless of whether you were high or not. I was taken to the local jail and put behind bars. I was told that within a day or two I'd be transferred to another jail, a bigger one. But upon entering the building, I'd been concerned that this wouldn't be the case.

I'd been put in a cell that was obviously built for one person. Two people (women) were already in it, each with a cot and a mattress. I was given a mattress to sleep on. Don't picture the big prisons you see on TV – this wasn't that. It reminded me more of a dungeon than a jail. The cement walls had been cracked and chipping. The floor had been permanently stained – was it spilled food? Someone's blood? Words, names and dates had been scratched into the walls, some written in blue ink, some painted on – with what, I'd wondered. Dirty and unclean is how it felt – the kind of dirty and unclean you can never wash off no matter how hard you scrub. It was a local jail. This jail was ten steps lower than the L.A. County Jail I'd been in already, which had been... not nice. There'd been no TV, nothing to buy from a commissary, and a tiny common area that I never saw people out of their cells to use. I'd had nothing but my own street clothes.

Unlike my experience in L.A. County Jail, I wasn't scared of the other inmates with me. It was just me and two other women in my cell, instead of twenty of us crammed into a 15 by 15 space. They were both non-threatening and friendly with me when I went in, and they'd introduced themselves and asked me who I was. As I got talking to them, I'd discovered through my cell mates that many of the inmates hadn't seen a judge and they'd been in there for six months or more – they couldn't afford bail. For those uninitiated in the jail system – if you can afford bail, you can pay it and get out of holding then wait for your hearing from home instead of sitting in jail for months while you await your court date. Oh my god – I could have to wait six months just to see a judge? The thought was terrifying.

Women had whispered with the male guards to be given a cigarette. Sometimes they'd get one. What did they whisper to get that cigarette, I'd wondered. In the middle of the night, I'd often be awakened by the sounds of a woman crying or someone yelling out. I felt like I'd been in one of the lesser-known levels of Dante's Inferno. Was it legal to house people like this? Crammed into filthy cells with no space to move or socialize? With no outdoor yard? Though I'd seen a phone hanging on the wall, only a few people had been allowed to use it. No one had offered me a phone call. The food? It was nothing to write home about, but I don't recall it being too horrible – it beat the hell out of the processed cheese sandwich at L.A. County Jail.

I'd prayed. I'd prayed and I'd prayed. God, please just get me out of here. Please don't let me rot in here for six months waiting to see a judge. I'd had no idea what was going on with my charges or what they'd planned on doing with me. No one had contacted me while I was there – not a lawyer, not a prosecutor, not a guard. At mealtime, someone would say, "Here's your food," and drop it in front of me. That had been the extent of what was communicated to me. If I asked a guard for answers through my locked cell, I'd received none. I didn't want to spend six months there waiting for an answer.

Perhaps four or five days later – I can't recall exactly, ICE (Immigrations Customs Enforcement) officers came for me. I'd been handcuffed and put in the back of a very fancy SUV. I'd known exactly what was happening when I saw the ICE officers. I'd be sent back to Canada! Nooooo! I cursed the name of the man I'd gone to for help. Goddamnit! This had been my own fault and I knew it! I should have kept to my internal promise – trust no one. The officers had stopped for fast food and gave me a burger and a drink. I was grateful for that. Jail food had sucked. As I'd eaten, I'd wondered if the ICE officers would have bought burgers for Mexican aliens. I think I'd been a novelty down there. All year long, the officers dealt almost exclusively with people from south of the border – Mexico, Central America, South America. I'd later spoken to other women, Latino women, and none of them had been given burgers and a drink if they were moved. I was special. I was from Canada.

What I'd figured out by this time was that they must have finally believed I was Tracey Rogers from Canada because that was the name I'd been arrested as, and that had been the name ICE used when they'd pick me up for deportation to Canada. I'm not entirely sure how they'd verified the information. It's possible that my mother may have called when I'd been picked up by ICE after she'd received a phone call from my friend Jane who'd let my Mum know what had happened.

They brought me to what I'd soon find out was my new home, the PCSO – The Pinal County Sheriff's Office, which was half jail, half immigration detention centre. Those sections were separated from each other in the building. It was a big modern jail. I'd been shuffled inside with my wrists handcuffed, but eventually the cuffs were removed. I had been fingerprinted then put on a bench in a long hallway to sit beside a bunch of Mexican women. When I was fingerprinted, I'd given them my real name. I had no idea what the officers were doing. Officers would go into one of the offices, come out, ask someone for more information, go back inside and disappear for a while. Everything had taken forever. They gave me a sandwich or two while I'd sat and waited to be processed.

Calling me back into an office, one of the ICE guys grinned at me and said, "We found you in California, Mary Auker." They knew my name was Tracey Rogers. They'd finally been able to connect the Cinco De Mayo Fiasco with my true identity. My stomach did a flip flop. Oh my god, no! I had no idea what my status was in California with my charges when I'd been let go on my own recognizance. I thought I had been charged with two felony charges of assaulting a police officer. Regardless of what my name was – Tracey Rogers or Mary Auker – if they were felony charges that would mean that I would not be going back to Canada but back to California where I'd probably have to go to Chino prison. Oh, sweet mother of god, no.

Chino was the main prison facility in California. It's where you'd be sent if you were convicted in California and given a sentence of over two years. Even I had heard of Chino, and none of the stories had been pleasant. The ICE guard continued speaking, "DUI on a bicycle, possession of pot, and two counts of resisting arrest."

"Um, is that it?" I'd casually asked. Yes, it was. Apparently, back in California when I'd been taken before the judge, my two felony charges for assaulting a police officer had been lowered to resisting arrest. Since the courtroom procedures back then had taken less than five minutes, I hadn't been told about the changes to my charges. The change in charges was a small miracle I'd been grateful for. While I was in the dungeon-like jail for the previous four or five days, the other women in jail had let me know how things would go for me. If I had felony charges, I would have to serve my time in the United States. If I had misdemeanors, I'd have to go back to Canada. How they knew all of this information, I have no idea, but I'd assumed some of them had been in jail before. My crimes had been misdemeanors since the charges had changed from assaulting a police officer to resisting arrest. DUI on a bicycle and possession of pot were also misdemeanors. That meant that I'd be sent back to Canada.

I was moved with the other women (most of them Latina) into a bunk area after we'd been given a new outfit to wear – a baby blue prison uniform with the jail name on the back. Even though we weren't technically in prison, we'd looked like prisoners right down to our clothing. I stayed in a bunk section for a few days. This was essentially a square room with a door and some windows. Had there been different furniture, the room could have looked like a typical classroom, minus the chalkboard, with banks of fluorescent lights, white walls, and modern windows. There'd been maybe ten bunks in the room. We'd been a handful of immigration detention women who were being processed but who hadn't been assigned a specific cell block yet. I hadn't spoken to any other detainees – no one I'd met spoke English. I had no idea what was happening as I'd been given next to zero information about my charges or how long processing would take. After a few days of waiting, I'd been moved into a cell block. It was at this point that the ICE officers had let me know that I was being deported.

I hadn't been happy about the idea of being deported, I had been terrified. Everything I had worked so hard to overcome – my fears and my phobias – were all back full force ever since the sheriff's office had stopped me on the road in Payson asking to fingerprint me. I had vowed to never return to Canada. I had envisioned a life in the United States and then I made that vision come to life. Unfortunately, I hadn't felt safe in the U.S. anymore either. Everyone had known who I was. Everyone had known my real name. The U.S. had no longer been a haven. Honestly, I'd started to consider how I could cross the border into Mexico illegally, so that no one would know where I was. My mind had been racing, trying to come up with solutions about what to do when the officers had told me I was going back to Canada. After days of not knowing what the hell was going on, wondering if I had to go to prison, go back to Payson, or be sent back to Canada, I'd had my answer. And I'd hated it.

The cell block they'd moved me to consisted of a huge two-story open room with cells along the far wall – a row of cells on the first floor, and a row of cells on that same wall on the second floor. A set of stairs led to the upper floor. In the open room, there was one TV and a whole bunch of steel tables with steel chairs attached to the table permanently. That was it. A guard took me up to my cell on the second floor. Inside, there was one bunk. My roommate who was in the cell at that time had the lower bunk, so I took the upper. My roommate hadn't spoken a word of English; she was from El Salvador. The bunk reminded me of going to camp when I was a kid...but the comparisons stopped after that. There'd be no swimming, no campfires for making and eating s'mores or hotdogs; childhood was a million memories away. I had been assigned a blanket, a pillow, a sheet, a laundry bag, and two sets of clothing that included pants, a shirt, a bra and underwear – one outfit to wear, one outfit to go in the wash. I'd put my stuff in the cell then headed to the common room.

As I descended into the common area, I'd felt many eyes on me. I had a feeling everyone was thinking the same thing: "What the hell are you doing here, white girl?" A few of them even came up and asked me that specifically. I'd laughed and said I was from Canada. Again, I was a novelty there. Scanning the room, I'd noticed another Caucasian woman. I made my way to her table and I'd asked if I could sit down. We were the only white women there. I sought her out instead of anyone else because if anyone was going to be able to answer my questions, it was likely to be her – she obviously wasn't being deported to Mexico or Central America and I was hoping she spoke English. So far, almost no one except the guards had spoken English to me and the few women who had, hadn't spoken it well. With a strong British accent, the woman had welcomed me to join her. Guess what her name was – Tracey! I'd had a million questions to ask her and she'd answered as many as she could.

She'd been in the detention unit for a long time so she was familiar with the system. I'd asked her about the charge that had been laid against me by the sheriff's office. "Oh, yes, they have to do that. Immigration can't just pick you up and take you away. They have to charge you with something," she'd said.

Tracey had been fighting her deportation and she'd suggested I do the same since I didn't want to go back to Canada. Coaching me, she'd let me know what I'd need to start building my case against deportation. I'd need letters of support from my Payson friends, tonnes of paperwork and a potential sponsor. I'd need to get copies of everything I could that would help make my case for staying in the United States. Every day the guards would come in with mail. Within a week of my arrival, I'd been receiving at least five letters a day from my Payson friends, sometimes as many as twelve or thirteen. Some women never received a single piece of mail the entire time I was there. I'd been blessed to have people to communicate with and I knew it.

My days had consisted of writing letters to everyone I knew in Payson. I'd also written letters home to my family back in Canada – to my mother, father, siblings. I'd put little doodles on every envelope and letter to make them look prettier. I'd also helped many of the women with their court paperwork and letters of compassion. A letter of compassion was something they could write and present to the court communicating why they should be able to stay in the United States. These women I'd been housed with weren't just 'illegal aliens' who had been picked up crossing the border; all of them had been taken from their homes based on charges they'd had years previously. They all had been living in the states. They had built businesses. They owned land. They owned homes. Their children had been born in the United States. They all had green cards and residency cards. Many of their charges were ten years ago, twenty years ago. It was heartbreaking to listen to their stories.

Just that year, the United States had changed its laws – if a non-citizen had ever had felony charges, even though they had served their time years ago, they were getting shipped out. It was horrible. These women had served their time. Though I hadn't served time, I did have charges against me in both California and now Arizona. I was not a legal citizen, and so, I'd been in the same proverbial boat. My heart felt the weight of their lives, all they'd achieved for themselves and their families during the years they'd been in the states. I'd felt compelled to help them as much as I could.

While I'd helped the ladies with their paperwork, I'd been compiling my own. Members of the LDS church had written me letters of support. So had my friends from the Payson Centre for Spirituality. Did you notice that the letters for the centre and the jail are almost identical? PCSO and PCS? The similarity wasn't lost on me. I'd noticed it right away when I'd gotten my prison uniform and I'd felt like I was protected by god. I'd taken it as a sign that one way or another everything was going to be fine...that there was a spiritual lesson in all of this.

I'd requested to spend time each week with a member of the LDS Church. A man from the church whose calling it was to have spiritual discussions with members of the church who were in jail or detention could come and speak with me. Honestly, I'd do anything to get out of the cell block for an hour, so if it meant talking to someone from church, I'd do it.

I had also been able to get copies of the LDS monthly magazine, Ensign, brought in for me. A Book of Mormon and a bible had also been provided for me to read. While I was there, I'd finally finished reading the Book of Mormon. My friend Wes, who had been my teacher for A Course in Miracles (through the spiritual centre), sent me reams and reams of quotes and sections of that book through the mail. I turned my attention to every spiritual piece of writing I could get my hands on, and I'd found comfort within them. Through this spiritual shifting, I had been able to see that there wasn't anyone to blame for my situation. Whoever had said something about me to the police, had done so out of concern and had every right to do so. The experience in the detention centre was humbling me in a painful but good way.

My friend Jane had allowed me to call her collect every day. It must have cost her a small fortune to do that, but she never said a word about it. She had been my lifeline; hearing a familiar voice telling me she loved me, helped me emotionally survive that experience. Prattling on about everything that was going on in her world, she'd tried to help me pretend my situation wasn't happening. If the two of us could just focus on what was going on in the world, and not in the jail, it would be like jail wasn't happening, right? For the small amount of time we'd be on the phone, it worked and I could focus elsewhere. But as soon as we'd hung up the phone, my reality would come crashing in around me. I'd turn around and stared blankly, hopelessly at the grey walls, the grey ceiling, the grey tables all around me.

I'd asked for a vegetarian diet because I was a vegetarian. But the detention centre would only make diet allowances based on religious reasons. So, I'd gotten my Mormon Bible and I applied for vegetarian meals based on religious grounds. The bible clearly stated in the Word of Wisdom that meat should only be consumed in times of necessity and starvation. No one had ever asked for a vegetarian diet as a Mormon before at that jail; there I'd been paving the way! The truth was I hadn't met a single vegetarian Mormon during my time in the US. It did clearly state for them to only eat meat sparingly and if necessary, but anyone I'd met ignored that. Often, I'd see meat served three times a day. It was anything but sparingly.

I only had a few visits the entire time I was in detention. They'd lasted around twenty minutes. Visiting in the jail had to be done from another building via a video feed. One day Bertha and John – the folks who had opened their home to me when I'd first arrived – showed up. I'd had no idea that they were coming. I'd been called into a room where I could see them and they could see me on a video screen. I cried like a baby when I saw them. Bertha was one of the sweetest, dearest women I'd ever met, and I didn't want her to see me like that – crying in a prison uniform. As we'd talked, I knew I might never see her again. I might never see any of my Arizona family again. It was devastating.

Upon my first visit to see the judge regarding deportation – which had been two or three weeks into my detention – I was asked if I was going to fight my deportation or not. I'd declared that I was going to fight my deportation. They'd offered me bail of $10,000. If I could pay it, I could go back to Payson while we worked through the court proceedings. Merriam and her husband Robert, members of the church, had offered to pay my bail. They'd always been very kind to me. Their generosity had never ceased to amaze me. While I was in the church choir, Merriam, the choir leader, had asked me what my favourite Christmas carol was. I'd told her the Little Drummer Boy was my favourite. Instead of pointing out that it wasn't a carol but a popular, contemporary Christmas song, she'd found the music for it so we could learn it and perform it. For the first time ever, the Payson LDS Church had performed Little Drummer Boy at the Christmas event with me singing my heart out in the middle of all of it. I'd considered Merriam a good friend. She's an amazing woman, with a heart of gold, and a mind like a steel trap.

But, I'd refused their offer of bail. I hadn't trusted myself to honour it. When I'd imagined being set free, I'd seen myself running away again, afraid. So, I'd stayed locked up. Even then, I'd known that my ability to say no was a good sign. Something had changed in me. The old me would have taken the bail money without considering that I could take off again because I'd be led by my fears. The new me had a budding self awareness that had known running off was a very real possibility, one that could hurt people I cared about by screwing them out of their $10,000 if I didn't return to court.

Two months into my detention, my time had finally come to see the immigration judge again. The court procedure had nothing to do with my charges, it simply had to do with my deportation. My misdemeanors would sit on my American records, but I wouldn't be facing any consequences of those charges at this time. I'd learned a little more about the procedures each time I was taken to another building to see the judge. I had been able to talk to an immigration court appointed lawyer for approximately five or ten minutes before seeing the judge, though no one had been more helpful than Tracey.

My friend Tracey had been ten thousand times more helpful than my court appointed lawyer. She taught me everything. Tracey had been in detention for more than nine months fighting her own deportation – she knew the system and had met the judge many times.

In court that day, I'd had a Latter Day Saint judge. I can't remember who told me, but I'd been told that the judge was a Mormon. I had dozens of letters of support. Jane had offered to sponsor me. I had proof of my time in the church 12-Step program. I'd been fully prepared to represent myself and fight my deportation. But something critical happened on my way to the courtroom. I'd decided, "I'm not doing this. I'm going back to Canada."

The courtroom had been small, with only a few rows of wooden benches for visitors. Most of the benches were empty. I must have been super emotional, because I don't even have a clear memory of who was there that day. I would have sworn it was Merriam and Robert, but I've been reminded it was Merriam, Jane and Mark (Jane's husband) sitting there on the benches. I'm in tears now, knowing that that memory has been lost to me. Payson is lost to me. In that courtroom I knew it would be a forever good-bye. I was going to lose all of it. Again, I was going to let go of everyone that was dear to me.

The judge asked me if I'd wanted to challenge my removal from the country. I'd told him no. Looking surprised, he'd asked again, "Are you sure you don't want to challenge your removal?" I'd said, "No, thank you." Before asking me a third time, he'd reminded me that I couldn't challenge the court after a third 'no' response – it was my last chance. Once again, I'd told him no.

The look of surprise on the judge's face had said everything. I'd been told that someone from the church had let this man know that a member of the LDS Church, Tracey Rogers, was going to challenge her removal – and I hadn't done that. My friends had also looked surprised, and disappointed too. They had expected me to fight to stay in the US. Everyone had. Everyone had written me letters to support me staying. I too had been disappointed in what the outcome of my going back would cause. I too was sad – sad that I'd have to say good-bye to my Payson family. I was scared – scared of returning to Canada. The demons I'd been running from when I fled Canada were still waiting for me at the border. I didn't fit in Canada anymore. I wasn't the same person who had left. Nothing felt good about my decision except that I'd known I had to get it over with. Whatever was going to happen, would happen now. Whatever fears I'd been running from would either destroy me or disappear like smoke in the wind.

Since I wasn't fighting my deportation, the judge declared that I'd be sent back to Canada as soon as possible and that I would be banned from entering the United States for ten years. The judge hadn't mentioned this because it wasn't in his jurisdiction, but my misdemeanors from California and Arizona would remain on my US record. I'd considered being banned from entering the US a blessing. Had I not been banned, my panic upon arriving back in Canada might have sent me right back across the border. The option had been taken away. If I did cross illegally into the US, I would face possible jail time.

The ban also meant that I wouldn't be able to visit some very dear friends in Arizona; people I'd considered to be family. My heart would ache many times for Janet, Annelle, Beverelev, Jane, Roger, Kerry, Leon and Bertha, MaryAnne, Wes, Merriam and so many more amazing people. I had so many friends down there who'd been a tremendous support to me. Each person I had met added value to my life, to my awakening. I wouldn't be who I am without them. I'm a better person because of my friends and family in Arizona. God bless every single one of them. I miss them terribly.

Had I not been banned, I wouldn't have stayed in Canada where I'd needed to rebuild my ties with my biological family, where I'd needed to rebuild my own life, where I'd needed to get over my phobias and fears. It had finally been time to face my PTSD and the unreal terrors I had created in 2005 and 2006 during my breakdown. It had taken my experience at the detention centre to really allow me to have the final strength to make the decision to return home.

I was going home to Canada. I had been terrified and relieved all at once. But it had been time. I had to go home. I had to face the music. If something bad was going to happen to me, let it happen. I couldn't run anymore. I couldn't be afraid. From the moment it had been announced that I was going back to Canada, my stomach became one big ball of anxiety, even though it had been what I had decided to do. For my life... for myself...for my continued awakening and recovery.

Due to a mix up with my paperwork, it took another full month before they could remove me from the United States. During that time, I'd communicated a bit with my Canadian family. I say 'a bit' because it had taken two weeks for each letter to go from Canada to me or vice versa. I spent a lot of time in my cell, alone, reading spiritual texts, and preparing myself to face my fears. I'd also talked with Tracey who I had built a friendship with. Few of the other women considered me a friend, although I had tried. I didn't put a lot of energy into trying to figure out why. I had spent a total of three months with ICE at the immigration detention centre. I'd had a very real, first-hand experience in a system that lacked sympathy, empathy and humanity. Of all the women I had been in with, the only one I knew for sure who was able to stay in the US was Tracey, the British woman.

Every day in detention had been another day of forced sobriety and clean living. Frankly, I'd appreciated every moment I had in detention. The last few weeks inside had really helped me prepare mentally for what was coming – Canada.

I could have left detention and flown home earlier if my family had paid for my ticket, but they'd refused to pay. I didn't blame them – it was a good call. I'd abandoned my family for over two and a half years. I was going to have to earn trust with them again and re-establish our relationships. The ICE had paid for my plane ticket.

My release date arrived. I hadn't felt ready. I'd felt anxious. But I'd felt my family in my heart and I couldn't wait to see their eyes again, to hear their voices again. Would they still love me? Would they understand me and everything I'd been through in those two and a half years of absence? Despite not knowing the answers to my huge questions, I'd known it was time to go home. I'd chosen to do this. I'd put on my big girl panties and braced myself for whatever Canada was going to throw at me. Two ICE guards escorted me to the airport and they sat with me until I'd boarded the plane to Toronto.

After watching me get on the plane, their work was done so they'd left. Me? I'd never been on a plane before! I'd been totally in that moment, excited and thrilled to be traveling on a plane! All of my apprehension about going home had left in a split second, as I realized I was going to fly for the very first time in my life! I felt like this was god giving me my wings. Something good was going to happen. Flying out of the country had been a good omen – a great omen. I had wings now. It was time to fly! I'd felt the low-belly pressure of the plane ascending and it freed the ball of anxiety that had taken residence there since my court date. I knew that what was ahead of me once I'd land in Canada would bring back the anxiety ball, but I did my best to focus on the experience of flying. Outside the windows, the clouds floated like large sheets of fluff. They calmed me. I thought about what I'd been through...how much I'd learned during my time in Arizona, and how much strength I'd gathered as my spiritual awakening bloomed while at the detention centre. Flying in the sky had been exactly what I'd needed to help me recognize my own ability to soar.

* * *

Before I'd left for Sault Ste. Marie, Amanda told me to stop in Bruce Mines at a place called Bobbers. Riding down Highway 17 (the Trans Canada Highway), I practically bumped right into Bobbers, and pulled my bike over. The ride was phenomenal – it wasn't quite over, but almost. Even though my ass ached, my legs needed to stretch and walk, and I wanted to keep riding, keep feeling the wind in my face, keep tasting Freedom, I knew I had to stop to eat and rest. Bobbers was fantastic! When my meal was over, I indulged in a butter tart – I had heard their tarts and pies were out of this world! And might I say that butter tart lived up to its reputation. Holy smokes – best butter tart ever! It was still warm when it was served to me, and it melted in my mouth when I devoured it.

After supper, I only had a short drive into The Soo – what Canadians often call Sault Ste. Marie. I had never been to The Soo before unless you count an overnight Greyhound bus ride where we'd stopped but I hadn't seen anything of the town. My GPS led me but I had a difficult time finding the correct street to park on due to some one-way streets. The Airbnb was a lovely little place, but the back of the building was desolate and adjacent to train tracks. That's where I was supposed to park my bike. I looked at Stella, I looked at the train tracks, and I hoped that I would somehow find somewhere else to park her. I'd have parked my car there without a single worry; but my motorcycle? Nope. It wasn't feeling safe enough for me to leave Stella there.

Loading up my gear and dragging it all into the Airbnb, I was thrilled to unload my stuff into a cute little retro bedroom. I was only paying $40 for the room, and as far as I was concerned, it was fab-u-lous. I felt something close to sadness at the end of each ride day; the fact that there was no more road to tear down, that it'd be time to park the bike, so staying in unique places to rest helped me handle the sadness.

After I took care of getting everything of value off my bike, I set about giving her a quick clean. I did this every day, sometimes twice. I'm proud to ride my bike, and nothing makes me happier than when she's shiny and clean, than when her chrome sparkles. It's impossible to give it a proper clean at every stop on the road, but what I could do was dampen a cloth to clean off the dirt and dust and use another cloth to buff her dry. I did that often. In my saddlebags, I also had some F11 which protected the finish and made Stella shine like a diamond.

When I was done with my daily cleaning ritual, I decided to knock on the neighbour's door. As she appeared, I asked if all of the parking spots up against the building were for residents and she said they were. She could see I was worried about leaving my bike on the street and she suggested that I pull it up onto the walkway behind the cars that way my bike would be locked in by the cars overnight. She assured me that I'd be able to get out by 9am at the latest in the morning. Perfect! With Stella locked in for the night, I felt safe going back upstairs and enjoying some R&R.

Inside my room, I did some research on the internet. My friend Kelly had suggested I go see some pictographs that were in the area. I looked them up to see where they were. She also told me about some falls that were on this stretch of highway, and that I should make sure to stop for gas in Batchawana Bay – if I didn't, I might run out of gas before Wawa.

The ride to Wawa the following day looked like it would be an easy one. I would only be travelling 227km which was under three hours of riding. I would have ample time to stop and see some sites and take my time. Confident that I had found everything I needed on the internet for my ride the following day, I crashed and went to sleep. I was exhausted.

DAY 6 – SEPTEMBER 16TH, 2019

CRAZY

On Monday, September 16th, like every other day on this trip, I woke up super early and was ready to go well before I was able to get my bike out and go. The best way I can describe the feeling I had is to say I felt like a kid on Christmas. When I was young, we'd be up by 4am digging through the stocking that Santa had left on the end of our beds. My sisters and I would run back and forth to each other's rooms showing off all the wonderful treasures we had received. By 5am we would be tiptoeing into our parent's room and waking them up to show them all the things Santa had gifted us. That's what every single day of my motorcycle trip felt like – Christmas. I was excited! I was happy! I couldn't wait to get back on my bike! I was seeing new places that I'd never seen before! Every day was a gift and I couldn't wait to unwrap it.

Around 8:30am, I was able to get my bike out from behind the cars. My first stop would be at an electronics store. Ron had wired in a phone charger to my bike battery, but something was making that connection unhappy as of the previous day, and the charger kept going in and out. Every time it would disconnect or reconnect, my phone screen would come on, and eat up way more phone battery than it would have had I not had a charger hooked up to it. To alleviate this issue, my plan was to find a portable charger that I could plug my phone into during my ride.

My quest for an electronics store brought me to Station Mall. I find that malls often give you a good indication about a city – it's size, it's demographics, and the kinds of things that folks are interested in. My opinion was that this mall summed Sault Ste. Marie up quite well. It wasn't as small as many I'd seen, but it certainly wasn't the mall of a large city. I wouldn't have been surprised to see moose wander by outside.

Inside, I found exactly what I needed for a fantastic price. One of the portable chargers was on half price for $25, and it wasn't a crappy one, but one with a higher-end storage capacity from a brand I trusted. Perfect! With my battery pack in hand, I left the mall. As I got to my bike, I realized I needed something else – tape. In addition to the wire shorting out, the phone holder itself had lost one of its knobby things that held the phone in place while I drove. Without all four knobby things, it was unbalanced and my phone kept shifting so that I couldn't see the screen for the GPS. Coming back out of the mall after visiting Dollarama, black electrical tape in hand, I set about the task of making a black knobby thing. Within a few minutes I had something that looked like it would work and I was on my way. I was kind of proud of myself at that moment for fixing my dilemma. No, neither were permanent solutions, but here I was on the road with slight gear malfunctions, and I had found a temporary solution to both problems. I realize this doesn't make me a rocket scientist, and no I didn't fix the engine of my bike, but I was adapting to my circumstances and making my experience as enjoyable as possible with my Red Green fixes.

You know, each time I told people that I was doing this trip, everyone said, "You're going all that way on your own?!" People were impressed. I guarantee you, if a guy said he was doing this trip, no one would use the same tone of wonderment when they'd say, "Wow! That's amazing!" I knew that what I was doing was something a great many women wouldn't do on their own, and that's cool, I understand why, completely. But by the same token, I admired the women who did do things like this on their own, and there are a great many of them as well.

I wanted to be that woman; the woman who wasn't afraid to drive on a motorcycle into the middle of god's country, by herself, and have an adventure. Fearless. It was my motto. And me fixing my little phone holder knobby thing and coming up with the idea of using a portable charger attached to my phone all day made me into that woman in my mind. My imaginary superhero cape was flying out behind me. I had my superhero goggles on. I was ready to save the world! Or fix a knobby thing. Or charge my phone while driving. You know... superhero stuff.

There are not adequate words to describe the ride between Sault Ste. Marie and Wawa. This was Nature's artwork at its absolute finest. Leaving the Soo was spectacular as the landscape was alive with colour. Trees lined the Trans Canada Highway for some distance as I left town. Reds, oranges, yellows, greens, and everything in between, created a fire of beauty for my eyes. Rocks, hills, winding curves, all mixed in with the beautiful trees, greeting me as I rumbled on my way. I have no idea if my feet were in the pegs or on the floorboards, all I knew was that was one of the greatest moments of my life. Tom Cochrane and the band Red Rider started singing in my ears – Lunatic Fringe. I consider this one of the greatest Canadian rock songs of all time. I was grateful that it was playing during such a wonderful part of my ride because the memories it brought back were anything but wonderful.

When Tom Cochrane wrote this song he was writing against the existing oppression of Jews in America. He sings of Hitler's "final solution." It's a song about backroom meetings and racism in action. Tom Cochrane was against all these things and had been deeply affected by meeting some folks who'd exposed him to the fact that this hatred was still alive and well in America.

Listening to the song brings me to a time of absolute craziness in a world of conspiracy and feeling hunted. By the time 2005 rolled around, I'd been taking insane amounts of ecstasy for almost three years. That year, I had also done a stupid amount of magic mushrooms – I'd gotten some really good ones at a wicked awesome price. My intention had been to do some now and again and have a stash for a while. Instead, they had been like a bowl of skittles – two ounces of mushrooms disappeared quickly. Add in a little cocaine here and there, some new chemical drugs on the market called CB2s, a ridiculously unhealthy lifestyle that had caused unnecessary stress and voila! I'd created a recipe for disaster.

In November of that year, I had a full-blown nervous breakdown. Initially it had been diagnosed as a temporary psychotic episode caused by prolonged marijuana use. But over the following five weeks as I'd been in and out of the hospital, I had been given a different diagnosis. One time was manic depression, another time schizophrenia, still another time bi-polar disorder. Every time they'd re-diagnosed me, my medication had to be changed. Unfortunately, the doctors had been missing a key piece of information – the amounts of drugs I'd been taking and the types of drugs I'd been taking. I hadn't told them the truth about my usage.

My breakdown had included paranoia and conspiracy. It had started the night the police first showed up on my doorstep to try to take me to the hospital. One of the cops hadn't had a proper name tag on and I'd been clear enough to realize that. I'd stepped back and asked to see an ID. He'd refused three times before he'd finally flashed a badge so fast that it could have been out of a Cracker Jacks box – and it probably was. I was terrified. Who the hell can show up on your doorstep looking exactly like a cop, other than cops? Panic had set in because it hadn't made any sense to me that 'fake' police officers were at my door. The panic never left.

It wasn't until 2012 (some seven years later!), when I'd been back in Canada that a counselor from the London area told me that at the time of my breakdown, the London Police had mental health professionals that would go out on mental health crisis calls with the police to help calm situations. They'd dressed exactly like cops – minus the badge, the nametag and a real gun. If someone had told me that back in 2005, it might have saved me a lot of problems, a lot of paranoid thinking, and a whole lot of heartache. For years, I ran from that experience. I'd created stories around that event and who the person was that had been impersonating a cop and trying to take me away. The stories I'd created involved the police, criminal organizations, my family and friends – a wide web of characters and plotlines out to get me.

After five weeks of going in and out of the hospital, I'd been released for the final time in January of 2006, but I hadn't been well. I hadn't started getting better until I'd made the choice to walk away from my life on September 11th, the same year. From the day of my breakdown until the day I'd walked away from my life I'd been terrified; my life had been a living hell. I'm certain it had been a living hell for family and loved ones around me as well.

Sometimes in Recovery, you'll be asked to pinpoint your 'bottom' – the worst point in your addiction – the point that made you say, "I just can't fucking do it this way anymore, this is crazy." That time had been it for me. My breakdown in 2005 that carried me into the fall of 2006 – that had been it. That nightmare had been the miracle I'd needed to change.

In the hospital, I remember I'd been petrified of everyone and everything. I remember I'd paced the halls for hours and hours, walking up and down trying to relieve my nervous energy. I remember I'd been so happy to see my family. I remember I'd been so angry to see my family. I'd said nothing. I'd yelled. I'd screamed. I'd whispered. I'd imagined horrible scenarios to explain everyday events. Everyone had been out to get me. They'd all been conspiring. Can't trust anyone...can't trust anyone...don't trust anyone...these words had run a loop in my mind

Eventually, I'd trusted someone – the other inmates. Ahem, I mean patients. We'd all been in it together. And we had all been screwed over by the people closest to us, right? We'd all needed to stick together because we were all we'd truly had. People who weren't patients had possibly been part of the problem, yes? And so very odd friendships had formed among us. We'd helped each other even though none of us had much substance to give. We gave whatever we could. I remember someone in my family had gotten upset about how many cigarettes I'd gone through because I'd been giving so many away, and it was costing me money. So what? Other people had needed cigarettes and they didn't have any. Money had been the last thing on my mind – the very last thing. In fact, I'll tell you, during my psychosis, money hadn't mattered one iota. There'd been something freeing in that.

One day, I had a pair of scissors for doing some crafts in my hospital room and I'd used them to chop off my long hair that had been almost to my butt. Why? Because I'd been mad. I had grown my hair long for someone else and then? Then I'd realized how angry I'd been about it. I hadn't wanted my beautiful long hair anymore.

There was a song that had helped me get through that horrible time. It was Lean on Me, by Bill Withers. A group of us had stuck together on the psych ward. We'd shared our conspiracies and we'd looked out for one another. I'd had people to pace the hall with instead of doing it alone. I'd started singing the song, Lean on Me one day, and soon, others were singing it with me. I'd known the lyrics to the song, and they'd been everything I'd needed to convey to my new friends. And we sang it together. And I sang it alone. And we'd encouraged others to sing it with us. I even remember the hospital staff had sung it a few times with us.

Music is incredibly healing and emotionally releasing. There are very good health and psychological reasons why people are so attracted to music. That song helped me through one of the worst times of my life. No, I take that back, not one of the worst times of my life – the worst time of my life. That was the moment in my addiction when things had been at their absolute worst. I never want to break down like that again. I'd spent five weeks in the worst of it. It had been serious, and it seriously sucked.

I'd wanted to die. I wouldn't wish that experience on my worst enemy. Nothing had made sense but a faint voice of reason in my mind.

I'd given value to this part of my mind because it housed one glimmer of hope and it was this – I'd known I wasn't healthy and that the things I'd been thinking and feeling were crazy. Truly insane people, I'd heard, usually lacked that awareness. Despite this knowing though, I'd wanted to leave the hospital. I had figured out what the doctors needed to hear in order for them to let me go home. But when I got home, I wished I'd stayed in the hospital. I believe I would have come to the right conclusion earlier – that I needed to restart my life – if I had stayed in the hospital which was a much healthier environment than what I was going home to.

You want to hear something really crazy? I am so grateful for my breakdown. I am grateful for the events that led up to it and I'm grateful for the events following it. All of it had been necessary for me to be able to do everything that came after. I needed the memories of being in the hospital and my breakdown that brought me there – they kept me sober. I needed the conspiracy that my mind created involving the police, and the terror that came with it – it chased me and helped me run to the place where I'd started healing. What had been the most nightmarish series of events in my entire life were also the greatest blessings, and the catalyst for amazing, awesome, incredible change. Remember that, readers. Every person, every event, every situation is an opportunity for growth and healing. We can miss the opportunities presented to us through trauma, if we don't also take the opportunities to heal. Hopefully, we can get to the roots of the problems. Adult trauma is almost never the root; we find the roots in our childhood or youth. Most adult relationships are triggers to where/when/how we were first broken.

In 2012, due to a whole bunch of synchronicities, my gut had told me that I should take the Addictions Counsellor program at the local college. In order to do so, there were a few prerequisites. One of them was a Psychology 101 class that I'd taken. I'd learned so much in that class. There were major sections of it that spoke directly to me about my breakdown. The textbook talked about genetic disposition and environmental factors. The long and short of it was this – people can have a genetic disposition to certain psychological issues. Some people will never experience them because they require a trigger. Stress, drugs and alcohol were noted as major triggers for many conditions, including psychosis. A person can trigger a psychosis and heal from it, if they avoid stressors.

By the time I'd taken this class in 2012, I was drug and alcohol free so nothing had been triggering my psychosis. In fact, my psychosis hadn't been triggered since early 2009. I was still experiencing PTSD symptoms, but no psychosis. Without drugs and alcohol, when my traumatic memories were triggered, I had the tools to cope with them – things like breathing exercises such as square breathing; being actively aware of my thoughts; EFT (otherwise known as Emotional Freedom Tapping); meditation, drumming, colouring, and talking to a friend or mentor. These tools allowed me to calm down in the same moment that the PTSD was triggered. I had an awareness of what was happening (that I'd been triggered) because I was stone cold sober. PTSD wasn't running my life anymore, I was.

And so, when things got triggered, I was able to calm myself down. In my experience, square breathing and other simple breathing exercises worked the best in the moment of PTSD and panic attacks. Breathing in slowly to the count of four, holding my breath at the top to the count of four, exhaling to the count of four and waiting to inhale again to the count of four, and then repeating this process many times, that was the square breathing technique that worked. Slowly, methodically, I'd healed the memories that had triggered the PTSD. I also wrote them out, talked them through, had counselling and desensitized myself to the memory. I faced the triggers and the attached memories one by one. The last one I recall working on had been in the fall of 2018.

Reading that Psychology textbook though had been a blessing. I'd realized that what had happened in 2005 didn't necessarily have to happen again – it was up to me. If I chose a lifestyle that was calm, relaxed, clean and sober, I'd have a great chance of never returning to that place of breaking down again. It was such a gift to know this! In 2012, I'd already been sober for more than a year, and I'd already had more than a pocketful of meditative practices in my coping toolkit. I had been off prescription medication for years. I was good. I felt good. I hadn't had any psychotic episodes since 2009 when the sheriff's office had picked me up in Arizona. However, I never did end up taking the Addictions Counsellor course. As it turned out, the Universe thought it would be super helpful for me to take the Psychology class and learn a whole bunch of useful information that would help me to stay well while also reassuring me that the nightmare didn't have to happen again. Thank you, Universe.

The song, Lean on Me, would continue to be an anthem in my life. Not just for getting through the hospital experience but for working on my sobriety with other addicts and alcoholics. This song would be an anthem for any time that life got hard because it always reminded me that we didn't get through the hard stuff in life alone; it was much better if we had our tribe with us.

I spent a lifetime building walls, not letting anyone in, and not knowing how to properly reach out for help. Very often for alcoholics and addicts, sometime during our youth or childhood we were left to fend for ourselves in some way or another – thus began the trauma of not getting our emotional and/or physical needs met. There was definitely a period in my life when my emotional needs were not being properly met. No one is to blame for that, it's just what happened. What I'd learned from that at the time, however, was that I had to look out for number one. If I had a problem, I'd needed to fix it. If I had a need, I'd had to find a way to meet it. Learning how to turn to others and work together to make things better, was new for me as an adult. It didn't come easily.

BAD POETRY

Cruising on my bike, the next song that came on was one that was dear to many people – Hallelujah, by Leonard Cohen. He and his works are Canadian treasures – he was a singer, poet, musician, novelist. When I think of Leonard Cohen, his poetry is what comes to mind – all his music was poetry set to song. He didn't write catchy lyrics, he delved into human experience with his words. His lyrics had multiple meanings. One could study his work for a lifetime and still not come to fully understand its depth.

While I was driving my motorcycle and hearing the gorgeous lyrics in Hallelujah I began to think about poetry. Writing had been a huge part of my healing, and in 2010 I'd started to write a lot of poetry – something I hadn't done for years. I do not consider myself a great poet however, I do believe I wrote a few poems that spoke powerfully to my audiences at the time I wrote them. Structure isn't my strength – the meaning and the message are. For some of those early poems, I wrote them when I was stone cold sober and for others, I'd smoked a joint or had a glass of wine first. Everything written after February 13th, 2011 was written in sobriety. On February 19th, 2011, I self published a book of my poetry. I was proud of doing that. Somewhere in the back of my mind, I felt like I had 'kind of' completed my mission to write a book. It wasn't The Book but it was a book that I could hold in my hands.

A few poems stand out for me as having something relevant to say in this story. I'm going to share my favourite poem first. It was one of the first poems I wrote in 2010:

LIFELINES

I am beautiful.
I was created by perfection.
I was created in perfection.
And any imperfection is merely a reflection
Of the road I have traveled, the tale my life has spun,
The battles I have fought, often losing, sometimes won.
The scars adorning my body, and my soul are not flaws.
They are the map of my lifeline, the meaning and the cause
Of everything I hold dear, and sometimes what I fear
They are the book I haven't written yet, the words I cannot say
Look deep into my eyes, they will show the way
To dig into my soul, my loves, my cares, my hurts, my sorrow
When you look there, you shall see yesterday today tomorrow
For they do not know the time, they don't even know the place
But they are the window to the beauty that sits upon my face.
Yes, I am beautiful.
Look into my eyes,
And see yourself reflected there
For you, yes you, are very beautiful too.

Tracey Rogers, 2010

I even love the way it looks on the page – when I centre this poem, it looks like a tree. To this day, I cannot say this poem from the heart without tears welling up while I do. I remember where I was on my journey when I wrote this. My self work involved steps to find the beautiful things about myself instead of all the flaws, all the mistakes. Instead of looking back at my life and seeing the pain, I was looking back and finding the hidden treasures, the insights, the things I had learned.

Every time I read this poem, I am reminding myself who I am and where I come from. When I wrote, "I was created by perfection… I was created in perfection", I was referring to our Divine roots. The Universe doesn't make mistakes. Each of us are here to live a Divine plan, but we aren't able to see that plan in full. There is no doubt in my mind that addiction was a karmic lesson for my soul. My life was set up for this lesson at a very young age – 12. The same number of steps I would have to take to sort it all out – 12. When I wrote this poem, I still wasn't aware of the full truth about my addictions. Instead of seeing my pain as ugly, the scars from my life as ugly, I was embracing all of them – all the parts of me that had been the most difficult to accept. I love this poem. I am beautiful. And so are you.

This next poem is significant because of when it was written in early 2011. It was as if I knew what was coming:

WHO I REALLY AM

Today is a perfect day to start again
And I don't mean pick up where we left off
I mean, start again, as if nothing has happened
As if there never was a day before today.

Anything I remember, was a past life
It wasn't here, it wasn't now, it wasn't the me I am
A mist forms over yesterday, blurring it
Smudging the lines between dream and reality.

I implore of the gods, to give me new eyes
Help me to see everything for the first time
Help me to release past judgments
Help me to start again, reborn, undone.

Years they spent molding me in their institutions
Trying to make me think, look and talk like them
Instead, an individual ran screaming from the building
Wild hair flowing, refusing to wear a suit.

But I learned there what I needed to know
How to survive in their cookie cutter world
How to blend in when I needed to camouflage
How to disappear when the man walked by.
I don't need it anymore, I don't want it anymore
All I want to do, is explore outside my door
I want to run and play, and when they say
I've lost my mind, she's going blind
To the world outside, it cannot hide
Her craziness, her stubborn laziness
She just won't be, what we want to see
We can't have that, others will start to chat
And decide they too, want to leave this zoo
And be someone unique, against the bleak
Grey sky we made, the green grass we laid

No, that will not do, we need her to
Conform with us, and get on the bus
Pop a yellow pill, sit and be still
Oh, such a tragedy, that she couldn't be
Like you and me, lost in the massive sea
Of faceless names, and human games.

Today, is a perfect day to start again
Today, is a great place to call square one
Today, I forget everything you taught me
Today, I remember who I really am.

Tracey Rogers, January 2011

This time in my life when I had been writing poetry was a time of self discovery, figuring out what I'd believed in, and how I'd viewed the world and myself. I was moving beyond what I'd been taught in Arizona, and I was using what I'd learned to shape my experiences. Having understood the structure of religion and the teachings of the spiritualists, I was able to mix all of those teachings with what I had learned on my own, thus creating and strengthening my own relationship with the Divine and with myself.

The Tarot card that correlates with this experience is The Lovers. Not only does it represent deep, intimate relationships which expose our vulnerabilities to a partner, it also represents a time of raw honesty, nakedness, exposition of our deepest emotions. Poetry allowed me to experience this exposition – I'd started to reveal the things that had hurt me, the origins of my walls, my fears, my hopes, my deepest, truest self. This was a vulnerability that I hadn't allowed since writing poetry as a teenager – except this time, I had a growing self awareness. In addition to that, The Lovers card represents 'passion'– not just romantic passion but things we are passionate about. If there is anything I am passionate about, it is the journey to the self – self love, self compassion, self awareness and the Authentic Self. Poetry played a big part in opening up the doors to myself. Poetry and writing are my passions. Finding words to express what I have never been able to express is a passion. I see myself as The Lovers while poetry unlocked my heart and allowed me to be vulnerable and open with the world.

The Lovers Card
Rider Waite Tarot deck

THE BEST IS YET TO COME

To match my mood as I rode along on my motorcycle, the Universe timed the next song perfectly – Good Life, by One Republic. When this song comes on I either have a huge, happy smile or tears of happiness stream down my face because I'm full of gratitude. Certain songs carry extra special meaning and memory, this is one of them.

In early 2011, I had moved to Windsor from London, Ontario. For a few months, I hadn't had a single drink or smoked a joint – I had been drug and alcohol free. Why? Because when I moved, I'd decided to start working on my Reiki certification. I wasn't entirely sure why, but I'd thought that I might have a business that included Reiki at some point. I'd wanted to get back into Reiki. I had loved what it had done for me in Arizona, and I had been doing some self Reiki since returning to Canada. It brought me joy. I loved it. I was dating a woman at the time, and she was renting a room at a yoga studio for her hypnosis practice. She asked me if I'd wanted to split the costs and do some Reiki there.

Let me backtrack for you for a moment. I had been dating a woman. Yep.

In May of 2009, US Immigration had kicked me out, and I'd landed back in Canada. It was a jarring experience for me. Firstly, I had been back to being Tracey again instead of Mary Jane. That had been weird at first. I'd been using my real name since being in detention but the full weirdness of using my real name hadn't really hit me until I'd heard my family use it. Tracey. How was I going to meld these two parts of myself into a whole person? I was part Mary Jane. Mary Jane went to church, she was spiritual, she was into crystals and Reiki and healing. And part Tracey. Tracey was crazy and out of her mind. Tracey had destroyed her whole life. Both these people were me. I had changed, big time.

But London had looked and felt the same. When I'd arrived in town, I felt like the last two-and-a-half years hadn't even happened. Listening to the radio, everyone sounded like they had a Newfoundland accent. Holy smokes, that's why people in the US knew I was Canadian when I talked! For the first time, I had heard a Canadian accent clearly. But I'd had an American accent. I'd sounded like I was from the south. My family? Sounded like they were from Newfoundland. It almost made me laugh, but not quite. I hadn't been ready to laugh yet. I'd been in cultural and spiritual shock when I returned to Canada. Two parts of myself had collided in the most horrible of ways.

One of the most difficult things about coming back to Canada was that my family only knew Tracey who had left almost three years prior. They'd wanted me back on medication. They'd wanted me to see doctors. They'd wanted to tell me what they thought I'd needed to do. They'd had no idea how my life had changed. They'd had no idea the new tools I had, even after I'd tried to explain it to them. Everyone had looked at me like I was still crazy. But I wasn't. I'd definitely been out of sorts, but not because of mental imbalance because I'd just spent three months in detention; because I'd lived under a different name for over two years, and because my family – the people who were supposed to know me best – hadn't known a thing about the new me. I hadn't known where to start, so for the most part, I'd kept it simple, told them about a few of the people I'd met, and spoke as little as I could.

More than that, I had been grieving as well. Not in a healthy way. I had been grieving in the way a broken person who always avoided her feelings grieves by trying to push it down and ignore it. Once again, I had left an entire family behind me. This time it was my Payson family. I had made some very close connections in Payson. I had opened up my heart, and others had opened up their hearts to me. And instead of holding onto those relationships from a distance, I had let most of them go. I had been banned from the US without much of a hope of ever being able to return. So, instead of holding on to what I had created there, I'd let most of it go. I had become a master of detaching from that which could hurt me. It was part of my survival skill set I had learned as a youth when my heart first got wounded.

Instead of allowing myself to feel my heart ache and break, I had shut it down and shut it off. I can still have that capability, if I don't pay attention. The hurt and the heartache doesn't go anywhere, it just festers and multiplies in a deeper, darker spot. I had let most of Payson go. I had detached, and in that decision I had let go of people who have incredibly dear places in my heart. I hadn't known how to hold onto the love. I hadn't known how to hold onto our friendship when the Universe was shutting me out and saying "never go back."

I had chosen to never look back as well. There is a place in me that remains hurt to this day because of the way I'd let that part of my life go. I wish I'd had better tools, but if I'd had better tools, I probably wouldn't have been running away from my life in the first place. It all happened for a reason, and so I cradle my beloved heart. I ask for my own forgiveness and compassion.

The first few months back in Canada had been difficult. I'd shared an apartment with a woman named Glynys. I'd met her through an online ad in which she was looking for a roommate. She'd helped me to get over the fears I'd had without even knowing she was helping me get over them – it was totally by chance. Glynys had a cat named Molly, and she left her front door open overnight so the cat could get in and out. The door being left open had freaked me out at first, but as time passed, I'd realized nothing was happening, and nothing was going to happen. My panic and my paranoia about being back in Canada had begun to subside a bit. What I'd been experiencing was nothing like my breakdown or a psychotic episode, it had been more like PTSD from the psychotic episode. Those fears I'd had during my breakdown had created a very real terror for me. Terror is terror, whether real or imagined.

I'd also spent a huge amount of time at my sister Sarah's. She was a godsend. My niece and nephew had made me smile an awful lot, and I'd enjoyed watching their family interact. I'd never been so quiet in my whole life as I'd been for the first few months back in Canada. I'd listened a lot. I'd watched. I'd allowed my old life to integrate with my new life in silence. I hadn't known what to do with myself. I hadn't wanted life to go back to the way it had been before I left – humdrum with no spirituality.

Eventually I'd gotten a job at a call centre. My life had started to balance somewhat, and I began to feel comfortable in my own skin again. After being home in Canada for about a year, I had started dating again. I had met a good one, Tim. But as soon as I'd started to feel close to him, I'd gotten paranoid. I'd begun to mistrust him. It was the same thing that had happened in Arizona when I had dated a few guys. Men had triggered my PTSD. So, I'd decided I that I must be gay. It wasn't a thought that I came to easily, but it seemed to be the only answer. Due to my trauma as a child and a teen, I'd figured that my ability to understand my sexuality was severely messed up (ironically, I was completely correct in that). Instead of banging my head against the wall continuing to struggle with dating men, I'd made the switch. Not long afterwards, I'd met a woman who lived in Windsor through an online dating site.

In hopes of bringing the two of us closer together, I'd moved to Windsor on February 1st, 2011. Two nights before I left London, I had an amazing dream about a hundred baby eagles. They were all in nests on an island I was standing on. Everywhere I looked, eagles – but all of them were young. I had never dreamt of eagles before in my life, and upon waking up, I knew that something awesome was going to happen for me when I moved to Windsor. Dreaming of eagles is always a good omen if you ask me, and dreaming of dozens of baby eagles, not quite out of the nest? Well this is a dream of hope and opportunity. I just knew something wonderful was waiting for me in Windsor. Waking from that dream, I'd believed that it was going to be a magnificent move for me.

I remember my Dad talking to me before that move. He had said, "What if it's a wrong move? What if you aren't happy when you get to Windsor?"

"So what if it is a wrong choice? At least I'll know then. I'm obviously not happy in London, so why not try something new? Worst case scenario, I move back," I'd responded. I had changed so much during my time in the US. I wasn't always aware of it, but it would come jumping out at moments like that one. The old me would have been paralyzed with fear, afraid of what? Losing a few bucks for a move? Having to move back or move somewhere else? The new me had been confident: Seriously, so what?

Immediately upon arriving in Windsor, I'd started working on my Reiki certification. My Reiki teacher in Arizona, Annelle, had taught us that a Reiki practitioner shouldn't do Reiki within three days of having drank alcohol or smoking drugs. She'd also taught us that one shouldn't smoke tobacco before Reiki either. The reason for this was that it affects our energy flow and the energy that we bring to our client. I took everything Annelle said seriously, and since I'd been doing Reiki every Tuesday and Thursday, that meant that I'd needed to keep sober and off pot while getting my certification. I'll be honest, it hadn't been very difficult for me by this point because I had spent a great deal of time clean and sober in Arizona. I had participated in a church run 12-step program. Even though I had not made a decision to quit forever, being sober was doable for me by 2011. My last 'binge' had been in California in 2007 – the Cinco De Mayo Fiasco. Also, while in the detention centre, I'd had more opportunity to stay clean.

I got a phone call one day from a woman I had met at a women's potluck. She said she'd wanted to meet me for coffee and had something to talk to me about. I had met her for all of ten minutes, so I couldn't imagine what she wanted to talk to me about, but off I went.

After a few minutes of niceties, Cory asked me if I'd ever been in a 12-step program. I told her I had in Arizona, but that it was a church type thing. She'd asked me if I was clean and sober currently. I explained that I hadn't had a drink or done any drugs at all for close to three months.

"Would you like to come on a 12-step retreat weekend?" she'd asked me.

I didn't really know what she meant, and when I'd asked some clarifying questions, I was given very little information. If I decided to go, she'd explained, I would have to trust her and just go. She wasn't allowed to tell me anything about the weekend, but she assured me that it would be good. She even offered to pay my way. I can't remember if that was $100 or $150, but since I'd been unemployed, the fact that she was offering to pay mattered a great deal. After agreeing to go – I was on a 'say yes to everything the Universe offers you' kick – I'd asked her why she had asked me, she knew nothing about me. She said that her intuition, her higher power, kept telling her to ask me. Otherwise, she'd had no idea why.

Much of that weekend I can't tell you about because that was part of the deal. If there is one thing I respect, it's anonymity and privacy within the Recovery community. But, there were a handful of moments that were crucial for things going well in my life, and that weekend was one of them. I'd walked away from it knowing that I had to make a commitment to being clean and sober. In Recovery, they teach 'a day at a time', but even that 'day at a time' requires some level of commitment – like an understanding that you are committing to stay sober. I had never done that. In the USA, I had assumed that I'd just needed to stay sober while I was there – that I was endangering my time in the US by drinking and doing stupid things. Back in Canada, I had stayed clean and sober for most of 2009, but had eventually drifted back to smoking pot more and more often, and having a drink of wine, more and more often. I'd stopped binging. I hadn't gotten drunk once since I'd been back in Canada, but I was back to wanting a drink or a toke or both every day.

What I was exposed to on that Recovery weekend was eye-opening. There were other people like me who had similar stories. Listening to some of the stories, I'd realized that there was hope for me. On Saturday night, I'd felt the presence of god, and if ever I have understood a message it was in that moment. I truly wish I could describe it to you. The magic of it. But I can't without breaking my promise. Loud and clear, I'd heard it though – I needed to be clean and sober. And it wasn't just a 'for now' thing, it was a forever thing.

I'd heard a song that weekend, and it was the one I mentioned above, Good Life, by One Republic. What I'd heard in that song was a promise that my life was going to be good. That I was not only going to recover everything I had lost, but I was going to find so much more than I ever had before. That's what I'd heard in the song. It has been forever etched in my mind as The Promises Song. The promise that everything will be better. The promise that it will all be worth it. The promise that I'm going to have a good life if I just follow these simple steps.

And that's why I smile, and sometimes even cry with happiness when I hear Good Life because I hadn't believed in a false promise. It had been true. My life is awesome. My life has been awesome for a long time now. It started getting awesome in Arizona, and it hasn't stopped getting more and more awesome. And you know what? The best is yet to come. I believe that. The best is always yet to come.

After that weekend, I went to a 12-step meeting. It wasn't the first meeting I'd gone to. When I was 27 or 28, I had tried to quit smoking pot. My addiction through the years was mainly to pot. I had been a chronic smoker who smoked first thing in the morning, when I could during the day, depending on work, and I'd smoked as soon as I got home until bed. I'd failed in that early attempt to quit after going to a few meetings because I'd been struggling with the whole 'higher power' thing. I had been an atheist and I just didn't get it. Had I truly wanted to get clean, I'm sure I could have found a way around the higher power thing. I had also not been supported by anyone in my life with my decision to quit smoking pot. It had been difficult attempting to do it by myself.

Here's a piece of truth for you – quitting any addiction is always a solo job, I don't care who you are or who is quitting with you. If we quit for someone else then the success of our Recovery becomes dependent on that person as well. That's dangerous water to be swimming in. I found I had to be willing to give up any friendship, any relationship or anything that stood in the way of my Recovery. It sounds harsh, but it's a lesson in learning to give our own health and well-being top priority. That's self love and self care.

It took me a few months to find the right support group, the right environment for me to feel comfortable talking about drugs and alcohol in Windsor. It would take me a number of years to unravel the reality of my addictions. It required a new level of self honesty and self understanding that I was still developing. It didn't happen overnight

The truth is, I don't think I was prepared to start talking about the reality of my addiction right away, especially as it had existed in 2005 at the time of my breakdown. Here's the reality, and it's still a hard one for me to talk about – I had been a meth addict, and I hadn't even known it. All that ecstasy I'd been taking every weekend? I now know it had been so heavily cut with meth that it might as well have been meth. I was getting it for $5 a hit – good ecstasy cost $20 then, sometimes more. After discussing the high I'd experienced and the side effects of my buzz with some other folks in Recovery, it was brought to my attention that whatever I had been taking was heavily cut with meth. That knowledge was a devastating blow and a moment of enlightenment all at the same time. No one walks away from a meth addiction unscathed. No one makes good decisions in the middle of that. I had been no exception. I was years into Recovery before I could admit that meth had been a part of my story.

In 2011, I stood up at a meeting and I said, "My name is Tracey and I'm an addict." It had taken me four years from that message I received on the Santa Monica pier guiding me to quit smoking, drinking, doing drugs and drinking coffee to get to this incredible moment. There I stood, finally taking that message as seriously as it should have been received in the first place. You know what? It was totally ok. I love the one who got the message in the time she needed to hear it. I love the one who so stubbornly wanted to believe she could somehow control her substance use. I love the one who never forgot what she heard that day back in California, and even though she wasn't ready to do it yet, she did it when she was ready. During the four years in between? I had prepared myself for making a more permanent decision by living the message one day at a time, and learning meditation, reiki and all the tools I would need to make my sobriety a reality.

In order to assist with my new choices, I'd told my closest group of friends at the time that they weren't going to see me for at least a year – I couldn't be around people smoking pot. I let everyone in my life know I had joined a 12-step group. Why? To make myself accountable. Leos, by nature, are a proud people, and I certainly am a Leo. If I publicly proclaimed that I was going to stay sober, I was going to stay sober, god damnit, even if my pride was the only motivation. I knew that much about me. Quickly, I'd found myself surrounded by sober people, people on the same path as me. Other folks I'd already known, having heard my public proclamations, let me know that they too were in Recovery.

I'm glad I did it that way right from the start. I was never ashamed to say that I was in Recovery, not from day one. I knew it was the best decision I'd ever made. I was proud of myself for doing it. So, what's the difference between me and other people first entering into Recovery who have a really hard time telling anyone because they feel ashamed? I'm guessing it has to do with the fact that that 12-step program wasn't really the beginning of my Recovery.

I'd been struggling with my addictions since California. Obviously I'd felt some shame because it took me four full years to admit that I had a problem – not just a temporary problem – but a permanent problem. I had also already been working on my self esteem, big time, since 2008. I'd been doing affirmations the entire time, reprogramming the way I'd treated myself and talked to myself. I had an awesome relationship with the Divine that was very personal and built from my own experiences. I'd felt loved by the Universe. I think that's what I'd needed – to feel loved first before I could own my addictions. I knew the Universe loved me – in spite of my sordid past – it wanted me to get sober and there was nothing to be ashamed of in that.

RECOVERY

Zooming by on my motorcycle, I passed a beautiful waterfall. Finding a road to turn around on, I made a loop and headed back. I found myself in the parking lot for Chippewa Falls. Wow! It was beautiful! There was a plaque explaining that this was the halfway point on the Trans Canada Highway. There I was!

Walking down nearer to the falls, I found another display. It was set up like an artist's easel as if someone was right there painting the falls. Upon reading the sign, I found out that it was a tribute to one of the Group of Seven artists, J.E.H. MacDonald. I love Group of Seven paintings. I had studied them long ago in public school, and I was always fascinated with their work. Canada certainly has something to be proud of in these artists. Needless to say, I was thrilled to find a tribute to one of them on my epic trip.

Carrying on down the road on my bike, I quickly found myself at the Batchawana Bay Voyageurs stop – the gas station. Kelly had told me to stop there and fill up my tank. She had also mentioned that they made great apple fritters so I should have one. After finding my seat in the back corner, I ordered a fritter and a hot chocolate. The waiter asked me if I wanted a meal too or just a fritter. I said the fritter would be fine. Turning on my phone, I messaged Ron to let him know I was safely through part of my trip, and then I checked my Facebook. My fritter arrived. Holy smokes! Did I want a meal too? This was a meal; the thing was huge! And it was delicious. Sugar, cinnamon and hot apple melting in my mouth. This was life! I laughed with the waiter about the size of my fritter then I went back to my phone.

After the meal, I wanted a bit more time off my bike, so I wandered around the property. There was a small variety store, the restaurant and a gift shop. All three had gifts in them, including t-shirts. I was on the hunt for a t-shirt or a hoodie because this was a unique little community that I might not be back to for a while. I eventually ended up in the gift shop. When I was in there looking for a shirt, I found a little pewter coin that had a moose on one side of it. Oh my gosh! I immediately purchased it. I had told everyone back home and on my Facebook that I wanted to see a moose on my trip. Since leaving Sault Ste. Marie that morning, I knew I was in moose country and the odds of me seeing one were increasing with every moment.

Since 2013, I'd been wishing to see a moose. Working with moose energy in my artwork, I had discovered that moose were one of the animals associated with self esteem. I referred to it as 'awkward grace.' Moose have a huge head that is almost too large for their body. Beneath this massive noggin are slender legs that look too small to carry their huge bulk. Atop their heads are a set of antlers so large they look like they could tip the moose over if he moved his head the wrong way. Awkward, ill fitting parts and yet, when put all together, the moose is majestic and beautiful. Graceful even.

When we work with moose energy, we can learn to appreciate those things about ourselves that we may feel awkward or non-accepting about. We can learn to love the things that make us uniquely us. In my mind, I believed that if the Universe gave me the gift of seeing a moose, it would be confirmation that I had arrived at the place of self acceptance and self love that I had been seeking for years. I had gone to Newfoundland in 2014, and everyone told me I'd see a moose for sure out there – they were all over the place. I was there for ten days, no moose. Not one! I'd started joking that moose were the "Great Canadian Myth," and they were all photoshopped. All the videos of moose were just guys in a suit. Any time I'd been in northern Ontario, I had hoped to see a moose in my travels. This trip was no different. I'd been keeping my eyes peeled for one since I'd arrived in the Sudbury region.

As I put my moose token in my pocket, hoping to manifest a moose with it, I told the shopkeep about my dream to see a moose. Everyone in the store started talking about moose – when they had seen them, where they had seen them, and where to go for the best chances to see one. Apparently, just up the road near Pancake Bay was a great area for spotting moose. But timing was also key for moose sightings. Unfortunately for me, evenings or dawn were the best times to spot these creatures and it was midday. I felt sad when they all agreed that they used to see a lot more moose years ago. They weren't sure if the population had gone down or if the moose had moved more North because of changing to habitats and people. I was sure it was a bit of both.

Still, I left the store feeling hopeful that I might see my moose. I didn't find a Batchawana Bay shirt I liked, but I did find a Canada long sleeve shirt I loved, so I purchased that instead. Outside, I found myself chatting with the gas attendant. Some locals had asked me where I was going on my bike, so I explained my little adventure. The gas attendant wanted to hear more about the Women Riders World Relay, so I told him, and let him know that in a few days we'd be coming back through here on September the 20th. He seemed excited and I tried to imagine what it must be like living way up in the middle of god's country. Promising him I'd be back soon, I hopped on my bike and drove away from the Batchawana Bay Voyageurs rest stop; full of apple fritter and happiness. Oh ya, and a moose in my pocket.

I knew what I was looking for next – the Agawa Rock Pictographs. These had been drawn by Ojibway people back in the 17th century or as late as the 18th century. Online I had found a description of how to get to them. I gathered that the hike to the pictographs wasn't too bad, but getting out onto the rock where they were could be treacherous. Turning my headphones on, I put my feet on the pegs and enjoyed the ride to the area. Oh my gosh was I ever enjoying the ride! I was driving through some of the most beautiful country I'd ever seen. The trees. The rocks. The colours. The water and streams and rivers. Everything was insanely incredible. To top it all off, my anthem for Recovery came on, Not Afraid, by Eminem. Eminem has struggled with addiction and he wrote an album entitled 'Recovery' after he started to face that demon head on. Off that album comes one of the greatest Recovery anthems of all time, Not Afraid.

The song is powerful for folks fighting through Recovery from addictions. I was lucky, my world was supportive of my decision to recover. Not everyone gets that blessing. I remember my Dad trying to offer me wine our first Christmas together after I chose to get clean and sober. He argued that wine was fine, I just needed to stay away from the drugs. No, it wasn't ok. One leads to the other for me, I had to tell him. When I didn't have access to pot, I drank. Period. Before I became a pothead, I drank. During my pot addiction, I hardly drank – just near the end – alcohol was not my drug of choice. Full abstinence from everything was the only option for me, and I knew that. No substance was worth risking my sanity for ever again. And alcohol was a depressant. Since I was working so hard to overcome tendencies towards depression, wouldn't having a glass of wine be beyond counter productive? I spoke to my Dad for a few minutes, and he never did that again – he never offered me another glass of wine.

I rarely use the terms 'pot' or 'clean' to people. I use the word sobriety and people tend to not ask questions. I've learned how powerful words can be when it comes to recovery and people's opinions and experiences around drugs and alcohol. As soon as I'd say that pot was my drug of choice, there were people who got defensive about smoking it. I'm not judging anyone else's decision to smoke pot every day. I don't care what other people do or why they do it. I know some people are managing pain. I know some people just enjoy giggling. Some are managing PTSD symptoms. I know some people use it as an anti-stressor. I know some people use it as harm reduction from more serious drugs. People don't need to argue with me that it's ok for them to smoke pot everyday – they have every right to do whatever they want to do.

Pot is one of those substances that has the potential to help some people and the potential to be a bad choice for others. I just know what's good for me. No one else knows what's good for me. Just me. I want to experience life fully, with no filters. I want to feel my feelings fully, with no filters. I want to have as much self awareness as possible. For me, that means no substances. Frankly, I couldn't care less what everyone else does and thinks is best for them. Have at it! I have no idea what's best for you. Enjoy your life, whatever that looks like to you.

I remember my first sobriety birthday – one year without drugs and alcohol. My last high and my last drink had been on February 13th, 2011. I had been with some girlfriends doing crafts and I partook in some joints and a bottle of wine. It had been a wonderful weekend, and as last highs go – it couldn't have been lovelier. I was with good friends and we had good fun. No one got wasted, and everyone had a great time. I had no idea it would be my last drink or my last joint.

I was so proud of myself – a whole year! I'd been going to meetings faithfully. I had been committed and I was doing the work. I had been doing my steps and life was getting better and better every day. Following through with what I had committed to myself was improving my self esteem. As I walked up to my table at a support meeting – a special table off to the side – there were gifts, some cards, and sitting right in the middle of the table at my spot were two eagle feathers. Oh my god. How did my sponsor know? He knew I loved birds. He knew I loved eagles, but I had never mentioned my yearning for an actual eagle feather. I had never spoken that aloud to anyone.

The way I understood it, eagle feathers were the greatest gift one could receive from the Universe. It was more than just a good omen – it was a symbol that I was on the right path, that the heavens were acknowledging my deeds, that I was worthy of an eagle feather. I was worthy? Of not just one feather, but two? It was my interpretation that one feather was for being clean of drugs, one was for alcohol. The Universe was giving me a very clear sign that full abstinence was a good choice. My sponsor was a good man and a good friend. I wish I'd known how to successfully navigate healthy friendships back then – I might still be able to call him a friend.

There is significance to all these dates – February 13th: my last drink/drug, February 14th: my clean and sober date. I had always considered 13 to be an unlucky number. When it became my sobriety date, that changed for me. Now, I consider 13 to be one of the luckiest numbers ever. I also pay attention when I see the number 13 – for me, it's associated with addiction. When this number becomes associated with an activity or a person, I pay attention. Even more significant, my first day clean and sober – February 14th – is my Mum's birthday. It's also the day associated with Love – Valentine's Day. My addictions are karmically tied to love and my Mum. I believe both of us can get off this particular karmic wheel - addiction. Our lesson has been learned. Neither of us have to go through this life lesson again because I've taken the time and effort to face the demon that is addiction. I believe that daughters karmically pick up where their mothers left off. So, what mothers heal, their daughters will not have to, and what daughters heal, neither mother nor daughter will have to come back in another incarnation to heal. It's my gift to you and me, Mum. Happy Birthday. I love you.

FIRE WOMAN

A song that always makes me smile is Good Feeling, by Flo Rida. This song came out in 2012 and was a wonderful reflection of how I was feeling that year. No, I sure as heck hadn't fixed everything, but I was working on it, and every day of life since 2006 had steadily improved one little bit at a time. What was I doing that made me so happy? In 2010, I'd started to intentionally put manifesting energy out to the Universe. What I'd wanted to manifest was a life full of doing the things I loved the most – Reiki, artwork, drumming, and making jewelry – my hobbies. When I had set this intention, I honestly thought the only way it could happen was if I won the lottery or married someone who was rich. So, instead of just waiting for a miracle to arrive, I filled my spare time doing those things. When I wasn't working, I'd do Reiki or arts and crafts. When I moved to Windsor in 2011, I'd immediately been offered the office space to do Reiki treatments, and I'd started doing them twice a week by donation.

Before I'd moved to Windsor, I'd become involved with the Windsor Pride Center and Diversity Training. Diversity Training was given to organizations in the city by the Pride community in an effort to bring awareness to LGBTQ+ issues, and to help build Pride-positive workspaces that were considered safe and healthy for the Pride community to go into. In addition to being a trainer for the Diversity Training, I'd started volunteering at the center as soon as I'd moved to Windsor. I hadn't been working yet, and I'd seen it as a positive experience for myself and for the people I would be helping.

In June of 2011, I'd attended a Women's Retreat Weekend on Pelee Island. The theme for the weekend was Courage. At that event, I'd sold my artwork, jewelry I'd made, and my book of poetry as a vendor. I'd never done that before. It was amazing! I'd sold over $1,000 worth of art, books and jewelry, and there had only been eighty women at the event. I'd considered it a fantastic success for a first try. That success motivated me to do more vending events and continue to put myself and my artwork into the world.

Twenty-eleven was the start of so many great things for me. Early in my sobriety, I decided to work on finishing my degree in English Literature. Dropping out of university back in my early twenties had been a huge blow to my self esteem and my dreams. Originally, I had been working towards an Honours Degree. I had almost all of the classes I'd needed to graduate, but in 2011, I'd made the decision to switch to a Bachelor of Arts which was a three-year program instead of four. I have never regretted that choice. Choosing to finish a Bachelor of Arts, instead of an Honours Degree, meant I was making a conscious and aware decision that I was no longer pursuing the dream of teaching high school because a three-year program was a barrier to that..

In June 2012, I received my degree and I'd finished what I started for the first time since the disaster that was my twenties. For years, I had beaten myself up in my head because I'd rarely completed my projects. I would start something, put it down, and never go back to it. Not anymore. When I'd received my degree from the University of Western Ontario, , I'd quietly tucked it away without much fanfare, but in my heart it hung on the wall of my accomplishments in a golden, bejewelled frame. I was proud of myself. I'd say it out loud, again and again. I'm proud of you! I no longer needed words of validation from my parents, I'd been able to give them to myself.

In the late summer of 2011, I'd gotten a job that kept me busy 30 to 35 hours a week. When I wasn't working, I'd do my hobbies. Two full days a week, I'd continued to offer Reiki treatments. I was loving life. My apartment had been tiny, but inexpensive, and my landlord and his wife were lovely people. Recovery was a big part of my life. I had new, sober friends. I had a cat that I named Serenity. Getting a cat had been a brilliant choice. I had heard someone at my recovery retreat weekend talking about how much getting a pet had changed their life because it gave them something to love and look after. I love Serenity to bits! She brings me so much joy and so many smiles. She was a rescue cat, but honestly, she rescued me. I firmly believe that Serenity played a big part in opening my heart. Serenity taught me how to love again.

Creating my artwork was extremely healing. I believed that I was working towards being a famous artist one day. Why I was doing it hadn't really mattered in the big picture. What mattered was that I was doing it and it was helping me heal. Through my artwork, I'd connected with animal medicine and spent hours contemplating the teachings they offered me. Beyond the spiritual guidance, I'd spend hours, sometimes days, doing a single piece of art. There were days when I'd get lost in work for twelve hours before I'd notice that I hadn't eaten or done anything else.

It had been a meditative practice and it got me out of my monkey mind – my busy, unhelpful thoughts. I'd enjoyed the peace I achieved while working on art. I had also begun to pay attention to the things I'd been drawing, to the energy I'd been putting into the art. The animal messages I'd been receiving through the art were beginning to manifest in my own life within a month or two of completing the piece. For example, things like my business, my relationships, and my personal development all had links to my art and the animal teachings. It was like I had been calling the energy into my own life with every animal I drew. It was like.... magic. Without even trying to do magic.

The same could be said for making jewelry and doing crafts. I would get so involved in the creation of a new piece that I didn't notice the time, and my thoughts weren't all over the place. My thoughts had been centred on my creation – what bead would I put on next? What energy did I want this necklace to have? What colour would look best with this scheme? More peace, just like the peace I felt when doing my artwork.

Two full days a week of giving Reiki treatments had been wonderful. I'd felt like I was working towards something with my Reiki. I had started contemplating a part-time or maybe even full-time reiki business, but I wasn't sure. The certification I was getting was a requirement for work so I needed to get certified first. A beautiful thing about doing Reiki was that I received everything I gave energetically. The chi energy that flowed through me to my client, I felt. And the things I'd been helping them heal, were healing in me as well.

After months of doing traditional reiki, exactly as it had been taught to me, I'd started doing something else with it. I'd started saying affirmations out loud for the client during the session. The affirmations I'd used were to help the client shift their beliefs in the areas of their life they were struggling with. I spoke the affirmations in first-person, that is as if the client was saying the words themselves – 'I am[insert affirmation].'I witnessed amazing progress with some of my clients and very little progress with others regarding the affirmations. What I can tell you about affirmations is this: the more you say them, the more effective they are, period. So, instead of only me saying them to the client once a week or once every two weeks, the successful clients were saying them on their own time too, every day. I had been attempting to teach folks a new way to think by offering them affirmations. But at the end of the day, the client had to change their thoughts on their own; I couldn't do that for them. I could only lead them in that direction. A side benefit had been that I was saying these affirmations while I was giving Reiki, and believing what I was saying – it created awesome changes in my own life as well.

In June of 2012, I had been at a pagan festival and there was a woman named ZsuZsa who ran Firewalk ceremonies. Everyone I knew who had done the Firewalk told me to do it; it was amazing. So, I went. As a group, we'd spent five hours building the fire, starting the fire, and then watching the fire burn. It was a ceremony, and everything had to be done in a very specific way. While we did this, participants had talked and shared.

It had been a healing circle. Some of the things that we'd talked about and shared became like kindling for the fire. Our letting go in sharing helped strengthen the fire we were creating. After much tending, the fire was finally down to red-hot coals. Because of how the fire had been constructed, the coals were all the same size. ZsuZsa had raked the coals creating a large pit. It was the time to walk across the burning coals.

It wasn't until that moment that I got scared. I knew if I'd picked a coal up in my hand it would burn me in less than a second. I'd watched as others walked across the fire. I thought, if they can do it, I can do it! I'd pulled all my courage up within me and I walked across those coals – eight full steps! When I'd gotten to the other side, I couldn't believe I'd done it! I'd walked through fire! Holy crap! I'd walked through fire! Then, I'd waltzed across the fire a second time because I couldn't believe I'd done it the first time. And voila! I was on the other side – I'd walked through fire again!

I consider that event life changing. Walking on fire appears to be impossible. I had a lifelong fear of fire – how on earth could I walk on it? My takeaway from that experience was if I can walk through fire, I can do anything. And that's exactly what I'd started to do – walking through my fears.

EVER FALLEN IN LOVE?

Very few country songs make it onto my music playlist, although there are a few I enjoy. One that I enjoyed started strumming in my ears as I cruised along on my bike, that is, Kenny Rogers' The Gambler.

In 2012, not all my relationships had been 'healthy', but all of them had been a source of great learning for me. Every relationship or friendship had offered something of value. When I say they weren't healthy that doesn't mean it was the other person who had the problem. I was part of the problem – in some cases a big part of the problem. Relationships and friendships had been one of the weakest areas in my life. My interpersonal skills had sucked when it came to healthy relationships. I hadn't known what that looked or felt like; I'd never had one. As I'd started to explore boundaries and my own limitations, I'd made some mistakes and I'd experienced mistakes by others. One relationship stands out in my mind from this time.

Two red flags had gone off at the start of the relationship. One, she had been married. Two, she'd liked to gamble. I hadn't learned yet about 'red flags' and how often I ignored them. However, that relationship had been an awesome teacher for me in that area. Dating a married person was an obvious red flag because there was deception right from the start. The gambling was a red flag because even though I had never gotten into gambling, I'd known that as an addict, it was dangerous ground. Many addicts will find any outlet for their addiction – if they can't drink or do drugs, then perhaps shopping or sex or gambling becomes the addiction. Both red flags had been waving. I saw them and I'd ignored them. I'd waltzed right in.

The whole relationship hadn't been a disaster. It had its beautiful moments. Both of us had been learning and growing. She had her reasons for straying outside of her marriage, and she'd claimed that she would be ending it soon. In the back of my mind, I'd known that being with her was not a good choice – it lacked good character on my part. And it had done nothing to help my self esteem that I was working so hard to rebuild. It hadn't helped my Recovery either. I'll get back to that part in a bit.

Near the end of the relationship, I'd finally given in to the temptation of gambling. I'd been watching from the sidelines for a full year. I knew gambling was a risk for me – gambling ranked right up there with drugs and alcohol for becoming a source of addiction gratification. For my first time, I'd taken the dice at the craps table and I'd rolled for close to forty-five minutes before I hit a seven. Everyone had been cheering, folks at the table had all been making money – even me – and it was super fun! I'd won money. I'd lost money. I'd won money again. I'd lost money again. I'd spent the entire weekend at the casino – we had a room, and from start to finish, the weekend had cost me a grand total of $60. Well, that wasn't so bad! I had a fantastic time and it had only cost me $60!

Do you know what I'd really been gambling? What I'd put on the table, all bets in when I'd rolled the dice? I'd been gambling my future. I'd been gambling my sobriety. I'd been gambling my sanity. I'd been gambling the life that I had worked so hard to rebuild. At the time this happened, I had been accepted into the Self Employment Assistance program, which was a program designed to help people like me – people who lacked the funds and the know-how to start a business. It assisted entrepreneurs with funds and know-how to get our businesses up and running. I had been taking business classes through this program. I had the guidance of professionals in book-keeping, marketing, sales, legal knowledge and more, for free. Financially, the money had come from maximum Unemployment Benefits for ten months so I could get the business off the ground. I had written a 75-page business plan to complete my acceptance into this program. And there I'd been – rolling the dice on all of it.

That same week, I'd gone to the poker room for the first time. I'd started gambling for money in online poker as well. In a three-week period, I'd lost $900 – $900 that I hadn't had. I'd been only weeks away from opening my new business. Walking home from the casino one evening, I'd walked down Goyeau St., past the Emergency entrance of the hospital. Ambulances had been lined up and one was coming down the road toward me. Sirens blaring, I'd felt myself fall back into 2005 – my breakdown. My head started spinning as I'd forced myself to walk past the hospital. It was what I'd needed to see, to hear, to feel. I'd needed a reminder in my mind and body and walking past the emergency room had triggered it. Gambling had only offered me my old life back – a life of addiction and mental health issues. I had not wanted that.

Old programs can be difficult to break. I broke one that day. Every part of my soul had been doing its damnedest to sabotage the best time in my life – I was sober, my business was opening – the future looked more than promising. A very old program said that I was a bad person and that I didn't deserve happiness. The choice to gamble that day had been motivated by the old program's best effort to validate this belief. And why not? I was with a married person. I was bad.

Somewhere between my first roll of the dice and the day I saw the ambulances three weeks later, I'd ended the relationship. What I'd told her was: "We're done because I love me." I know she had no idea what the hell I'd meant by that. But I'd known. I had to put my sobriety first. I had to put my mental health first. I had to make choices that were motivated by the program that was "I love me."

I don't look back on that story with any shame. I made some mistakes. Was it a failure? Yes. An epic fail. But I'm allowed to make mistakes. If I'm paying attention, I will only make them once now. I figured something out about mistakes a few years ago. I feel, very strongly, that one of the main purposes of incarnating on earth – the reason for life – is to learn and grow. When I look back on all the learning I've done in my life, my greatest learning came from my greatest mistakes. Those mistakes that were so huge they ripped my heart out, I learned extremely valuable things from. And when life is going perfectly and I'm not making many mistakes? My lessons are much more subtle. I had to go through some of those big ones to get it. Understanding this has helped me on my path to forgiveness – both for myself and others. I'm here to learn, and I learn through mistakes – it's all part of a greater plan.

What was the overall lesson? Beyond a deeper awareness of my potential to self sabotage, I'd learned about red flags. Red flags are when you have those thoughts that say, "this guy's going to cheat on me," or "gambling is an addiction and dangerous for me," – thoughts that come up as warnings in the rumble of voices in our heads. But we walk right in and participate anyways, despite these red flags flapping. A year or two down the road, we may find ourselves saying, "I knew this was going to happen." Because we did know! And we justified the red flag away. Perhaps because we didn't trust our own intuition or because we had no proof of the red flag or most often, because we so desperately want this to be the thing we're looking for instead of the thing that it is. Now when I see a red flag, I try my best to listen and make my decisions based on that red flag. I don't always succeed. Any time I don't pay attention to the red flag, I pay for it down the road, and then I have a good laugh at myself when I get over whatever just happened. Hindsight is a flag store, isn't it?

They say you shouldn't get into relationships before you've done one full year in Recovery. Everything that had gone wrong in that relationship had been a brilliant example of why. I had no idea what I was doing. I had no idea how to have a healthy relationship. In fairness, I don't think they did either – otherwise they would have been divorced instead of having affairs, amongst other things that I won't get into here. It had been a case of two good people making some questionable choices.

Overall, 2012 had been a good year. I had good feelings. I had taken the steps to open my own business! I had been learning how to establish boundaries in friendships and relationships. I had been recognizing my own failings. I had been able to look back on my past with honesty. My life had been full of Reiki, artwork, tarot, crafting and

Recovery. I'd taken big steps forward. I'd never ever had so much joy and goodness in my life before – all based on healthy choices I'd made for myself, out of love for myself.

A CHANGE WILL DO YOU GOOD

Winding my way through the mountains, somewhere past Batchawana Bay, on the way to Wawa, a cover song came on, It's the End of the World As We Know (And I Feel Fine). The original version was by REM, but this version was by Great Big Sea, a fantastic Canadian band. This song reminded me of when the world was ending for me on December 21st, 2012. I've been through a few 'end of the worlds' in my lifetime but this was the big one. The Mayan calendar ended on this date. Though some people were preparing for cataclysmic change, I had absolutely no fear of it. Something inside me had known it was just symbolic. Many in the community thought that it would be a great time of awakening.

For me, my awakening first began in 2006 – when I'd found god. I believe when I'd found god, it created a huge shift in my life. Everything I'd believed in started to shift – how I'd viewed the world, how I'd viewed 'coincidences', how I'd viewed energy, how I'd viewed my entire life and everything that happened in it. Slowly over time, as I'd unlearned more and more of what I'd been taught, and learned more and more from what the Universe was showing me, I'd seen a connection between all people, all events. I'd started to believe that things weren't so random and chaotic.

I'm going to share another very personal story here, one that will help illustrate the kind of connections I'm talking about. It had started not long after my awakening. It was September, 2006, around the 23rd or so. I had a dream, a very vivid, real dream. In this dream, I'd felt a booming knowledge that said: "THIS IS YOUR LIFE", throughout the entire dream, I'd been watching, almost like a TV show. I knew I'd been watching my own life. I'd seen myself on the steps of what looked like a gothic-style church. It was grey and drizzly rain. There were men all around me in black robes. Someone was putting a black robe over my head, and as that happened, I just knew I was being made an Anglican minister. Then I woke up.

When I awoke, I'd been amazed with my dream because I knew it was about my life. I'd remarked to myself, "Huh! I'm going to be an Anglican Minister? I don't see that, but stranger things have happened." I'd floated the idea around in my head that day, and it started to seem entirely possible. I had just had a spiritual awakening a week or two before; who knew what path life was taking me down?

Two days after my dream, I'd ended up in an Anglican Church. I hadn't known it was Anglican until I was inside and I saw a pamphlet. I'd been there because the church was huge, and I'd been looking for a church, any church. I'd decided I needed to get baptized, just in case the Christians were right – I didn't want to die unbaptized and be banished to the pits of hell. I'd found the Dean's office. He'd been in. I'd asked him, "Do you have a

Book of Days for the Anglican Church? Like, the significance of each day?" He said he did as he'd scanned his bookshelf, found the book, and handed it to me.

I liked to look up the significance of my birthday in books like that one, just to see. I'd opened the book to my birthday, August 17th. Then clear as a bell, as if I'd been back in my dream, I felt the same booming knowing in the message: "THIS IS YOUR LIFE." I had to check that I was awake because it felt so much like the dream! I'd started reading and the information was about a guy named John Stuart. He had been the first Anglican Minister in Upper Canada to minister to the Mohawk people.

As I'd sat reading, I'd realized that the dream I'd had wasn't about me becoming an Anglican Minister, it had been about me being an Anglican Minister. Oh my god! The Hindus were right?! There is such a thing as reincarnation? I knew at that moment it was true, and I mean, I knew it. The feeling I'd had during the dream and then sitting in the Anglican Church cannot be properly explained. It had been a knowing; a loud knowing I could feel on a soul and cellular level. A deep...remembering based on a past lived experience.

The rest of my conversation with the Dean had been insignificant. He couldn't baptize me unless I became a member of the congregation and donated a certain amount of money to the church for the service. I hadn't had time or money for that. I'd just wanted some holy water dropped on my forehead. I'd wanted to turn my life over to god. Did he really have to make a big deal about it? Couldn't it be done, like right there, right then? Nope. But perhaps the significance of that interaction hadn't been about the baptism, but about my dream and the story in the Book of Days.

I'd walked out of the church, stunned about my new revelation. Oh my gosh, reincarnation was for real! It's not that I merely thought reincarnation was a possibility, I'd known it was. My experience had been that influential. The knowledge had been that booming. I'd only ever experienced that a few times, and when I had, it had been impossible to mistake. I just knew.

I'd found out a few more things about John Stuart. He had first lived in the New York area. During the American Civil War, he'd helped some of the Mohawk people cross the border into Canada. The ones who'd been left behind in that area were decimated during the war. He had a long career teaching the Mohawk people – as long as twenty-five years. He'd gotten involved with Joseph Brant, a Mohawk leader, for a while. Apparently he'd even tried to get the bible translated into Mohawk.

This information had helped connect some things in my life. I had grown up about three miles off the Oneida Reserve. I went to my first pow wow when I was eleven, long before they had become culturally popular. My Dad had found out one was happening, and he'd piled us all into the pickup to go check it out. I remember parts of it very vividly. The first thing I remember is the drum. The sound of the drumming went right through me – it felt like... home. The moment we'd gotten out of the truck, we could hear that drum and it didn't stop. It had gone right to my heart. I recall feeling almost dizzy, but not dizzy, out of my body.

Something I'd noticed quickly was that we had been the only white family there. This had been the first time in my life that I recall feeling... different...a minority. It had made me very self conscious and I'd felt like I didn't fit in. We'd watched some dancing and we went to some booths where people were displaying their crafts and items for sale.

Now and again, my father had surprised me. Looking back on this event, it was one of those moments. When we were at the pow wow, he'd taken us to as many of the elders as he could. They'd been in dance attire. My father had us kids sit with them and ask them if they could teach us about their dance outfit. The very first word I'd learned was 'regalia.' I'd learned that their regalia wasn't made of random items. We were shown the hoof of the deer from a man's first hunt; items a family member had sewn for him on his wedding day, and other very personal, significant items from important moments in his life, all of it regalia. His regalia hadn't just been an outfit created to 'look cool', it had been the story of the person's life.

I recalled that in school at that time in my life, I'd been taught about the 'taming of the savages' in Canada in the 1600s. A year later, I'd meet Don, the First Nations man who molested me. I remember I had asked him about a book that was on his table one day. It had something to do with Residential Schools. I'd already known by then, at age twelve, that the schools were houses of horror. He told me he had attended one of those schools. He didn't want to talk about it.

In my teen years, half of our high school population had been First Nations students that were bussed in from three reserves. For the most part, they'd socialized amongst themselves, but I did get to know a few Native kids during school. I remember always being sympathetic to First Nations issues. I remember arguing with people who put Canada's Indigenous people down and said they needed to get their shit together. I argued that when an entire group of people is institutionally broken, when their culture is decimated, you can't bring it back overnight by simply handing bands some money.

I'd been irate about the residential schools. I'd been irate about their rights not being the same as other Canadians. I'd been irate that we weren't doing more to fix what colonization had broken. And I hadn't known exactly where this sympathy came from, outside of a general love of humanity. I don't recall ever having it taught to me. It hadn't come from my parents though my father had been curious about their culture. My feelings about them had felt innate, like something I'd been born with. Something had awakened in me at that first pow wow when I was eleven and had heard the drums. I'd felt a deep connection I could never explain.

When I'd been trying to compute the possibility of reincarnation and its connection to John Stuart, it had made sense, a whole lot of sense, when I'd remembered my childhood connection to First Nations people and culture. John Stuart must have been sympathetic too, even if his thinking had been wrong by today's better understanding. If I was a reincarnation of John Stuart then his soul was my soul, right? It would make sense that I'd feel residual sympathies from his lifetime in my own lifetime.

In 2006, I'd considered John Stuart a wonderful guy who must have helped the Mohawks a lot. Later, during my spiritual growth and teachings in Arizona, I'd learned about karma. I'd started to re-evaluate the karmic connection between John Stuart, the Mohawks and me. I had been molested by a First Nations man when I was twelve years old. That man had been raised in the Residential School System. John Stuart had been one of the first people to start teaching the Natives about a Christian God in the 1700s and attempting to give them a European education. Technically, John Stuart had planted one of the earliest roots of the Residential School system. Had Don been a part of my karmic cycle reaching back to John Stuart? Karma teaches us that we will see all things from all angles and that every action we make has an equal reaction from the Universe.

I spent a few years doing shadow work, believing that my soul had probably done almost everything there was to do. Reincarnation means we will experience all things at some point in our life cycles. We don't show up in our first incarnation understanding murder and rape, and all things horrible. Over the reincarnated lifetimes of our soul's journey, we will be raped and we will rape. We will be murdered and we will murder. I worked on forgiving the worst crimes my soul could have possibly done. I spent days, weeks, months in contemplation about forgiveness and karma, and learning about how these actions and beliefs operate. I wondered if my soul felt so apologetic for things that it had done in other lifetimes that I'd spent subsequent lifetimes choosing to punish myself with difficult life experiences and traumas – a kind of penance, if you will. At no time had I gained memories about John Stuart other than during that one dream.

After much meditation on these topics, I came to this conclusion: I have no idea what John Stuart did and didn't do that isn't recorded in the history books. I do know that part of his karma, at least, is very good concerning the Mohawk people as he did help many survive the American Civil War. I do know that he educated the Mohawk people and tried to translate the Bible into Mohawk. What this made him, however, was one of the roots of the Residential School system. That doesn't mean that his intentions weren't good. That doesn't mean that he didn't believe he wasn't saving their souls and helping them arrive in God's Heaven, which as far as he was concerned was a positive thing. In my heart, I like to think he believed what he was doing was the best thing he could do for the Mohawk people. Almost everyone has great intentions but that doesn't negate the sometimes-harmful results of these intentions.

Being molested is an interesting ending to one of my karmic teachings. Karma teaches that the ripple effects of actions in one lifetime can be felt seven generations later. The results of these actions can push forward that many lifetimes and be experienced in a later lifetime. The results of what the early church in Canada did to the First Nations peoples? Horrendous. The outcome of those choices that at the time felt like the right thing to do, ended up decimating a whole culture. What Canada's indigenous people have endured is unconscionable. It's amazing that their culture is still managing to revitalize in spite of it all, in spite of colonization's attempt to stamp it all out. And it's beautiful. Nothing brings me more joy than to hear their native languages spoken openly again, their songs sung proudly, their drums thumping like an undying heartbeat. I wish the First Nations community as a whole nothing but success.

Some people couldn't share this story, this belief of past lives and karmic connections. Perhaps they'd feel ashamed or embarrassed to associate with it. I carry no shame for these beliefs. I didn't create or destroy the residential school system. I didn't translate anything into Mohawk. I have no true memories about John Stewart outside of that deep knowing I felt through my dream and my karmic work. Any meaning I've made about those bizarre events in September of 2006 has been my own creation. I'd wondered for a while, if one of the reasons I'd created these connections was because my 11-year-old self felt such a positive, deep connection to the elders and the drumming at the pow wow, I could join those feelings into my karmic understanding of why I was molested and also because 12-year-old inner child has never stopped feeling responsible for what happened to her – most children feel responsible for abuse they endured until they have gone through counselling and trauma therapy.

She's not responsible. Don's actions were criminal and awful. I do not condone any criminal behaviour. But what I have now that I didn't have before is a super awesome, first-hand experience about why it's important for me not to judge other people, ever. There is a larger picture at work that we are unable to see in our short lifespan. I believe fully in reincarnation. In choosing that spiritual path, it is important for me to work through forgiveness for everyone, and to let go of my judgement while at the same time healing my own trauma because I have no idea what my soul connection is to the people who I feel have wronged me. I have no idea, on a spiritual level, in the big picture – bigger than the 80 years I'll likely get here – what is going on or why. The man who just robbed me may be returning karma to me from twenty lifetimes ago because I robbed him or someone else. I do know that things happen in this life for a reason and I am almost never privy to that reason. I can mourn my inner child who was damaged, who had her innocence taken from her. And I can also forgive the man who did it. My forgiveness does not mean I'm condoning his behaviour. It means that I am going to let go of it, so I can allow myself to be free of the anger, free of the hurt, free of the judgement – all of these emotions being results of Don's actions. His actions are between his god and himself.

What if every time I forgave someone in this lifetime, I am actually forgiving myself for something my soul did 500 or 20 lifetimes ago? What if both of us – Don and I – can get off a karmic hamster wheel of me hurting him, him hurting me, me hurting him, forever in a karmic cycle, by me just saying, "I forgive you"? What if I never have to repeat this cycle again? Wouldn't that be nice?

I always cringe when I hear people say, "Karma's a bitch, you'll get yours." If you really believe in karma then that understanding would suggest that whatever is happening right now that is making you say, "Karma's a bitch," is karma coming back to smack you in the ass from a few lifetimes ago. People struggle with this because they often think of karma as only existing in this single lifetime they are living. They can't imagine (or understand) why someone is stabbing them in the back now. It's why I strive for forgiveness. I don't want to keep playing the karma game lifetime after lifetime wondering why I keep getting smacked in the ass. I don't wish people's karma on them, I wish them healing. I wish them opened eyes. I wish them well.

Karma is a difficult energy. I personally believe it's similar to what the Buddhists teach – to understand something, you must experience it. To me, that means experiencing everything, from every angle so that we fully understand it. How can I judge Don? I didn't walk in his shoes. What are the chances he was molested as a young boy by a priest or teacher in the residential school? What are the chances he was beaten for speaking his native tongue? What are the chances he was made to feel inferior? With or without the concept of karma, I'm certain that Don experienced a horrendous childhood. I hope he has found healing in the spirit world since the time of his passing.

We all have a unique set of experiences that make us who we are, that make us do the things we do. I'm not condoning violent and harmful behaviour. Not at all. All of it needs to be dealt with in the courts. Victims have every right to feel wronged, to feel angry, and to want justice. It's important that we feel those feelings, work through them, and for the love of god, get counselling. My story is an example of how all of this is possible.

At the end of it all, in order to complete the healing, we have to let the anger go. I have a toolbox full of tools that have helped me forgive, and this story about karma is just one of them. Why is it important? Because when my life fell apart and I ran away with nothing but the shirt on my back, the one thing I prayed for every day was to find peace. Forgiveness plays a huge part in feeling peace. You may find peace through Jesus, through understanding karma, through Ho'oponopono – there are many ways to find your own inner peace. For me, forgiveness is key. If there's one thing I've spent a huge amount of time trying to master (and I'm damn close), it's forgiveness. It's one of the keys to the Universe. It might not be one of your keys, but it sure as hell is one of mine. And it brings me one heck of a lot of peace. I don't have to understand why everything happens right now, I just accept that it does, and I believe that after this lifespan, I will understand it better when my soul and god sit down to review the life of Tracey Rogers. I trust that the Universe has a plan and that the plan is good.

I started telling this part of my story because It's the End of the World as We Know It came on my headphones, and I wanted to explain a 'shift' I experienced. I shifted from being angry and feeling like a victim to learning how to forgive and be a survivor, a thriver. This was one of a million examples in my own thinking that had shifted and changed after 2006. It doesn't mean I'm right and you have to believe what I believe, but I've found a set of beliefs that work for me. Find a set that works for you. I believe in the Universe, in karma, in forgiveness. These are some of the life-changing tools in my toolbox.

* * *

As December 21st, 2012 approached that year, I had known something was going to shift but I hadn't known what. As I had mentioned earlier, in the fall of 2012 I participated in the Self Employment Assistance program to help me open my business. I had heard about it before I moved to Windsor at the beginning of 2011. I had kept the information tucked away already knowing I had a desire to open a Reiki business – that had been why I had started doing my certification as soon as I moved to Windsor. From June of 2011 until the fall of 2012, I'd sold my artwork, my jewelry, my book of poetry, and I'd offered Reiki for donations. By mid 2012, I'd felt ready. It had been time to consider opening a business beyond vending and art fairs.

My opportunity to begin the Self Employment Assistance program (SEA) had come in the fall. I'd attended some pre-program classes and developed my early business plan. The first version was forty-five pages long. After submitting it, I'd eagerly waited for a response to find out if I'd officially be accepted into the program. I had been on a boat slowly trolling on the Detroit River, heading out to Peche Island with a group of Recovery people (eleven of us altogether) when the call came in. We'd been having a wonderful day together; that was one of the gifts of sobriety. My cell phone rang. I'd picked it up. I'd been at the front of the speed boat having turned my back to the group so I could hear the call. The person had identified themselves as being with the SEA program, and just as they were saying to me that I'd gotten accepted into the program, a blue heron flew in front of the boat, five feet away from me at the most, at eye level. Wooooohoooooo!

I'd already been familiar with heron medicine and magic as I had had so many experiences with herons my entire life. I had looked up their mystical meanings many times. For myself, any time heron shows up, it's offering an opportunity. Herons are flexible; they bend with the wind. Heron people will always find a niche they fit into. Heron is peaceful, it brings tranquility, but it also knows when to move – always at the perfect moment. Standing perfectly still like a statue, it will dart its long neck out like a flash of lightning and snatch unsuspecting fish from the waters.

Life had been offering me an opportunity with that phone call. The sign had been clear as the blue-sky day. And the importance of my sobriety in that offering was made very clear to me by the company I was keeping at that precise moment. It had been a truly incredible way, place and time to receive the amazing information about the program. All signs had pointed to success with my small business!

On December 6th, a few months later, I opened my business, White Feather Holistic Arts. My entire world had shifted in amazing, awesome, magical, fantastic, wonderful ways. Simply opening the business at all was a major shift. I had to walk through many fears to get to opening the doors. Questions of worth and worry had plagued my thoughts. Was anyone going to come into my business? Why would people come to me for Reiki instead of someone else? Was my artwork good enough to sell? Who would buy my artwork? Were my tarot readings good enough? Who has $60 to spend on a reading? Not me! Oh my god, I signed a three-year lease? These were some of my thoughts...and the financial fears, well I had financial fears galore!

I sat myself down one day and forced myself to look these fears in the face. "What is the worst-case scenario here?" I'd asked myself. The answer surprised me. The worst-case scenario was that if the business failed, I'd be right back where I already was, working jobs I didn't want to work at. That had been the worst-case scenario I could think of. Best case scenario? My dreams would come true and I'd love what I did for a living. Choosing the best-case scenario was a no brainer! What the hell was I risking? Absolutely nothing.

Once I'd opened the doors, I'd spend hours and hours working on affirmations to continue to build my confidence:

I am loved.
I am worthy of love.
I am worthy of having a great job.
I am worthy of feeling happy.
I am worthy of knowing comfort in my life.
I am a successful business owner.
People love my artwork.
People appreciate my reiki services.
Many people can afford my services and products.

And so on. I had a full page of them that I'd read over and over and over for weeks and months. When the business had first opened, I had time to do my affirmations, so I did them. I'd already been doing affirmations for years so I was well-practiced in the tool. Louise Hay, in her book, You Can Heal Your Life, teaches about affirmations, about how they are new ways of speaking to yourself. As I have already mentioned, when I lived in the trailer at Roger's, I had the space covered in little yellow sticky notes with a different affirmation on each one. It took years to reprogram my wrong thinking - negative statements about myself, limiting beliefs, fearful doubts. And so, I've spent years working on my affirmations. It was worth it. Because I'm worth it.

I'm a child of the Divine Universe, a child of God, however you want to put it. As a child of the Divine, I am Divine. And I don't mean that in a prideful, haughty kind of way, like 'I'm better than you.' No no, so far from it! You are a child of the Divine too. You are Divine. And since I've realized that everything has changed. I treat myself so much better now, choosing things that will lead to me being happy, being comfortable, having the life I deserve to have. I treat other people so much better now, knowing who they are, and who I am. We're all interwoven. We are all part of something so much bigger than ourselves.

That was the end of the world – my old world, my pre-2006 world – as I knew it. All these ways of thinking had developed firmly into my work at White Feather; relating with the public, with myself, with god, with the Universe. My own understanding of how the Universe operates – my beliefs– became so much clearer in my mind and heart. My knowledge deepened. The things I just know, deep down in my soul, are so much easier for me to access now. My intuition is electric. My business blossomed through workshops, drum circles, tarot readings, artwork, conversations with customers (who became friends), helping strangers, listening.... really listening for the first time in my life. It's a whole new world I live in since those doors opened in December of 2012.

Thank you, Universe. Thank you for never giving up on me, even when I did.

MIRROR MIRROR

A road sign let me know that the Agawa Pictographs were coming up. I pulled my bike into the parking lot and got myself orientated. I left my chaps on, but I took off my leather jacket, leaving it draped across the saddle of my bike. When I leave my bike and jacket unattended like that, my club patch sits right where anyone walking by will see it. Nope, my club isn't scary in any way – the most law-abiding, down to earth bunch of people you could ever meet. But I think people think twice about stealing when they see a patch on the jacket.

Grabbing my good camera, I started walking down the path. What a beautiful day, what a beautiful forest! There was a clear path through the trees with signs to make sure people didn't get lost leading to the pictographs. The grade of the land was going down and then further down. I knew I would eventually end up at Lake Superior. Partway through my walk, I came across this huge chasm in the rock where the entire wall was split, and through the other side of the chasm, I could see Lake Superior. A woman was there with her dog and she was trying to take a picture. I offered to take a picture of them together, and then she offered to take a picture of me.

Noticing my chaps and boots, she asked me where I was headed on my motorcycle. I started to explain the Women Riders World Relay, and she stopped me exclaiming, "No Way! My friend Julie is going on that! She's up in Thunder Bay and she's doing that leg of the relay!" I knew Julie from the Facebook groups. We'd all been introduced to each other online, sort of, and her name was in a lot of the postings. "Wow, what a small world," said Michelle. Yep. What a small world indeed. Here I was, hiking out by Lake Superior looking for some First Nations pictographs, and the only person I ran into knew what the hell the WRWR was!

After taking some photos of each other, we headed down to the pictographs. When we got to the spot, I wasn't overly excited about crossing over. I would have to walk on rock that was slanted, and if I slipped, I'd land right in Lake Superior. If I'd been using my brain at that moment, I would have taken the time to take my chaps and my boots off and gone barefoot. Barefoot is the safest way to go when you don't have the proper kind of rubber on your boots for hiking over rocks. Motorcycle boots have a hard rubber, meant to last if it got dragged on the asphalt. That is not good hiking rubber.

Hiking rubber, for these kinds of rocks anyways, needs to be soft and dig into the rocks, grabbing them. Even though I knew all of this, I headed out on the rocks anyway.

Being super careful, I made it to the pictographs which were just a few feet away from the rocky crossing. I took a quick moment to connect energetically. I put my hands up on the rock, but away from the paintings, and I allowed the rock to enter into me. I thanked the people who had painted the images. I sent my love to them. I had nothing physical with me to offer, so I offered my love, my prayers, and hoped that that was enough. I pulled my head back as far as I could so that I could see the pictographs and capture them on my cell phone.

There was a canoe, a horse and a lynx-looking animal. I'd read that some of the images were believed to be manitous. The images were amazing! There wasn't room for me to take a photo with my good camera. There wasn't room for anything! One step back and I'd be sliding right into a very chilly lake. To get photos of me with the pictographs, I'd have to inch my way back to safety. Michelle (Julie's friend), didn't venture onto the rocks. Frankly, I can't blame her. It was treacherous and I'm shocked that Parks Canada hasn't built some kind of a platform or something, bolted into the rocks. Though, I suppose their only chance of preserving the space was to keep it nearly inaccessible.

Michelle and I walked back up the path together, but we took a different route up a very steep set of stairs that were put into a huge crack in the rocks. I asked her what she'd done before visiting the pictographs, and she explained that she had driven some rescue dogs (puppies) to a shelter in the Soo. Having a big enough vehicle, she figured it was the least she could do to help the poor pups. I promised to say hello to her friend Julie as I got ready to get back on my bike. She left with her dog. I was ready to take off when a retired married couple pulled up in an SUV beside me, and we started talking. Of course, we started talking about motorcycles, and inevitably, the WRWR. After sharing my motorcycle joy, I honked, waved and pulled out of the lot.

I've read online that some of the pictographs are said to be much older than others, perhaps more than a thousand years old. Apparently, there are hundreds of images. I only saw a few and these ones were said to have been created in the 17th or 18th century. Possibly drawn when John Stuart was walking the earth between 1740 and 1811. I wonder what he'd think of them still here on the wall a few hundred years later.

The pictographs were my favourite sightseeing stop on my trip. They were incredible. The site was beautiful. I love history. I love Nature. I love First Nation's culture and history. I made a mental note to thank Kelly for the suggestion because any trip through the area would have been incomplete without seeing the pictographs!

This was what the road trip was all about. This was why I had taken eight days – more than enough time – to drive up to Thunder Bay. I wanted to be able to dally along the way, to have shorter ride days. To stop where I wanted to stop and see what I wanted to see. To adventure according to my own pace and the many little gems that friends suggested I see.

I continued down Highway 17 awed by the scenery around me, awed by my day so far. The speed limit was 90km an hour. I drove 90km an hour, much to the chagrin of most of the other vehicles going the same direction. There were a few reasons I kept to the speed limit. First of all, I was sightseeing and I wanted to take in the magnificent landscape. It really was spectacular; one of the most beautiful riding days I'd had. I was also keeping my eyes peeled for moose. At every swampy or marshy looking area, I slowed down and scanned the landscape for a moose. I felt certain that somewhere, sometime on this trip, I was going to see a damn moose! The third reason for staying at that speed, or lack thereof, was that this was the curviest road I'd ridden on, and I was doing it by myself without another rider ahead or behind me to connect with if something went wrong.

The roads went up and down and around as they snaked through that mountainous landscape. Curves were a part of riding that I wasn't 100% confident with yet, certainly not at high speeds. When I was riding with groups back home, I was the one who was going the speed limit through almost every curve, which I realized, could have been a disappointment for the folks behind me who were forced to go the speed limit too. But they did, and they did it without a single complaint. Why? Because the rules of the motorcycling world include that we ride to the level of our weakest link in a group. I'd only been riding for just over a year. I was often the weakest link and I was ok with that. I didn't feel pressured by anyone to ride differently or faster than I did.

As I drove through this landscape, I was super grateful that Ron and I had gone on a bike trip to Manitoulin Island with Kelly and Todd on the long weekend only a few weekends before. On that trip, we had driven on some very curvy, fun roads, and I had practised speeding up on the curves. I had also gotten some valuable night riding experience – in the pitch black. Until that trip, I'd had very little night-time experience on the bike, and what I did have was mostly near cities, where the glow from the city lights keeps the roads semi-bright.

I had a scary moment on that trip. We had gotten off the ferry to the island just before 10pm. It was cold and dark out. We were riding in formation, and honestly, I was not comfortable riding at the speed we were at. Cursing under my breath, things got worse. I started to feel my leather vest, the one with all my patches, flapping a bit on the right side. How could that be? It was tight against my body. Then a string flew up in my face around my helmet. At that moment, I realized that the leather lacing holding my vest together at the sides must have come undone. There was no way to pull over, nowhere to pull over, and no way to flag the other riders – they couldn't see me in the dark.

Things got worse. My vest started flapping all over the place. I was praying and cursing at the same time. When we did finally pull over maybe twenty or thirty minutes later, I stopped, got off my bike, and looked at the damage. The lacing was gone but everything else was intact. Kelly came over to help me. Todd wondered what Kelly and I were doing. Kelly shouted "Wardrobe malfunction!" I laughed. Grateful that we stopped and relieved that no major damage had occurred. Everything that happens is either a blessing in disguise or the lesser of two evils. This incident was a blessing in disguise.

The result of my leather vest tragedy was that I replaced the black lacing with purple leather lacing – purple is my favourite colour.

Listening to my playlist can be a jarring and bizarre experience at times. My musical collection is eclectic and all over the place, just like my spiritual beliefs and the core of who I am. Up next, with the wind blowing around me, sky watching over me, rocks encircling me, motorcycle rumbling underneath me was By Thy Grace, by Snatum Kaur.

This song brings me peace. I feel close to god when I sing along with the simple lyrics. Grace has been an ongoing theme in my Recovery. Grace gives us the room to be imperfect. Grace allows us to try again. When we get sober, (from any addiction – sex, gambling, drugs, alcohol, shopping, etc.) at some point we have to get honest with ourselves. Whether it's through the 12 steps or some other series of spiritual awakenings. It's almost impossible for an addict to stay sober and not do this. If we don't like ourselves, why stay sober? And if we don't know ourselves, truthfully, how on earth do we expect to stay sober? Good hard introspection, self evaluation and shadow work led me to understand that there were parts of me that I needed to work on, parts that I wanted and needed to improve.

This truth didn't reveal itself easily. I had a whole hell of a lot of ego standing between me and my weaknesses. What I discovered as I worked on these parts of myself was that these coping mechanisms – that's what most of my weaknesses were – stemmed from my subconscious. None of them were consciously or maliciously created. I was unaware of what the roots of most of my behaviour were. That doesn't make it less harmful. In my youth, some of my needs had not been met, and so I'd started figuring out how to get those needs met through unhealthy coping mechanisms.

Self awareness was the key for me. I had to be aware that I had the potential to participate in behaviour that wasn't...the best I could do. For me, that awareness started in 2011. I'd been working on sobriety and I'd gone through my steps a few times already. I'd started to see myself, usually through other people. What I mean by this is, if I witnessed a behaviour that I didn't like in others, I would hold a mirror on myself to see how or if I behaved the same way. Some perfect examples – do you remember some of the folks from the US I talked about? Chris, the hotel manager, my boyfriend Rob? Glenn in his green RV at the camping area? I had been able to see their alcoholism the moment I'd met them. What I'd failed to recognize was that they were mirrors for my own alcoholism. The Universe had surrounded me with alcoholics – classic Law of Attraction, but I hadn't been holding up a mirror on myself then, so I hadn't seen myself in them.

I'm not going to name any of the people that I was holding the mirror up to in 2011 through to 2013. If an addict wants to get a good look at herself all she has to do is start hanging out with people who have addictions – active or not. I'd made some big mistakes during those two years, but I'd also grown in leaps and bounds. I'd started to be aware of these huge mistakes though usually not right away, and that was okay. It took the time it took for me to become fully aware.

I'd gained such a deeper understanding of myself and my actions. I'd started seeing the emotional roots of my decision making. And I'd learned from them. I'd worked on all of it in the hopes that I wouldn't have to repeat the mistakes. In the process, I'd been hurt too. Being hurt taught me something else though. It was during the times of hurt and pain that I'd learned to create boundaries for the first time in my life. It had been a painful learning curve, but well worth it.

What do I mean by boundaries? I mean, clearly outlining in relationships or friendships what is ok and what is not ok regarding personal intimacy, communication, space – all the core parts of relating. Defining boundaries requires learning how to say 'no'. It requires learning how to live with other people's disappointment. It also requires learning how to enforce consequences when boundaries are not honoured. Part of the process of learning about how to create boundaries was a result of breaking other people's boundaries. I certainly wasn't a victim in any of this, nor was I a villain. I was learning and growing. I was learning how to apologize and I was learning how to ask for an apology.

All these processes, all the work, had been previously put into the category of 'bad' in my internal program. In years previous, I couldn't look honestly at boundaries, apologies, healthy relating because I'd thought it made me a bad person. If I'd admit to making a mistake through an apology, I was bad. If I'd refused to do something a partner really wanted me to do, that I didn't want to do then I was a bad person because they were disappointed in me.

However, the more I practiced these new ways of relating, the more I began to understand that they didn't mean I was bad. Certainly, there were parts of me that were broken, but establishing boundaries meant I was mending. Of course I didn't know how to have a healthy relationship – I had never in my life seen an example of that. My first sexual encounter was as a child with an adult. My following significant sexual encounters weren't much better. I grew up in a home with an alcoholic parent. None of these facts excuse my behaviour, but they make room for me to have compassion for my mistakes, for my unhealthy relationships, for my self sabotaging. Having compassion for myself motivated me to change what I could and work on the parts that were broken.

These were a few years of revelations for me. I was gaining a deeper and deeper level of self awareness. I was beginning to learn how to catch unhealthy behaviour, by myself, before I acted on it. I got to the place where a lot of it I could catch in my thought processes instead of after it had been acted upon. That's not to say that to this day I don't do things that I reflect on and say to myself, "That wasn't the best I can do." What it does mean is that at this time in my life, I do try to be aware of my behaviour and I try to correct it when I fail.

For me, having a healthy self esteem doesn't mean being a perfect person. What it does mean is that I'm being a self-aware person and I'm learning to show myself compassion. If there are traits in my personality that I'm not fond of in others, maybe I want to spend some time trying to correct that behaviour in myself. And if I make an error and that behaviour comes flying out anyways, I've learned to have some kindness for myself instead of beating myself up for it. If I catch myself saying, "Oh my god, why did you say that? You're horrible," to myself, I can put my hand over my heart and say, "I love the one who just said that." And I give myself some love. I'll try not to do it again. I watched a lot of Matt Kahn videos to learn about this type of self compassion work. I wish he'd started teaching earlier, it might have saved me some time.

I highly recommend shadow work and mirror work to everyone. I discussed mirror work a bit already – it's the practice of healing in myself what I see in others. The shadow is the 'darker side' of our personality. Our shadow holds the potential to do all things classified 'horrible' that human beings have ever done. It includes those traits we cannot stand in others as well as the traits we cannot stand in the self. Shadow work involves embracing that darker side of human potential, sending it compassion and healing, sending it love, and finding room to accept it. The purpose of shadow work is not to engage more in shadow type behaviour, but rather, the opposite. It is so that these 'shadow' traits/behaviours will cease to surprise and/or sabotage us when we least expect them.

Each of us has a shadow self that has acted out in one way or another whether it showed up as manipulation, anger, lies, infidelity, jealousy, greed, envy, gossip, fear, etc.. If I take the time to acknowledge the potential to behave these ways within myself, and send that part of myself some compassion, when the trait shows up, it's less likely to surprise me. If I don't acknowledge it, it can pop up without my even being aware it's popping up.

Shadow work can be extremely difficult, even traumatic to work through. I recommend doing this work with a professional, someone with a degree in counselling or psychology. Every single person on this planet, addict or not, could greatly benefit from this type of inner work. Twelve steps programs are greatly helpful too. In the steps, they use the terms 'character defects' and 'shortcomings.' I use different words for these terms now. I'm a fan of the term 'survival tools.' Because honestly, many of the traits we learn are learned to help us get through experiences when we don't have better tools to do so. Unhealthy behaviours are coping mechanisms. Even our addictions – they are coping tools. I'm not sure I would have survived what happened in my youth if I hadn't had certain traits to numb my pain. One suicide attempt was one too many.

With mirror work, I like to pick the person whose personality I struggle with the most and see if I can see myself in them. Here's a great example. Everyone hates a liar. Ask a group of people what traits they dislike the most in other people and lying is always near the top of the list. Yet, I beg you to find a single person who has never in their life told a lie. That's a big part of why people hate liars so much. We've all told lies. We all hate being lied to. But, remember being a kid and sneaking an extra cookie? Or telling your friend her dress looked great when really you thought it was ugly as sin? Or telling your parents you were going to sleep when you were reading your book with a flashlight under the sheets? Or how about the time you called into work and said you were sick when you weren't? It's possible that you felt badly telling these lies – small, medium or large sized. Perhaps it hurt your self esteem when you did it because you knew you were lying but you made the choice to do it anyway. Your face might even have turned red because you were ashamed of lying.

If you can learn to embrace the liar, admit that the potential of the liar always lies within you, because it does, then your chances of being sabotaged by the liar are much less. Your chances of the liar popping out when you least expect it, well your chances go down greatly if you can learn to accept the part of you that is very capable of telling a lie. Your hatred for liars begins to shift to compassion; you learn to accept the possibility of being one. The same rings true for every other difficult personality trait. Every single human being is, on some level, capable of doing anything another human being has done. The potential is within us all. If you can embrace that shadow self and accept the shadow as being a real potential, you can disarm it, and take its power away. It's part of self awareness – acknowledging your own potential.

You're welcome to think I'm crazy or off the mark with this. But my self esteem has gone from being nearly non-existent to thriving. My self loathing has turned into healthy self loving and self awareness. Shadow work and mirror work helped me to get here. It helps cultivate the kind of self love that allows every single one of us to be imperfect, to be wounded, to have quirks, to have 'survival tools', and hopefully use those tools much less, by having an awareness of them. Practising shadow work helps me forgive others much more easily. It helps me forgive myself. It helps me to embrace acceptance – and I'll tell you what – acceptance is the key to peace and happiness. Through my awareness of self, I am better able to see others completely as their whole self – instead of only seeing their good or their bad. And I have compassion when I see them. I see myself in them and I see them in me.

I see me fully now. I accept me as a whole person, not just the shiny parts I'm willing to look at with ease. Within myself, I can see the sinner and the saint. By seeing these parts wholly, I get to choose the part(s) of me that makes choices. And, it's no longer the broken version of me, it's the healed woman.

SCHOOL'S OUT

Katy Perry sang Roar confidently and loudly into my ears. Singing to myself under my facemask, I felt empowered, I felt strong, and I felt just like Katy must have felt when she wrote it. I love it! This is a great song when you have a job to do and it requires some strength to do it. It came out only a year before the time I would need it in my corner to give me courage. I'm particularly fond of it because of the 'roar' – I am woman, hear me roar!

I first heard this song around the same time I was going through a legal battle. The battle started in June of 2014. I had a weird dream. In the dream, I was in a motorboat with a bunch of friends from high school. While we were driving the boat, we saw other boats under the water. They were driving too, but beneath us. I was staring down into the water because it was bizarre to see boats moving under water. All of a sudden, a huge boat appeared beneath us and it started to rise up and out of the water. As it surfaced it looked like a humongous pirate ship. It had the jolly roger flag, and the entire boat was a giant skeleton – the hull had massive rib bones forming its shape and holding the whole thing together. Jewels and gems covered it from stem to stern, sparkling in the sunlight. I have never seen such a formidable pirate ship in any movie during my life. Without knowing how I got there, I was talking to the pirates who were dressed in suits on the deck of the pirate ship. Everyone got along. It was a peaceful meeting.

I journaled the dream as soon as I got up because it wasn't like most of my dreams. I knew it was significant, and that it had meanings I needed to pay attention to. What I gathered from my understanding of dreams was that something was going to surface in my life; something from my subconscious. Whatever surfaced was also associated with my emotions. Whatever it was that was rising up was going to be huge. And it was going to be a gem of a discovery. I hadn't associated the gems with money – I'd associated them with value. Something of great value was going to surface. Because the boat had been made of bones, I wrote in my journal that I thought that whatever was coming could be a skeleton in my closet – something from my past.

The dream was so amazing that I went to work and talked to both my workmates about it. I also talked to a few friends about it. I couldn't fathom what on earth was going to surface that hadn't already surfaced for me by then. I was sure I'd worked through all my crap by 2014.

In September of 2014, I had a series of clients and friends come into White Feather and tell me about their childhood traumas with sexual abuse. Two names would pop into my mind every time. The first name was Don and I'd dismiss it with, "nope, I've really done that work. That is a healed place." The second name was Kaiya and I'd dismiss it with, "That was different. It wasn't like that." But the synchronicity kept pursuing my mind, and eventually Kaiya's name kept surfacing.

I knew I was supposed to do something about what had happened with Kaiya. My gut said so every time someone mentioned childhood sexual trauma. I'd been spending time with a friend who I was helping emotionally as they worked through the legal system because of childhood sexual abuse trauma. Because of this, my mind automatically considered the law regarding my own childhood trauma, not only towards counselling. The law had been in my face at the time. My intuition had said to seek out a lawyer. At the same time as I'd applied for getting counselling, I'd consulted a lawyer friend as I had no idea where to start. Should I pursue something criminally? In civil court? I had no clue. My friend gave me the name of a lawyer in London who had dealt with a great many Catholic Priest abuse cases. I wasn't sure I'd wanted to pursue a civil case with Kaiya. I wasn't sure what I'd wanted to pursue to be honest. I put very little thought into it at the time. I'd been running almost solely on intuition and instinct.

Before deciding whether or not to hire him the lawyer I'd been referred to asked me to write out a timeline of every event I could remember related to the case, including my drug and alcohol use. I had never taken the time to review this phase of my life. I had ignored it, much like I would a skeleton in my closet. The one and only time I had brought it up with a counselor was when I was in my twenties. The counsellor reported what I'd said and it almost cost Kaiya her job, and I hadn't wanted that to happen. I felt like I'd been responsible for making sure she kept her job. Not only that, I'd felt responsible for the other people who had known about it at the time and not reported it.

When I drew out the timeline, I'd felt sick. I remembered tiny little details that I'd pushed into a dark corner for years. It had brought me no comfort to see it all written out. As an adult, looking at the timeline in such an objective way, I could see things I hadn't been able to see before. What the timeline revealed was a kid reaching out for help about previous abuse; a kid looking for attention; a kid finding that attention in a very unacceptable way. I could clearly see a suicide attempt followed quickly by a sexual relationship with the teacher, and immediate changes to a friend group and to substance habits. I saw a steamroller that had crushed me through to age eighteen until I'd ended the relationship and dove into my adult years from a terrible starting place.

I'd spent a few days in tears and in anger. I had never seen the relationship like that before. Before, I had only been able to see the love. I had only seen the concern she'd shown for me at the time. I had only seen Kaiya's good intentions. I had only seen myself as mature for my age. But when I'd drawn the timeline and I'd started writing about my experiences, I'd been able to see so much more. I could see the damage, the lack of self awareness that a fifteen-year-old girl can have. I certainly did not see myself as a mature adult, but a messed up kid who'd made mistake after mistake in her life at that time.

When I'd continued the timeline further into my adulthood, I saw how the relationship had affected my other relationships. I saw how my depression had bloomed. I saw how the relationship had linked to horrible lifestyle choices I had made. Sex, sexuality and self esteem – all of this had been affected.

It had been the drawing out of the timeline that sealed the deal. After a few weeks of sitting and just being with what had surfaced, I hired my lawyer on and became fully invested in pursuing a clear conclusion to this saga from my youth. What I was seeking was healing. What I had seen in the timeline clearly proved to me that I had unresolved issues because of the relationship with Kaiya.

The fact that I'd initiated a lawsuit generated an inner battle for me for more than a year. I struggled with feelings of responsibility – that is my own responsibility and role in the relationship. My psychologist had been certain that that teacher had used classic grooming (when one initiates and cultivates a relationship that culminates in sexual abuse) – which implies a maliciousness. I could see where he saw that, but I'd still been unable to wrap my mind around it. I believed she had been trying to help me – that she'd thought I was gay, and I'd just needed another gay person to love me. It had been my fault that she'd believed I was gay. This is what I had always believed. When I was fifteen, before any of this had started, she'd told me that she thought my problem was that I thought I was gay. Instead of saying no, I had said yes. And that moment right there, that answer, possibly changed my life history. What would have happened if I had told the truth and said, "I've never been attracted to girls?"

Around the same time as I was working through all of this, one of my nieces had been having some personal problems. I had been spending some time with her and talking with her. She was fifteen, almost sixteen. And do you know what I'd seen? I'd seen a kid – not even close to an adult. I'd tried to imagine an adult thinking that what would help her would be to get sexually involved with her. And it hurt my spirit to even try to imagine that. Staring back at me, every time I'd looked at her, I'd seen my fifteen-year-old self. For the first time in my life, I'd been able to accurately see myself at age fifteen. Disturbing is the only word that describes my reaction. How could any adult look into those young eyes, those confused eyes, those hurting eyes, and think that an intimate relationship was the cure?

Somewhere in all my counseling and observations, I'd finally seen the truth of the matter – I'd seen what I needed to see. It didn't matter. It didn't matter if Kaiya had been trying to help me or if there had been grooming. It didn't matter if I had been lying about being gay. None of it mattered. What mattered was that she'd broken the law and abused the position of authority that had been entrusted to her. There are no circumstances that ever make it ok for an adult in a position of trust and authority to be in a sexual relationship with a youth in their care. Zero. I hadn't been responsible for her job or for the other teachers who knew about it or for my counsellor who had also known about it. I hadn't been responsible for any of them. Their actions, twenty-seven-years previously, had been the problem. My actions had never been illegal. I hadn't broken the law.

During my court process, there'd been a time period when I was angry with all the adults who hadn't reported what had been happening. Why had no one reported it? I know the answer to that, and it's one that still doesn't sit well. Times have changed. But back in the 1980s when this had happened, I don't think anyone who knew about it was able to see a woman as a predator or a perpetrator. I can say without a doubt that if it had been a male teacher under the identical circumstances, everyone, including my mother, would have reported it. It took me twenty-seven years to look at it with a clear set of eyes and clear understanding because my predator had been a woman. In addition to that, the world had been just beginning the process of trying to become more open and positive towards the LGBT community.

My Mum hadn't known how things worked in gay culture. She had trusted advice that had been given to her. In an attempt to understand the times a bit more, I've spoken to gay women from the same age group as Kaiya, and so many either had a personal experience or knew of someone who had their first lesbian encounter with a teacher, a professor, a coach or a person in what would be considered a position of authority. Adding to this, I'd spoken to straight friends from the same age group and asked them if they ever heard about teacher-student relationships in highschool, and almost everyone was able to name off a few people they had known who had dated teachers in highschool, and some of them even married eventually. Being of a different mindset and time does not excuse bad behaviour, but it helped me understand how it all happened, and how it went unreported by so many people.

In the mess of the whole legal affair, I had a revelation. I'd been responsible for my own actions and the consequences of my own actions. I hadn't been responsible for the consequences of other people's choices and actions. In my Recovery, I had learned how to take responsibility for the results of my choices. In fact, like many recovered addicts – I'd actually taken too much responsibility. I hadn't been responsible for some of the people closest to me who had also made their own horrendous choices, but I'd felt responsible. Like many recovered addicts, I could see how I had failed, what I had lost, how I had hurt others...but I'd failed to see how others had failed, lost and hurt me. People like Kaiya.

She wasn't a bad person. I'd refused to believe that she was or that she is. I believe she came from a different time, with a different set of beliefs about the gay community – it was cloaked in secrecy and people trying to avoid losing their jobs and being outed. I believe that her choices back then had been horrendously misguided. I do believe she was trying to help me, even though my psychologist never saw it the same way. I believe she thought she was helping a young woman to 'come out' during a time when being gay was much more dangerous than it is now. But her intentions – good or bad – do not undo the damage caused. There are very good reasons why there are laws against what she did. The fact that during the legal proceedings she still seemed unable to see the relationship for what it was was frustrating to me.

During the lifespan of a lawsuit, there is a process called Discovery. The Discovery is when most or all evidence is brought forth by both sides. Documents are submitted, photos, medical information, financial documents, and more. The most important part of it for the plaintiff and the defendant is being questioned (though grilled is a more appropriate term!) by the opposite team of lawyers for a predetermined amount of time. Any questions they want to ask can be asked, and the other lawyer can try to object to certain questions.

Honestly, it was a horrible experience and an empowering experience all at the same time. Three lawyers had sat across the table from me, and my lawyer had sat beside me.

"Why didn't you say no when the 42-year-old man asked you into his house at age 12?", had come barreling out of one of the lawyer's mouths. Questions like this had been tossed into the mix with some tedious, boring material. I'd known what they were doing. They'd been attempting to lay some blame on me, and they were attempting to scare me away from the courtroom that we could progress to in a year or two. What had been empowering about it was finally being able to tell my story after twenty-seven years. I knew Kaiya (who hadn't been present in the room) would read my statements. I'd wanted her to read how the relationship had negatively impacted me. I'd wanted her to understand why we were going through this after so much time.

Her Discovery, which I read because I wasn't present for it, revealed a lack of fully understanding the impact of her actions. Perhaps it would be too much for her psyche if she fully grasped how terribly destructive her choices had been to my life. But it's really hard to forgive the self if you never look the reality of your choices in the eye. It's the kind of stuff you take to your death bed otherwise, unresolved. I don't wish that on anyone.

Partway through my counseling, my psychologist had asked me what I wanted from the lawsuit. "I want thirty minutes in a room with her, so I can explain the impact that she had on my life, my self esteem, my self image, my sex life, and my understanding of self," I'd responded. My psychologist looked at me with a frown and told me it was unlikely I'd get that. He explained she would probably never fully understand.

I wasn't legally pursuing what had happened as revenge. It hadn't been out of selfishness. It hadn't been out of anger. I'd just wanted to heal what was still broken. I had still never had a healthy adult relationship. I told my counselor that was one of my goals – to finally have a healthy relationship. I'd desperately wanted to know what that looked and felt like. I'd experienced issues that were directly related to that time in my life. My sexual confusion had never ceased to be an issue in my life – not from the moment I had ended my relationship with her.

I had an "Aha!" moment one day, just over a year into my counseling. I realized that it didn't matter whether Kaiya ever 'got it.' It didn't matter if she ever understood how this had affected me. That was Kaiya's business, not mine. What mattered was whether I understood how it had affected me. Was I going to walk away knowing myself better, and having better self awareness? What would the results of this case be in my life? Would I have a greater peace with my greater understanding? Answering these critical questions enabled my focus to change. I accepted the fact that the lawsuit was completely ok for me to pursue, and I took the opportunity to heal as much as possible, on the school board's dime while they paid for my counseling.

I will take a moment here to explain in a bit more detail how exactly this relationship affected me and caused damage. For twenty-seven full years, I questioned my own sexuality and my own understanding of self. I had believed Kaiya when she told me that "almost all women who play a lot of sports are gay." I had believed Kaiya when she told me that "bisexual people just refuse to accept the fact that they are gay. They are in denial." I was young...I was fifteen years old and very impressionable. For all of those years, twenty-seven of them, I had refused to look for a moment at that relationship. It was blocked and repressed from any healing I'd done. I felt responsible for four people either keeping or losing their jobs. I participated in the relationship. I put their careers in danger. I'd fully believed in the false narrative of the relationship created by Kaiya.

In a significant adult relationship spanning years of my life, my misunderstanding of my own sexuality led to an incredibly destructive set of choices and actions. A set of choices that would have been made entirely different if I had understood my own sexuality better. A set of choices that deeply wounded two people. I'd spent years in the abyss of addiction – a pattern of addiction that I can actually trace to starting approximately one month after the sexual abuse with Kaiya had started. Can I blame her for my years of addiction? No. I bear some responsibility once I became an adult and didn't heal what motivated the addiction. But it was disturbing to me to see the direct relationship between the abuse and addiction in my timeline. I will never know for certain whether or not my path would have been the same without her.

I had a phobia of being a passenger in cars with most people until after my counselling started with the lawsuit. I had no idea what the root of that phobia had been until I took myself back to when Kaiya had driven me around in London. I would have to lay the seat down and hide so that no one would see a teacher and student together. To this day, I get overwhelmed with anxiety visualizing that memory.

In 2010, I came out as gay thinking I had finally figured out all of my problems, that Kaiya must have been right; tomboys like me were gay. There is no part of me that believes my sexuality wouldn't have been easier to figure out if a trusted adult hadn't abused my trust, and filled my head with all sorts of out-dated, bullshit understandings of sexuality. Since the time I was in a relationship with Kaiya, I have experienced anxiety, depression and PTSD symptoms. All of these issues improved greatly when I finally got counselling beginning in 2014. I struggled the entire time, (even to this day) about how to classify what happened with Kaiya. It took months in counselling to use the word "abuse" to describe it, but I still naturally fall to using the word "relationship." I can look back at fifteen-year-old me and see the reality of who I was – emotionally immature, surrounded by walls, angry, with a huge chip on my shoulder, desperate for attention from my parents, suicidal, depressed. Yet still, I want to call it a relationship because there is a part of me that will always feel like I had more control than I actually did if I think about it that way. I had been old enough to feel responsible.

Any time I want or need to remember my fifteen-year-old self objectively, I spend a few minutes talking to a fifteen-year-old. I am easily able to question how the hell any adult could do what Kaiya did to a kid? Because a fifteen-year-old is a kid. My counsellor and I felt that dropping out of my fourth year of University had been intricately tied to the abuse. It is no coincidence that at that exact same time, I had requested a meeting with Kaiya, myself and my counsellor because a decade of deep depression had begun. On a more personal, intimate level, my sexual relationship with Kaiya had initiated a twenty-eight year pattern of sexual dysfunction. At the time we'd had our first sexual relation, I'd faked my first ogasm. I had done that because it seemed she wasn't going to stop a session together until I had an orgasm. This had quickly led to faking multiple orgasms because once she was confident she could make me orgasm, she'd wanted to see if she could make me orgasm multiple times. And I'd faked it, I'd faked it all. Glorious amounts of totally faked orgasms.

I had had orgasms before Kaiya, real ones, with two previous boyfriends. But I never had a real orgasm with a partner again until after my counselling had started in 2014. Why did I fake them for all those years? Because it made me feel more loved, more loveable – my partners had loved that I'd had multiple orgasms. For twenty-eight years, a piece of me had died inside every time I faked it. I had made attempts to come clean about the orgasm issue a few times over the years when an opportunity presented itself. I had made feeble attempts to stop faking, but I hadn't been able to. Try as I might, I could not orgasm with a partner.

Once I'd started counselling and I'd become comfortable talking about the problem, I'd started to work on it by having honest conversations with my intimate partner. It had caused frustration and anxiety. Sometimes I'd end up in tears during love-making. But it was worth it because now, my sex life is honest and real, and I am able to climax with a partner.

I've already mentioned this, but another result of being in the relationship with Kaiya was that I had massive trust issues. During the Discovery phase of the lawsuit, tonnes of pictures, poems and cards had been presented by Kaiya's legal team. I don't know if she'd thought they would help her case. I'd been shocked she had given it all to her lawyer. In amongst all of it was horrible poetry that I had written as a 15-year-old. I say horrible because it was horribly written. It made me laugh and cringe at the same time. It also made me want to be sick when I'd looked at the content of the poems. The word trust had been written over and over. I could feel my fifteen-year-old self reaching out for someone to trust. My heart had broken when I'd read my words.

My psychologist and I had spent many hours discussing trust in relationships. I'd clearly had virtually none. Making the connection between Kaiya and my trust issues had been an easy, obvious line to connect. As much as it doesn't matter whether Kaiya will ever be able to see the reality of what happened, it is vitally important to my own healing, to my own understanding of self, that I have compassion for how things got as messed up as they did. I can't blame her for the disaster that was my adult life, but I certainly can have compassion for the roots of where it all began. Trust had been a major root.

One of the more difficult things I'd worked through during the lawsuit was The Big Box of Fun, as I'd called it. It had been anything but fun. In a massive, heavy legal box were my medical records, doctor's visits info, hospital notes, psychologist and psychiatric reports, hospital admittances, educational history, and anything else the legal teams had collected for court. It held the paper trail of my life. When I'd received it in the mail at White Feather, my lawyer told me I needed to read the entire contents at least three times. Was he kidding? This thing was gigantic!

On my first pass through reading my entire recorded life, I'd bawled my eyes out and was overcome with grief. Documentation about my suicide attempt at fifteen was in there; counseling appointment notes from when I was a young teen, doctor visit information, records about a few hospital visits over the years – none of them resulting in being admitted to hospital; and then all the stuff from 2005 and beyond. As I'd read the nurse and doctor' notes, I'd been horrified. I'd wanted to curl up in a big ball and disappear.

The patient they'd written about in late 2005 and 2006 was batshit crazy. I knew I hadn't been well during that time, that I'd been psychotic, but this was the first time that

I'd been able to look at the depth of my psychosis fully. It had all been written down for me to read and face. Going through the memories, including the stuff from my youth, had hit me like a tonne of bricks. I couldn't breathe, my stomach had tightened, anxiety had shaken through me. Kaiya had even been mentioned in the nurse's notes after my suicide attempt at fifteen. It angered me to see that when I was fifteen, I had made a weak attempt draw a line between her and my suicide. I'd felt anger because a part of me knew, even then, that the relationship was taking dangerous turns, but no one had been able to put two and two together. My fears about the conspiracy in 2005 were in the doctor's reports from the hospital. Everything was in those notes – every real thing that had ever hurt me, and every imagined conspiracy that had never existed. But I'd done it. I'd made it through The Big Box of Fun. I'd cried a hell of a lot of tears, but I knew I had to read through it all – three times. All of what was in that box was going to come up in court.

I'd waited a day or two before I read through it all again. That time? There'd been some tears, but they'd been tears of relief. The shock had been taken away after the first read. On the second read, I'd thought to myself, my god Tracey! You're amazing!!! It's a miracle that you're even alive and that you survived all this shit!!! This box... this box is the record of everything you survived! And not only survived, but here you are, sober, strong and recovered, a successful business owner, and so much more, fighting for yourself! Way to go Tracey!!!

That's right. If you had your own Big Box of Fun, you'd be absolutely amazed at what you've overcome in your life. You'd pat yourself on the back. You'd be a Rockstar! It doesn't matter if your story looks totally different than mine, the process is the same when we venture into our personal histories. We all have a Big Box of Fun that holds a record of everything we've overcome – the hardest stuff, the stuff that almost destroyed us, but didn't.

My third read through the box had merely been for memory's sake, so that if I'd need to recall any of the information in court, I'd be able to.

My astrologer, Dan Alice, told me in early 2015, that I was in the middle of my Saturn Return (he had no idea about the lawsuit), and that a cycle that had started for me when I was fifteen was coming full circle. Saturn Returns are a 29.5-year astrological cycle. He told me that my Saturn Return would complete itself in the late fall of 2017 or at the very latest, early 2018. But he was pretty certain that it would end before the year 2017 ended. He saw nothing but success in the outcome. Amazed, I'd stared open-mouthed at him as he explained all of this to me. How on earth had he known that I was completing a cycle that had started when I was fifteen based on my birth date and time alone?

By late 2016, I'd had a court date set for November of 2017. It had been the last thing on my mind. My mother was dying.

In September of 2016, Mum had some health issues so she went to the hospital. It hadn't taken too long for the doctors to discover a collapsed lung, a massive growth on one lung, and a plethora of other issues. It had taken six weeks for a full diagnosis, but we'd known. Mum had stage-four lung cancer. To receive the news officially had been devastating. From the time she'd been admitted to the hospital until the day she left this earth, I'd seen her almost every single day. While she was in the hospital, I'd drive three hours each day to make that visit, and when she was moved to hospice, I'd drive an hour and a half a day to be with her. I'd cut my work hours down to the bare minimum, and only did what I had to do. My co-workers and my employees had covered all the hours at the store.

I'm going to tell the story of the end of my mother's life in another part of this book. She deserves her own, very special, very honoured section. My mother is more important than lawsuits, lawyers and money.

The opposing lawyers had wanted to interview my mother in the hospital before she died so they could get her statements. My family and I had made sure that didn't happen. I hadn't given a crap if it could cost me the entire court case – there was no way that her last memories would include a group of lawyers asking her where she was while I was with the teacher or why hadn't she known I was being abused or why, when she did find out hadn't she reported it. Screw that. My Mum had done her best during that time in my life. And nope, it wasn't "the best", but it was "her best." She had sought out advice from professionals when I was sixteen and I'd told her about Kaiya. Every professional had advised her not to report it. My Mum had the best intentions concerning the decisions she'd made at the time, and she hadn't made the decisions alone.

My Mum passed, February 5th, 2017.

I'd spent time mourning my mother's passing and dealing with my grief. Sooner than I would have wanted to, I had to return to legal matters – lots was happening. I'd had to fully grasp a teaching in the spring of 2017. For years, I had been preaching to clients about the concept of not taking things personally. It was based on one of the four agreements from Don Miguel Ruiz's book, The Four Agreements. I really thought I had the understanding and the teaching down, but I'd learned during the lawsuit proceedings that I did not.

I'd been getting upset by legal processes. I'd been getting upset with the choices and actions of lawyers. And it had made me angry. Any time I'm angry, I know it's because really, I'm either hurt or I'm afraid. Anger never sits alone as an emotion – it always sits over hurt or fear. So, why had I been hurt? I'd been hurt by the things the lawyers had chosen to do during the lawsuit – things I'd believed were downright insensitive and uncaring. One of the legal parties had included my mother in the lawsuit as a fourth party. They'd sued my Mum on her deathbed. As I'd sat pondering one day, trying to figure out why I'd felt so angry, it dawned on me – I was taking their actions personally believing that they'd anything to do with me. The lawyers and everyone involved in the court case would have made the same choices, done the same things, said the same things, regardless of whether it had been me or any other plaintiff in a case. They'd done what lawyers are trained to do. A lightbulb had turned on with that realization.

I'd finally gotten it. Everything you say and do says something about who you are. It doesn't have anything to do with me. Everything I say and I do says something about who I am. But still, we take things personally. People don't do stuff 'to' us as much as they do stuff, and we react and we choose to be affected. A person could do the exact thing whether we were in their life or someone else. For example, a friend lies behind your back and betrays you. That's aggressive language to describe what happened. Another version of the same reality could be that a friend told a lie to make themselves look better. Their lie is affecting you, but how it affects you is up to you. The lie has nothing to do with you. It's a reflection of who that person is, that's it. There is nothing personal about it – they would lie to another person because that's the kind of person they are, and they need to make themselves feel a certain way. When I look at people's actions in this way, it makes it a lot easier for me to come to a place of acceptance concerning people's bad behaviour. Their choice has nothing to do with me – it's affecting me, and I decide how and what my reaction will be. The sooner I can let it go, the less it affects me.

I'd found peace in this teaching. In fact, I'd found a hell of a lot of peace in it because I'd started applying it to every single hurtful place in my life. My Dad hadn't abandoned me when I was twelve as I had told myself for years – my Dad had divorced my Mum. That was the fact. That was what happened. He'd had no idea how to successfully navigate his relationship with me through the divorce, and neither had I. He would have done the same thing whether I had incarnated as his child or any other soul in the Universe had been his child. He did what Bob would do. Plain and simple.

Don's abuse hadn't been personal, he would have done the exact same thing with any other vulnerable young person. Don hadn't done it to me because I was 'me.' He'd done it because I was a present, vulnerable child and he took advantage of what he saw as an opportunity. Yes, it greatly affected me. You see, children take all this stuff very personally – they internalize it. As a child, I'd internalized what happened by asking myself what was wrong with me that that person acted this way? Why did I get abused? Why doesn't my Daddy love me? These questions lived on inside me into adulthood. Other people's behaviour is a reflection of them, period. It was time for me to stop taking it personally. Since that time, in the spring of 2017, I have stopped taking other people's behaviour personally. I finally, for the first time since I was a kid, understood what belonged to you and what belonged to me.

I hadn't been responsible for Kaiya's job, for Susan's (the counsellor I started seeing after my suicide attempt), for the other two teachers who had known about Kaiya and I. I had taken legal action in response to the results of their choices, not mine. Their choices made them legally responsible for their actions. Furthermore, if I chose to sue Kaiya, the results wouldn't be up to me at all. It was up to the legal courts to decide if she did or did not have a legal responsibility for her choices and actions. As well, by legal definition, it followed to question whether the school board bore any responsibility in what occurred?

My choices and the consequences of those choices, belonged to me, including the consequences of choosing to sue. If the courts ruled in my favour, great, if they didn't, great - but I could own the consequences either way. Yours belong to you. Eureka! Understanding ownership of choices had been one of the biggest blessings that came out of this entire saga. Peace was all I ever wanted.

In November of 2017, the lawsuit ordeal was over, exactly as my astrologer Dan had predicted. It was settled out of court. I am forbidden discussing the terms of that settlement. What I will tell you is what I did at that time. Using money from Mum's inheritance, I took myself on a trip to the Dominican Republic so that I could digest everything that had happened since October, 2014. I was able to spend time thinking fully about my Mum because court was over. I also bought myself a cherry red 2010 Yamaha V-Star 650 motorcycle with the intention of getting my beginner's license in the Spring. In January of 2018, just a few months later, I took scuba diving lessons and got certified in the ocean in Bonaire; all courtesy of Mum. I started to check things off my bucket list, one by one. If my Mum's death at a fairly young age had taught me anything, it was to do the stuff you want to do today, not tomorrow.

* * *

I will never know for sure what anyone's intentions were thirty years ago. I will only ever know my own. The bottom line is I've learned that it doesn't matter. Regardless of whether Kaiya was trying to help a messed up 15-year-old kid or whether she had a darker personal agenda – it doesn't matter. She broke the law. Her decision to break the law left me scarred with a plethora of issues that would take me three full years of weekly counselling, and a hell of a lot of self work to untangle and pull into the Light. These scars affected my adult relationships. I don't hold Kaiya responsible for my adult years, although the law might have. Kaiya and I have karma from somewhere before this lifetime. And I hope whatever things we both needed to see and learn, we've seen and learned in this lifetime.

I hope her heart has been able to heal, I really do. Something like this doesn't just wound one person, it wounds everyone involved. I had to go through the legal process that I went through for my scars to get healed. I never would have sat through years of counselling sessions, and unravelled what I needed to unravel without choosing to go forward with the legal proceedings. Once upon a time in my life, in fact, for twenty-seven years of it, I hadn't taken the steps toward a civil suit because I'd felt responsible for everything in the first place. One of the greatest things I'd learned in 2017 was about what belongs to you and what belongs to me. The consequence of your choices belong to you, your words and your actions belong to you. The consequence of my actions belong to me, as well as my words and my actions. During my counseling, I'd been able to come to a place of acceptance and deeper understanding regarding my sexuality which had been a point of confusion for me since age fifteen. The shame that was attached to sexuality had become untangled as well. After thirty years of holding secrets and lies inside of me all of them were in the Light.

I'm not sure there was ever a villain in this story. I don't think so. But it bears repeating because this is the kind of shit that can keep us high and drunk for years if we don't bring it into the Light. This is the kind of stuff that can keep you hating yourself because you don't understand yourself and the choices you're making. A sexual relationship, at such a young age, with an adult in a position of authority, messes you up in ways that no human being is able to heal by themselves. If it's a same-sex relationship that can add more baggage and more damage. After three and a half years of sobriety, I loved myself enough to face that personal demon, and bring it into the Light. And then? The emotional program that had been running in the background for years and years had finally been dismantled. That program would no longer make choices for me, from a place of unawareness. Every scar, unhealthy trait and trauma I heal gives me awareness and engages my awakened abilities to make better and better choices. It's worth it to do the work.

I couldn't have gotten a lawyer and experienced the court case earlier than I did. I'd needed to have three-plus years of sobriety under my belt. I'd needed to have a good sense of self awareness. I needed to heal some of the stuff that got healed early in my sobriety before I would have the courage and/or the ability to work through the court process. It was stressful, and it required me to use all my spiritual tools to not lose my shit during the journey. I hadn't handled the entire thing with grace – just ask my lawyer – but I'd handled the entire thing. And it wasn't just the legalities and court process; my mother's passing had been right in the middle of it. I'd devoted three years of intensive counseling to work through my demons. What I'd experienced in those three years is the stuff that could have driven a more newly sober version of myself back to drinking. I am proud of myself for working through the entire thing as well as I did. I could hear my Mum saying from the other side, "I'm proud of you, honey."

Roar. There is no fight left in me when I sing this song. Just a big smile and a whole lot of forgiveness for everyone, including Kaiya, including me.

The Judgement card in Tarot fits perfectly into that time in my life. In a different deck that I use, it is called the Karma card. I find it helps me to fully understand the meaning of The Judgement card. When I say Karma here, I mean those lessons we incarnated to learn. I personally think of them as a soul contract we agreed to before we arrived. In our lives, the unfolding of karmic lessons begin in our childhood with the hurts, the traumas, the loss of innocence, the things that we will have to overcome later in life. For some people, this happens through horrific events, and for others it can be much more subtle. For example, it could be as simple as our mother always telling us it's important that we look pretty whenever we go out. A karmic lesson? Yes, it develops when that woman grows up, and places her entire self worth and self image on how she looks to others. Self worth will end up being one of her teachings, if she is awake enough to listen. How could that unravel? Maybe she gets cancer, and ends up losing her hair, and through that process, she learns to love herself for who she really is on the inside – with or without her hair. I can see her now, screaming to the world that she doesn't give a flying fuck if they like her grubby garden clothes or not; she's happy in those garden clothes. Karmic lessons come in all shapes and sizes.

Me? There were so many lessons tied up to those two-and-a-half years from my teens. Most significantly, I learned about responsibility. I learned how to own what I was responsible for, and not what others were responsible for. When people now do something that I would have called backstabbing in the past, I realize they aren't stabbing me in the back as much as they are making a self preservation choice that they would make regardless of whether it is me or someone else. And my mistakes? Same thing. My mistakes are never about other people, they're always about me. Forget what they've done, am I ok with what I've done?

The Judgement card fell into my life during the three years of legal proceedings, and in the end, I walked away with peace, healing and forgiveness for everyone involved. That's what the Judgement card is all about. There is a letting go with this card. We live, we learn, and we let go.

The Judgement Card
Rider-Waite Tarot deck

HEAD OVER FEET

I was getting close to Wawa, according to my GPS. I still hadn't seen a moose. Why no moose, god? I didn't feel like it was a big request...it was doable, no? But no moose. Keeping my eyes peeled along the roadside, I kept looking, and I kept listening to my tunes. As if god was picking my tunes for me, the next song that came on filled me with Love – Counting Stars, by One Republic. This song belongs to my husband Ron and I. It's our song. I'd known Ron for five years as an acquaintance and a friend. Every now and again, we'd see each other. We met at a birthday party in 2011, right after I'd moved to Windsor. At this party, there were many Reiki practitioners, holistic practitioners, spiritualists, psychic readers and people who were into a lot of the same stuff I was into. Ron and I ended up standing near each other in the room and we got talking. I was curious and pleasantly surprised to find out he had been trained by Dolores Canon in past life regression, and that he was a trained hypnotist. We got talking about how past life regression works and the kinds of things he would discover when doing it with people. Fascinating!

That night, Ron and I had talked for close to three hours, and I had been disappointed when our talk came to an end. Shortly after, he'd invited me to a Reiki Share, and he also invited me to the Holistic Network. He never asked me out, never hit on me, we just knew each other within the holistic community. Now and again he would come into my store – he'd supported me as did many in the community, when it opened. I remember he'd bought a piece of my artwork, and he'd attended a few meditations and workshops at the store. That had been it.

In the years following, my astrologer, Dan, had been telling me that in March of 2016, I'd meet "the one" – a very important romantic relationship would start in my life. As the time approached, I'd laughed. Even when he'd said it again in January of 2016. Not a chance Dan! I give up! I was pretty damn happy with my life, in fact, I'd loved it. I'd loved my job. I'd loved my friends. I'd loved my hobbies. And I'd loved my freedom. I was finally where I had always wanted to be – at peace and happy.

In February of 2016, Ron came to one of my work meditations at the last minute. I'd whispered to him, "You know, you're supposed to register. I've already turned some people away because it's full. But I love ya, so I'll let you in." I'd found out later from him that he had just decided to re-enter the dating world three weeks prior. He'd stared at me for most of the meditation because I'd said, "I love ya." After the event, I'd invited him to the sobriety dinner I was hosting the next week to celebrate five years of my sobriety. He'd accepted, and the next time I'd seen him was at El Mayor restaurant for the celebration dinner. People thought they were coming to have a meal with me, and that they'd be paying for it. I was happy to see how many had come – close to 40. However, I had a meal prepared for everyone, and the cost was on me. I had been so happy to be in a place in my life where I could afford to do that – maybe not everyday, but I could afford to pay for this celebration.

I was so joyful that night. I was so proud of myself, and I had every reason to be. For five consecutive years, I had not had a drink or a drug of any kind. My business was a success, and I had been self reliant through it all. There was no one else to pay the bills if I'd failed, this had all been on my shoulders, and I'd done a good job of it.

Ron brought a card for me that night – a birthday card for a five-year-old! I'd laughed! You get a lot of those at sobriety birthdays. I'd been surprised that he was familiar with the custom. After the supper, he asked me if I'd like to go out to dinner some time soon. I said I'd love to, and that I'd have to get back to him with a date once I had a look at my calendar at work. My celebration was on February 13th, 2016. Our dinner? We'd set it for March 3rd.

After that lovely dinner together in March, I'd said to my closest friends in an online chat, "I think I just had a date," but I wasn't 100% sure. He hadn't kissed me, but we'd both been more dressed up than we usually were when we saw each other. It had felt like a date with all the talk about relationships and family and personal history. I'd texted him and said, "I really enjoyed dinner. We should do that again soon." That had cinched it.

Up until that time, my main problem, which had stopped me from fully investing and fully loving in a relationship, had been with trust. I hadn't trusted anyone, especially men. But this...this had been different. I'd known him for five years before our first date. I'd known a great many of his friends in the community. We had been out many times together and he had always been a good guy. There was a pre-established trust that I'm quite certain was the reason the relationship could progress.

Our song that was playing, Counting Stars, dates back to our early dating. We had been on our first motorcycle ride together out in the county on his bike. The song came on the radio, but I'd never heard it before. I remember liking it instantly. When I'd listened to the lyrics later, they were perfect. Just like in the song, Ron and I were spending copious amounts of time together, we were staying up all night talking, and enjoying each other. When I wasn't with him, I was thinking about him and about us. It had been years and years since I'd felt like this. I had dated some wonderful people, but something had been missing...it was the 'big click and I'd clicked with him.

Something bizarre had happened after that first motorcycle ride together. I had a client come into my office and tell me about a disturbing thing he had seen on the 401 the day before. He said he had been driving along and he'd seen a motorcycle in his rear-view mirror. There were two people on the bike. The motorcycle had pulled up and started to pass him on the left. And then it had just disappeared. He'd panicked, thinking they had been in an accident. He'd slowed down, he'd sped up, but he couldn't find the motorcycle. He had just seen it beside his car. Afterwards, he'd checked the newspaper and online, he'd listened to the news, but he couldn't find anything about a motorcycle accident. I'd asked him what time it was when he'd seen the bike, and if he could describe the bike. At the exact same time that Ron and I had been on the 401, the client had seen the motorcycle. And the motorcycle he'd described? Was exactly like Ron's red Goldwing. You know, I had been giving Reiki to Ron during the ride at that point. And we were flying high on new love. Is it possible that our energy was so intense, so out of this world, that we'd literally blinked into another dimension for a moment? I like to think we did. It's very romantic.

GOOSES AND MOOSES

When you drive into Wawa Ontario, before you see anything else, you are greeted by the most gigantic Canada Goose you've ever seen in your life! I had no idea it was there until I saw it! Before I go into my Wawa experiences, let me tell you about Goose's animal medicine. Back when pens were made from feathers and the quill of the feather held the ink, the most common feather to use was a goose feather. This is why the goose will help with any creative writing projects. Goose is protective. Goose teaches us to work with others to complete our tasks as they fly in V formation. Goose is associated with bravery – ever seen a goose go at an animal ten times its size to protect its turf or its young? Goose has the spirit of the warrior.

Thank you for the giant goose Universe, it was exactly what I needed to see. I knew what it meant as soon as I saw it, and it was a remarkably good omen. Having just decided that my bike trip would turn into the frame for The Book, a goose the size of a dragon was beyond perfect.

By the time I got to Wawa, I was in the most incredible mood of my life. The feeling didn't stop until the trip was over. I'd been on the road since September 11th, and every day the ride and the experience got more beautiful, more incredible, more inspiring, and just, more. My heart was so full, and it was getting fuller by every second! A giant goose?! The totem animal for creative writing?! Are you kidding me?!

Finding my motel, The Wawa Motor Inn, just down the road, I pulled up to the front and got my room key. I arrived nice and early. I had turned a two-and-a-half hour drive into a six hour drive by stopping at places, going on a hike, having an apple fritter, talking to locals, and taking my sweet time on the highway. Still it wasn't much after 4pm by the time I got into my room. My plan for the evening was this – check out the general store across the road, have dinner at the motel restaurant, The Goose (of course!), and well before dusk, head out on Highway 17 towards Thunder Bay. I'd been told that dusk was the perfect time to see moose on the highway.

Taking off my chaps and motorcycle gear, I headed across the road, on foot, to Young's General Store. The lady at the motel had told me that the giant Goose and the General Store were the two must-see sites in town. I'd already seen the Goose. I smiled as I darted across the highway. Young's General Store had an old west look, and I could see why it was a must-see in Wawa before even going inside. As I got closer, I noticed there was a giant taxidermied moose on the porch! No way! By moose standards, I could tell that this wasn't a big example of a moose, but still, it was a moose!

I had a brief conversation with the Universe right then and there. As lovely as it was to see a stuffed moose in Wawa, it wasn't what I had in mind when I had asked to see a moose on this trip. We have to be clear about what we're manifesting, and so I let the Universe know that I was looking for a live, free ranging, wild moose.

Heading into the store, I was greeted by a large space, packed full of northern treasures, tourist traps, and Canadiana merchandise. I loved it! A giant pickle barrel full of the biggest dill pickles I've ever seen was near the entrance. I quietly hummed The Pickle Song by Arlo Guthrie, under my breath. There was an ice cream bar to my left, along with some displays full of candy, and lots of gifty type items spread throughout the rest of the store. I wandered around for some time, trying to see if there was anything I wanted to buy. There wasn't really much for me, but I loved all of it. I had very limited space on my motorcycle – beyond limited – and so whatever I took with me had to be special and it had to be the thing I wanted, not just some thing I grabbed. I scoured through their shirts and t-shirts for a women's v-neck for myself, but I saw nothing I wanted. Nothing for Ron jumped out at me. It was ok, I had purchased a headband tube thing from the Visitor's Centre where the Goose was located. It said Wawa all over it, so I had my piece of Wawa clothing. I purchased something to nibble on and headed back to the motel.

Opening the doors to the Goose Restaurant, I discovered a country-style, logger-type bar. It was decorated with an all-wood interior – big wooden beams, taxidermied animals on the walls, and a big wooden bar in the middle that ate up half the room. Around the outside of the wrap-around bar and stools were tables for patrons who were there to eat. That was me, a meal eater. I only talked to one other couple while I was in the restaurant – a man and his wife. He'd already been talking when he approached, but he was friendly. He proceeded to tell me there was barely a room to rent in town. He had had to pay $300 for one of the cabins down the hill behind the Motor Inn. Apparently, he could sleep 8 or 10 people in his rooms.

I suggested that maybe he should set up shop for the night and find some other people who are looking for a room, and share. He turned to his wife, who was now at their table, and said, "See! Even she thinks we should rent the room out," and he walked over to his own table laughing as he went. I had felt that my $150 a night was a lot until that little interaction; I was instantly grateful for my $150 room.

Having some time to kill before going out on my motorcycle, I put a post up on Facebook:

Northern Ontario News: This just in! The Trans Canada Highway #17, between Batchawana Bay and Wawa was brought to a crawling pace today as Tracey Rogers of Windsor, gawked at beautiful landscapes, waterways and searched for moose. Rogers claims that moose are a myth and claims it is The Great Canadian Conspiracy. More news later at 11.

I was feeling humorous and I was in a fantastic mood. I knew I had slowed the highway traffic down with my look-for-moose-and-nature speed, but I'd done my very best to let everyone get by me as quickly as possible. Nothing could have made me happier that day than driving the speed limit around every single one of those amazing, beautiful, awe-inspiring curves – each corner revealing some new incredible view beyond it.

After supper and Facebook, I saddled up wearing my warmest gear, and readied to go on a moose hunt. I knew that what I was doing had some risk and it was potentially dangerous. If I did see a moose, it was likely to be on the highway, and the last thing you want to see on the highway is a moose. Vehicles never win. Moose don't really win either. No one wins. It's just a mess, and people often get very hurt. Motorcycles? Even worse. I didn't want to see a moose on Highway 17; I wanted to see a moose off to the side of Highway 17. I wanted to see a moose in a bog or a marsh or a swamp. I wanted to see a moose 'considering' coming up onto the highway, just down a bit in the ditch.

So, off I went, down Highway 17 towards Thunder Bay. The sun was above the horizon, and I had a good amount of time still in the light to search around. And that's exactly what I did. I ended up taking a few side roads off Highway 17 thinking that maybe the moose would be more likely to show up there, where less cars pass by. I rode at a slow speed, below the limit, and I looked left to right. I peered deep into the bush. Looking miles out, looking close, looking everywhere.

I'll tell you something, I have good eyes when it comes to spotting wildlife. I'm a birder, and the same day I got into birding was the same day someone took me out for a drive in the snow to look for a snowy owl. I learned that day how to spot a white snowy owl sitting in the snow, half a mile or a mile away. I know I'm not as good as the guy who taught me – Paul – that man has eagle eyes, but I do know that something I've developed since is a very keen eye for spotting anything in the landscape that doesn't belong. Especially birds and animals that are trying not to be seen.

But...there were no moose. The sun had gone below the horizon. There was still lots of light, but it was time to start heading back. As it turned out, I miscalculated dusk and how many kilometres I had to go to get back to Wawa because I soon found myself riding in the pitch black. I was none too happy about this. This was dangerous. The last thing I wanted to see now was a moose! I prayed to god and the Universe and all the angels, "No moose, please!" I couldn't even see the ditches, let alone beyond that. All I could see with my bike lights on was the road and the line on the road. That was it. That meant that if I saw a moose, it would be on the same road as me, and that wouldn't go well. Praying the entire way, heart pounding, it felt like it took forever to get back to Wawa. I'd gone much further than I thought. I didn't see a moose on the drive home, and I thanked the heavens for that as I dismounted my bike outside of the motel. That was it for me – I was exhausted! Time for bed.

DAY 7 – SEPTEMBER 17TH, 2019

WORTH IT

After waking up super early, I went down to the breakfast room. It opened its doors at 6am. I was already showered, dressed, and packed to go. The continental breakfast was satisfying. I was happy to fill up on eggs and toast, have some apple juice, and chat with a couple of the guys who were there having breakfast too. Wawa, Ontario is not where you'd expect motels and hotels to be sold out, but they were. It's not like there are a whole tonne of them there to start with, but you'd think there would be enough for the middle of the week in September in Northern Ontario. I had heard that down the road there was a tonne of construction. I'd see it on my ride.

In the breakfast room there was a TV, and the TV agreed with my internet weather report – I should have a good day, rain free. Wow! I dared not even mention the weather out loud. I'd been having such incredible luck with it! Rain was moving throughout the province while I was on my trip, but not on me. Other than thirty minutes or so of misty rain outside of Port Dover, I'd seen none.

It was light enough outside to give my bike her morning wash down after I got back to my room. Wetting a cloth from my saddlebags, I used it to remove all the bugs from the previous day, all the dust, and any dirt. I shined the windshield up as clean as clean could be. That was most important to me – the windshield. Sometimes I cleaned it multiple times during the day – at rest stops and gas stations. The reason? I looked through that windshield, and I didn't want to miss a single moment of the beauty up here. I didn't want to see mountains through bug guts. And the bugs up here? Man, they were like small flying animals! These were not like the bugs I see down near Windsor or even Owen Sound. These bugs meant business!

After putting on a quick small dab of F11, and shining up her beautiful wine-coloured paint, Stella and I were ready to load up and go. Loading up meant packing my Frogg Toggs, my heated gloves and vest into the saddlebags, and strapping my luggage pack onto the backrest. I used a bungee cord to hold it all down so it wouldn't budge.

I was proud of myself for the way I'd packed for this trip. That luggage pack only holds so much, and my saddlebags were packed tight with riding gear that I needed to have with me. Every single item with me was necessary – no room for frivolities. Two pairs of jeans, one pair of activewear pants, one pair of long johns, eight pairs of underwear, four long sleeved shirts, five t-shirts, five pairs of socks, one zip up hoodie, one bra, one pair of sandals, one tiny cloth purse. That was it for clothes for twelve days, plus the most basic toiletries I could get away with. I knew I'd see a laundromat if I needed one in North Bay, and I was certain I'd see one in Thunder Bay because I was staying there an extra night with a hostess from the WRWR. I know folks who could pack even lighter than that if they had to, but I was pretty damn happy with myself. I'm someone who likes to take fifteen extra outfits when I travel, just in case I run into any type of social situation possible. There were no extra outfits, no extra shoes.

Before heading out I grabbed my phone from its charger, and my last-minute things. One of those last-minute things was the pewter moose coin I'd purchased the day before in Batchawana Bay. I flipped it over, and for the first time, I saw it had words on the back as well as the picture on the front! It said, "Live Large." Riding eight days solo was living large! Participating in the WRWR was living large! One of the expressions I loved using was "Life isn't a dress rehearsal, so start living it!" And I was living it!

I'd been living it for a while now. I felt inspired reading those words. Stopping to consider the trip I was on was inspiring. Instead of always looking to others for guidance on how to live an inspiring life, I knew I'd been living a life like that myself for a number of years. Friends had watched me step out of my comfort zone time and time again to try something new, to do something daring, to go on an adventure. I loved living large and I loved that the Universe associated those words for me with the moose on my coin.

My attraction to moose had to do with self esteem, and now living an adventurous life was being attached to it as well through significant words on the coin. I know that my adventures helped on my self love journey. Every time I'd tried something new, I'd felt good about myself. Even though I felt like it could almost kill me, I'd been proud of myself when I finished the West Coast Trail. Hopping on a motorcycle, in spite of the phobia I'd had of them for years, had added to my own confidence in myself. I was not feeling afraid of motorcycles any longer. Taking scuba lessons and jumping into the ocean, confident in my ability to apply what I'd learned in my classes – that too improved my self image. Anything and everything I did that challenged me, whether it was opening a business, going on an adventure, dipping my toes into the waters of trust and relationship, learning how to do a tarot reading and having the confidence to put it out there to other people, selling my own artwork and creations, going to the United States without a plan and having an amazing experience there, surviving on the street when I was homeless...all of it rebuilt my confidence and improved my self image.

In 2005 and 2006 I had broken into a million pieces with zero self confidence. Every moment since then has been an effort in rebuilding my self confidence. The big difference this time was that it wasn't being built on shaky, sandy ground. This time I was healing, I was sober, I was making better decisions, I was self aware. This time, I was honouring myself. Live large!

The drive from Wawa to Thunder Bay was 478 kilometres. By car, Google listed it as a five hour and sixteen minute drive. When riding a motorcycle, always add a bunch more time onto that number – well, I do, anyways! Motorcycles have to stop more often for gas. Motorcyclists often need to stop and stretch their legs a bit, and walk around to avoid their butt hurting from being in the saddle. These things add time to a trip. As an aside, there are a bunch of challenges bikers can participate in called the Iron Butt. The idea with these challenges is for a rider to ride as fast and hard as they can for a long distance. There are multi-day rides that also include sleeping. In 2019, a woman named Wendy Crockett won the Iron Butt. This was the first time in history that a woman won that challenge! She had to ride 11,000 miles in 11 days. Wendy, you're a legend.

Setting out on the road, Stella and I were ready for whatever the day had in store for us. The skies were bright and blue that morning, and the scenery, once again, didn't disappoint. Trees, forests, water and mountains spanned as far as the eye could see! I cannot neglect to mention the ravens and crows up north. They appear to be everywhere. Watching. Creating mystery. Creating magic. Ravens and crows are magic. They show up when magic is being worked or needs to be worked. Ever since I first got interested in animal medicine, I have loved crows and ravens. They are teachers, and they bring sacredness wherever they go. The North is full of ravens and crows. The North is full of magic.

Highway construction quickly turned out to be the theme for the day's ride as construction crews scattered along my path. I didn't mind. At no point during the trip was I in a rush and needing to be anywhere other than where I was. Extra stopping on the highway was just another opportunity to stand up, stretch my legs and wiggle around to get the blood flowing.

My first stop for the day was in White River. I already knew who was waiting there for me – Winnie the Pooh! Oh my gosh, how fabulous was that?! My friend Kelly had been there earlier this summer, for the Ripple Relay with the Women Riders World Relay, and she had a picture of herself with Winnie the Pooh. I wanted one too. Like, who doesn't want a picture with Winnie the Pooh, right? Oh, Pooh bear, thank you for all of the wonderful stories when I was a child. I'd loved Winnie the Pooh and Tigger too! I loved Piglet and Eeyore. And don't forget Rabbit.

So why is Winnie the Pooh in White River, Ontario, you might be asking yourself? Because that's where the real bear, who inspired the entire series of books and stories, came from. The bear had been orphaned and raised by people in White River, and eventually the bear was purchased and renamed "Winnipeg Bear", after the purchaser's hometown. The name shortened to Winnie, and the bear ended up in England. Christopher Milne, the son of A.A. Milne had named his stuffed bear after Winnie, a Canadian black bear he saw frequently at the London Zoo. A.A. Milne's inspiration for the entire Winnie the Pooh series was based on his son's stuffed animals. And that is how an orphaned black bear from Canada inspired one of the greatest children's books of all time.

Fast forward and you find yourself in 2019 with Tracey Rogers driving her motorcycle Stella up onto the walkway so that she can take a picture of her bike in front of Winnie the Pooh in White River, Ontario. My inner child was beaming from ear to ear! I was laughing and giggling to myself the entire time. I'm sure you're not supposed to ride your bike up onto the walkway, but it was 9am in the morning, who was going to tell me not to? I started to take pictures with my phone and my real camera. And then I saw him, a young man who was emptying the garbage cans in town. He was ten feet away from me.

"Hey... do you mind taking a picture of me and my bike please?" I asked him. Explaining that he had no idea how to use cameras, but that he'd be happy to, he took a few pictures for me. Thank you!

After gassing up, I hit the road. My next stop would be Marathon for gas as far as I knew. I wasn't aware of anything that I needed to see there, and the day was still young, my belly still full.

Sinead O'Connor's beautiful voice filled my head, as Take me to Church started to play. How could I write my story without including something by Sinead? Very publicly, she battled with her demons and mental health. She's a warrior, and I just love her. I appreciate that she put her experience out there for people to see. Mental health issues are far too often swept under the rug or whispered about in the back room. People are starting to speak out and it's awesome because that is needed.

My mental health had been my worst demon. Of all the things I had to look at under the microscope, it had been the most difficult. There's a stigma attached to mental health issues, and that includes addiction. I've done my best at different times to help break that stigma in my own little world. I'm not afraid to talk about my past and the things that happened. For me, mental health and addiction were intricately woven together in a tapestry of destruction – it's not a new story. Here's a little science for you that I read in a book called The Addiction Solution by David Kipper, written in 2010. When neurotransmitters aren't firing properly, certain drugs and substances will mimic the neurotransmitter that isn't firing correctly. Depending on which neurotransmitters aren't working properly, a person will have an inclination towards different substances that get them firing again. They fool the body into thinking it's receiving the chemicals that aren't being released properly. Alcohol, cocaine, opiates, etc. are some examples of substances. When the body receives the drug, it thinks the neurotransmitters are firing, and so the body begins to crave the drug more than the real body chemicals because the reaction is instantaneous. Humans love instant gratification.

Why explain this science? Because I'm interested in helping lift the stigma off both addiction and mental illness. There was a chemical reason I liked alcohol – my serotonin did not release properly in my body. I know this because the only antidepressant that ever worked for me was Celexa, and it's an SSRI. SSRI's increase the level of serotonin in the brain. Alcohol mimics serotonin, so someone like myself, with a serotonin release issue, is going to be vulnerable to alcohol and easily crave it. Some studies have shown that low doses of marijuana can increase serotonin levels, however, that research is not conclusive from what I understand.

When I got sober in Arizona, one of the first things I'd started paying attention to was the food I was eating. I'd stopped eating foods with processed sugar. I'd stopped all caffeine intake. I'd also become vegetarian and I'd greatly reduced my dairy intake. Caffeine and sugar give us an energetic boost. The bad news? That means they can create a post-boost crash as well. For someone like myself who is very sensitive to moods and emotions – these things weren't good. Anyone who considers themselves energetically sensitive, emotionally sensitive, prone to mood swings, prone to sadness, I would suggest you consider removing caffeine and sugar from your diet, depending on your dietary needs.

Caffeine is a tricky one – people attribute it to helping with migraines and headaches. This can be true, so no blanket statements can be made. My own experience? When I'd quit caffeine, I had horrible headaches for weeks. But once I'd removed it completely, I didn't get headaches at all. That is, unless I'd drink caffeine. During the rare times I'd started drinking coffee again (like when I was driving to see Mum three hours a day for months), my headaches had returned, but only when I didn't drink coffee the next day. Non-concentrated apple juice or an apple makes an awesome replacement for a coffee in the morning. There are numerous studies that show a direct link between dairy and depression, and for some, even gluten and wheat can be associated with depression.

I hadn't understood at first why the message I'd received on the beach in Californian had originally been to quit smoking, drugs, alcohol and coffee – but once I understood how the boost and the subsequent crash of caffeine affected me, it had all made sense. Through a combination of quitting sugar, quitting caffeine, quitting drugs and alcohol, exercising regularly paired with my spiritual regimen of meditation and doing meditative hobbies like artwork, reiki and drumming, I'd been able to kick my depression.

Not everyone can kick their depression or their mental illness without prescription drugs. Always get a doctor's guidance if taking prescription drugs or getting off of them. There's nothing wrong with being on prescription drugs. I would still be on an SSRI if I was experiencing depression. Many diagnoses and their healing journeys require medication. And they require gentleness with the self. They require a level of acceptance so that we aren't fighting against who we are, but instead finding compassion for the one who experiences the challenges. If you are bi-polar, for example, Matt Kahn is a potential guide who can teach you to put your hands over your heart and say, "I love the me who is bi-polar." He can teach you how to send yourself some love and compassion with intention. This practice is gentle and a healthy, spiritual alternative to saying, "God! Why does this still happen? Why can't I be normal?! What's wrong with me?!", when you're experiencing difficult symptoms. It's not that we love being bi-polar, it's that we love the one who is bi-polar. We don't have to love the experience, but we can love the one surviving the experience. It makes the experience much gentler if we can try to nurture ourselves through it.

I have a special place in my heart for anyone experiencing mental health issues. It can be a personal hell. My breakdown, my psychosis was the worst thing I'd experienced. It caused severe PTSD afterwards – that's how real the terror had been during the psychosis. My experience with the teacher that went unresolved for years had caused PTSD symptoms along with worsening my depression. The only way I had been able to work through the PTSD was by addressing them both directly and forcing myself to slowly and carefully relive events that caused them. I had to take myself back to the night the police came to pick me up and work through each moment of it. I had to take myself back to the hospital when a nurse jammed a needle in my ass as I'd screamed and yelled that they were killing me and relive it. I hadn't done it all at once, far from it. One baby step at a time, I'd faced my triggers until none of them were left.

My depression lasted for more than a decade. That too falls under the mental health umbrella. It had begun at age fifteen, not long before my suicide attempt, then resurfaced in my early twenties. I didn't fully overcome my battle with depression until I was fully sober, and I had gone through my steps for the first time. Coming to terms with my addiction and coming to terms with my past was a huge part of my clearing my depression to the point where it was no longer an issue. The work I did in Arizona had helped a ton as well. Learning about my thoughts, with the help of Eckhart Tolle's books, and becoming aware of the never-ending dialogue in my head had been the first step towards reigning my mental dialogues in. Through meditation practices, I began to stop my negative thought patterns and replace them with positive, uplifting thoughts – hopeful thoughts.

No single thing was my cure for depression. It was one long-fought battle that utilized many different teachings. The battle required self discipline – being aware of my thoughts did not just happen. It required healing every single thing that had ever hurt my self esteem. I had to come to terms with my sexuality and my sexual past. Facing my depression required me to build a level of acceptance with every aspect of my past. It required owning my choices and the consequences of said choices. My diet changed, my habits changed – shifts affected every part of my being. It was worth all the work. I consider myself lucky that I was able to get to where I am.

Not everyone will have the same results even doing the same work. Every mental health scenario is different. I'm quite certain my depression was a combination of the trauma from my youth, the sexual confusion that sat in my subconscious for twenty-seven years, a neurotransmitter that wasn't firing properly, a busy monkey mind that always leapt to the worst possible outcome, a lifestyle that conflicted with my soul purpose and my authentic self, heavy pot use, and an unhealthy lifestyle. I will always consider myself 'prone to depression.' For me, it's vitally important that I keep this within my sight, no matter how long I go without experiencing it, that way I will always keep myself away from the dangers and activities that can trigger it.

I love Sinead's song Take Me to Church. I love the message. The lyrics are about taking the sin out of mistakes. It's a song about learning to love yourself instead of searching for love somewhere out there or from someone else. It's a song about forgiveness and healing and life and laughter. It's a song about my own healing journey.

STUMBLIN' IN

After singing along with Sinead, another song came on that I sang with. Next up was Head Over Feet by Alanis Morissette. I love this song. I love Alanis. I'd been hearing this song more and more on the radio. Many of her songs speak to the anger and disappointment I've felt in regards to past relationships, but this song... it spoke to the healthiness I felt with Ron.

We moved in together in 2016. Living together had been a gigantic step for me. I hadn't been able to share my space with a man for years. Due to phobias that still lingered with my PTSD, I hadn't felt safe with a man having access to my home and the intimacies of my life. I'd trusted Ron because of our friendship. I'd even broken my one-year rule. I had a rule when dating that I should never move in with someone before one year into the relationship. I'm a firm believer that you don't see who a person really is until at least six months or one year into the relationship – people can put up a front for about that long, but not much longer. Things like do they yell at waiters when their food isn't cooked right or do they get jealous when you go out with friends? Important stuff like that. But I'd had a pretty good idea of who he was, and I'd trusted my gut. From day one, living together had been wonderful.

After my court stuff had finished, Ron and I took a three-week trip to Scotland. I'd promised my Mum before she'd passed away that I would go there for her. Our trip was magical! We saw so many castles and standing stone circles, pieces of history, beautiful landscapes – to date it's been my favourite trip. While we were having a quiet moment together by Loch Lomond, he'd gotten down on one knee and said, "Here on the bonny bonny banks of Loch Lomond, I doth proclaim my love for thee." At first, I had no idea what he was doing, but as he continued, I'd realized he was proposing. He'd taken a beautiful vintage setting ring out of his pocket, and slipped it on my finger as I'd said, tears streaming down my face, "Yes!" Oh, it had been the most romantic of proposals from the most romantic of men. It had been perfect!

What is it that makes this relationship good? Makes it healthy? I'm able to be my authentic self with him, and he's able to be his authentic self as well. We'd both been happy people before we met. At the time, I couldn't imagine meeting someone who could make me happier than I already was. I'd loved my life before we met, but I'd loved it even more after we'd started dating.

Ron was an adventurer. He'd travelled Route 66 by himself on his bike. He'd been east and west on his motorcycle. He'd been to Peru. He had scuba dived. This guy had been living his life. And so had I. Neither of us were looking for someone to make us happy – we'd both wanted a partner with whom to share our happiness. And that is a great starting place for a relationship. I don't have the power to make anyone happy, and neither does he, neither do you. It's not my job to make someone else happy, and it's no one else's job to make me happy. That job is mine. Personal responsibility and ownership, remember?

When he wants to go with the guys hunting for a week, off he goes. When I want to go for three weeks to edit a book I'm writing at a cottage, off I go. Neither of us is busy trying to make the other person feel guilty for pursuing their goals. And we share some goals and interests too – motorcycles, scuba diving, holistic and spiritual practices, travel. After years of having no idea what a healthy relationship looked like, I have a pretty good idea now, and all the work to get here was worth it.

There had been a method to the Universe's madness. Everything had to happen in the order it had happened. I had to get sober. I had to work on my self esteem. I had to learn to really like myself. I had to become financially independent. I had to be happy and in a healthy relationship with me. The career part was important for me, and I'll tell you why. In my work, I meet a hell of a lot of people who are unhappy in their relationships and marriages. They tell me that the only reason they are still together is because of money that they don't know how'd they survive financially if they were single. I believe money had been one of the causes of my mother being upset when my father wanted a divorce – she hadn't worked for years and had no personal income at that time. She had been full of financial fear. I am certain that subconsciously, money had something to do with my resistance to leaving my old life behind. Now, the concept of being financially dependent on another person is not an idea I relish. I've been financially independent since 2006. And I like it.

I'd also had a fear about marriage. The fear was financial. I didn't want someone else's financial situation to become my financial situation. While single, it had been easy to control my own money situation, but marriage requires trust. But, I'd created boundaries to protect myself and moved forward anyway. I knew where this fear came from – it was rooted in when I became homeless and had nothing. It has taken me years to rebuild a life for myself, and I have little desire to do it again. I love myself enough to create boundaries that give me a feeling of safety and trust – even within my marriage. (For the record, my spouse is financially stable and responsible.)

Alanis's words speak so powerfully to me every time I hear them. I spent many years in unhealthy relationships. For me, they included addiction, codependency, poor communication, infidelity (my unfaithfulness), poor lifestyle choices, and all the ugliness that goes along with all of that. I had no self awareness, so I hadn't realized my consent and active participation in the unhealthiness. I had been oblivious until it blew up into something I can only look back on now and say with confidence was an act of mercy. It was merciful that the Universe...my choices... had offered me an out.

When Ron and I started our time together, I'd already been in counselling for a year-and-a-half. I'd been clean and sober for five years. I'd been doing self esteem work for almost a decade. I'd been aware of my own emotions, my motives, and my choices. There had been no blinders this time, like there'd been in the past. I hadn't been hiding anything from myself. Because I'd been able to see everything – that is, everything about each of us that could make or break a relationship, I'd actually been able to see the potential for truly healthy love.

And after a decade of struggling with the idea of being in a loving, healthy relationship, I'd jumped in... I'd jumped right in! Because this time, I'd been aware and awakened. And if I'd ever need to jump out again, I'd know how to without burning the whole Tower down. I hadn't been so desperate for love that I would stay in something that didn't feel good. In fact, I hadn't been desperate for love at all. I'd learned how to treat myself well, and with respect. And what I'd discovered was another human who could and would treat me the same way, and who I'd adored treating that way in return. It had been such a new understanding of love for me. A love full of friendship and fun, and at the same time, rational and sensical. It feels incredible to be aware of all of that. It was a conscious decision to be in a relationship with Ron, not a drunken stumble-in.

GIVE AND TAKE

My motorcycle ride was moving along nicely. Blue skies still hovered above me as Stella carried me forward, closer and closer to my goal destination of Thunder Bay. I stopped in Marathon for a gas fill up, and a leg stretch, and I moved along, knowing I had a long day ahead. Feet in the pegs, music pouring in my ears, I once again allowed myself to get lost in it. If Everyone Cared, by Nickelback played from my song list. I adore this song and its message too! I imagine a better world every time I hear it. I like to think that I'm doing my best to try and help this world be a better place for the community around me.

I rarely attend any kind of meetings for sobriety or addiction at this point. This was a hard decision to make. It had been drilled into me that once I go, I go forever, and if I don't, I risk my sobriety. Alas, my sobriety is firmly in front of my view, and I never allow it to get out of my view. I speak to sober people all the time at my work, through my work, and in my personal life. Sometimes a meeting is just two or three sober people getting together and being real with each other, and I experience that (and more) nearly every day in my work. It's not that I feel I need to justify my absence, that's not my point. My point is to remind folks that there are always different options, different ways of getting to the same place. If one thing doesn't work for you, find something that does.

Recovery from anything is hard work. It requires focus, and it really helps an awful lot to have like-minded people around you, sharing their experiences. Something good about 12-step meetings is that they help the new folks meet people with years of sobriety under their belt, but the newcomers help the old-timers by reminding them of where they've been. The truth is I knew I wasn't helping anyone in my final time there. There was no part of me that was enjoying the process or feeling fulfilled by it. I'd felt obligated, and if there's one thing I can't stand, it's feelings of obligation. I want my Recovery to be full of passion, full of happiness, full of my heart. Early in Recovery, that had all been there. As time moved along, my own personal growth had started feeling stifled. Like many other areas of my life, I do something passionately for a while, giving 200%, and then my attention gets diverted and I need something different.

The song I mentioned is about giving, so how do I give? I give through my business, offering stories of personal experience when people who come in seeking answers. Simply listening is a major way I give. On my website, I am open about my own Recovery and I invite people to come have a discussion with me about it, and they do. Not everyone feels comfortable going to 12-step programs, and that's ok. I advise people to find something – Smart Recovery, a counselor or psychologist, a 12-step meeting, a support group for addicts – but find something. Recovery is difficult to do on your own. I have gone to meetings with people new to Recovery just to help get them in the door. My business gives back to the community through donated time and events. I doubt I would be alive today if it wasn't for shelters in Toronto, so I donate locally to support similar establishments remaining open and available.

Do I give back because I feel that if I don't, I'm a bad person, or I'm unworthy? No. Not at all. I give back because I want to. There's no obligation there. I firmly believe that giving should never feel like an obligation. If it does, don't do it or sit and ponder why you are giving back. Are you doing it to feel worthy of your existence here? Are you doing it because you feel you are not enough if you don't? Are you still paying penance for your past mistakes? I give back simply because it feels good. I love to see others succeed. But when my well is dry, and I'm burnt out or I don't have anything left to give, I don't. There were a great many times on my healing journey when I just didn't have anything left over for anyone else. I was barely making it by myself, and during those times, I gave myself the Grace to not rush out to save the world.

I hear oodles of clients who tell me, "I gave and I gave, and when I needed them, they gave nothing back." I'd like to stop and ponder these words. Why did you give and give? Was it really giving, if you were looking for an exchange down the road? Was it really an unwritten contract for an exchange – if I love you, please love me back? Here's what I teach, what I believe, and how I act on this belief: I make sure I meet my own needs. I make sure to get the exercise I need, the food, the free time vs. work time, all that stuff. When I do these things my well of energy is full. In fact, it usually overflows. And with that overflow and some of the energy in my well, I can give to others. When the well gets empty? It's up to me to say no to some requests from others and refill my well first.

There are going to be times in life that are an exception to this. When my Mum was ill is a great example. She came first in terms of energy expenditure, but I made sure to get sleep, eat properly, and be as healthy as possible. My mental health demanded it. If you have a relationship where you feel someone is always taking, taking, taking, then it's up to you to either put up boundaries or to put distance between you and the other person. The other person's behaviour is beyond your control. What is within your control is how you interact with their behavior. If they take too much, then it's your responsibility to have a conversation about it. It's your responsibility to put some boundaries up and say what's ok and what isn't. If these boundaries aren't adhered to by the other person? Then it's up to you to enforce consequences. Period. Sometimes those consequences can be drastic and end relationships either permanently or temporarily. If you don't do this, then you have made the choice to give, give, give. You'll choose to live with that dynamic. The other person isn't the problem – your choice to continue to give and give and give is the problem. Our part is the only part of the equation we have any control over. This is one of the places that empowerment comes from.

Let me just add something here though. When I suggest that other people aren't the problem, but rather the way we interact with them is the problem, I'm not suggesting that people with unhealthy or violent behaviour aren't a problem. They are. Their actions are dangerous, unsafe, terrifying – the list goes on. Being able to recognize the types of behaviours that warrant a serious 'no' in terms of how we interact is also a key component to creating a healthy relationship. Violent or harmful behaviour is always a problem.

Once you're able to step away, though, once you've started to heal, continuing to focus on their bad behaviour won't bring you any closer to avoiding it from happening again. What will bring you closer to true healing will be focusing on why you allowed someone to treat you that way. What part of you was so devalued internally that you allowed the unhealthy behaviour to go on for as long as it did? That's the root question we ultimately need to ask and find answers to. How you can improve your self worth so that you demand better treatment from those around you all the time is an ultimate relationship goal.

I'm not sure if I'm supposed to return to a 12-step life at some point, to attend meetings and everything again. At this time, I don't see it. It feels forced and my heart isn't in it. More important to me, due to my own history and my own experience, is continuing to learn how to love myself. I firmly believe my addiction issues were a symptom of my self hatred, not the other way around. My sobriety and my self worth are intricately woven together, and it's impossible for me to separate the two. So, my sobriety remains my highest priority in my life. It is more important than family and friendship needs, more important than marriage needs, more important than work. If I'm not sober, there is no family, there are no friends, there is no work, there is no marriage. There is no happiness. My sobriety is the one thing I'm allowed to be selfish about.

The lyrics of this song mean more to me though than just giving back. They remind me of who we are – all of us. I firmly believe that if every single person on this planet recognized their own divinity then all the unkindness would go away. We would be able to treat each other and ourselves with respect and kindness simply by acknowledging our own Divine nature.

Some people go to Church and worship Jesus every weekend of their lives without ever considering what Jesus being the son of god really means. You are the son or daughter of god too, or a child of the Universe, if you prefer! Jesus knew who he was. He acknowledged his own divinity, and through that he was able to do miraculous things. You too can do miraculous things. If you are a reader of the bible, it even says that you will do greater works than he! Jesus just wanted to awaken the world to who we all are – children of the Divine. We are Divine Beings. And when we awaken to that, we awaken to our greatest potential! Jesus was wide awake and self aware. He encouraged people to awaken to that too. Though I don't follow the Bible, I understand it as a wonderful set of allegories and teaching lessons. I find tonnes of spiritual truth within it. I don't deny the Bible either though – who the hell am I to decide what is Truth and what isn't Truth? My own path is unique. It belongs to god and I based on my experiences. And, I've found Truth in every single path I've studied.

I'm not here to pick your spiritual path for you – we all have a unique path, and we all have our own thoughts about how the Universe operates. My spirituality and my relationship with the Divine has played such an important role in my healing. I shook hands with god in 2006. I believe that god spoke to me and told me to get sober in 2007. I experienced someone else's understanding of god through the LDS Church, and that helped me get sober. I was led by god to that Recovery retreat in 2011. I believe god sent teachings and love through the people I met in my Recovery. And that doesn't mean that every person I met in Recovery was perfect, all love and light and stuff – far from it! But they said things I needed to hear. They propped me up when I needed lifting. They were my cheerleading squad in Recovery – even the ones who didn't necessarily like me. They also called me on my bullshit when my ego was running the show. Every one of them wanted to see me get sober, and it had nothing to do with us liking each other. We had a common goal in recovering that kept us accountable to ourselves and each other.

My spiritual beliefs have shifted somewhat since then, but the results of my beliefs have not. I still believe in the Divine, but it doesn't really have a name or a face, and it's not singular. It is everything, including you and me. I have friends in Recovery who are atheists and if they say Higher Power it means something different to them than it does to others. Some of them see each member in their Recovery program as their Higher Power, and they listen to what others have to offer through their stories and sharing. Higher Power doesn't have to mean "God." It can mean something outside of yourself that is helping you. Period.

For me to get strong in my own Recovery, I had to first put some faith in something outside of myself. By doing that, I became stronger within myself. By trusting this outside-of-myself entity/energy/phenomenon for a long period of healing time, I learned how to trust my intuition, my gut instincts, my inner guidance. I am most often able to tell the difference between my ego and my Higher Self. My ego will tell me why having a drink right now probably wouldn't be the end of the world, and that because of my strong spiritual practices, I could test these waters and be fine. Hell, I hardly even drank at all in the few years before I quit for good. My Higher Self is the one in the background very quietly saying, "Why even test that? Remember the hospital?" My ego is the one telling me that smoking pot made writing so much easier, made the words flow without even trying. My Higher Self is the one telling me that I'd rather not ever fulfill the dream of writing The Book if it means doing something that has the potential to trigger mental health problems for me. I love me. Every choice I make now has this question at the root of it – "Does this choice reflect self love or self sabotage?"

There is such a gratitude written within this song that I can't help but feel inspired by it when I hear it. Riding my motorcycle, I belted out the lines, "I'm singing Amen, I, I'm alive!" My life is good. I want to share that goodness with others. I want other people to know the goodness I am experiencing. I want others to feel what I'm feeling. Every time I teach a class at work, I pack in as many tidbits to true healing as I can in the hopes that someone is listening and applies what I said into their life. Even it means they find just a little bit more peace in their life. Often people take the time to tell me how much something I taught them has changed their life. And that's why I do what I do. That's why I include this in my story.

Maybe no one will read it, maybe it's just for me and my own healing? But maybe someone will read it, and when they do, it'll be packed with as much information and personal truth as I can pack into it. Maybe just one of my experiences will bring a shift of some kind into their healing journey. Nothing will bring me more joy than knowing that my story helped someone else heal. It gives meaning to the madness. I've said it before and I'll say it again, I believe everything happens for a reason. In my life that reason is so I can help walk others through the same kind of shit that I had to walk through. There's a meme on Facebook that says, *"I love when people that have been through Hell walk out of the flames carrying buckets of water for those still consumed by the fire."* (Stephanie Sparkles). *"We're all just walking each other home."* Ram Dass

MAGIC MAN

Something of concern was happening on my motorcycle ride. The blue skies disappeared into fog. It was just getting thicker and thicker by the moment. The weather change wasn't gradual, it happened immediately! I'm not talking about some misty morning fog. I am talking about the kind of fog that brings the Trans Canada Highway to a virtual standstill. I was able to see approximately seven feet in front of Stella. I couldn't see oncoming traffic until it was almost on top of me. My hands gripped the handlebars so strongly, I started losing feeling in my fingers. To say I was scared would be a gross understatement. This was the kind of fog people died in.

A trucker had seen me as the fog descended, and I knew he was right behind me, but he was keeping his distance. No one could get between me and that truck. The trucker knew I was driving at a snail's pace and he honoured that by giving me all the room that I needed. I couldn't see him but I knew he was there. He couldn't see me but he knew I was there. He felt like an angel sent to protect me. For me, fog represents magic, mystery and the sacred. It's where the things that we feel, but can't know for sure, exist. I've got a tale that I would like to share, and it feels like it fits right here, nestled in the mist.

In 2016, a counsellor suggested that I could benefit from attending Paths of Courage, a retreat up north. Paths of Courage was designed for men and women who are survivors of sexual assault and sexual abuse and it was paid for by Ontario medical coverage. Men and women (separately) attend during different weeks. I'd agreed to attend. Each day, we did group work that had been very difficult essentially guiding participants into the core of their trauma. I had been surprised and shocked by what surfaced during my own work. We'd been asked to hand our cell phones in at the beginning of the week. I'd handed in a phone, but had another one I kept. I had just started dating Ron and the thought of going a week without talking brought me no joy. I hadn't needed to talk for hours, but I'd wanted to let him know I was good, and how things were going. Halfway through the week, my conscience got the better of me and I'd told the facilitators about my 'other' phone. Normally that would have resulted in being sent home, but since I had brought it to their attention myself, and I'd been participating in every other way, they'd allowed me to stay.

I'd felt horrible. I'd felt ashamed. I'd felt bad. And that was the core of my trauma that had come out during my healing sessions – the trauma behind feeling bad. Since age twelve when I had been molested, I'd felt bad about myself. I'd felt ashamed and flawed. I thought I had healed that feeling of shame, but I hadn't because it surfaced over and over. There I was, almost in my mid 40s, and shame hadn't left my belly. Identifying it that week had helped me tremendously. Being aware that the emotions lingered inside of me had helped me not make decisions and choices based on them. I'd cried, screamed, and curled up in a fetal ball as my body let go of the 'bad' it had still been holding onto. It had been time to let go of the bad.

Another moment that stood out in my mind was having to do a blindfolded exercise with a buddy. While I was blindfolded, my buddy had to guide me around outside with words while I'd leaned on them to maneuver me around the terrain. I'd hated it with passion. I'd wanted to look under or over my blind fold, but I didn't. I'd even ended up in tears at one point during the blindfolded walk. The feeling of having no control had been horrible.

I'd realized through that exercise how distrustful I was of anyone's guidance and help; anyone's but my own. The timing couldn't have been more perfect. The entire reason I'd been at the retreat was because of my court case. One of the fallouts of the relationship with the teacher had been a huge lack in my ability to trust – though the opposite had been true during the relationship. When I'd read the poetry I wrote when

I was fifteen, I'd read and clearly seen the trusting words (the need for trust!) of a kid. I had placed all my trust entirely in the wrong person. There'd been a direct connection between that relationship and my ability to trust.

I had similar experiences in some of my adult relationships. The fallout from these? A powerful belief in the voices that said: trust yourself and only yourself. Trust your own guidance. Trust your own gut. My own self guidance continues to trump anyone else's every time. I'm not convinced that's a bad thing. I've become well practiced in following my inner guidance and responding based on that important information. Compromises, boundaries, and open communication have become key components in the healthy relationships I have, and I couldn't have cultivated these abilities without first knowing how to trust myself.

When I try to explain trust to clients, I tell them this: You don't have to learn to trust other people, it's important that you learn to trust your own gut about other people. If you see white flags, great! Go for it! If you are seeing red flags, don't do what most of us do – ignore them. Even without knowing why there are red flags, trust the fact that your gut is waving them. Proceed with caution, if at all. Every situation I can think of in my life concerning unhealthy relationships with guys or girls included major waving red flags way before the damage happened. Yet I'd waltzed right into the relationship anyway.

At the retreat, in addition to trauma work, we'd also made a walking stick, we did a drum circle, we did yoga, we did crafts and other spiritual activities. I'd loved it! At the end of the week we were to do a Healing fire with Glen. Glen, a very spiritual man, was a counsellor for the men. I'm not sure if he considered himself a medicine man, but I did. If I'd ever seen a medicine man, he'd have been it. Just being in his presence felt healing. We were to write out the things we wanted to let go of, and then release them into the fire. During the event, Glen had told us that he was a Mohawk from the area. We all did ceremony that night at the fire. Healing was offered to all of us in this process. This fire had been a symbolic gesture of healing and closing a traumatic cycle.

I'd stood there, my jaw agape. Oh my god. This man was Mohawk and a healing cycle had been coming to a close. Glen was from the region that was once known as Upper Canada – where John Stuart had been. Glen was Mohawk – from the same group of people that John Stuart had taught and converted to Christianity. I had been at this retreat to heal from what happened with Kaiya which was a direct result of what had happened with Don, a First Nations man. If John Stuart and I shared a soul, his learning was coming to completion through me. He had lived out his own actions, and the results of those actions some 250 years later had come full circle. I had stood at a healing fire with a Mohawk medicine man telling me that the healing was done. The karmic circle was complete. We could all be released from this teaching. Magic. Sacredness. Mystery. The message hadn't been lost on me. Standing there at the fire, 250 years of karmic teaching coming to a close, my own childhood trauma coming to a healed place, the song Electric Pow Wow, by A Tribe Called Red, started to scream inside of me. I was free.

GIRLS AND BOYS

My ride through to Terrace Bay felt like it took forever, and it probably did. It should have been about an hour ride, but having to ride 20km/hour, tops, because of dangerous weather, it took much longer. I couldn't see a thing as I rode into Terrace Bay. I wasn't even sure if the parking lot I was pulling into was indeed, a gas station, until I finally saw the pumps through the fog. Happy as hell to get off my bike and stand on solid ground, I thanked the Universe for getting me there safely as I filled up my tank.

As I was about to go in and pay, a woman bounced excitedly up to me and said, "Hey! You're going on the WRWR aren't you?!" I let her know that yes, I was! "I'm Helen! I'm going too!" she said and she started telling me about her friends who were participating as well. They'd be doing the ride from Thunder Bay to Wawa on the 19th. After chatting and getting each other's info, I asked her where I could go for a good bite to eat. I was planning on staying for a while to let the fog figure itself out. After telling me where the restaurant (Drifters) was, Helen asked if I would like her to guide me there. Yes please! I hopped on my bike and followed her car through the fog across the road. When I got there, she said she'd be back shortly with Kendra, her friend, and they'd both have lunch with me.

Drifters had that local, northern Ontario feel with lots of natural wood. I found a spot where there was a place I could charge my phone, and I sat and took the place in. Folks in the restaurant smiled at me and seemed friendly. I could tell that everyone knew everyone – I was the exception. I put a post on Facebook about the killer fog, messaged Ron, then I looked at the menu. Kendra and Helen came in and sat down with me. They both were wearing jeans and looking very comfortable. I was happy to start getting to know them.

When I got talking about moose and how badly I'd wanted to see one, Kendra told me a story about her own moose experience a few years before. She and some friends had been riding near this location, and a mama moose with a young moose both walked onto the highway. Everyone had been able to avoid them except Kendra, who had to swerve between the two moose, but as she did so, she caught the mama moose's hind legs. When the ambulance had arrived, they had an open body bag on the stretcher. The attendants had told Kendra that they usually pick-up dead bodies when they get a motorcycle-moose call. After inspecting her, they were getting ready to take her to the hospital. Instead, she'd signed a release waiver, hopped out of the ambulance, and asked her friends loudly, "How's my bike?!" She'd managed to get to town that night, though her bike was quite damaged.

Hitting a moose on a motorcycle and surviving to tell the story is quite a feat! Hitting a moose on a motorcycle and getting back onto a limping motorcycle and riding away from the scene of the accident! Fearless! My admiration for Kendra grew instantly. She and Helen were some of the first WRWR riders I met, and I just knew I was going to be surrounded by more brave, awesome women once this ride started in Thunder Bay! She hit a moose and still rides! Roar!!!

While we ate lunch, the fog finally lifted in Terrace Bay. I was told that sometimes the fog stays all day, so I was grateful to see the sky again. Hugging Helen and Kendra goodbye, and thanking them so much for introducing themselves to me, I carried on my merry way, anxious to make up some lost time.

I wasn't five minutes out of Terrace Bay when the fog descended again. Oh, for the love of god, really? I couldn't wait it out because I had no idea if it was ever going to lift. Turning my music right down so I could hear everything, I drove into the fog. I wondered why the Universe would do this – everything happens for a reason, right? I decided that this way, I'd have some new things to see on the way back with the WRWR. This was an entire section of a very beautiful part of the world that I hadn't seen before and I still hadn't seen, because of the fog. There would be something new to see on the way back with the relay. I also decided this: I was being given a chance to be brave and do something difficult. If my entire ride was a cakewalk, what was the fun in that? That's the way my brain operates.

A big part of being happy is being grateful, and looking for the silver lining behind every cloud. There is not one event in my life that doesn't have a silver lining. Even my childhood trauma and my years of addiction had silver linings. There are blessings, knowledge and learnings that come out of all the events in our lives, if we are open to receiving them. I am open now. It's a skill worth honing. I used to be negative and wonder "why me?" But as my Reiki teacher Annelle taught me, consider this question instead: "why not me?" Ha! She was a wise woman.

Back into the fog I drove. My music was off. My vision was limited to seven feet in front of me. Another foggy tale came to mind. There'd been a place where things were unclear and unknowable. This had been a very personal place for me. It was a major part of what I had to heal and come to terms with – my sexuality. As a teen, I'd spent three years in counselling, mainly working through the Don stuff, but also working through some family stuff. When I'd left the teacher at age eighteen, I'd believed that my main interest sexually was with men. Though I'd been aware that I could get emotionally attached with women. I mean, I had done so with the teacher. Throughout my teen years, I had fooled around with quite a few boys. There'd been physical attraction there, for sure. I had been coaxed into accepting a gay relationship, and a gay lifestyle with the teacher, even though I had known I had such strong attractions to boys my own age.

What I had needed more than anything was to hear someone say, "I love you." The relationship had nothing to do with sex for me. But because that sexual element had progressed, I had been unclear – was I straight? Bisexual? I hadn't been sure. In my early 20s, I'd started to experience very deep depression, and when I seemed unable to pinpoint the source of my depression, the question would pop up in my mind, "was I really gay and denying it?" At age 27, I'd explored the possibility when in a same-sex relationship which I wrote about earlier. Being gay hadn't been the problem. The truth was that my confusion about my sexuality had been connected to my depression.

My sexuality and my self esteem were related – with roots reaching back to deep shame and Don. To root in lies, secrecy and shame with Kaiya. The stuff with Kaiya had never been dealt with properly with a counselor. Any treatment I'd done back during high school, with my counsellor Susan had been about Don, not Kaiya. At that time, I'd believed I had been in love with Kaiya. The fact that I'd been in love with her was a huge part of the problem. I'd loved the person who breached trust in the most horrendous kind of way. It took me years to put that all together.

As I've already mentioned, since beginning my new life in 2006, I've been with both men and women. Men feel more natural to me, and where my physical attractions have always been. However, I'd be a liar if I said I didn't find women attractive. I'm just not drawn to them in the same way. After three full years of counseling during the lawsuit, I still walked out unable to define my sexuality. If someone had asked me what my sexual orientation was my answer would have been "It's mixed up, and the result of some really messed up experiences as a youth. I'm not straight, I'm not gay, I'm not bisexual. I'm undefined and unlabelled." That's the best answer I could have given. My psychologist hadn't been happy with that answer. He liked to think that I was straight, and that there would have been no confusion if Kaiya hadn't intervened. There could be a world of truth in that statement, but I'll never know for sure because she did intervene, and it is part of my history.

I was a tomboy, big time, when I was a kid. I hated playing with dolls. I loved playing in the dirt, riding ATVs, exploring in the forest, catching crayfish, target shooting with Dad's 22 rifle. But I was told by Kaiya that most tomboys were gay and just didn't know it. I believed that because I trusted the person telling me. Since the court proceedings initiated in 2014, I've explored my inner tomboy again, and I've embraced her. For years, stuck in the back of my mind was the belief that tomboys were gay. I had buried my inner tomboy for years because of it. When my addiction got really bad, in my late twenties and early thirties, I became more feminine. I wore more mini-skirts. I grew further and further away from my authentic self. I'm not a mini-skirt kind of woman. But I tried to be, and it just got…it got messed up. I got messed up. Everything got messed up.

I'm so relieved that I feel comfortable in my own skin again. I'm relieved that I can connect with my authentic self and allow her to shine. And there's no way in hell that I would have found her while smoking pot every day. Nor would I have found her without all the counselling during court. I'm ok without defining my sexuality. The truth is it's no one's business except mine. And my husband is a big enough man to understand all this stuff and meet me exactly where I am, as I am. He's a big enough man not to try to exploit it in a way that could hurt me.

I had to understand all of this before I was ever going to fully embrace my authentic self again. I had to unravel all the guilt, all the responsibility, all the trust issues, all the tomboy voices – all the everything that had gotten messed up in the situation with Kaiya. I had to deal with it all before I could ever be me again.

My conscience doesn't struggle at all anymore with my decision to sue her. I struggled with it during 2014 and 2015. The results of the suit itself were inconsequential. It was the results of the counselling that mattered. It was the fact that I had the strength to sue her that mattered. Taking legal action had been the physical symbol of my refusing to take responsibility for her behaviour anymore. And one of the added bonuses? I was finally 'ok' with my sexuality. I was able to embrace my inner tomboy again. And smack dab in the middle of all that counseling, I became intimate with the man who would join me in the first truly healthy relationship I've ever known. His patience while I learned how to do that was divine.

I wrote a poem back in late 2010. I think it fits here nicely:

MUSINGS

What do you want to be when you grow up?
I want to be me.
But no, seriously, what do you want to be?
Seriously, I just want to be me.
Why do we have to be something else, something more
Why can't we just be ourselves?
Today I want to be a musician, and bang on my drum
Tomorrow, I want to paint mad-crazy love
And when the colours have all been used
I will write an ode to painting.
My destiny isn't to wear a title made by men
My inheritance is far more divine, eternal.
When God was a child, did someone ask Her
What do you want to be when you grow up?
Did He have to choose to be a boy or a girl?
Did She have to go to St. Michael's School of Theology?
I bet He just woke up one day and said
"Today would be a fabulous day to paint in the sky!"
And with Joy on Her face, She painted the world.
No one paid Him to do it. He just did it.
Because music, and colour, and madness, and life
Was screaming to come out of Her soul
Love was what He wanted to be when He grew up.

Tracey Rogers, 2010

Even as early as 2010, before my sobriety began, I had been aware that my need to define my sexuality and how I identified my sexuality was a problem. This poem was my attempt to remove the labels and to remove my need to define myself. What did Tracey want to be when she finally grew up? Tracey wanted to be Love. Tracey wanted to be happy. Mission accomplished, Tracey.

Riding through the mountains, fog embracing me on every side, I was terrified, yet still moving forward. The fog would have to lift eventually, right? I continued to pray to the heavens, my Mum, the angels, my Granny, my Aunt Sue, and anyone who would listen, to keep me safe, and if they could, could they please lift the fog? But riding through was important. I was scared, and I still did it. That's courage. That's what healing takes – courage.

We're scared of what we're going to find when we go digging to heal things. We don't want to look those demons in the eye. It hurts to look, and we know it's going to hurt to heal. But we dig anyway. I rode through the fog for years – from 2006 to 2017. It was terrifying at times, and yet at the same time, my life got better and better. I was terrified during my breakdown. I was terrified to set out and create a new life. I was terrified when I was homeless. I was terrified to leave my life and go to the US. I was terrified to come back to Canada. I was terrified to open a business and risk more failure in my life. I was terrified to do my 12 steps. I was terrified to face the demons I faced during counselling about Kaiya. But I still did it. And I give you my word that walking through my personal fears was worth it! Oh my god, was it worth it! My life is good, and it's been good for a long time now. It's better and better every day since September 11th, 2006 – when I took my first step towards healing.

TWO OF US

Let's go back into the mystery, magic and sacredness of the fog again, and talk about my Mum. My relationship with my Mum had been difficult for me to reflect on for years. I loved my Mum. I got a lot closer to her in my teen years when my father and I had drifted apart, but that closeness hadn't lasted very long. Around age eighteen, I'd become aware of the fact that Mum was drinking a lot, more than I had known. Many times, I'd spoken to her about it. The situation had frustrated me. I'd watched her relationships disintegrate because of her drinking. I believe it had affected her work life as well.

Mum and I couldn't emotionally connect. At first, I'd believed it was all on her, but when I got clean and sober, I'd realized we were two peas in a pod. For years I'd pointed at her drinking and seen the problem. But I'd had a joint in my hand – the same hand that was pointing the finger. For years people said to me, "Oh, you're just like you Mum!" They'd said it with love. I certainly looked like my Mum, which was the compliment they were giving. I took their comments as compliments until after my trip to the US. when I'd gone to my first 12-step meeting and said out loud, "My name is Tracey and I'm an alcoholic." Then when people said I was just like my Mum, I'd heard something completely different. I'd heard, "You're an alcoholic."

It hadn't been a bad thing. It had been a powerful motivator in my Recovery. The day it dawned on me that my habits were leading me down the same road as my Mum, I'd been scared shitless. Mum had isolated herself. She had a hard time finding and keeping work. Her family relationships were less than they could have been. She'd lacked connected friendships. She'd been alone with her glass of wine. I don't say any of this to disrespect my Mum's memory. I love my Mum with all my heart, all my heart. But her story, our story, is so important for me to convey. The day I saw myself in my Mum, I knew I had to get and stay sober. Period. Pot or alcohol, it didn't matter – the results were the same for me. Pot had stopped me from connecting fully with myself and others. It had kept me from healing my past. It may not be the same for all people, but for me, it very much was about disconnection. Furthermore, any time the pot hadn't been available, I'd turned to alcohol.

During my sobriety in 2011, I'd been able to create a slightly better relationship with my Mum, although it would never reach its full potential. Even though I'd been learning not to judge others or do their inventory through the 12 steps, Mum's situation had still frustrated me. There was a part of me that hoped very much that Mum could witness my healing journey and choose to want it for herself. I had wanted my sobriety to be a beacon of hope for her. That never happened.

In September of 2016, Mum had gone into the hospital with swollen legs and problems breathing. After doing a few tests, she'd been released. But within a day or two she'd been back in. They'd discovered a collapsed lung, a 10cm tumour on her lung, and fluid around her lungs. I'd known right away her diagnosis was serious. My immediate reaction was to be angry – not in her presence, I didn't allow her to see it, but I'd been angry inside. Why hadn't she gone to the doctor's for years? Why had she still been smoking like a chimney? Why had she still been drinking so much? How long had her lung been collapsed?

I was angry that she had allowed herself to get this sick before doing anything about it. My anger was doing a powerful job of hiding my fear and my hurt. I knew my Mum's life was in danger, that her illness was possibly terminal. It would take six full weeks to get a proper diagnosis. In my mind and heart, I'd treated her illness as terminal from the moment I'd heard about the 10cm tumour. I hadn't said anything about it to my Mum. I'd kept my mood as positive and upbeat as possible around her.

Approximately one week after hearing about the tumour, the anger went away forever. The judgement went away. All the judgement I had ever felt towards my Mum disappeared like fog blows away with the wind. Compassion moved in. My only focus had been to be there for her. To love her. To make sure she felt loved and knew she was loved. As this happened, I remembered the New Year's Eve list I had made for the things I wanted for 2016. On that list had been "To Expand in Unconditional Love." Why had I asked for that, you may wonder?

I don't have kids, and I think that mothers know how to unconditionally love better than anyone else on this planet. Moms can love their kids through the worst of things, even murder. Many moms never stop loving their kids. I don't mean to say that moms are the only ones capable of unconditional love, nor do I mean to suggest that all moms know how to unconditionally love, but they have been the best examples when talking to people about love. Mum had loved me unconditionally. I'd put her through hell in 2005 right through to 2009. From my breakdown to when I'd returned home from Arizona. She'd loved me through all of it. I'd wanted to know how it felt to love someone in that kind of way – the way a mother loves her child. That's why I wrote it on my list.

Sitting in my office at work one day, I'd picked up Rosy, the rose quartz skull that I had purchased in 2016. I had asked Rosy to teach me Unconditional Love when I brought her home. It's said that crystal skulls have personalities and they contain knowledge. If we meditate and spend time with them, they will reveal knowledge to us. Allowing her to lay heavy in my hand, I'd looked into Rosy's eyes and said, "Please help me navigate this with my Mum. I don't know how to do this." And I believe she'd helped me. I believed I'd navigated my Mum's end of life well. All the answers of what to do and what to say had come naturally as they were needed.

When Mum's hospitalization began, I took everything I could off my schedule. There were certain events and classes I still had to attend or teach myself in the following weeks, but after that, I'd tweaked and changed White Feather's calendar. Some classes had been removed. I'd stopped taking any new clients for tarot and Reiki, and I'd made sure staff was scheduled every day, so that no hours were assigned to me to have to be in the store. Each day, I'd driven to Newbury hospital where my Mum was. It was a 1.5 hour car ride there. Her care team had tried to convince us (my sisters and I) to take Mum home with one of us, but none of us had been prepared for that kind of situation. I have questioned a few times if I should have had her at my home, but I believe that everything worked out as it should. She'd received excellent care where she was in a small hospital. Every day, at least one of her daughters had spent time with her.

Mum hadn't been ready to die. She was scared to die, and she'd told me so. Mum didn't really know if she'd believed in god. She hadn't believed in heaven or hell. She'd thought maybe things would just end, forever. So, I'd shared an experience with her. This is what I'd said, all of it was true:

"Mum, earlier this year, we hosted a medium named David Schultz who does a lot of events with us. Mediums make contact with spirits and passed loved ones. That night, he said he had a woman come through who was painting, and he asked if anyone present had a loved one who had painted. Three of us put our hands up. David then described the paintings. Mum, he described Granny's paintings to a T! He had a message for me from her about continuing to work on my art. He described your Mum. How she was frugal, and kind and reserved. After that, he said that he saw Grandpa standing beside her. He said Grandpa was quiet. David said Grandpa passed about 20 years before Granny and I told him yes, that was correct! He then told us that he saw Grandpa during the war in Europe, but not in a soldier's uniform. He was definitely there during the war, but not as a soldier. [Mum interrupted me here, saying, "That's right! Daddy was a civil engineer during the war in London, but he never was in the army."] David then went on to describe Grandpa's workroom with all his tools, and he described old tools, just like the wood plane of Grandpa's you still have. And at the end, David said that he saw Grandpa reaching deep into the pocket of the baggy pants he was wearing and pulling his hand out and offering something to me, but David couldn't see what it was." At that point, I did exactly what David had done, and reached deep into a pocket and held something out, as if to show it to Mum.

"Lifesavers!" my Mum had exclaimed.

Every time we'd see my Grandpa, the first thing he did was dig deep into his baggy pant's pocket and pull out Butterscotch Lifesavers. He would then give one to each of my sisters and I. Grandpa had been famous for that.

Mum's eyes were as wide as saucers.

"How did he know that, Tracey?" she'd asked me.

"Mum, he saw your parents because they are still here, they just aren't in body anymore," I'd said. I'd explained that David knew nothing about Granny and Grandpa. I had never told anyone about the lifesavers.

Mum had a perplexed look on her face."Huh," she'd said. And that had been it.

The next day, I went in to see her. and Mum said,

"I was thinking about that psychic guy you told me about yesterday. There's something to that, isn't there?" she'd said.

"Yes. Yes, there is something to it Mum. I believe so very much!" I'd responded. I'd proceeded to tell Mum about all the bird signs I had gotten over the years from her mother, my Granny. You see, I have wonderful memories from my childhood of sitting in Granny's garden with her, watching birds. Each bird that came to the feeder, she would ask me to identify. When I couldn't identify one (even though she could) she would get out her Birds of North America book, and help me find the bird and discover its name. I had forgotten about those memories until partway through my healing journey. Since the Oneida Family Healing Lodge, I'd been aware of birds, and they had given me signs to help guide me. I told my Mum about all the experiences I'd had with birds, and that I just knew it had been Granny bringing the messages and signs. Mum had nodded her head. I could tell she'd been digesting it.

I have expressed my gratitude to David again and again for the gift of the vision he'd had that I could then give to my Mum. When Granny and Grandpa had come through at that event in early 2016, I'd thought it was very touching and cool, but I had commented afterwards, "I'm not sure why they came through for me right now. I know they are there. I talk to Granny all the time. There were people here tonight who needed this more than I do." Well, they hadn't come for me, they'd come for Mum. They'd known what was coming later that year, and they'd known I would help their beloved daughter Jill by retelling the vision. And it did help. Mum began seeing signs from Granny everywhere.

I was given the gift of four months with Mum. There were only a couple of days that I was unable to go for at least an hour or two. For the first time in my entire life, I'd been putting someone else's needs above all my own. I couldn't have done this without sobriety. Things got more difficult as Mum's illness progressed and her health deteriorated before our eyes.

Something I'd caught myself doing at the beginning of this experience was wanting to control the situation. It had bothered me who visited Mum and who didn't. Other people's choices regarding Mum had bothered me. I had spoken to dozens...dozens of dozens of clients over the years about codependency and the desire to control and fix situations that weren't ours to control and fix. This had been a classic example of codependency, and I'd started to give in to my need to control and fix the situation!

I didn't get down on myself or beat myself up for it. Instead, I'd worked on my behaviour. No one else had noticed it. No one had pointed it out to me. I'd caught it on my own. That had been something I was proud of. Progress, not perfection. It was none of my business whether other people had visited Mum as often as I thought they should. My decisions about how often I'd wanted to see Mum were my business. How often they'd wanted to see her (or not) was theirs.

The next four months would be about me and Mum. That was it. Not Mum and her other family and friends. Just Mum and I. I'd allowed myself to create the experience to be just that. I focused on assisting Mum in whatever ways I could. I focused on telling her all the things I'd still had in my heart to express to her. I poured my gratitude out, letting her know how thankful I'd been that she hadn't given up on me through the difficult years – my teen years, the hospital in 2005, the trip to the US.. I'd let her know that I was aware how hard that had been on her. I showed patience and kindness, even though some days she hadn't had any patience and kindness to show me. Radiation had been very unpleasant for her. I'd asked Mum questions about her youth that hadn't been answered in her memoirs.

Allow me to take a tangent for a moment. Yes, my Mum wrote her memoirs for my sisters and I. Her memoirs consisted of everything she could remember about her early childhood in postwar England, the homes she'd lived in, the schools she'd attended, and the foods she'd eaten. She wrote about her family, her teachers, her studies, her friends. She included information about her family ancestry; a feat she'd worked on for close to twenty years. She even had family letters that were of value for proving our lines of ancestry. Mum wrote about coming to Canada on her great adventure with her best friend, and about hitch-hiking and backpacking through parts of Europe during her university years. Her relationship with my father she'd written about in detail. The births of her three children and what it was like being a Mum filled many a page.

She even wrote about the divorce, including her thoughts about her post-divorce years. Of all the things my Mum ever gifted me, besides life itself, this set of memoirs was the greatest gift of all. It was ninety pages long, single spaced. I wouldn't say Mum was poetic or creative in her writing, but she was very detailed, and I appreciated every single one of the fine details. If you're looking for something special to give your children – write your memoirs. It has nothing to do with writing well, and everything to do with giving your kids a window into who you were before you had children, the family ancestry, and the legacy of your life. Plus, it gives them something solid to hold onto and pour over, when you're no longer on this Earth. My Mum revealed her adventuring soul in her memoirs. It turns out I'm a chip off the old block.

I believe it was early December 2016, we received confirmation that my Auntie Sue's cancer had returned. Auntie Sue was my Mum's only sibling. She had battled cancer already for years, but we thought she had won. For the past few years, she had been in relatively good health and we'd all been so grateful and relieved for that. But it had come back. And apparently it was throughout her body. That was never good. Auntie Sue had been like a surrogate mother to me at times. She had been emotionally there for me at crucial times. I had a special relationship with my Auntie Sue. I felt like my world was crumbling around me. My Mum was leaving this Earth soon, and I'd feared for my Auntie Sue as well. I didn't have any other aunts or uncles that I had been close to. The news had been devastating for all of us, including my Mum. Neither of them could go visit each other. Toronto seemed like a galaxy away with both of them in hospital beds.

On Christmas Day, I'd visited Mum even though she asked me not to. She'd wanted me to 'just enjoy my Christmas.' I don't think she understood – I couldn't enjoy my Christmas without spending time with her. The thought of her in a hospital bed...It would be bad enough leaving her on Christmas Eve and part of the day on Christmas. Ron had cooked up turkey and goodies for Mum. Some of it she had been able to enjoy. I'd reminded Mum of our Christmas back in 2006 when the two of us had spent time together at her house without anyone else knowing I was in town. It had been our secret little Christmas together. I cried as I'd told her that it was my favourite Christmas out of all the amazing Christmases I'd had over the years. That one had belonged to just her and me. And it hadn't been about presents or stockings or turkey. It was just like Dr. Seuss wrote in How the Grinch Stole Christmas:

"And he puzzled and puzzled 'till his puzzler was sore. Then the Grinch thought of something he hadn't before. What if Christmas, he thought, doesn't come from a store. What if Christmas, perhaps, means a little bit more."

No one had taught me the truth in those words more than my Mum. I learned that in my heart in 2006 and again in 2016 during my two, extra special Christmases with Mum.

Shortly into the New Year, on January 11th, Auntie Sue passed away. Mum couldn't go to her only sister's funeral. My heart had shattered into a million trillion pieces by this time. Ron had been a rock for me. I couldn't lean on my Mum. My god. Mum had been incapable of expressing what was in her thoughts and her heart. Emotional connection was never her forte, but I knew she'd been hurting. I knew she'd been trying to process what was happening. I'd sat with her and processed it with her as best as

I could. We'd taped the funeral so that Mum could watch it if she wanted to. She'd watched part of it, but not all of it. It had been too hard for her.

There had been a lot happening with the lawsuit at that time. Cursing lawyers under my breath, I'd set the legal stuff aside and spent every moment I could with my Mum. She had been moved to Leamington Hospice and had been treated like a queen. She'd been treated very well in Newbury, and her care was over the top in Leamington. Mum had mentioned she wanted a haircut to me one day. I'd set about the task of making that happen with hospice. They'd arranged for someone to come in, and for Mum to get lifted out of her bed into a chair. It had been a painful, difficult process, but she was happy to be upright for the first time in a long time!

That day was 'Mum & Tracey' day! We had her hair done, and she'd promptly flirted with the doctor who remarked about her new hairdo. I showed her the entire Hospice building, which she hadn't seen. We had lunch together, eating food of her choosing, in the dining area. Sunshine had poured in the windows, and we'd watched birds at the feeders outside on the patio. I couldn't have imagined a more perfect day. It had been such a gift.

My sisters were both there the following Sunday. We'd all had a wonderful day together – Mum and all her children. Our graduation photos had been hung on the wall. Mum clung to a stuffed elephant that she named Huffy that I had given her. There were pictures of her grandkids and some personal items placed around the room. We had done what we could to make it feel like home. Hospice encouraged us to do that. There'd been a pull-out bed in the room that I'd used many times to catch some zzz's while Mum was sleeping. Mum couldn't believe how well they treated her, and she'd commented that she couldn't believe it wasn't costing her any money. She was born into a harsh world where everything had been rationed. Lack was all around her during World War II. But at the hospice, we'd made sure that when she left, she would leave a world that was nurturing, kind, abundant and free.

Just two days after that, Mum's medication had been changed because she was having some pretty intense delirium. Her dosage became very high, and she'd been heavily sedated. On Saturday February 4th, I'd gone home exhausted and hungry. When I'd gotten in my car to leave, a song came on the radio that was singing something like "I'm leaving here tonight". The next song was another song with lyrics that said "goodbye." Sitting alone in my car in the parking lot, I'd said out loud, "Oh god, you shouldn't even go home, she's going to pass away tonight." But I chose to go. I'd needed food and a shower. My intuition could be wrong, I'd hoped.

At 11:45pm that night, I'd received a call saying that the family should be at the hospice. I'd asked if she was dying, but they wouldn't answer the question with a yes. Everything else they'd said led me to believe that the answer, indeed, was yes. I'd called both of my sisters and told them what was happening. Sarah said she'd be there as soon as she could. Michelle said she'd come the next day – she'd been driving back from Toronto when I'd called.

When I arrived, Bonnie was there. Bonnie is a First Nations woman who I have done ceremony with in the past, and with whom I had attended a couple of her spiritual events. Bonnie explained that Hospice had contacted her to come in case the family didn't arrive. Her volunteer position was simply to be with people at a time like this. But, she hadn't been called and to do it before – that had been her first time. It was so special that she'd been there. I'd hugged her and she left me to be with my Mum, telling me that she would stay nearby.

I held Mum's hand and I talked to her. Mum was struggling to breathe. She had not been conscious for five days. About forty-five minutes later, Ron had arrived, saying that he couldn't sleep while I was here. He held my hand. He held my Mum's hand. We both talked to her. At times, I saw my Mum's eyebrows go up at very specific things that I'd said. I knew she heard me. I'd prayed. We'd prayed. I let Mum know that it was ok to go now, we were all going to be ok. I had already promised Mum that I would always look after my sisters. Mum had been worried about my younger sister; Sarah was Mum's baby girl. I told her she was going to see her Mummy and Daddy and Sue. My understanding of how death works is that Mum had already been seeing her family, long before that moment. They'd been with her, helping her to cross over.

After 3am, Mum took her last breath just as I'd said "Amen" in a final prayer. I knew it was the last prayer I'd say. I called a nurse to come and assist. They'd noted the time of death. And Mum was gone. Forever. Mum had given that moment to me. Sarah had arrived just five minutes later. Sarah just knew that Mum had wanted to protect her baby girl from that moment. I'm certain that was true. And I'd known that Mum and I had a karmic tie that required me to be there at her transition. She was me. I was her. And everything I'd healed in my ability to love her fully had healed my ability to love myself.

Bonnie came in and she'd pulled a medicine card for me and my Mum. Squirrel had been pulled for my Mum. Squirrel was the medicine animal for resourcefulness and saving for a rainy day. For me, Bonnie pulled Bear. Bear was the medicine animal for mothering, nurturing, protecting. Mum had gifted me with the gifts of both of those animals. Mum was frugal and had taught me how to pay attention to my pennies. And like the Mama Bear, she had always nurtured, protected, and looked after me.

After we were done with what needed to be done, Bonnie asked if she could do an Eagle Feather ceremony with my Mum to help her in the transition. I'd said yes. That moment was between god, Bonnie and my Mum. I hadn't been part of it. And it had been perfect. My Mum hadn't had strong spiritual beliefs, but she'd loved First Nations culture and artwork. Like me, she had felt a connection there. An eagle feather ceremony had been divinely perfect. God, the Universe... some force of the Divine had placed Bonnie in Hospice that night. For that, I am forever grateful.

In the parking lot at Hospice, Ron had gotten into his car, and I'd gotten into mine. When I'd turned it on, the following words sang out of the radio, "Please forgive me for all I've done / So I bet my life, I bet my life / I bet my life for you." Then the song had ended. I had never heard it before, and if I had, I hadn't listened. It wasn't familiar. But I'd felt like Mum was talking to me through the song at that moment.

It has torn me apart to write this section for you. But it's important that I did it. That was one of the most important moments of my life. My Mum brought me into this world. My Mum taught me Unconditional Love. She allowed me to Love her Unconditionally in her final months. And I helped my Mum leave this world knowing that she felt loved, that she knew that her children loved her, and that she knew that any mistakes she felt she made over the years did not matter, not one iota.

Do you know a miracle when you see one? I do. Getting through my Mum's illness and passing, getting through my Aunt's illness and passing while going through the motions of a court case – without having a drink or taking a pain-killer or smoking a joint. That's a goddamn, bona fide miracle! And that's the miracle of Recovery. Right there.

I'm sure there were many moments in 2017 that I could have handled with more grace, but I handled them. The day before my Mum passed, I remember being in her room, bawling my eyes out, devastated with what was happening in front of my eyes, and I realized there was a full bottle of red wine in the room. In a drawer, there were some pot cookies my sister had brought in for Mum to help her with pain. And I remember thinking how nice it would be to numb my pain, right then and there... just take a drink... just have a cookie. Something. I hurt so badly. My heart felt like it was being imploded over and over and over again. But I didn't. I sometimes wonder if Mum chose to leave when she did because she wasn't sure how much more hurt I could take before I cracked.

The following day, I'd searched online for a song with the words "I bet my life." I found out it was by a band I'd already loved – Imagine Dragons! The song was I Bet My Life.

Oh my God. My Mum was singing to me in the car just moments after her passing! But it wasn't her singing about only the things she'd done, she was singing about the things I'd done too. I mean, right down to the lines, "Now remember when I told you that's the last you'll see of me / Remember when I broke you down to tears." Those were the exact words I'd said when I left Canada – I told her I'd never be back. I was leaving for good.

This song forever belongs to me and my Mum. It's our song of forgiveness. We are two peas in a pod, my Mum and I. Anything I saw in her, I could see in me. And that I was able to see her differently hadn't been a bad thing. It had been an awesome thing. I learned how to Love her unconditionally, and in doing so, it brought me closer to Unconditional Love for myself. By loving her unconditionally and allowing her the grace to be human and make mistakes in her life, I was in turn, allowing myself... finally, after all these years, to give myself that same Grace.

Thank you, Mum. The things you taught me throughout my life, and in those final four months were some of the greatest gifts of my life. And more than that, you gave me LIFE. The gift of life is the most precious of all things.

I love you Mum. I miss you.

THROUGH THE YEARS

And so, I find myself feeling driven to talk about some other difficulties that need addressing; namely, my relationship with my Dad. You know, our parents are our greatest teachers. It doesn't matter whether they are making good or bad decisions, either way, their actions teach us. The truth about my Dad is this – he's a great Dad and he always has been! Yes, he's made mistakes. Welcome to the club, we're all members. If my Mum's passing taught me anything, it's that mistakes made years ago don't matter.

The first twelve years of my life are full of memories camping as a family, going to the Western Fair, Hallowe'en fun, Dad driving me to soccer, basketball, volleyball, music, and god only knows where else. My memories are full of laughter and tickle fights, silliness and mad antics. Dad was my hero. I looked up to him and trusted him more than anyone else on the planet.

Neither of us maneuvered through my parents divorce well. My Dad wasn't an expert at saying healthy things when things got tough. His own parents had been emotionally cool and detached. He said things that felt hurtful a whole bunch of times. He made the wrong choice, a bunch of times. So did I, but I was 12... 13... 14. I was always able to cut myself some slack for the mistakes I made then because I was the kid. He was an adult. He was supposed to know how to do this, wasn't he? Well, we didn't. And I built a huge wall between us after the divorce. The wall got higher and higher with every moment that disappointed me.

By my late teens, it would take me literally two to three weeks to recover from a visit with him. Something minor would set me off. I'd see a family photo without me or my sisters in it, and I'd be hurt. He'd tell me about a trip they were going on, without us, and I'd want to punch him in the face. That's how I felt. I'm not going to sugar coat this. Because it's important. And over the years, it didn't get better, only worse. I would accept monetary gifts at Christmas and birthdays. I went to him for financial help during university. He gave. I received that help. But nothing he did ever changed my heart. Until I was in the hospital in 2005. That's when things finally started to shift.

My father had stood by me like a rock. Every day for the five weeks I'd been in the hospital, my Dad had visited. Every day he'd bring me Tim Horton's coffee, and coffee for a bunch of my friends too. The gesture hadn't been lost on me. When I was fifteen and had attempted suicide, I'd been crushed by the fact that he hadn't been the first one to the hospital, even though he'd been the first one called. That pain had lingered, but in 2005 and 2006, he'd been there for me. He'd been supportive, and he did everything he could to help me through that horrible, scary time. Once I was out of the hospital, my Dad had done everything he could to encourage me to leave my current life and start again. He'd never stopped coming around, and he'd never stopped being concerned about my well being.

When I took off in October of 2006, and not a single person knew whether I was alive or dead for months, I knew my father had been beyond distraught. And yet, when

I'd arrived on a plane, kicked out of the United States in May of 2009, guess who had picked me up at the airport? My Dad.

My Dad rocks. And I have done everything I can, and I will continue to do everything I can, to Love him Unconditionally. I wished I'd done it sooner with my Mum. If I don't Love him Unconditionally now, I know I'm going to have wished I had. Our relationship is imperfect, but it's still damn good. I had to get my ego out of the way for that relationship to happen. Once upon a time, this section wouldn't have looked like this. I would have trashed my Dad and said things to prove that I was right and he was wrong. No one had been right, and no one had been wrong. In our past, we'd both lost.

In learning to Love my Dad Unconditionally, I've also learned to Love my stepmom Unconditionally. Yvonne has done her very best over the years to try to keep our family together. Like the rest of us, she too made mistakes. And like the rest of us, she too deserves Grace for that. The most important thing about Yvonne, for me, is that she loves my Dad and my Dad loves her. They are happy together, and they both deserve that happiness. I'm not sure what he'd do without her, quite frankly. It took years to heal our relationship, but the more I've grown up, the more I've appreciated Yvonne. I don't think I was willing to really get to know her when I was younger. I'd only see what I'd wanted to see. I'm grateful for her patience with our relationship.

You know, I was having a conversation with my Dad one day about 'soulmates'. I believe one of my exes had come up in that regard. I told my Dad, "Soulmates don't always stay together forever. Soulmates are people who teach us our biggest life lessons, like the karmic lessons. Sometimes it's forever, sometimes it's for a season." And my Dad looked at me thoughtfully and he said, "Huh. You and I must be soulmates."

I almost fell off my chair! I believe that was one of the most profound things I'd ever heard my Dad say. I'm not even sure he remembers saying it. But I sure do! Dad, we are soulmates. I have no idea what I taught you. I hope it was more than patience and humility. You taught me some of my best lessons, and I thank you for that. I Love you, Dad. You're still my hero.

Family is hard. It's some of the hardest stuff for folks to work through on the healing journey. The end result looks different for everyone. Some people end up divorcing family members and cutting them out of their lives. Some people mend fences. Some people struggle with it until the day they die. I'm very blessed. My family is full of good people. Not all of us are great at family, but we do our best, and our best looks different for each of us. I'm grateful for my big, beautiful, awesome family.

Often, self forgiveness is part of the equation with family. Letting go is often part of the lesson. Acceptance is always part of the lesson. And remember, acceptance doesn't mean that we accept bad behaviour, it means accepting the way a person is, and then learning how to let go of trying to change or fix it. Acceptance is the end of the struggle against 'what is'. Our family members aren't going to change by us badgering them over and over again about how we think they should be. They are exactly who they should be, whether we understand the reason for their incarnation or not. When working with clients, I like to express the following, when they are trying to rescue someone or fix someone or change someone they love:

In my own life, I've been at some horrible, horrible places – in the gutter horrible. And looking back, I know I was exactly where I needed to be in every one of those awful moments, in order for me to learn what I needed to learn and be who I was going to become. It doesn't mean I liked where I was, but I was where I needed to be. When I look at someone else who I think needs to change or see something or heal or be rescued, I remind myself that they are exactly where they need to be, in order for their life to unfold, and their lessons to reveal. I let go of trying to control that process. It doesn't belong to me to control. If they ask for help, I do what I can to facilitate that help, and I let go of my expectations of what the result of that will be.

Applying this thinking in my own relationships, whether at work or at home, has brought such a deeper peace to my life. I don't have to rescue the world – it was never a job assigned to me. Everyone is exactly where they are supposed to be, and I'm not usually privy to knowing why – that's between them and the Universe. If I have difficulty being around someone else's energy, I'm not going to attempt to change them, I am going to change how I respond to them including whether or not I allow them into my space. That is what is within my power to change – me.

ME AND YOU AND YOU AND ME

Like magic, the fog lifted just before Marathon, but it was right around the same time the roadcrews appeared everywhere along the Trans Canada Highway. This ride was giving me lots of time to think between the slow crawl in the fog and stopping dead in construction. I was out of the fog so I turned my tunes back on!

Happiness came to me through the music while I rode through construction and looked at the glorious landscapes. Next up was You're a Superstar, by Love Inc. This song makes me smile with my heart, every time I hear it. It came into my life in 2010 or 2011 even though it had been written years earlier. This was an anthem for my journey towards healthy self esteem, and it has stayed with me all these years. Listening to it on my bike took me to that squishy, huggy place where I was learning to say nice things to myself and treat myself the way I deserved to be treated.

Healthy self esteem is not about thinking you are better than anyone else. It's about having an accurate view of yourself and still liking yourself, regardless of what you see. It's about treating yourself well and not self sabotaging. Healthy self esteem is about working gently on the traits you want to change without judging yourself harshly during the process. If self esteem is based on a false view of the self, it will eventually crumble when the shadow self comes flying out unexpectedly.

I'm at a spot in life now where I make much fewer mistakes, but when I do make a mistake, I can own it, I can apologize. In addition to that, I have compassion for the part of myself that made the mistake. That was an impossible set of tasks for me once upon a time. Everything that went wrong had been someone else's fault. This way of thinking was connected to the deeply entrenched belief that I was bad. If I admitted that I had made a mistake, it reinforced the belief that I was bad. But by not acknowledging my mistakes and blaming others, it created a vicious cycle of making me feel even worse about myself because deep down inside I knew what was my fault and what wasn't my fault.

The other beautiful thing that happens when I make a mistake now, (even a doozy!) is that I find compassion for myself immediately in the process. Even though my initial response, still to this day, is to start to knock myself down for making the mistake with loud thoughts like: "how could you be so stupid!?" and "Why are you so insensitive?!" Thing is, I catch these thoughts now. And I put an end to them. I take a moment to put my hands over my heart and say, "I love the one who just did that," and I send myself some compassion. "I love the one who was talking negatively about herself because of her mistake," I say, and I send myself some compassion.

I don't care how silly you might think this sounds. I guess it's related to how much you want to change your life or not, eh? Me? I had to change. I almost killed myself with my shitty self esteem. For most of my life, I'd made bad choices after bad choices resulting in a barrage of self sabotaging. Even when I got clean and sober, I'd still made some very self sabotaging decisions.

True happiness without healthy self esteem is a difficult thing to achieve if we aren't ignorantly happy to start with. "Ignorance is bliss" is a true statement for quite a few people – they can be happy without ever doing any self introspective work. Good for them! There's nothing wrong with that – that's fantastic. But growing numbers of people aren't happy, are experiencing anxiety, depression, mood swings and general dissatisfaction. Self introspection is necessary for creating and sustaining a healthy, happy life.

Me? I'm a Superstar. You know why? Because I survived what almost killed me. I'm a Superstar because I never gave up on myself. I'm a superstar because I worked my ass off to climb up, inch by inch, rock by rock, memory by memory, to fix what was broken. I'm a Superstar because I showed up on Earth, even though I knew it was going to be hard. I knew my path was not going to be an easy one, and I showed up anyways. I'm a Superstar because I go out of my way to point out to others why they are a Superstar too. One of my personal missions in life is to help others learn to love themselves. Reach for the sky and hold your head up high!

The song, All My Friends, by the Revivalists came on. Apparently, this song is about the lead singer's struggles with alcohol during his 20s, and his friends that helped him through it. When this song plays, I am reminded of the friends who have helped me over the years. I've had amazing friends throughout my lifetime, even during the worst years. But want to know something I'm not very good at? Maintaining friendships. I'd love to find a way to figure out how so that I am good at it, but I don't feel particularly skilled at friendship. I find it more difficult to keep friends as a sober person than I did when I was using drugs and alcohol. I rarely allow myself to be vulnerable with friends. A small handful of people get in past all my walls, and I mean very small. Once they're in... it's still not guaranteed that we will always be friends.

Just like I couldn't recognize or experience healthy life-partner relationships, healthy friendships fell into that same boat. I had no idea what that looked or felt like. All my friendships had been riddled with drug and alcohol use, and through most of them, I had been an active addict. Active addicts don't make great friends. Recovering addicts aren't always great at making and keeping friends either – some are, some aren't. My behaviour has improved. I know how to be thoughtful and how to be healthy in friendships, but I allow few people in close enough to build strong ties. I can pinpoint the time in my life when the pattern had started. It was when I'd changed schools in grade seven, and then again in grade eight, and then again in grade ten. Not to mention the change from elementary to secondary school which for me had been in grade nine. I had changed schools four years in a row. Add on top of this a new distrust of my father and being molested by Don. I'd permanently changed within myself over that time. I'd started to detach, and not in a healthy way but as a coping mechanism.

I have a small handful of friends I trust with my life – some of them ride motorcycles. I mean, I have a thousand friends on Facebook, but what does that really mean? How many of those people know me intimately? How many of them do I spend time with? How many of us talk on the phone? I've been hard on myself regarding friendships in my life. Part of me wishes I could do a better job of having awesome friendships... but a very authentic part of me likes to be left alone so I can do my own thing. I'm not unhappy having few friends. In fact, almost all the things I do, I love to do alone. And it's weird because in my active addiction, I always had to have people around. I couldn't ever do things by myself.

When my business first opened, I'd just loved all the connections I was making! Now? I appreciate the quiet. I appreciate the silence. I seek a walk in the woods with my camera. I seek a ride on my motorcycle, by myself or with a bike buddy or with my husband. I'm not an introvert. But I'm not an extrovert either, like I thought I was for years. I'm an extroverted introvert? I'm an introverted extrovert? I'm not sure. I love the time I do spend with friends and I love my time to myself. Amazing how much sobriety changed that.

It's perfectly ok that I don't go out of my way to have lots of friends and constantly be out with other people. When I didn't like me, of course I didn't want to just be by myself. I needed others to feel validated, to feel worthy, to feel loved. I'm perfectly capable of providing all of that for myself now. I recall it being very difficult at first when I took off to the US, and then when I came back. I didn't have friends to rely on at all during those times. I also recall getting so comfortable with being alone that I didn't want to go out with others much. After returning to Canada, I did a heck of a lot of crafts, artwork and jewelry making during my getting-to-know-and-like-me time, by myself, and it worked wonders. Now? Now I'm happy to be by myself doing something I enjoy or doing nothing at all. I'm also happy to go out with people and enjoy life together – just not all the time. I need the me time. I like the me time. And that is growth for me. I value all my friends, and I appreciate what they add to my life. I'm grateful for every single person I have ever called friend, even if it ended badly.

There is a part of me, hidden deep down inside, that wishes I could maintain friendships better. This is a very vulnerable place for me, in fact, this is one of the few places that still hurts... like... really hurts. That skill I have that allows me to detach, at one time in my life, it was a saving grace. It helped me survive some very painful experiences. I can honestly say, it saved my life more than once. But once I learned how to do that, it became more than a challenge to stop doing it, to stop detaching. It's like the ability is as natural as clearing my throat. It has become part of me. I remind myself that it helps me to do the work I do. My inner work makes some of it easier on my heart. But that doesn't stop this trait from hurting me. I have never claimed that my Recovery is complete, and this is one of the places that hasn't fully recovered. Buddhism teaches detachment, but not the kind I speak of. Becoming detached from one's emotions removes us from the full human experience. My heart got scared to fully engage in emotion, and I've had to work terribly hard to learn how to not do that. I'm a work in progress.

POCKETFUL OF SUNSHINE

Construction was the theme of the ride between Wawa and Thunder Bay. Just when I thought I saw the last of it, more would appear ahead. I had bursts of open highway and free riding, broken up by long stretches of rock blasting, highway widening, and road building. Nipigon was my next big stop after Marathon. The first thing I saw in Nipigon was a huge, massive bridge that took up the skyline! As I crossed the bridge, I saw that there was a large gap in the highway, a paved section, that didn't belong to either direction of the road. It was just wasted space in the middle. Without thinking, I pulled my bike into that gap, parked it, got off, and grabbed my phone quickly. I needed to take photos. I wish I had taken a few more minutes to get the 'perfect shot' but I was nervous that law enforcement might come and usher me along. I snapped a quick pic and got out of there.

From Nipigon, I drove straight through to Thunder Bay. Along the highway, I saw road signs for the amethyst mines. I definitely wanted to stop at one of them! The mine that caught my eye was called Panorama Amethyst. Watching for signs, I exited the highway where it directed me. The mine was 8km ahead, so off I went. Probably about 5km in at the most, the road turned to gravel, a poorly taken care of gravel road at that. I stopped my bike and turned around. This wasn't the kind of road I'd take my bike on unless I absolutely had to. I was disappointed. I wanted to be able to bring back some amethyst that I knew for sure was from Thunder Bay because I'd collected it myself.

For years people had told me stories about coming to the Thunder Bay area to get their own amethyst. I'd done my own rock-hounding up in the Ottawa district before, getting myself rose quartz, smoky quartz, amazonite, mica, and a few other things, in addition to getting sodalite in Bancroft, Ontario. It's not that I didn't have tonnes of amethyst already, it's that I like to get rocks, even rocks found on the beach, from places I visit.

I had been preparing to teach my Introduction to Crystals course for the first time in 2013 when some memories flooded in about crystals in my life. We'd still lived in London, so this had been before I was eight-and-a-half-years-old. I used to ride my bicycle to Lambeth most sunny Saturdays to go visit a rocks and minerals speciality store. It wasn't a metaphysical shop like White Feather, but more like a geological shop that was concerned with the science of rocks and minerals. I remember the owner had spent hours with me on Saturday afternoons telling me about the different rocks and how they were formed. My young mind had been captivated. I'd loved rocks – even then – it was why I'd ride my bicycle a few miles just to go visit the store.

You know, I don't believe that I'd ever purchased a single rock from him. And I'm sure he didn't care. I know I don't care when people come in and just want to talk about rocks and crystals at my store. I am more than happy to share all the information and knowledge I can. And when kids come in wanting to learn, I get out the most interesting specimens I can – enhydro agates with water trapped inside the stones, elestial smoky quartz, folding over itself, fulgurite – fossilized lightening, and anything else I know I would have enjoyed seeing as a child.

When I'd arrived in Arizona, people started giving me rocks and saying "Here, hold this. It will help you." I'd walked around with pockets full of rocks because people said the rocks would help me with my life. Eventually, I'd been able to take a workshop on crystals in Payson, and I'd learned that all the stones had different metaphysical properties that could help me heal different things. I'd begun to research stones. I'd discovered that the stones people had given me had healing properties for the exact things I'd been working on healing, without them actually knowing what I'd been working on healing.

That's when I'd started to put some faith in crystals and stones, when I was in Arizona. To this day, I continue to experience amazing things and experience incredible insights when I work with certain crystals with intention. Believe it or don't believe it. But remember – what you believe is what you'll experience. So why not open the doors to limitless possibilities?

Getting back on the highway from the gravel road, I continued for the last 20km or so to Thunder Bay. Instead of going straight to my hostess's house, I stopped in at the Harley Davidson shop. I wanted to find a Canadian flag for my bike for the Women Riders World Relay. As I pulled in, another lady was saddling up on her bike getting ready to go. She introduced herself as Ruth, saying that she wasn't going on the official ride, but she was going to be there with us in the morning to see us off on the 19th when the relay left Thunder Bay. I was barely in town and already meeting riders! I was saddened to learn that she had just been widowed that year, and that was part of the reason she wasn't joining us. Her life was a little topsy turvy, and she hadn't been sure that she could do it in time for registration. I asked if I could give her a hug. She said yes and seemed grateful as we hugged each other. I held back tears. Thanking me for the hug, we promised to look for each other on Thursday morning.

Inside, I was unable to find a Canadian flag for my bike, but they suggested I try a dollar store or the airport. Oh, good idea! I asked if they had any Thunder Bay patches or pins for my jacket but they didn't have those either. Damnit! What I did buy was a Harley shirt which I have never done in my life. I don't ride a Harley – my bike is a Honda. Harley shirts are expensive if you ask me. You are paying extra for the name. But they had this purple shirt with teal green writing on it. The same colours as my business colours! My two favourite colours! A long sleeve shirt with Thunder Bay Harley on it, I was sold at $72! Why not? It was a special trip and I just spent a full week getting there by myself. I earned an extra expensive shirt.

As soon as I said that to myself, it dawned on me that I had driven all the way there. I was there!!! Oh my god! I'm in Thunder Bay! I screamed in my head. I had just gotten my license last year, and I just rode for a week all by myself! Inside, I was doing cartwheels and flips! I wanted to cry. It's funny that I hadn't even realized before that moment that I had reached my destination. For a few months, I'd been going on and on about how I was driving up to Thunder Bay, and when I finally got there? I didn't even acknowledge it right away! I think I was still in get-stuff-done mode. I needed flags and pins and patches, of course!

So how did I feel at that moment of realization? I was proud of myself. I didn't need anyone else to tell me they were proud of me. I was proud of me! It had taken some guts and courage to ride my bike all the way up there by myself, not knowing what the weather would be, not knowing what kind of people I could run into, not knowing what difficulties I could face. Damn straight I was proud of myself!

Moments like that one, they are how I continue to build my self confidence because I can remind myself that I can do anything I set my mind to. For years I sought that validation from outside of myself, needing to hear certain people say they were proud of me and rarely hearing it. Now? I take the time to pat myself on the back when I do something good. I acknowledge and validate my experiences, and no one can take that away from me. Honestly, I don't give a shit if you're proud of me or not. I don't care if you like me or not. I like me, and I'm ok with who I am. Your validation is no longer required.

The Fool's journey was nearing completion with my arrival in Thunder Bay. The Fool had been traveling since September 11th, 2006 when she closed the door on an old life and set out to find a new one. In Thunder Bay, the Fool transformed into The Sun tarot card archetype. The Sun card is a wonderful, positive, uplifting card. Representing a time in life when we have found our joy, when we have become perfectly comfortable with the self. The Sun card reminds us that our joy radiates onto others, almost like a contagion. When we are in our purpose, when we are comfortable in our own skin, others feel that, and it invites them to do the same.

The Sun card
Rider-Waite Tarot deck

Riding up to Thunder Bay was a success. Not only had I proven to myself that I could achieve this on my own, I became inspired on this trip to write The Book that had been shouting at me to be written for thirteen years. I embraced my purpose. That's the Sun card, embracing happiness, joy, being in our purpose, being unabashedly ourselves, innocent, pure, and open to the success that has always called us. The child you see riding naked, happy, bouncing on the back of the horse – that's me on my motorcycle arriving in Thunder Bay for the Women Riders World Relay on my trusty steed Stella.

I left the Harley Davidson dealership and went to the airport still on the hunt for Canadian flags. Jackpot! At the airport gift shop, I found small little flags on sticks. They would do. I could attach two of them to my luggage holder. While there, the ladies were asking me about my adventure and I was happy to tell them all about the WRWR. They were excited to hear about it.

"Oh, my friend Julie is going! You'll meet her!" One lady said.

I laughed and explained I had already met Julie's other friend, Michelle, down by the Agawa Pictographs. I jokingly asked if Julie knew everyone. I was told, yes, and we all laughed.

Heading out of the airport, I put Monique's address into my GPS. It was time to head to my lodgings for the night. Within ten minutes, I pulled up to her house, and was ushered into one of the nicest working garages I'd ever been in. The garage was functional, obviously used for storing and maintaining motorcycles, but it was spotless! The floor was made of some kind of thick, hard rubber. Along the wall was the tool area with tools put away neatly, many of them in a large tool cabinet. Two motorcycles were already in the garage, and there was lots of room for my bike and more. As I turned Stella off and removed my helmet, Monique greeted me with a warm hello and a big smile.

Monique was one of those natural beauties who didn't have to do a single thing to brighten up a room – she made it look easy. She's a gal with no pretension who is kind. There's no way you'd ever feel less than when you're with her. Right away, I felt welcome and that's not always the case for me with a total stranger. You see, I didn't know Monique at all other than by a few words exchanged on the Facebook WRWR Canada page. When she found out I was coming up a day early to Thunder Bay, she'd offered me a place to stay for both nights. I took her up on her offer for the first night. The second night, I was staying at the hotel with my friend Joanne, who was also coming up from Windsor. Some other women from out of town for the WRWR would be staying at that same hotel, so I thought we might meet some more of the riders from out west there too. Monique offered me a lovely room in the basement, and gave me free use of the house, including the laundry room. I was very happy to get some things in the wash so that I would have a full wardrobe for the final five days of my adventure.

I struggle meeting new people when there is no one I know around to bring some comfort. If I have a friend with me, I'm fine. But by myself, with all new people, I feel self conscious. It brings me some anxiety. Folks who know me might find that odd. I often present as very confident, and I'm great in front of a crowd. But that crowd is most often filled with people I know, so the anxiety isn't there. As I looked around Monique's home, I had a dialogue going in my head, one that was very quiet, but I became aware of it. In my thoughts, I was commenting to myself about how lovely her home looked. How I wish I had the ability or even the desire, to decorate a home that looked like it was right out of a magazine. Some people seem to fit in with the Universe so easily, they just look like they belong, like they have always belonged.

But I stopped my thoughts right there. The truth was I had no idea what Monique's life was like, or any stranger for that matter. I had no idea what she struggled with, what hurdles she'd faced in her life. This reaction of mine was a very natural reaction... telling myself the narrative that some women have always fit in, and have always looked like they knew what they were doing in life. Of course, there was absolutely a chance that Monique felt awkward too when meeting new people. For sure, she had her own narratives playing on triggered loops in her head too.

As a child, I hadn't cared that I didn't fit in. I hadn't been one of the popular kids with a gaggle of friends. After my parents' divorce, I know I'd tried to fit in more – to find my place as one of the cool kids, though I'd never aimed for popularity. As an adult, I relied on drugs and alcohol to make me feel at ease when meeting new people or when in awkward social situations. With a beer or two in me, I'd settle in to feeling at home.

But I don't do that now. I choose sobriety. Yes, I'm comfortable in my own skin, but I still feel awkward as hell around most new people. I do my best to never let that show. I push myself through the social situations instead of fleeing like I want to. I force myself to stay and do my best to feel more comfortable. It helped that I had my own space to go to at Monique's house so I could settle in alone too. When I retired to my room, I gave myself some compassion and love. I knew I wasn't feeling at ease yet, even though Monique and her then-husband were perfectly wonderful hosts with no expectations. It wasn't about them, it was about me. People don't have to do a single thing to make me feel awkward, I just am awkward at times. I've accepted this part of myself, and it gets easier and easier for me to deal with (even if it takes some time in the actual situations) as my life moves forward.

It's ok that I'm awkward and I feel like an outsider whenever I meet strangers. I don't have to struggle against that anymore, it just is what it is. And the more I accept it, the easier it becomes. I have tools for managing it – much like what I was doing right then – retreating to my room for a few minutes to check Facebook, to ground myself with familiarity, to send myself some love, and then head back to try to connect with strangers. I knew I could do it.

And I did! Monique was a wonderful host. She served a fantastic meal, and I felt more comfortable as the evening went on. Monique's then-husband took the little flags I bought at the airport and strengthened up the sticks so they wouldn't get wrecked before my ride in two days.

DAY 8 – SEPTEMBER 18TH, 2020

FEELS LIKE HOME TO ME

The day before the big day! Monique offered to show me some of the sites around Thunder Bay, and I was excited to get out and do that with her. Our first stop that morning was at Mount McKay. Mount McKay belongs to the Fort Williams First Nations people. We were greeted at the entrance by a wonderful woman who let us in and only charged us for the price of one car instead of two motorcycles since we were together. In Ojibwe, the location is called Animikii-wajiw. Locally, it's spelled Anemki-waucheu which means Thunder Mountain. Apparently, sacred ceremonies are still done on Mount McKay. It is only since a road was put in that non-Natives have access to the area.

The ride up was lovely and quick. I noticed some statues along the way and when we dismounted at the top I let Monique know that I wanted to stop and see the statues on the way down. We had a fantastic view of Thunder Bay and the surrounding area. There were a few memorials at the top. One was a white cross with "In Memory of Local Indians who fell in the Great War 1914-1918" on a plaque. Below it had lists of the names of "Forgotten Soldiers." Officers on the top plaque and general ranks below. I said a quick prayer of thanks for their sacrifice as I stood before the cross. We also saw the chapel that had been built in 1888 and restored in 1939 that was dedicated to Rev. Father Joseph Heber. I took pictures of the dedicated monuments; Monique and I took some pictures of each other. I also posed with an eagle statue – of course!

On our way back down, we stopped at the statues of First Nations women that were in a clearing. I was very attracted to this spot. It looked like a lovely place to put a blanket down, set out some crystals, and maybe do a prayer offering ceremony to the people who I feel intuitively, have always seen this place as sacred. Mount McKay sits so high up above the surrounding landscape, I could envision young men in times past, coming here for first rites or camping alone on a vision quest. I felt good energy on Mount

McKay, grounding energy. I felt the presence of many who had been there for a very long time, maybe thousands of years. The sacred is everywhere. It is all around us if we just get still enough to feel its presence.

Monique took a video of me riding my bike down around one of the curves before we left the top of Mount McKay. Then, we were off to see other sites around Thunder Bay.

After leading us down back streets and side roads, Monique pulled over to ask me if I needed to gas up, but as she pulled over, so did a police SUV. With its lights on. My heart sank. I knew what we were being pulled over for. We had rolled through a whole bunch of stop signs instead of coming to complete stops. A serious faced police officer stepped out of the vehicle. He walked up to us and asked if we knew why we were being pulled over. Both of us shook our heads no.

"You didn't come to a stop at the last two stop signs," he said.

In my head, I was thinking, "We didn't come to a full stop at the last 10 stop signs!" but I wasn't going to say that. I know when to be a smartass and when not to be with cops. At the border, in the airport, in that situation – not being a smartass is a good choice. The police officer asked for our driver's licenses, insurance and registration. Digging through my saddlebag, I found everything and gave it to him. Monique was only able to produce her registration and insurance. She'd left her ID at home. Oh dear.

I started babbling on about the Women Riders World Relay, and how I'd never been to Thunder Bay before. I told the officer how women from around the whole world were participating in the race – the largest motorcycle relay ever! Babble, babble, babble. Monique stood there smiling, looking cute, cool and guilty, all at the same time. Officer Rivet (as we discovered his name), of the Anishinabek Police Services, went back to his vehicle, and ran our info through his computer. Monique and I whispered to each other as we waited. Monique said she'd never been pulled over on her bike and she was shocked that we had been. I wondered for a moment if it was because I was wearing a club jacket. Maybe he'd wanted to know what club I belonged to, but I kept that to myself.

When he emerged from the vehicle, he gave us a little lecture about coming to a full stop, then said it was our lucky day – he wasn't going to give us fines. He did take a moment to explain how much our fines would have been though, if he had decided to give them to us – over $600 and 6 points. Ouch! Truth be known, I've come to a complete stop almost every time since our little interaction!

Our next stop was at Kakabeka Falls. It was a bit of a ride to get there as the falls were about 30km west of Thunder Bay. The name comes from Ojibwe, Gakaabikaa, which means 'waterfall over a cliff.' I love waterfalls. I love water. I feel re-energized when I get around natural waterways. Waterfalls have high energy as they pour over and down into the rocks. I can feel the power as I stand near them. And so, when we got there, I stood near the rushing water fall allowing the power to flow all around me. Monique stood quietly with me as I took in the moment. We both spotted a bald eagle above us and flying nearer. I had my good camera with me, so I grabbed it, and not having time to adjust my settings or prepare for the shot, I aimed it up in the sky and snapped one picture.

I'd taken a hell of a lot of eagle photos since 2015 when I got my first quality camera. Some of the photos I have are awesome, I'm not shy to say that. The photo I took that day with Monique isn't the best shot I've ever taken, by far, but it very may well be my favourite because of the moment I'd taken it.

I had just ridden my motorcycle up to Thunder Bay – a week-long ride – and I did it by myself. I'd never done anything like that before. I was about to go on an adventure that only a few thousand women around the world had signed up for – and I was one of them! It wasn't just any relay, it was the largest male or female motorcycle relay ever – and I was part of it! Then the Universe sent me an Eagle. An Eagle that said, "Well done! You're soaring now!" I'd been able to get out my camera and capture the Divine moment not just for me, but for you – the readers of The Book I was destined to write.

Eagles bring messages from the Divine because they fly closest to the heavens. Eagle medicine is that of the Thunderbird – powerful, strong, far seeing. I'd seen a couple of eagles already on my trip, but this one was extra special. He came in close – that photo was taken with an 18-200mm lens which is not a large zoom. He was right over our heads spreading his mighty wings in a divine wave from the Universe!

It had required serious healing for me to make it to that point in my life, to be on that motorcycle adventure. But it wasn't just about the motorcycle trip. It was about eight-and-a-half years of sobriety. It was about healing the crippling phobia I'd had of anything to do with motorcycles. It was about overcoming my PTSD. It was about coming into my power, which really blossomed, near the end of 2017 when I'd finished the court proceedings.

Coming into my power meant being able to fully own what belonged to me and letting others own what belonged to them. It meant being self aware and no longer allowing old, outdated emotional programs to run my life. Being in my power meant owning the consequences of my choices. It meant accepting myself, all of myself. Being in my power meant coming into my authentic self and feeling comfortable in my own skin. This ride... this ride for me, was a celebration of all of that. And the Universe had been kind enough to send an Eagle so close I could almost touch it. I felt the spirit of Annelle there, my Reiki teacher. I felt the spirit of my Mum, my Granny, my Auntie Sue. My ancestors were watching and cheering me on.

Monique and I rode down to the marina on Lake Superior after our encounter with the eagle at the falls. Lake Superior was gorgeous but the skies were misty. We were barely able to make out the Sleeping Giant, but we did. A part of Ontario parks, when viewed from town, the peninsula very much resembles a warrior laying down. There are wonderful legends about Nanabijou, The Sleeping Giant, in the Ojibway culture. The short version of the legend says that the giant Nanabijou was turned to stone when he revealed the location of a great silver mine to white men. I saw so much beauty and yet felt so much sadness all in the same place.

After the marina visit, we went to Bliss, Monique's favourite eatery, for lunch. Deciding to lunch on the patio, we found a table outside. Without having a moment to collect my thoughts, I was approached by a young woman who appeared to be homeless. I don't mean to be judgemental with that comment. I recognized the look from first-hand experience. Usually, the first thing I notice is the many bags a person is carrying. The woman was carrying many bags. When you're homeless, you have nowhere to put your most prized possessions, whether it be a family photo or a tube of toothpaste, so you carry them in bags with you everywhere.

The young woman asked me to buy her a meal at McDonald's which was just across the parking lot. There I was taking twelve days off work, riding my bike to Thunder Bay, just for the fun of it – of course I could buy her a meal! We went into the McDonald's and I ordered a Big Mac meal. The woman was standing at my side. The staff member turned around to her manager and whispered something. They both looked right at the woman I was helping, had a quiet discussion, and then I heard, "Go ahead."

I had no idea how many people each day that woman asked for a Big Mac Meal. I had no idea if she ate them herself or took them to friends or sold them to someone else for money. All I knew was that I felt such sadness for her. I could tell that she didn't always get served there because the staff had considered denying me the meal.

There but for the grace of god, go I.

I always keep that message in my heart. I don't know why I was able to fix my life, and some people aren't able to. I am blessed with my family. I am blessed with the right people who walked into my life. I am blessed with a determination, that even in the middle of complete insanity, never wavered, and helped me to pull myself out of my darkness. It's in my blood. It's in my soul. I acknowledge that I am blessed to be where I am in life. At the heart of my healing is gratitude. We have a choice every day to focus on the positive or the negative. We can focus on obstacles or we can focus on possibilities. There but for the grace of god, go I.

I handed the woman the food. She thanked me and wandered off down the road. Angels walk among us. Every person I meet is god. I do my best to stay conscious of that. I went back to the restaurant. While we ate, numerous homeless groups of two or three people passed by us. I noticed a high number of First Nations people amongst them. I've looked up the stats online. In 2018, 66% of homeless people in Thunder Bay identified as First Nations. This is not a singular example of this problem – it exists in many cities across Canada. The cultural revitalization helps, it really does – so many First Nations people have been healed by being able to practice ceremony again, to speak their language, to engage in sweat lodges, and to return to their spiritual roots. But it's a slow process, and it takes time – it takes generations to make positive change. We need to do more as a nation. I'm not sure I have the answers...we just need to do more.

When a culture is systematically rooted out, destroyed, made illegal, and entire generations are mistreated and abused in institutions – like Residential schools – the results of the nightmares endured cannot be "fixed" by tossing some money at it and offering unguided help. Every home, every family needs to heal. And if a person grows up in a dysfunctional home that was broken by the system, we cannot expect it to heal itself in one or two generations.

To everyone who I have listened to who is impatient about the time it takes for an entire people to heal, let us replace our impatience with empathy. Let us replace it with compassion. Let us replace it with learning and understanding. Let us replace it with better solutions.

After visiting all the sites I had visited in the previous two days – the Pictographs, Kakabeka Falls, the Sleeping Giant, Mount McKay – and being filled with such love and appreciation for those places, it seemed fitting that I saw the other side of the coin. The side that reflects a very harsh reality for a very real, living, breathing, culture – one that isn't stuck in the legends, the myths, and the magic but in the reality of their struggles. This side of the coin deserves more than just our admiration and curiosity. The First Nations are the rightful keepers of this land.

After we finished eating, I said good-bye to my wonderful hostess Monique. She headed home, and I headed to the hotel for the night. All my gear was already packed on my bike, so I headed right over. At the Days Inn and Suites, I was greeted by wonderful staff who were happy to say hello to any and all the WRWR riders. A most awesome woman at the front desk, Donna I believe, allowed me to keep my bike under the cover of the roof in front of the hotel. Truth is, I always try to find a covered overnight space for my bike, in case the weather turns foul. Stella is a bit of a diva that way.

After settling into my room and unpacking my belongings, I headed out in search of local amethyst. Following my phone GPS, I ended up at a lovely little gift shop I'd found on Google that claimed to sell amethyst. Well guess who I found?! None other than Lorna, the owner of the Panorama mine! Lorna, an elderly woman who looked far past her working years, was tucked into the back of the little shop. It was her and her husband's mine that I had been trying to see the day before. What luck! I hadn't chosen their shop on purpose – thank you synchronicity! They had lots of bags of raw amethyst chunks, but I didn't want that much. I only wanted five pieces to bring back to Windsor with me. I asked Lorna for just the five pieces. She walked back to her lapidary table, chose some pieces, and brought them up to show me. Perfect! Ever so grateful to have found what I was looking for, I tucked my treasures away into my saddlebag, and headed back to the hotel.

That night I was expecting Joanne from Windsor to arrive, along with Ashley, from the Netherlands. Joanne was a member of my riding club, the Canadian Motorcycle Cruisers. Ashley had come across just to participate in the Canadian leg of the WRWR, and to see some family while she was there. Joanne had met her in the Facebook group and had offered to ride up to Thunder Bay with her. I was looking very forward to meeting Ashley, and I was anxious to meet any other riders – the official leg of our relay ride was tomorrow! Oh my god!! Tomorrow I was going to participate in the largest motorcycle relay ever! With amazing women!

I waited until past supper time for the gals to arrive. They didn't. So I decided to head over to the restaurant and grab some dinner. Leaving instructions at the front desk to allow Joanne into our room, I left hoping I would see her soon. I was eating dinner at a place just across the parking lot, and as I was finishing up, I got a text that they arrived in Thunder Bay, where was I? Quickly, I strode across the parking lot and into the hotel.

In the lobby, I saw a few women decked out in WRWR t-shirts so I rushed up to introduce myself. How exciting! Everyone was meeting for the first time, yet we treated each other like long lost friends and relatives. I had no anxiety about meeting these women. You know why? Because I arrived at the hotel first, and so it felt like my home base. I felt like I was welcoming them. My anxiety is weird like that.

I headed up to my room and found Joanne. I gave her a great big hug even though we didn't know each other very well yet, we hadn't spent much time together in the club. Exhaustion was written all over her face. She'd traveled up to Thunder Bay in two days – record time – by heading across Manitoulin Island. She and Ashley were hungry for dinner, so I went with Joanne to the lobby to meet Ashley. I was introduced to Ashley by Joanne. Beautiful with a warm smile, dancing eyes, and enveloped by a free spirit, I instantly felt drawn to Ashley's energy. Over the next few days, I would have wonderful opportunities to get to know them both better. All I knew of Joanne was that she was a small business owner like me. She was in my riding club, she loved to stitch and sew things (she had sewn my patches on my vest for me), and she had a dog. Three days from then, I would know so much more about Joanne, through our talks, our ride, and our shared experience.

DAY 9 – SEPTEMBER 19TH, 2019

Excerpt from Colette Tindall Edeling's Facebook page

WOMEN RIDERS WORLD RELAY DAY 205
THUNDER BAY, ON – WAWA, ON

Date: Thursday, September 19th, 2019
Start location: Thunder Bay, ON
Start time: 8:30am
Leaving time: 9:30am

Route Highlights:

Meet at the Terry Fox Monument for photos to acknowledge another journey across Canada. Kickstands up and it's a long tour along Lake Superior. Most of this route is a bucket list check-off for many motorcycle riders.
The photo opportunities will be incredible!
The day will end at the motorcycle friendly Wawa Motor Inn for the night.
Ending location: Wawa Motor Inn, Wawa, ON
Ending time: 17:30pm
Approx mileage: 477 km

WITH A LITTLE HELP FROM MY FRIENDS

Wide awake well before my alarm, I was buzzing with excitement as I stared at the ceiling. It was as if it was my fifth birthday, and I knew that cake and presents and surprises awaited me downstairs, but I wasn't allowed to get out of bed yet! Wow, Tracey. This is your life! Did you imagine back in 2006 when everything fell apart, that one day you'd be doing things like this?! Did you imagine you'd even still be alive? No. This was not how I pictured my future.

What about after you met god? Is this what you imagined then? The truth is, even at that time I didn't know what my future would hold. I thought my life would be over much sooner... like, by the end of 2006 or 2007, at the latest. But I kept living, didn't I? The Book didn't happen right away. In fact, it would take thirteen plus years to explode out of me. Still, slowly but surely, things just got better and better. Then one day, I'm laying in a hotel bed in Thunder Bay, Ontario, on a 12-day motorcycle trip with new friends, and at first glance it seems like I have no idea how I got there. But I got there!

And I always believed it would be good. I knew the Universe had good things in store for me, I just didn't know the specifics. I'm so glad I believed in the possibility of goodness because I'm positive that's what made it happen – my devoted belief. Most of my life, I had believed what my Dad told me when I was young: Life's tough all over kiddo. That belief had been stamped into my psyche at a very young age. Until the day I'd stopped believing it, it remained true.

Something else dawned on me as I scrolled through my Facebook waiting for an appropriate time to wake up my roommate. The date. September 19, 2019. Back in Arizona when I had been camping in the woods, I'd had a little booklet of astrology information. I remember reading that for Leo's, the number nineteen represented 'magic.' The information had stuck with me. Since then, I've always paid attention to the number nineteen with 'magic' in the back of my mind. Every New Year's Eve, I choose a theme for the upcoming year in hopes that the theme would manifest somehow. I themed 2018 the Year of the Gift – and boy had that ever manifested! In 2018, I got engaged, I got my scuba diving certification in Bonaire, I got motorcycle lessons, I traveled to Scotland and so much more.

On New Year's Eve 2018, I chose the theme 'magic.' Twenty-nineteen would be The Year of Magic. I just knew in my soul that 2019 would offer lots of magic – it included a nineteen! Ron and I were married, and that was magic but I just knew there would be more! That I was sitting there in Thunder Bay waiting with anticipation to participate in something amazing and unique – the magic was manifesting again. The numerology for September 19, 2019 – 91919 – it didn't get much cooler than that!!! Magic. Everything was magic. Thank you, Universe.

As soon as the alarm went off, I jumped out of bed, and hopped in the shower. Our morning went quickly. Joanne, Ashley and I headed up to the Terry Fox Monument for the morning WRWR gathering. At the helm, using my GPS, I led Ashley and

Joanne on the ride to our location. As we drove up the lane to the monument, my heart thumped wildly when I saw dozens of women, bikes, cars, cameras already gathered in the parking lot!

"WOOOO HOOOOO!" I shouted as I rolled into the lot on my bike. My shouts were echoed by the shouts of other women and men there to greet us.

I wasn't off my bike for two minutes when one of the organizers came up to me and handed me a beautiful, big Canadian flag to put on my bike. Double WOOOOO HOOOOO! Taking the small ones off and putting them in my saddlebags, I grinned with delight as the new, larger flag found a very welcome home at the back of my bike. I was also handed a Thunder Bay pin and a Lake Superior patch to put on my jacket. No way! Everything I had wanted but couldn't find the day before was literally being hand delivered to me. A patch, a pin and a flag – thank you, Universe! I'm not sure why I waste my time looking for stuff at airports and stores at this point – I should know the Universe has my back!

My phone in hand, I snapped selfies with and introduced myself to as many women as I could. It was thrilling to learn who everyone was. Some of the ladies were local, and a large group was from out west. They'd been riding for a few days and were continuing on with us.

I want to make mention of something. The police. The day before, I had taken my picture with Officer Rivet, and that morning, I had my photo taken with another officer who would be escorting our group onto the highway. Progress can seem small sometimes, but when I look back at the big picture, it's truly incredible. My experience with police had come full-circle.

When I had been taken to the hospital during my breakdown in 2005, I mentioned that I had a horrible experience with a mental health worker who had been dressed as a police officer. That experience had created a phobia about police that lasted for years. It had lasted until a counsellor had explained to me that sometimes police bring uniformed mental health workers on calls. That information had come six years later. So, for six years I had been terrified of the police. Seeing them had triggered my PTSD symptoms. Another seven years after that breakthrough, I was at a place in my healing where I could comfortably take selfies with the police! For me, this was a major accomplishment.

What qualifies as accomplishment differs for all of us. Here on the relay, a woman named Colette Tindall Edeling had already rode for two-hundred days of the relay. Some women were doing one day, and that was huge for them. They may have never ridden without their partner, or even out of their own neighbourhood. Some women were cancer survivors and wanted to seize the day. Some women were doing one leg – a part of a day – and that was monumental. One woman was riding across Canada and blogging about it (Duca Chica). Each of us had our own hurdles. Every woman had a story to tell and it included the 'why' of our participation in the relay.

For me – it was my longest solo ride ever – eight days. For me, it was about getting on a motorcycle in the first place. For me, it was a little thing that conquered a big thing

– like hugging a police officer. It was putting myself out there and doing something big with a group of incredible women. This ride represented the conquering of every phobia and fear I had. This ride was a culmination of all the work I had done to rebuild my confidence after having it shattered in 2005. It's important that we acknowledge our hurdles instead of comparing them to others. If I compared myself to some of the other women on this ride, my successes might seem small. Hell, Colette had mortgaged her home for the relay! But personal progress isn't up for comparison – we all start at a different spot in the game of life. Sometimes, just getting out of bed in the morning is crossing a hurdle...or stepping out the front door and entering the world...or going on a first date after a divorce. Progress looks different for all of us. I take time to acknowledge the hurdles I've crossed. It's important, and it helps me build my self love and my self compassion.

Before we were ready to go, one of the women from out west, Wendy Funk, made an announcement. She pulled out a bag and asked if we all remembered seeing the opening ceremonies for the Women Riders World Relay in Canada back in Vancouver. She reminded us of the woman, Marlene (aka Diesel Brajak), who had painted stones for the Canadian riders. We all remembered. The stones had been traveling across the country with the riders. These words from Mar had been passed along with the stones:

The rocks were hand picked and hand painted with the 4 sacred colours of the Medicine Wheel. This represents many things but I have given these in the spirit of the balance of the four parts of who we are. Physical, mental, emotional and spiritual. May our Medicine Wheel and our bikes always be balanced. Ride safe my sisters!!

The bag was then passed around so we could each take a stone. Mine was beautiful and so precious to me. Priceless.

Wendy came up to me afterwards and asked if I was riding for a few days. I told her I was. She handed me the bag and asked me if I would keep passing the stones along until we ran out. She would forward the words from Mar to me on my phone. I was to get in touch with Mar as well. I felt honoured and humbled at the same time to have been given the task. It fit nicely with who I am spiritually.

Group photos were taken, tonnes of them. Interviews with the local press were conducted. Riding formation was established. Then it was time to be off – Women Riders World Relay, here we come!

I wasn't at the front. I wasn't at the back. Joanne, Ashley and I were nestled around each other in the middle of the pack. My tunes were playing and I was in my glory! More Than a Feeling, by Boston serenaded me as we headed towards Wawa. What I loved about this song wasn't about the lyrics as much as it was about the music and the way it made me feel when I listened to it. This song feels like happiness. It feels like rock and roll.

Listening to the lyrics, I considered how I'd slipped away a number of times. Any lover I'd slipped away from, in my opinion, was lucky that I did. And I don't say that because I don't like me... but if I'd left, I knew it was because I knew we wouldn't have worked. We can't fight to make someone stay where they don't want to be. Well, I mean we can but it's wasted energy, and it will likely end in a whole lot of unhappiness and frustration. Likewise, I don't have to take it personally when someone doesn't like me anymore, for whatever reason. I'm strong enough with who I am.

There is so much truth in the expression, "You can't please all of the people, all of the time." If everyone likes me, I'm doing something wrong. I don't go out of my way to offend anyone, but by me being myself, and being authentic and true to me, chances are, somewhere along the line, some folks are not going to like me. I spent a lot of years pleasing people – trying to be what I thought people wanted me to be. When I found out someone didn't like me, it would drive me nuts until I found out why so that I could change it. In my early relationships, I'd conceded on so many things, without my partner even having a clue that I had. Also because they hadn't asked me to. I had just done it, believing I'd make them happy.

That's on me. I've put a great deal of effort into becoming aware of my pattern to people-please. I do my best to stop it. I catch myself sometimes, but that's ok. Progress, not perfection, right? My go-to reaction when someone doesn't like me is still to want to find out why, so that I can change it – but I catch myself now and I stop before I tell myself there's something wrong with me that I need to change. It's totally ok if nine out of ten people like Tracey. In fact, it's ok if it's less than that. In my heart, I know I'm a good person. I know I'm doing my best. I know that I am self aware. I know that I've done a hell of a lot of work to listen better, to be thoughtful, to engage with others. And any time I feel weak or that I'm not perfect or I lose my shit – I give myself Grace. I don't have to spend my whole life fixing me or creating some better version of myself. I can just be me. Like it or leave it. I'm ok with that. Plus, I have created, and will continue to create the best me possible.

I was excited as we rode that morning not only because I was livin' the dream, but because I knew that I was going to get to carry the baton later that day. This baton had travelled through fifty-plus countries already. When we signed up for the relay, our names went into a draw to be a Guardian of the Baton. Inside of that baton, was a scroll that every Guardian had signed – women around the world. My name would be on it later that day. I'd already had my picture taken with it at the Terry Fox Monument before we started our drive.

Only four Guardians would carry it today, and my name had been drawn to be one of them. I was thrilled when I'd been told! I felt like I won the damn lottery. Over twenty women rode out of Thunder Bay that day, and I'm sure every single one wanted to carry the baton. I had considered giving it up for someone else – but no one had asked me to. One thing I've learned in my healing is that if I want something, I have to ask for it. I have to use my words and let my feelings be known. It's called communication. In the past, I'd felt resentful for things I hadn't been given, but I'd never actually voiced out loud and asked for them. My bad.

I try to allow others room for the same lesson – to learn how to use their voice. If you want something, you're going to have to vocalize it. I'm not a mind reader, most people aren't. I'd dated folks in the past who'd resented not getting something they never actually asked for. As much as I'd been able to see their point, that I should have been able to just know what they needed, I'd also realized that, no, I didn't always know what others needed.

I had a hard time identifying my own needs, let alone anyone else's. It's important that I not assume that others know what I need. I have no idea how other people's experiences have taught them about their own or other's needs. I've learned how to create boundaries around needs by establishing communication in my relationships. If my friend or partner feels they have a need that is not being met, it's important that they communicate it to me. Please don't expect me to magically know all your needs because I'm not that person. Some people may be, and that's great, but it's not who I am. I know that. I communicate that. I manifest healthy relationships.

Our first gas stop was in Nipissing, Ontario. Twenty plus bikes pulled over, though not all of them needed to gas up (some tanks were much larger than others). Our Road Captain for the day – a woman who had volunteered to lead the group - watched carefully to see when everyone was finished getting gas. Then she threw her hand up in the air with two fingers outstretched, and shouted, "Two minutes ladies! Saddle up!" She was not messing around! Within two minutes, she was heading out with the other lead bikes, and away we went. A few women weren't ready for the departure, but they caught up. I would come to appreciate this style of riding more over the next two days – gas up and go.

Being a road captain is a big responsibility, in my opinion. I had a few people ask me why I didn't volunteer to be one for the WRWR. The answer is simple – I didn't have enough experience. A road captain should be someone who has been riding for a certain amount of years or a certain number of kilometers. In addition to that, they should have road experience leading large groups, hopefully with their local club or friends. I only put 5000km on my bike in my first year – that's not enough to be leading large groups, especially if said large group has never ridden together before.

Recognizing my own limitations is an important task for me. I've always been a natural leader when it comes to groups, but it's important to know my strengths and my weaknesses. I wanted to learn from these women, to grow from their experience, to listen to their advice, and to watch how they handled their bikes. It wasn't about me leading others it was about me being part of a group that was accomplishing something together with the best motorcycle leader at the front. Not me. It's one thing for me to be brave and courageous and lead myself on an epic trip, it's an entirely different thing to lead a group of women in a way that may leave the group exposed or unsafe.

In the next leg of our ride, we started to hit more challenging terrain: hills, curves, mountains going up and down and around. Whereas I had taken this road at 90km/hour on my way up, these ladies were taking it at 105km/hour. This was pushing my boundaries for riding. It was important to keep up with the group and keep us all together, so I kept to the pace. I loved it! And it scared me. I could feel my heart racing a few times as I banked the curves quickly, leaning over on my bike and pushing my handlebars away from my body. Our road captain and the other ladies who were from this area – Thunder Bay and Wawa – they were used to these mountainous curvy turns. These were their stomping grounds. Me? I'm from Windsor Ontario, the flatlands. We have to go out of our way to find a few curvy roads. In fact, there's a half mile road in Windsor called Canard Lane, it has a whole bunch of S-curves, and on a nice weather weekend day, hundreds of bikes ride it because it's the one of the only fun, curvy roads in town. But up there, up in the North, they had a rider's bounty for fun roads, interesting roads, all complimented by beautiful vistas, waterways, and heavenly sights.

My feet were in the pegs less that day and were instead planted on my floorboards for complete and total balance. Pegs, for me, were more for long, open stretches, and when these would appear, my feet would go up. There's something about the pegs I really like. Pegs are so you can stretch your legs out into a different position. This is both for comfort and so that your legs don't seize up. My pegs were in such a spot that I could stretch my legs straight out if I wanted or I could put a slight bend in my knee and rest my legs that way. Both positions were good and helped keep the blood flowing. Still, there's another reason I dig the pegs.

I'll tell you a secret… I kind of feel cool when I put my feet up in the pegs. When I'd look at other riders, even before I had my own bike, I'd always thought it looked cool when I'd see riders with their legs stretched out on the pegs. I feel cool when my feet are in the pegs. And if I'm a dork for admitting that, then so be it, I'm a dork! Me on my bike… it's all about how I feel on the road. It's about forgetting my worries. It's about feeling free of everything. It's about feeling in control. It's about engaging with myself in such an authentic way! If it makes me feel cool to put my feet up in the pegs, then hallelujah!

Lunch was in Terrace Bay at Drifters, the same place I had stopped for lunch with Kendra and Helen a few days before. It was awesome to get a chance to talk to some of the women over lunch, and to spend time with my friend Janice, who I had done some of the Ripple Relay with in June. The best part of all though was that I had the baton and the carrying case for it. Amazing. I felt so much emotion. I was so full of joy to be a part of this! The baton and carrying it represented so many things. It was like a trophy for thirteen years of hard work. That's exactly how it felt. It was like a thumbs-up from the Universe.

I also felt like I was carrying it for other women who weren't there yet on their journey, but would be and could be. I asked Janice to step outside with me to help record the moment. At that point, it was just Janice and I because the others were eating lunch. At most major stops, the baton was moved from one Guardian to another. Only a small number of women would carry the baton, compared to the number of women in the relay. Every woman who got to strap it on her bike or her back, looked like someone who just won the lottery when she took it into her arms. The baton was our holy grail. I wanted a video because I knew it would be the most important moment of the entire trip for me. Standing in the parking lot, Janice turned on the phone camera. I was wearing my jeans, my chaps, my WRWR Guardian t-shirt, the three-bird pendant with my Mum's ashes hanging down onto my chest, and my purple and pink face cover around my neck.

Holding the baton out for the camera and Janice, I said these words:

Alright, so I am carrying the baton, this baton which has gone all the way around the world. Thousands of women have carried this baton, signed this baton, and I'm carrying it today between Terrace Bay and Marathon. And um (here is where I pause, all choked up, fighting back the tears), I'm so happy and so proud to be able to do this. I'm proud to be able to be part of this event. I'm proud to be able to represent the women in Ontario here who are carrying this baton. You know, the organizers of this event have said that it's about, you know, promoting women bikers and getting gear and all that kind of stuff, but for me, it's more than that. This is for (fighting tears as I speak again) every woman who has never felt free at some point in her life. Riding these bikes is all about freedom and that's to me what this is. When I'm carrying this (shaking baton in air), I'm carrying this for the women in the world who aren't free yet. I want you to be, Sista!! Thanks, God for this opportunity.

My words were entirely unplanned. They came out of my heart in that special moment with me and the baton and Janice. I could have babbled on for hours about everything that baton meant to me. How the baton represented the moment I forced myself to move past the liquor store and just go for a walk instead of relapsing and having a drink. It represented me hiking for miles and miles through the hills in Arizona, working off my anxiety instead of having a cigarette or a joint or a drink. It represented years of affirmations, reprogramming a lifetime of negative self talk and limiting beliefs. It represented pulling myself out of bed and forcing myself to get the day on, even though I just wanted to curl up and cry all day. It represented me running terrified through the streets of Toronto thinking horrible people were after me. The nine months of hell after my breakdown before I gained enough strength and sanity to walk out the door. The baton stood for facing my financial fears and signing a three-year lease for a business I had no idea how to run. It represented me sitting at a table in front of three defense lawyers and answering their questions about why I'd allowed myself to be abused by an adult male when I was twelve years old. It culminated with me hopping on the back of a motorcycle even though anything connected to a motorcycle had been a paralyzing phobia for years.

The baton represented my freedom. My personal empowerment. My triumph over myself, my negative thoughts, and my fears. The baton represented a new story that I could tell in which there was no victim, there was no villain...there was a woman in emotional control of her own life and choices. And more than anything, it represented an authentic desire to help and support other women in their journeys toward the same awakened experiences too.

Janice helped me strap the case onto my back. I felt like King Arthur strapping on Excalibur. I felt like a warrior – Rainbow Warrior Goddess of Love! The case carried the precious cargo of the baton, and a few other items crucial to the relay. As I said, I'd met Janice during the Ripple Relay. Janice was one of my motorcycle heroes. She'd been riding for years, and had been all around the world on motorcycles. She epitomized the free woman to me. Always one to wear all her gear, even in the middle of summer, she was a walking spokesperson for motorcycle safety. I'm sure she'd shake her head at me if she saw me hopping on my motorcycle without my leather jacket in the warm weather. I was thrilled when we'd met up in Thunder Bay for the main relay. Everyone needs a Janice in their life... a strong woman, a good role model, and a hell of a nice person. Having one of my motorcycle heroes strap the baton onto my back, well that was just another piece of awesome magic.

Before we left, I got a selfie of myself with Colette Tindall Edeling. In the picture, I can see the baton case on my back and the strap coming across my shoulder. I spoke to Colette for a few moments. I had been giving her distance since the morning, even though I very much wanted to meet her. She was from Australia, but she'd been on the relay since day one when the event started from Scotland with Hayley Bell (the creator of the WRWR) and a few other ladies. Colette had mortgaged her home so that she could take a year off and do the entire Women Riders World Relay. I figured that everyone wanted to meet her and talk to her as much as I did! I thought she must be exhausted. The relay was over two hundred days in. I couldn't imagine getting up and doing this every day for two hundred days. I told her I admired her for what she was doing – it was epic! She said, "You only get one chance to do this stuff. Live your life to the fullest! Money is just money." Exactly Colette! Oh my god, exactly! This ain't a dress rehearsal – show up and be counted! That moment, that kind of inspired speaking and connection... that was why I was on the ride in the first place. I wanted to meet and ride with women who grabbed life by the balls. I wanted to ride with women who had been to hell and back, who still smiled and made the most out of every day! I was riding with my heroes, a whole bunch of them.

Between Terrace Bay and Marathon, baton strapped to my back, one of my favourite bands came flooding through my headphones. I turned up the sound for Whatever it Takes, by the Imagine Dragons. This is the song I put on when I'm pushing myself to be more than I already am. When I'd failed my first motorcycle riding test, I'd played this to pump myself back up. When I'd be pushing through writing and needing some ooomf to get back into the flow, I'd put this song on. I understand myself now and what makes me tick. I love to be challenged. The challenge is what drives me and what keeps me moving forward in life.

I've had a hard time being settled in my life. Since the business became successful, I have my house, a healthy relationship, a car, my bike, I travel. What more is there? Can I just sit and strive for... peace? It feels like it's almost impossible for me. Since 2006, I have given my all to recreate a life for myself. Within six years of being homeless, I opened the doors to White Feather. And in the seven years that followed, I worked through all of my shit, I hiked the West Coast Trail, I bought my first car, I purchased a home, I learned how to scuba dive, I started riding a motorcycle, I sought out my ancestors in Scotland, I helped my Mum transition, and I achieved sobriety.

In the past, I tried to write this book because I wanted to get it published. I'd wanted it to 'fix' my life for me. But not now, my life is fixed. The Book offers me huge satisfaction because I did it – I wrote it! I completed my mission. The satisfaction will continue if even one reader tells me "your book changed my life." My goal was to write The Book I'd want to read, and as I rode my bike, carrying the baton, I knew it was going to happen. I just knew that the time was nearing. I hadn't written a single word at that point, but I finally had the frame for my story. I finally achieved the healing I'd needed to get my words and my message out.

I was free. I was free to say whatever it was my heart needed and wanted to say. I was no longer held back by what I thought people wanted to read. I was no longer held back by worrying about whether anyone else would like it or not. There was no underlying financial concern that had previously motivated me to try and write. There was no concern about what my exes or friends would think. There were no fears constricting my words. I hope my story helps. I really do.

Writing this book helped me. It really did. Writing this book helped me prove to myself that I'd let go of everything that needed letting go of. My anger and bitterness disappeared into the white space of the pages. I wrote without being motivated by a need for validation about my life story. I kept the story about me and my experience. It was utterly empowering.

Things ran like clockwork at each stop on the way to Wawa. We gassed up, we ate, we got back on the road. Fifteen minutes ahead of schedule, we arrived in Wawa at the huge Canada goose. Joanne, Ashley and I spent most of the evening together, checking out Young's General Store across the way, and excitedly sharing our thoughts about the day. Laughing, reminiscing, being exhausted together...I felt elated. Day one had been a success. There was a get-together at the Wawa Motor Inn for dinner. We all signed the baton and the banner that would continue traveling around the world. It was a great opportunity to connect with some of the women we'd ridden with all day. I couldn't tell you everyone's name, I met so many beautiful folks, but I'd ride again with every single one of them.

Joanne and I retired to our room before 9pm. We checked our phones and Facebook, and then we sat and talked for a while. We didn't know much about each other, except that we were both small business owners. Joanne's place is called SculptedYou – it is a body contouring business. Joanne's main goal is to help people strive for a healthier lifestyle, and a healthier body – her contouring can assist them on that journey to healthy living. We got to talking about our husbands and how we met, our life before our current spouses, our ex's, our struggles. This is how I connect by letting someone in, just enough to give them a glimpse of who I am, where I've been. It's not the whole me. I leave out a lot of the most vulnerable stuff, but it's an open door into my world. It's a cautious but kind start.

As we lay staring up at the ceiling in our beds, Joanne asked me where the name of my business came from. The full name of my business is White Feather Holistic Arts. I get asked that question a lot. It's a funny story. Back in Arizona, I'd gone on a day trip to the Natural Bridge with my good friend Leon. It was a beautiful spot with a creek, a little valley, and rock that formed a natural bridge. The moment we arrived I'd felt like I was on sacred ground. The place was special; the energy was high. Leon and I walked for a while and decided that we would each do a meditation. He'd gone to find his own spot, and I had done the same.

I sat down beside a tree, closed my eyes and emptied my thoughts. About fifteen minutes into the meditation, I'd been highly relaxed, in a trance-like state. My arm lifted and I'd touched the tree beside me. As soon as I'd made contact with the tree, as clear as I bell, I'd quietly heard the words in my head, "Welcome Home White Feather." I'd come out of my trance instantly. Holy smokes! Welcome home White Feather?! My name is White Feather? I didn't know what it meant, and I didn't know why the place was 'my home.' I had been 2000km from home.

I am White Feather! At first, the name made me think of angel feathers and doves – of peace, and love and all that good stuff. I'd decided to embrace my new name. Six months later in my trailer at Roger's, as was the norm every morning, I'd been awakened by a crowing rooster just a few meters from me in its pen with all the chickens. As I was slowly coming out of my sleep, I had a thought, "Chickens...chickens have white feathers. I live beside a chicken coop. Did the Universe call me a chicken by calling me White Feather?!" That had made me feel quite differently about the name! I'd struggled with the name for a while after that as I'd struggled to find the meaning in the message during my meditation.

Online, I'd looked up what a white feather signified in the United Kingdom (my ancestral heritage) and sure enough, it denoted cowardice. It was derived from cock fighting. The Universe had called me a chicken, a coward. It had been fitting. Perfectly fitting. I had run away from my life, and I was hiding in Arizona. I had been terrified to go home. I had been acting the coward. Despite the other seemingly negative layer of meaning, I'd still held onto the name after that; though 'White Feather' had lost its appeal. Fast forward to 2012, when I'd been getting ready to open my new business, two names kept jumping out at me: 'Inner Child Creations' and 'White Feather Holistic Arts.' You know why I picked White Feather? Because opening a small business took balls. It took courage. By putting the name of cowardice on the sign out front, I was flipping the bird to the Universe and saying, "Fuck you. I'm not a coward!" And that's the story of White Feather.

The Eh! Team
UNITES US
Nous Unit
EXCITES US
Nous Excite
ADVENTUREOUS
Aventureuse
COURAGEOUS
Courageuse
#WRWR2019

DAY 10 – SEPTEMBER 20TH, 2019

From Colette Tindall Edeling's Facebook page:

WOMEN RIDERS WORLD RELAY DAY 206
LEG 1 - WAWA TO SAULT STE. MARIE

8 am: Leave Wawa on hwy 17 to Sault Ste Marie, 230km ride, approximately 3 hour ride (Rest stop at Chippewa Falls at Batchawana Bay, approximately 65 kms north of Sault Ste Marie, photo op, Beautiful scenic lookout and waterfalls and stretch legs, 10 minutes)

11 am: Arrive Great Lakes Honda for event, 1 hour stop,
415 Pim Street ,Sault Ste Marie

WOMEN RIDERS WORLD RELAY DAY 206
LEG 2 - SAULT STE. MARIE, ON - PARRY SOUND

Date: Friday, September 20th, 2018
Start location: Great Lakes Honda, Sault Ste. Marie
Start time: 11:00am
Leaving time: 12:00pm

Route Highlights:
Leave Great Lakes Honda on hwy 17 towards Sudbury.
Very high chance of 5-10 km off road section between Massey and Nairn Center. The baton will travel off road for those with bikes capable and the rest will follow parallel on the highway. Stop in Sudbury for a possible photo with Big Nickel, 15 min tops then on to Parry Sound for the night.
Ending location: Parry Sound, ON
Ending time: 6:30 pm
Approx mileage: 467 km

MAGIC

I was up bright and early again the next morning. I lay in bed playing on my phone until it was time to get up. We had a big day ahead of us with a 700km ride planned. That morning at breakfast, a gal named Vanessa braided my hair for me. I had asked if anyone could braid my hair. I don't know how to braid my own hair and can barely do someone else's. This was Vanessa's only day of the relay. She was doing it on a dirt bike as was her friend Liza. Both were into off-road riding, and there was a special off-road leg designed just for the two of them.

As we gathered before the ride, I took out the bag of stones I'd been given, and explained to the ladies what they were. I read Mar's words aloud, and the new riders who didn't have a stone yet were invited to choose one out of the bag.

This day would be a day of lessons for me. I sure didn't show up as my best self. Well, I may have started out on the right foot, but it didn't last long. Everything about the day was disorganized. It started late. The stops ran late. We had to miss Sudbury Harley Davidson, even though they had prepared a barbeque for us. Where the previous day had gone seamlessly with everything totally on time, everyone in sync, everyone riding like a boss; this day felt awkward, and dangerous, and more than a little unorganized.

Ashley, Joanne and I met another woman that day, Donna, and the four of us stuck together. We laughed about the stuff that was happening as we waited (and waited) at the gas and food stops. There's not much else you can say about it when shit doesn't go right – 'it is what it is' or 'just go with it' tried to stay at the top of my mind...but I bitched some. I did it with friends, not the whole group. I tried to get the leaders moving by calling out a "hey, let's get moving" as we went way over time at each gas stop. The thing was that having to stop every 100km or less wouldn't have been so bad if folks stopped, got gas, and saddled up to go. That didn't happen once.

No one deserved my frustration. No one was in the wrong. It was what it was. And I was frustrated. Hand over my heart: "I love the one who's frustrated." That's what I'd needed to do that afternoon, but I hadn't. I did take time to do it later when the day was over. I'd love to say that I'm a perfect person, that I don't get frustrated, that I don't get bitchy, and that I handle every situation in the best way possible, but that would be a flat out lie. I could have handled the day so much better than I did, and I forgive myself for not having done so. Likewise, I'm grateful I didn't handle it worse. I'll do better next time. And...if I don't, that's ok too. I'm allowed to be run by my emotions now and again. There are consequences to handling things poorly – I come off as a bitch, for one. Hah! Yep. I'll try to do better, but I'll forgive myself if I fail.

So, that day while we were waiting for Liza and Vanessa to complete their off-road trail, the group was at a large complex somewhere or another that had a Trading Post gift shop, a Tim Hortons, and a few places to grab a bite. Joanne and I went into the gift shop looking for something for Ashley. Joanne wanted to send her home with a gift, and I thought that was a great idea.

While looking for a gift for Ashley, I came across a beautiful moose necklace and earring set! "LOL, I suck at buying gifts for other people! Look what I found for me!" I said to Joanne, and laughed. Joanne knew I wanted to see a moose – everyone knew I wanted to see a moose! It was all over my Facebook and I'd been talking about it as well. Heck, it had been on my Facebook since 2014! The truth was that I'd given up on seeing a moose on the trip. We were coming down into the lower north which was moving away from the most likely places to see a moose near Wawa and Thunder Bay. If I couldn't see a moose, I'd get myself some jewelry. I found a small dream catcher with the traditional medicine wheel colours on it – black, white, red, yellow – for Ashley. I tucked both purchases away quickly into my saddlebag so that Ashley wouldn't see I had purchased something.

I mentioned that we met Donna that day. This woman was awesome! Another hero for me on the road. Donna was a cancer survivor. She was a badass. She had just gotten her bike license that same season, and here she was doing the relay for a full day. A 700km day is a long day for an experienced rider. For a new rider, 700km is monumental! Someone asked me, "Why would she go if she was such a new rider? Isn't that dangerous?" Because Donna knew tomorrow wasn't guaranteed. Cancer survivors, more than anyone, knew the truth of that statement. There may not ever be another relay. There may not be another riding season. We have no idea what tomorrow will bring. So, hell ya, she signed up for the relay because she knew it was a once-in-a-lifetime opportunity, and she wasn't going to miss it. That takes balls. Donna was the kind of woman I was hoping to meet on the relay – a woman who lived big!

I was tired. It was getting dark and past the time when we were supposed to be done for the day. Our arrival time in Parry Sound was supposed to be at 6:30pm. The sun had set beyond the horizon and we still had almost two hours to go.

And then I saw it.

A MOOSE!!! OH MY GOD, A MOOSE!!!! My left arm went up in the air waving wildly. Others were pointing at it too. I started to stamp my feet excitedly up and down on the floorboards doing an impromptu happy dance. I couldn't slow down or stop because I had to keep the group ride moving, but, oh, he was magnificent, massive, with a full, huge rack of antlers on top of his head. This was the bull moose of bull mooses! Even better, he was no danger to our group because he was across the highway with a median between us. Still, he was very close so I could see him perfectly. My heart was pounding. I saw his huge, hulking body mounted on top of legs that looked too small to hold his heavy weight. His head swung up for a moment, and I was able to look into both of his eyes. They were god's eyes. Big dark pools of blackness, ready to pull me in to swim in the unknown of eternity. It was the wisdom of billions of eons looking back at me. And it all happened in a split-second flash.

"Whoooo hoooooo!" I shouted. I let out some screams of joy too! Prince was playing on my headphones – I made a special note of that. I love Prince. Sexually ambiguous. A genius. Totally comfortable in his own skin. Wildly out of the box. Authentic.

These are traits I prize in people. He was perfectly purple for my moose moment.

I would like to take a moment to point something out. In my saddlebags was the moose jewelry and the dreamcatcher that I had purchased earlier in the day. I also had the moose coin in my pocket. Somehow that dream catcher worked magic with the moose earring, pendant and coin giving me my moose sighting. My dream to see a real live moose came true that day. This was a dream I'd had for a great many years. The Universe granted me the magic to see the moose on the most magical of journeys. A dream catcher, some jewelry, a pewter coin – I had no idea I was helping the Universe to weave a spell when I tucked them together into my saddlebags and pocket.

When we stopped for gas, I ran up to the leader and Road Captain with a huge smile.

"Forget any bitching I did today about being late! We were perfectly on time! A moose!!! Wooo hoooo!" I said to her as I laughed. I hugged her. Laughing back with me, she shared my excitement about the moose. I'm sure she'd seen a million moose because she lived up here, but she generously shared in my joy.

What a lesson! Everything happens for a reason. I need to remember that sometimes. If we had been on time that day, I never would have seen my moose. Because we were late, there he was waiting to say hello. Thank you, Universe. The frustration of the day slipped from my consciousness (like a moose snort). I was floating on cloud ten – far above cloud nine. I'd seen a moose! It hadn't been just some silly dream, but a deeper, important must for my heart and soul. I love nature. The moose represents some very powerful energies that I admire. Seeing a moose existed in the same giant spiritual energy as being gifted an eagle feather. It was a wonderful omen from the Universe. A great gift to let me know I was exactly where I was supposed to be. I felt like god was saying, "You're here. You finally made it. Congratulations!"

At that last gas stop, Donna revealed that she was not comfortable riding in the dark at the speed we were driving. This was her first night-time riding experience. Damn! I wasn't too keen on night riding either, but I had gotten some experience over the summer before the trip. Joanne let the Road Captain know about Donna's situation and asked that we slow down just a bit and bring it back to the speed limit.

As we were all pulling out of the gas station, Donna's bike stalled. The leader saw this, but likely thinking the bike would start in a minute, she rode on, as did a few other women. After a little fiddling around, Donna's bike got started again.

I looked at Joanne and said, "Do you want to lead?"

Joanne was already in the lead position.

She looked at me with wide eyes and said, "Um, no."

About a dozen women were behind us, and the lead bikes were getting way ahead of us. No one looking back at me volunteered to lead.

"Ok, I'll do it," I announced; the courage to take on the lead zipping into me as I said the words. I checked that everyone was ready, and off we went. I had never led a group like this. I drove what I thought was the speed limit, 90 km/hour. My bike speedometer could have been off because I found out later that I was going closer to 85 km/hour.

No matter, I stayed at that speed because I knew Donna wasn't comfortable going any faster. Yes, we all wanted to get to the hotel and get off our bikes by that point. It was late, but group safety comes first.

Janice, not knowing it was me up front, rode her bike up to me with the intention of taking the lead. I would have given it, but when she saw it was me, she stayed back behind me and motioned for me to keep leading. It was dark. A dozen women were depending on me to lead us safely. All my focus was 100% on my task.

After about half-an-hour, we found the other three bikes that had gone ahead. They had pulled over to wait. They pulled out in front of us to lead again. But the Road Captain sped up to 105 km/hour again. I kept my speed at 90km/hour. Eventually the lead slowed down, seeing that the rest of us were going slower. It may have been frustrating to some other riders. We all wanted to get in. But the code is that you ride to the level of your newest rider. I didn't care if anyone else was pissed about our speed. I didn't care if anyone thought I was a shit leader. What I cared about was that Donna felt safe on her bike. And she did. And we all got there. Donna thanked me, and I felt a surge of happiness for my choices.

As we rolled into Parry Sound up to the restaurant where everyone was meeting, we were greeted by whoops and hollers and cheering. A crowd was waiting for us! Many of the crowd were women who would be joining us the following morning. My friend Maria was there. She was the Canadian Ambassador and I rode with her in June on the Ripple Relay.

When I got off my bike, I felt a wave of exhaustion slam into my body. This wasn't kind-of exhausted. This was fall-over-dead exhausted. It must have been written all over my face because someone tried to hand me a beer. I said no thank you, but mentioned I was starving. A sandwich appeared under my nose, and I happily accepted. I didn't stay long at the restaurant. Ashley, Joanne, Donna and I rode back to the hotel and called it a night. Joanne and I started tired-laughing in the hall on the way up to the room. Tired-laughing is when you are so exhausted that when something even minorly funny happens, you start laughing and can't stop. I was letting out the entire day's frustrations in one big belly laugh. We were dragging our luggage up the stairs, and it was banging and making a racket. For some reason, we just couldn't stop giggling. Then as soon as we closed our room door, we heard someone else who was going up the stairs drop their luggage. We heard it crashing down the stairs which sent us into further fits of laughter.

I fell onto the bed. While Joanne took a bath, I made a short video about the moose. I wanted to capture the feelings that were still dancing inside of me about that moment. You can tell I'm exhausted in the video, but my joy and my happiness come shining through with the laughter in my voice, and the pure elation at having finally seen a moose! I was too exhausted to journal. I was too exhausted to do much else. I called Ron to tell him the highlights of the day (the moose! the moose!), and after wishing him good night and telling him how much I loved him, I crashed into a wonderful sleep.

photo: Tim Butcher

DAY 11 – SEPTEMBER 21ST, 2019

WOMEN RIDER'S WORLD RELAY, DAY 207

LEG 1

7:30am – KSU (Kickstands up) Super 8 Parry Sound
8:45 – gas stop, Shell, Creemore
9:00am – KSU to Mildmay
10:15 – rest stop in Mildmay at Sandy's restaurant, and gas up
11:15 – KSU – heading to Grand Bend

LEG 2

11:15 – country ride to Grand Bend Motorplex
11:45 – Renegades Diner, Bayfield
12:45 – KSU – heading to Hwy 21 and a short trip with views of Lake Huron before hitting the strip at Grand Bend Motorplex
13:30 - Arrive at Grand Bend Motorplex. If you have ever wanted to try something completely new & different now is your chance!
15:00 - KSU and off to Hamilton. If time permits the ride will go along Hwy 2 instead of the 403.

LEG 3

15:00 - KSU from Grand Bend Motorplex16:15 - Stop in Woodstock, 101km, 1 hr, for fuel
18:00 - Depending on timing (baton MUST keep moving) & size of group either follow Hwy 2 or the 403. End Day at Super 8
Checkered Flag diner to follow, hosted by the MCC.

SHINE ON

Once again, I woke up way too early. Getting four to five hours sleep a night was beginning to wear on my system, and yet, there I was, wide awake every morning by three or four. I lay there for a while and rehashed the previous day's events with special highlights on the moose. I played on Facebook for a bit, checking all the posts online for the WRWR. We were already making the newsreels in the local press. As soon as I saw Joanne was awake, I hopped out of bed and into the shower, ready to start another day!

As part of my morning ritual, I cleaned Stella and made her nice and shiny. After getting my luggage strapped on, I was ready. Making my way to the breakfast room for my continental breakfast, I ran into lots of women preparing for the fantastic day. This was the 'big numbers' day with over forty-five women on the leg – double the amount I'd ridden with the previous days. Maria, today's organizer, had designated groups with Road Captains. There wouldn't just be one Road Captain, but three or four, and a sweep person for each group (sweep or tailgun is the last rider in a group ride). I hadn't volunteered, but I'd been asked to sweep for our group. My friend Janice would be leading.

Joanne wasn't joining us. She had decided to ride with Donna back to Sudbury. She was concerned because Donna was such a new rider, and she wanted to make sure she got back safely. I asked Joanne if she wanted me to ride with them. I'll be honest, I was happy she refused. I was asked to sweep for one of the groups, and I'd have hated to give Maria one more problem to deal with. Also, Ron was supposed to meet me in Grand Bend, and my friend Kelly was joining us in Mildmay for the relay. I was excited about seeing them both! I was proud of Joanne for doing such a good deed, it was generous and kind. That's who Joanne is.

As we neared the starting time at 7:30am, it was clear that things would likely run about as smoothly as the previous day, except this time, I had an awesome sense of humour about it. I didn't care. I laughed as our KSU (kickstands up) time rolled by and we still didn't see our group leader. Waiting around, laughing, chatting, meeting new riders, I realized the weather was going to be warm enough to take off my chaps, so I did. I was so grateful. I hadn't taken them off since my very first day of riding. Chaps are heavy and they make washroom breaks a hassle.

While I was rolling up my chaps, a woman came up and handed me a brand-new tube bandana (it can be used as a face cover, a headband), or about ten other different ways. I, however, always used them for headbands or face shields. This one had a Canada flag on it. I jumped up, looking at her in surprise, and I said, "This is for me?"

"Yes, I brought a bunch, this is my last one," she said. I scooped her up in a hug. Asking her what her name was, she answered, Jennifer Pickle. I immediately started singing, "I don't want a pickle, I just wanna ride my motorcicle. And I don't want a tickle, just wanna ride my motorcicle. And I don't wanna die, just wanna ride my motorcy----cle." It's an Arlo Guthrie song. Since I was eighteen and I'd first heard that song, any time someone asked me if I'd wanted a pickle, I'd start singing Arlo's Motorcycle

Song. It makes me laugh; it makes me smile. By the time I got my motorcycle in 2017, I'd been singing it for about twenty-five years. The funny thing was, I never knew I'd ride a motorcycle one day. I laughed and said to Jennifer, "I bet you hear that song a lot!" She laughed and said she heard it way too often.

When I ride, I wear one bandana tube over my hair to protect it from rubbing inside the helmet, and when it's chilly, I wear one on my face. Wearing my purple Windsisters tube over my hair, I replaced my pink and purple generic face shield with my new Canada flag tube. I LOVED it! I positioned it so that the red Maple Leaf was right square over the centre of my face. With my big Canadian flag still streaming from the back of my bike, and now my face mask, I had completed my Canadian Biker look! Woot woot! Women Riders World Relay – Canadian edition!

Maria rushed out to the parking lot looking frazzled. She'd been dealing with some last-minute changes and administrative stuff which is why she was late. I gave her a hug and reminded her to breathe.

"It's ok, we start when we start, no worries," I told her. Everyone huddled into a group, and we got our morning directions. I had exactly enough stones left for each of the women starting the ride for the first time that day, but only if I gave my own to one of the ladies. So I did. She tried to refuse, and I explained, "The gift is in the giving, please don't deny me my gift." She looked at me with understanding, took the stone, and said, "How could I refuse then?" She gave me a hug.

We rolled out of the parking lot about forty-five minutes late, and I was smiling ear-to-ear. There was so much joy in my heart! We were a huge group. The sun was shining, music was dancing through my ears, I had my new face shield on, and I was riding my motorcycle. What else could a woman ask for?!

Our first gas stop ran late, and it was decided that we would be cancelling our lunch stop. I texted Ron to let him know to meet us at the Motorplex instead, and off we went again. Not long after we left that gas stop, something happened. The lead bike and the truck that was with us for the day in case of gas emergencies or mechanical problems, led off left down one road, but my road captain, Janice, stayed right. Here's what I know about group riding – you always follow your Road Captain, even if your Road Captain is lost – the group stays together. So, staying with Janice was a no-brainer. I had no idea if she was right or not. The Road Captain behind us, took the rest of the group off to the left, and so our riding group was alone. We were down to about fifteen bikes of the forty-five we'd started with. I was laughing a belly laugh under my Canadian flag face shield. I knew that Janice didn't use a GPS. She would write a map, and put it under a mesh wrap on her gas tank so she could see it– she was old school. I also knew that the route we were taking that day had been changed multiple times in the previous week, and road captains were probably having a hard time keeping it all straight in their heads.

A song that wasn't on my playlist, started singing my head – Tom Sawyer, by Rush. I could hear Alex Lifeson's guitar crashing, and Geddy Lee belting out the famous Canadian lyrics as drummer Neil Peart banged on his drums like a madman. My feet went up in the pegs. I was smiling the goofy smile of a woman living her dreams, and as we cruised down country back roads, I decided that this was my favourite part of the ride. I loved this. And what was this? It was freedom. It was adventure. I had no idea if we were lost or on the correct route. I had no idea what this would do to the overall day. But it felt like an adventure, and we were off on our own, making our way through unfamiliar, yet beautiful backroads. We rode by cows and horses, farms and forests. Hobbits go on adventures. I like hobbits. And I like adventures. I felt like a modern-day Tom Sawyer.

My playlist was apparently aware of what was happening because a song just as perfect for this moment as Tom Sawyer came on to match what was happening. Trooper We're Here for a Good Time sang in my ears. Exactly! Such wisdom in this simple Canadian classic! Life is short, enjoy it! When things are good, let them be good! Don't fill the sunny days with worries about the future or regrets about the past. And man, was the sun ever shining. The sun had been shining for my entire trip. Here's the truth – the sun shines every day in my life, no matter what the weather is doing. Yes, I have gone through some hard things, and there have been some tough days, but I don't make those days heavier than they have to be. When the tough part is done, I try to let it go. When things become difficult, in the middle of it all, I remind myself that there's a blessing in disguise. When I remember to do these two things, the tough days are easier, and the difficult events don't plague me with worries. I just trust. I trust that everything will be fine. Know how I know that? Because I've been through a lot of shit in my life, and in the end, I was always fine. I have a 100% success rate of surviving everything life has thrown at me. So do you.

As taught to me by my Reiki teacher, Annelle Henson, Dr. Mikao Usui created 5 Reiki Principles which are taught to every student. They are as follows:

Just for today, I will not worry.
Just for today, I will not be angry.
Just for today, I will count my many blessings.
Just for today I will do my work honestly.
Just for today I will be kind to all living things.

I teach my students that if they can apply one of these principles to any situation they are not happy with, they will have an easier, happier life. And if they aren't sure which one applies to a situation – always refer to the middle one – Just for today, I will count my many blessings. When we are in a state of gratitude, it's impossible to feel anything else. And I don't just mean listing off a bunch of things you are grateful for. "I'm grateful for my cat. I'm grateful for my job. I'm grateful for my family. I'm grateful for..." Because we can do that without feeling gratitude. We are just making a list. What I recommend and what I do myself is include the 'why' in what you're grateful for. For example, "I'm grateful for my cat" turns into "I'm grateful for my cat Serenity because every time I come home, she will look me in the eyes, and roll over onto her back, exposing her belly. And she will lay there, flopped like that, until I bend down to give her a belly rub." And I can't think about that without smiling in my heart. A smiling heart is a heart that feels gratitude.

Gratitude lists like this help me immensely when I am going through a difficult time or feeling anxious or depressed. Gratitude as a means of healing is a coping tool I learned naturally at first, before being taught about it. It happened when things were extremely hard. I was homeless. I'm not sure that I had ever properly felt gratitude in my entire life until that experience. But man, when I got into a bed with clean sheets for the first time after almost freezing on the streets for three weeks, I laid in that bed for hours, filled with gratitude. The entire time I was in the homeless system, I was overwhelmed with gratitude. I couldn't stop being happy because gratitude was oozing through my entire body.

I was grateful for warm food. I was grateful for clean clothes, for a shower, for a computer to use, for a snack between meals, for a safe place to sleep, for my three-dollar Walkman, for a book to read. Every single thing I was using throughout the day, I felt gratitude for. And that feeling stayed with me, quite literally, for years.

During my time in California, I was grateful every day for the sunshine, the beach, the people, a kite stuck in a tree waving at me all day, skateboarders rolling by, people walking and laughing, ice cream, hot dogs, my jobs, my cool beach clothes, my new friends, a beer, a joint, a bicycle.

And then in Arizona, oh my gosh! In Arizona. You see, I started to get sober there, and I saw life through new eyes for the first time. One of the first things I remember about moving into Payson was the little tiny wild purple daisies that were everywhere. Daisies are my favourite flower. Purple is my favourite colour. The Universe had sent me to a town to do my healing that was covered in wild purple daisies. Not only that, but it looked very similar to Muskoka which had been my happy place for years – all rock and pine. Every single time I went for a walk, I thanked the Universe for the daisies and the rocks and the pines. I hardly had two dimes to rub together, yet I had a very comfortable home, and a whole bunch of people who treated me like family. I was able to support myself through jobs, which I know were found for me generously. I had books, I had friends, I even got myself a $50 computer that worked. Almost every day I was filled with gratitude from the time I got up until the time I went to bed.

Things manifested so easily for me during those times – in both California and Arizona. I am positive that genuine gratitude is the secret to manifesting. When we are filled with true joy, the Universe wants to bring more of that to us, and so it does – that is the Law of Attraction. I've never had to spend time visualizing things I desire for them to manifest – it's always been done through the energy of gratitude and joy. And you can't fake that. We can work on it, we can develop it – gratitude is something we can actively create within ourselves, but we can't fake it. I spent a few years doing reiki, making jewelry, and creating artwork, and the next thing I knew, BAM, an opportunity to open a business, without me having a penny or credit to my name, materialized. Why? Because I loved doing Reiki. I loved doing artwork. I loved making jewelry. And so, the Universe manifested a business in which I could do as much or as little of each of those as I desired.

Even better? Teaching. Since grade two, I had wanted to be a teacher. There had been a great sadness when I dropped out of my fourth year of university and let go of that dream. It plagued me and I'm certain it was part of my deep depression for years. I was teaching a Reiki class at White Feather one day when it dawned on me, "Oh my god, I'm a teacher! My dream came true!" I felt Pure joy. And I love teaching Reiki. I have the ears of my students for a full day, and I cram as much positive teachings into those nine hours as possible. I talk about all things Reiki, but I also talk about ways to be happier, how to not feel brought down by other people's energy. I talk about self compassion, and I offer as many tools as I can give them in that time.

Nothing makes me happier than when I see a student or a client start to 'get it', and their life changes for the better. Every moment of my job is worth it when someone comes up to me and says, "Tracey, I want to thank you. My life has changed so much since coming here, and I'm a lot happier," or whatever it is they are experiencing. I hear that often enough so I know I'm doing a good job. Universe, thank you for letting me do this job. As jobs go, it's awesome.

We're here for a good time, not a long time, so try to enjoy the sunshine while it lasts.

TRUE COLOURS

One of my favourite songs for motorcycle riding came on my headphones while we were on our adventure trip with Janice that day – Freebird, by Lynyrd Skynyrd. Certain songs are just naturals for being awesome when you're on your bike – this is one of them. I associate deeply with this song. When I hear it, I hear me leaving an old way of living behind me. It wasn't easy for me to leave an entire life in 2006. But looking back on it from 2019, man, was it worth it.

The lyrics, they have meaning for me. "And this bird you cannot change,"– that's Me. The real me. She wasn't a drug user, she wasn't a drop out, she wasn't a sad, miserable person. This bird that cannot change, the core me, is smart, funny, she enjoys life, she loves helping, she is courageous, an adventurer, a creative, she loves her family, and she has a heart of gold. But my core self had been wounded as a child, and the wound expanded with choices I'd made during my years using drugs. No one else was responsible for those choices, but me. I'd wounded myself, nonetheless. I moved further and further away from who I really was with every drug I ingested, every drink, and every sabotaging decision I made. I hurt others and I wasn't true to them, but most importantly, I hurt my self love, I hurt myself, and I wasn't true to me. Oh my god, did I hurt me. Every time I cheated someone in my life, I cheated myself. Every time I made a selfish decision that hurt someone else, I took a knife to my own heart and cut out another piece of it. My soul aches, just contemplating all the things I did that were untrue to me. But I've also never forgotten that smart, confident little kid who declared she'd never do drugs.

My dream of becoming a teacher died when I'd dropped out of university. A piece of me died with that dream. I'd had dreams of traveling. I'd had dreams of writing. For years, I'd been involved in sports – soccer being my longest lasting sport of fourteen years. I had let go of my music – something else that was near and dear to my heart. Music had been an integral part of my childhood.

Who I became when I did drugs was never who I was in my core. She was the wounded self. The most beautiful parts of me got lost in the sea of drugs and alcohol. For those who only knew me during my heavy using years, age fifteen to thirty-three, I offer my apologies. You didn't meet me. You may have seen glimpses of the real me. But mostly, you met a very wounded, damaged, hurting, sad, broken version of me. It would take me years to uncover, to recover, all those lost parts of self that had gotten drowned out by drugs and alcohol.

There was a grieving process in my Recovery. It could only happen after I was done making amends with others and working through how I'd hurt other people in my life. When that work was done, I had to grieve the loss of my core self during all those years. I had to grieve the little girl who'd moved from Innocence to a harsh reality when her parents divorced. I had to grieve the little girl who'd met a very wounded man and was molested. I had to grieve the youth who had gone to someone trusted for help and ended up being hurt in such a loving way that it would take twenty-seven years to unravel to the core of that mess.

Alone with my writing, with my healing work, and drawing pictures, I would grieve the me I lost for over nineteen years. I wouldn't dwell there forever, but it was something I had to do. No one deserved an amends from me, an apology, more than me. And I don't give a rat's ass if anyone from my past thinks that selfish – it's not. There is no other person on this planet, more deserving of my love, my time, my compassion than me. Those reading this – give yourselves permission to do the same. No one is more deserving of your love, your time, and your compassion than you.

There is not a single person on this planet that knows the whole me – everything I've ever done, said, thought, considered doing – other than me. And because of that, there is not a single person who can offer me truly unconditional love. The same goes for you – no one knows everything about you – except you. If you want to experience pure, unconditional love in this lifetime, you are the only person who can give it with full knowledge of every damn thing you ever did, that you looked back on and wish you hadn't... every thought... every choice. Love all of it. Forgive all of it. Shift all of it into a place where you just know it was meant to happen, so that you can learn the things you came here to learn.

I love me. I forgive me. I'm a free bird.

HEROES

I enjoyed riding tailgun and being sweep (sweep and tailgun are terms for the last rider of the group)! I had the most fun when we were on our own adventure – not lost but taking our own way. That section of the ride brought me so much joy. Just like carrying the baton and seeing the moose, that part of the ride was my favourite part of the entire relay. As we pulled up into Mildmay, I saw everyone else was already here. The corner by Sandy's restaurant was a sea of motorcycles. As I was parking Stella, Kelly came up to me. Kelly! I was so happy to see her and to get to do more of the WRWR with her. Kelly is another of my motorcycle heroes. She's quite possibly the coolest chick I know. And what makes her cool? She doesn't freak out. She doesn't give a shit what everyone else is doing or thinking. When something goes horribly wrong, Kelly is as cool as a cucumber. She knows how to handle shit when shit happens. She has a heart of gold that she only lets a few people see. I feel blessed to call her friend.

After chatting with a few folks in the street, I went inside to find some food. I was hungry. When I entered the restaurant, people were happy to see us and I loudly declared, "There is no such thing as a wrong turn; only unplanned adventures!" That was my attitude the entire day. I saw the blessing in everything that was unfolding.

During our lunch break, the time came for the baton to be handed to Kelly. She had earned that privilege of carrying the baton during the Ripple Relay in June. I turned on my phone camera and recorded Kelly taking the baton out of its case.

"Here's Kelly, getting the baton. Kelly who took the coin all the way across Ontario – you can do it! You're on film right now, Kelly!" I said. As she pulled out the baton, people cheered from around the room.

"Goosebumps," Kelly simply said as she held the baton proudly above her head and smiled from ear to ear. She's one of the most humble women you'll ever meet. A quiet warrior.

I found out over lunch that our group was the only group that had been on the correct course – everyone else who went left at the corner, went the wrong way. Janice hugged me and thanked me for believing in her. I let her know I didn't know if she was on the right course, I followed her because she was my Road Captain, and that's what you do. My trust for Janice goes much deeper than trusting that she is on the correct route. I trust her to be fine, even if we are on the wrong route. In fact, that leads me down another road of thought. The Trust road.

I've learned how to trust that I'll be fine, even if I make the wrong decision. I talk about this one a lot when I'm doing tarot readings for clients. In the cards, I can see if someone is struggling with a decision. People are so afraid of making the wrong decision. And so, they stand there, in the place they aren't happy in, afraid to move forward, just in case it doesn't work out. I visually demonstrate how this works. I stand still in a spot, and I point ahead of me – "I think that's what I want to do." I point to the left. "I'm not sure, maybe I want to do that." I point to the right. "That's an option but I don't know." And so, I just stand there. Demonstrating what it looks like to be afraid to make a choice. "Here I am, staying in my unhappiness, afraid to move." I just stand there. I wait. Finally, I jump forward, "Screw it, I'm trying this!" But when I land, I say, "Oh, I don't like this," and I hop back to the spot at the left. "Oh, this feels good, I like this." Sometimes we have to figure out what we don't want before we know what we do want. But doing nothing will never lead us to that knowledge we will gain if we shift.

So, I trusted Janice's choices. It's not that I knew she was on the right route, it's that I trusted she'd lead us well and we'd be fine, even if we were on the wrong route. It's a good attitude to take in life in general.

After an overly long lunch, we were off to the Grand Bend Motorplex. We would be making a long stop there as well. Ron was supposed to meet me. I was looking forward to seeing him. It had been ten days since we'd seen each other! Once again, riders got separated from the group, but not our team. Janice kept us on the right path once again, and we stayed up with the pack. As we rounded the corner into the Grand Bend Motorplex, I saw Ron, my friend Jannette, and Kelly's husband Todd! They were filming us and taking pictures. I was so happy to see them! While I was focusing on parking my bike up against the Motorplex wall, Todd, Jannette and Ron came running up to my bike with rags in their hands and started shining Stella – as if I were at a pit stop in a race and they were my pit crew! I laughed so hard! They were making fun of me for always shining my bike. I felt so loved in that moment. I felt so lucky to have such good friends! After hugging each of them, I started telling them all about our adventures.

Todd and Jannette. Let me take a moment to share my heart as I introduce you to my friends. Todd should have a patch on his vest that says, 'PR Officer' because from the moment we joined the CMC bike club, he made Ron and I feel welcome. Back when we didn't know anyone, he would make a point of coming up to us and talking with us. Todd's got a wonderful sense of humour and I love spending time with him and Kelly. They're an awesome team. We'd had a kick ass time with them on Manitoulin Island on the Labour Day weekend. It was fantastic getting to know them both better than we did already.

Jannette is another friend from my club. She and I have spent some time out on our bikes just the two of us. Jannette has a heart of gold that she wears on her sleeve. I'm blessed that she's taken the time to help me open up as we've become friends. She's a super cool chick, and the kind of person who'll have your back. Actually, all my bike friends are the kind of people who'll have your back. It's part of why I love riding with the club so much. And I'll have their backs too. That's what friends do.

The next event was racing down the drag way. First, two drag bike racers readied at the starting line. One of the riders had the baton. They did burn outs to entertain us and get us riled up, and then they lined up for the race. The Motorway lights were used to start the race, and they had the Official Times billboard showing us the race time! The rider with the baton won, of course! After that race, women were invited to race their bikes down the drag way. It was a once in a lifetime opportunity. I'm not a racer, nor did I have any interest in taking my bike up to dangerous speeds, so I stayed put as an audience member. It was fun to watch Ashley and Maria race down the track. Other ladies raced as well. Right after the event, I realized I could have gone up to the starting line, slowly pulled out at the light, eventually taking it into third gear at the most and cruised down the track – taking the race at my speed. But I didn't think of it at the time. During the races, Kelly, Todd, Jannette and myself hung out together while Ashley hung with the racers.

After it was over, the WRWR riders took a group tour down the track and back to the entrance. Then it was time to go. I kissed Ron, gave him a big hug, and I thanked Jannette and Todd for being there as I gave them big hugs too. I love my motorcycle family.

The rest of the day went very much like the start of the day, groups got separated numerous times. At one of the stops, there was even a bike mishap. With everyone parking at a gas stop, one of the bikers made a mistake and hit another bike. Sarah, the woman whose bike was damaged at no fault of her own, was clearly upset at first. Who can blame her? She wasn't even sure if her bike would be rideable for the rest of the day. I believe it was her clutch handle that was broken off, along with bent parts by the brakes. However, the situation was handled with grace by everyone, and luckily, Sarah was still able to ride. The mishap added more time to our day. It is what it is. I didn't stop smiling. I couldn't stop smiling! I was on such a high riding with a bunch of my friends – new and old – that nothing would wipe the happiness off my face.

Some riders were feeling the length of the ride though. Maria was exhausted. She experiences severe chronic pain, and this was her longest ride ever in a day. I could tell from looking at her that she just needed the day to be over. Things were disorganized, and Maria didn't have the strength to keep trying to pull things back on track.

She looked at Kelly and said, "Can you please take over – take over the route and lead this ride to The Checkered Flag in Mount Hope?"

Being the rock star that she is, Kelly nodded her head, pulled up her GPS on her phone, and set about the task of learning the route well enough to lead it.

The group waited at that gas stop for some time, so everyone was ready to go when it was (finally) time to go! Kelly took the lead. I fell in behind her with Ashley. This was the last leg of the Women Riders World Relay for me. When we reached our destination, The Checkered Flag, I wouldn't be continuing with the group any further.

Kelly rode like a boss. My tunes were cranked, and I was soaking in every last bit of the experience that I could. Our ride ended up on the 403 for the last bit, and this is apparently where some of the ladies were separated from the main group. We were flying down the highway, and somewhere along the route, riders got separated into at least one other group, maybe two. My headphones were screaming the song, Who Do You Trust, by Papa Roach.

Who do I trust? It's not a long list. There are very few people that fall into my 'trusted' category. My family. A very few friends in my inner circle. Trust is something I don't give out easily. What I trust is that humans will be humans. They will make mistakes and sometimes they will do things that feel hurtful. I don't take it personally anymore when people do something underhanded or uncalled for. They aren't doing it 'to' me, they are just doing it, and it's affecting me (or not). Their actions speak volumes about who they are, not who I am.

After years of working on it, I do trust me. When my life blew up in 2005 and 2006, I lost any shred of self trust I had, and believe me, there wasn't much to start with by that point in my life. Years of bad decisions led me to not trusting my own guidance. I was relieved when I met god in 2006 because I felt I could trust god. I couldn't trust myself. I had screwed my life up in the most colossal way. But I'd needed to surrender my distrust, to give myself a break. That's why I followed the guidance I was receiving from god so willingly – if god said get sober, I got sober. If god said go to California, I went to California. For quite a few years, I continued to say, "god told me...." or "the Universe told me...." as to why I made certain decisions.

For example, the Universe told me to open a business. In the time that followed, it started to dawn on me that my intuition was also guiding me. My intuition felt connections between certain events, saw them as synchronicities, and urged me to 'go for it!' The lines between what god told me, what the Universe guided me to, and what my intuition knew I should do have been blurred now. I don't know what the true Source of my inner guidance is, and frankly, I don't care because it doesn't matter. All I know is that it guides me very well. My sense of timing in both my personal and business life is pretty damn awesome. I jump when I need to jump. I jump out of the way, when I need to jump out of the way. I just know when someone is not going to be a positive connection for me, and I follow along when there's something that will be good in my life.

My gut instincts have led me into a successful business, a healthy relationship, and situations that grow my life in positive ways. It doesn't mean that every interaction is sunshine, rainbows and unicorns, but it does mean that every interaction moves my growth and life forward in positive ways. There have even been a few times where I've lost my cool with someone, and at first I beat myself up a bit for not handling it well. But then I show myself some compassion for my reaction, and voila, it ends up that cutting ties when I did was the perfect thing to do – it could have been disastrous if I didn't. There have also been times when I've lost my cool and regretted it. Those moments turn into lessons. Situations like that are fewer and fewer as my life moves forward.

Just because I'm not sure who is running the show anymore – god, the Universe or my Higher self – doesn't change my spiritual connection with the Universe. I know the Universe has my back. I know the Universe blesses me everyday in a million different ways – some of them seen, some of them unseen. I trust my Higher Self to step in when my ego is trying to take the reins. My ego slips out sometimes, but I usually rein it in within a few days, sometimes sooner.

The distinction I'm making is this: the ego is all about I/me. The ego is very self centred. It's protective. The ego gets scared very easily by anything that's unfamiliar.

I laugh when I hear people say, "I no longer have an ego." I call bullshit. Everyone has an ego. Our personalities are the ego. The ego pays the bills. The ego looks both ways before you cross the road. The ego keeps you alive when danger is near. The ego knows it has to go to work in the morning. So, I'm not too hard on my ego – my ego and I, we have to be friends.

I don't want my ego running the show when someone criticizes me or when life becomes challenging. I definitely don't let my ego try to convince me that having a drink would be fine. I don't want my ego in charge when it comes to dealing with peers in the business community or to create feelings of being better than people. The Higher Self though, it looks beyond the little picture of 'me' and 'I'. The Higher Self is able to see what the best solution is for everyone involved. The Higher Self is able to see the growth and the good in difficult situations. The Higher Self is able to catch the ego when it's about to make a fear-based decision.

I believe that we all have a Higher Self that is connected to our soul's mission and is interwoven into the web of connection that exists between all lifeforms. Some folks will become aware of the Higher Self and some won't. And that's ok. It's not that some people are more advanced or further along on 'the path' than others, it's that our soul missions in this incarnation are different. The people who my ego wants to look at and think, "my lord, they have a long way to go to enlightenment," might be there specifically to teach me not to be judgemental. That's part of their whole soul mission. How do I know that's not true? They could have passed every test there is for a soul to pass, and may have come back just to teach me something. In fact, for all I know, I'm the slowest learner in the entire Universe, and every single human I meet is an angel playing a role to help me 'get it' and meet my full soul potential.

Who do I trust? I trust the Universe. I trust that no matter what happens to my physical body, that my soul will be fine. I'm untouchable. I trust that everything is happening for a reason, and I don't always need to know what that reason is. I trust my inner guidance to choose a good life for me. I trust that All is Well because all is well. And when I'm feeling out of sorts, I remind myself that All is Well. There's a plan, and the plan is good.

ALL GOOD THINGS

Exiting the highway, we very quickly found ourselves in the parking lot of The Checkered Flag. Kelly got us there within fifteen minutes of our expected arrival time, which was miraculous. I saw Joanne and Kevin's bikes there. Kevin is Joanne's husband and must have joined Joanne somewhere along the line. Joanne was back from her drive to Sudbury with Donna. In the parking lot, some people were waiting and they cheered us in! Our group was relatively small compared to the size of the group that had left from the last stop. Kelly, Ashley, Joanne, Kevin and I found ourselves a high table to stand at in the bar, and we shared the day's adventures with each other. Janice joined in a few times as we talked excitedly.

There was a lot of laughter, a tonne of smiles, and happiness everywhere. The setting was so freaking awesome. The Checkered Flag is one of those super cool establishments that is a 'must stop' anytime you are within thirty miles of it. It's decorated with low lighting and cool stuff hanging everywhere – the walls, the ceiling, the bar. There's something interesting to look at everywhere you turn including a 3D white tiger jumping out of the wall, flashing signs, and jerseys! There's also old advertising posters and oddities; weirdness and coolness all around. The ceilings are very low, so it creates this feeling of being in a cozy, close atmosphere. I loved it!

I made sure to talk to Colette again before leaving. Wishing her well on her journey, I told her I had no idea how she was doing what she was doing. I'd been on the WRWR for three days and I was exhausted! Colette laughed and said it was tiring many days, but she was enjoying the experience and making it work. She looked happy. Tired, but happy. I get that. I respect that. Go Colette! You rock woman! Thank you, for inspiring other women to take a risk, to take a leap of faith, and do something wildly outside of the box.

I experienced something I didn't expect that night at The Checkered Flag. When we arrived to cheering from a crowd of folks waiting to see us, I knew it was the end of the ride for me. My epic adventure was over. I only had the ride home tomorrow left in my journey. As I stepped into the bar, for a moment, a thought flashed through my mind: Man, right now is the perfect time for a drink to celebrate. I'll be honest, it's a rare, rare day that I get a thought like that – like, once every five years or less.

When I'd opened my business, which was a hell of a lot of work, I remember feeling the same way. At times of true, great accomplishment, it seems appropriate to celebrate with a drink. Ironically, a drink is what would smash the accomplishment and turn everything to shit again. I don't think it's my self sabotage that brings up the thought. I believe it's a lifetime of programming – internally and externally. Societies and cultures around the globe drink in times of celebration. I can't deny that I felt a twinge of sadness when the thought crossed my mind in the bar that evening.

Sometimes I think it would be nice to be 'normal' and smoke a joint outside with the girls or have a beer to celebrate twelve days of awesomeness. I wonder what that would be like, to not be me, to not be different from most people? I have no idea. I haven't known a life without addiction since I was a child. It seemed harmless when my drinking shifted to pot use. I hardly drank for years during that time. Unfortunately, my experimentation hadn't stopped there. Add cocaine, ecstasy (cut heavily with meth), mushrooms, LSD, other chemicals and you had a recipe for disaster.

I don't know what it's like to not struggle with doing things to excess. The urge to gamble, to binge eat (especially when I'm emotional or stressed), to work myself to the bone, or the opposite, to take too much time off, all of it points to the fact that I am a textbook case for an addictive personality. And thank god for Reiki, meditation, crystals, amazing spiritual authors, breathing exercises, A Course in Miracles, drumming, self compassion, arts and crafts, scuba, my motorcycle – all the things that centre me. Because of having and using these tools, my life doesn't have to be run by my compulsions anymore. Food seems to be my cross to bear at this point – and it's a difficult one because I can't abstain like I do with drugs, alcohol or gambling. I have to eat. And so, I do my best with it, and I show compassion for myself as I struggle. If I eat more ice cream than I know I should, I try to do better, but I also forgive myself for this because it's better than the alternatives I could turn to. Beating myself up for it isn't going to help the situation, it's only going to make it worse. Feeling bad about myself makes me want to choose more self sabotaging behaviour – it is always counter productive.

I came to earth to learn, and man, am I learning through my mistakes! Mistakes are wonderful tools for growth. It did me a world of good when I stopped identifying with the word sin. In its original form, before translation, the word sin derived from the Greek word for spear throwing, which meant missing the mark – not being on target. When you describe it that way, instead of giving it all the heavy biblical connotation that comes with it, it's a lot easier to swallow. I've missed the mark oodles of times in my life, and that's ok. I'll keep practising my aim and get closer to the target!

DAY 12 – SEPTEMBER 22ND, 2019

HOMEWARD BOUND

Kelly and I shared a room that night. In the morning, I was happy to mill about outside with the riders who were continuing on the WRWR. I laughed out loud as it became clear that their day would not start on time. Breathe. Enjoy the day, ladies! Adventure awaits! I chatted with friends I might never see again. I chatted with Kelli – a woman I met the previous day who was continuing on the ride today. She wore this super cool green glitter helmet, and for some reason, she just made me smile and laugh every time we spoke. She had a great attitude and a killer sense of humour. That morning in the parking lot, she rolled her eyes and muttered, "It's like nailing Jello to a tree," as folks were trying to get organized. I burst into laughter – a deep belly laugh. I had never heard that expression before, but I'll tell you what, I'll never forget it!

Ashley was outside with her cousin who had joined her – she too was done with the WRWR. We hugged a lot, talked about visiting, and I told her to give her Mom a big hug for me. I'd become friends on Facebook with Ashley's Mom when I did a Facebook chat one day so they could talk. I do hope to make it to the Netherlands to see Ashley and ride together again. She's a badass woman with a super sweet heart and gentle spirit. I'm blessed to have made her acquaintance. All of us kept saying, "Fucking eh!" It was the one piece of Canada we wanted Ashley to not forget! I was going to miss Ashley, but I knew I'd see her again, in this life or the next. Soul sister.

Joanne, Kelly, Kevin and I saddled ourselves up after we had waved the WRWR riders out of the parking lot, and took videos and pictures of them too. It felt a little odd to be waving goodbye instead of riding off with them. I was envious. I wanted to be on the ride still. Before I had signed up for the relay, I had considered doing all of Canada – having my bike shipped out to British Columbia, and then riding all the way to New Brunswick. It was only ten full days of riding. But it was a HUGE ride. I asked myself if that's how I wanted to ride all of Canada for the first time – without being able to stop and see the sites. The answer was no, and I also didn't want to put that many miles on my bike without being able to stop along the way. My next consideration had been to ride the Thunder Bay to New Brunswick leg, but again, I decided against it.

September 23rd was the Autumnal Equinox. Every Solstice and Equinox White Feather hosts a big drum circle to celebrate. If I missed this one, it would be the first miss ever. Community looked forward to those circles. For the outdoor circles in the summer and fall, we have between two hundred and three hundred people join us. My friend Nelson leads the drumming while I lead the spiritual end of it, and we both get the crowd all pumped up and energized. We're a good team Nelson and I. He's a wonderful human being, so full of love, kindness and connection. And man, does he love the drums! I'm truly blessed to call him friend, and to get to drum with him as often as I do.

So, no, missing the Fall Equinox drum circle for anything less than doing the entire WRWR Canada ride wasn't an option in my mind. So, three days it was, and honestly, it was enough! As we rode out through the backroads towards Kelly's brother (we were going to drop in to say hi and have lunch), I decided that three days was the perfect amount of time. I was physically exhausted from sleeping so little for the overall thirteen nights of my trip. I had met some amazing women – badass women – during the ride, and I felt so blessed to be a part of the WRWR. The Universe had granted me a leg with the baton. I had seen my friend Amanda and my brother Bob on the way up. I met fabulous strangers during my travels, animals had offered me their energy in the form of huge statues, birds flying over my head, animals along the highway. There hadn't been a single mishap of note. I got to ride with Janice again, and two other members of my bike club. My friends Kelly and Joanne had been able to join me on the ride. I went further North than I had ever been in Canada. My longest solo ride had changed from one full day to seven full days, and I'd put almost 5000km on my bike during this trip alone.

I was a participant in the world's largest motorcycle relay event ever! I pushed my own boundaries and grew. I discovered the inspiration for The Book. The Book that had given me the motivation I'd needed to get through the hardest times of my life. Anyone who knew me in 2006, would have said I was batshit crazy, and rightfully so. I was not well. But I knew I was going to write a book. Knowing that I would write it one day carried me through homelessness, running to the US, being kicked out by immigration, getting sober, starting my own business, and facing all my demons from the past. I wasn't crazy. I never was crazy. I had a breaking down, a breaking up, a breaking open. I had a breaking through! It was a breaking of everything I knew into a whole new world, full of possibility and magic. That breakdown was the hardest time in my entire life – the crumbling of my Tower – and it was the best thing that ever happened to me. So, go ahead and call me crazy, but as I rode towards home that day, I knew I was going to write my book, finally. I knew that my dream was going to come true. And I knew I wasn't crazy. No more so than all the dreamers who dreamed so hard that their dreams came true.

The visit with Kelly's brother was lovely. He and his wife were fantastic people, and they owned a beautiful Koi fish farm. I was happy to discover he was into Tarot reading, and he had just received his Masters in Reiki. What a wonderful journey he must have ahead of him. Rain threatened on the way home. Kelly had already broken off from our group as she lived in Woodslee. Kevin and Joanne had told me to follow them to near Essex, but as we came up to one of the 401 onramps, I decided to break off and take the fast way home.

The fast way was the 401. Taking this route was going to save me twenty minutes or more and possibly keep me out of the rain. As I pulled on to the 401, I wasn't nervous at all. I pulled the throttle back and got myself up to 115km an hour. It wasn't until I got home and was processing the whole trip that it dawned on me how monumental that moment was. I had chosen to go onto the 401 by myself, and I wasn't nervous at all! Wow!!! That was new. I had avoided every major highway on the way up to Thunder Bay. It's not that I'd never been on the 401 before, but I never went by choice, and I sure as hell didn't like it. I'd never felt comfortable on it. Incredible! My thirteen-day journey had strengthened my riding confidence and expanded my comfort level. Sweet!

While I was by myself on the highway, rushing home to beat the rain, a song came on that fit nicely with this last leg of my trip – Ahead by a Century, by the Tragically Hip. Few things are more Canadian than the Tragically Hip (maybe hockey or syrup!). This song held a special place in my heart. On the eve ringing in the year 2000 (remember Y2K?), I'd gone to see the Tragically Hip in concert. It had been my second time seeing them live. The show was insanely awesome, magical. I'd been high as a kite on cocaine and ecstasy. Though I'd still considered myself an atheist, I'd had a spiritual moment that night. As the clock turned to midnight, the stadium had filled with glittered paper raining down on the audience. My seat was behind the stage, and there were a group of children– maybe the band's? Maybe the crew's? Maybe both – all dressed up, and dancing in circles in the glitter. I'd witnessed a perfect moment of bliss. I'd seen god dancing in the glitter.

The song, Ahead by a Century is about many things, but one of the meanings wraps around the dreams of childhood getting lost and becoming illusions as we grow up and face the harsh realities of adulthood. It's a song about living life to the fullest, reminding us that life isn't a dress rehearsal. As the song played through my earbuds, I realized, this is my life. My life hadn't turned out the way it was 'supposed to' – at least by any protective standards. My childhood dreams barely had space or time to breathe as they were quickly shattered by the trauma of abuse. I had to face 'grown up' realities when I was just a child, and the results of that created many illusions as I tried to cope as an adult.

But just like the message in the song, we can choose to make things better. We can smoke out the hornets that stung us, and create new dreams. We can live here, now, today, and show up for life. There are many parallels between the song and my life; it's quite amazing. Sometimes hearing it makes my heart ache for the dreams I had that died in a blur of drugs and darkness of self loathing. The truth is that in the middle of the blur of drugs and the darkness of self loathing is god dancing in the glitter. I can choose to write an ode to the tears. I can and do create new happy memories, new dreams, and I live the most amazing life I can, choosing to love me every step of the way. This is my life.

Pulling off the 401 onto Dougall Ave, I was only a few minutes from home. Already feeling emotional from the previous song, I immediately started bawling my eyes out as my headphones started to play Crimson and Clover by Joan Jett. It was the perfect song for the Universe to choose for me to hear at that moment, just a few blocks from home. You see, this song is my favourite song of all time. When I was eight years old, I decided that the original version, by Tommy James and the Shondells, was my favourite song. I loved the warbling in the music that made it sound like they were singing under water in the middle of the tune. When mp3s first came out, the very first song I downloaded, out of all the music in the Universe, was Crimson and Clover by Joan Jett.

During my using years, I had no spiritual connection with the song, I simply just loved it. But when I woke up, and started becoming more self aware, I started to take a look at all the songs that had strong emotional connection for me – and this was one of them. When I decided in 2010 that I was gay, I thought, "Oh, now this song makes sense! It's about the woman I'll meet and fall in love with one day". That was 100% right. I was the woman I'd fall in love with one day. "I don't hardly know her, But I think I can love her." I'm still getting to know the real me, but I will tell you something, I do like her. I love her. And I understand her a hell of a lot better than I did ten years ago. The closer I get to my authentic self, the more comfortable I am in my own skin. This journey of self discovery will never be over. I came into this world alone, I'll be leaving it alone, so there is no other person on this planet more worthy of my understanding, my compassion, my connection, my attention, and my love. Healthy relationships start with me. Know thyself, and to thine own self be true.

ON TOP OF THE WORLD

The final card in the Major Arcana of Tarot – the highest card in the deck – is The World. This card represents the completion of our journey, our task, our goal. A card of success and achievement, it denotes a time when we have a feeling of closure. The Fool's journey is complete. Everything has come full circle.

With my hands over my heart I tell you this: I do not love everything I experienced in this lifetime, but I love the one who survived it. Congratulations on ten years of sobriety and clean living, Tracey! You rock my socks. This book is my gift to you, dear child of the Universe.

The World Card
Rider- Waite Tarot Deck

ACKNOWLEDGMENTS

THANK YOU TO ALL OF THE INCREDIBLE WOMEN who participated in the WOMEN RIDERS WORLD RELAY, and a special thank you to its creator, Hayley Bell. Thank you to my friends Kelly, Joanne, Ashley, Janice and Maria who made the experience extra special for me, with their cool chick awesomeness and beloved badassery.

I would like to thank Stephanie Renaud for doing some of the initial editing for the book, and for her contributions to the book's direction.

A heartfelt thank you to Conni Ma'iingan. There were some difficult First Nations conversations in the book, and it was vitally important to me that all was conveyed appropriately. Thank you for your input Conni.

Many, many thanks to Chris Edwards and the team at Walkerville Publishing for for their creative work with the book design and layout, in addition to organizing the printing and publishing of the book.

A big thank you to my husband Ron. He was a great sounding board through the entire process, and I appreciate all his input and his patience with the time I spent working on this book.

I would like to thank my family and friends, who allowed me to include personal recollections from our lives and were gracious in their inclusion in the book.

Thank you to Tim Butcher for allowing me to use photos from the day at the Grand Bend Motorplex. His photography was spectacular, and it added a special something for all of us who were able to participate in that event on September 21, 2019.

Mum, you're not here to read this, but thank you for always believing in me and for supporting my goals and dreams. You waited so patiently for The Book, always knowing it was on its way, and always knowing it would be awesome. I wish you had been here in the physical realm to read it, but I felt you on my shoulders throughout the entire process of writing and publishing.

And one last Acknowledgment. Tracey, thank you for never giving up on this dream. Thank you for learning how to believe in yourself. Thank you for choosing sobriety and making this possible. Thank you for learning how to love you – you were always worth the effort.

A SPECIAL ACKNOWLEDGMENT & MAGIC

VANESSA SHIELDS, a poet, a writer, an editor, a magic maker. I've known this woman since 2011, and always called her friend. Vanessa is one of the people who always believed in me. We met at a women's retreat entitled, "Courage," and that word has defined our friendship, and our lives. Vanessa is a wildly courageous woman. As she opened her own business, Gertrude's Writing Room, I witnessed her courage, her bravery, and her fierce belief in herself and her gifts. Like me when I opened my business, she had to walk through all her own worst self doubts and fears. I admire this woman greatly.

I came to a spot with my book, where I knew it wasn't ready, but I knew it was good. I was at a loss as to what steps to take next. I had already had an edit done, and it just didn't...taste right. Covid had just crept in, the world was shutting down, my income was disappearing with my closed business doors, and in swoops Vanessa and she said, "Let me read it. Maybe I can give direction."

After we finished the edit together Vanessa reminded me of the artwork I did a few years back for her – a piece of totem art. Unbelievable is the only word I can use when I'd seen the painting again.

Spider weaves our dreams and our goals into creation. As the spider, we create our own vision, and we weave it into reality. Horse is present on the spider's body in this piece, it represents a few things, but most of all it represents Freedom. Horse is also the noble servant, helping out the world around him, not because he has to, but because he wants to. Wolf reminds us to stay strong in our individuality as he howls by himself at the moon, but also reminds us to never forget the pack. The wolf has friends, many of them, and those friends help him to survive. The ladybug brings us this quiet message, "Your dreams will come true, but in the Universe's divine timing. You might have to wait a bit." In the corner of the artwork is a sack of spider eggs. Each one of them a dream, a creative project, waiting to come true and be brought into the web of creation.

Remember how I said in the book that the artwork I drew kept coming true for me, that it kept manifesting into the real world without me attempting to make it happen on my own – like it was a form of magic? It's pretty amazing to me, that this, of all things, is the artwork I created at Vanessa's request a few years ago. Our stories have been intricately woven together into a piece of magic.

Thank you, Vanessa. I could never have finished this without you.

TRACEY'S TIMELINE

1972 – Arrived on Earth, London Ontario, Canada.

1980 – Moved to a hobby farm with my family at age eight. Attended Southwold Public School.

1984 – My parents divorced when I was twelve.

1985 – Moved to London with my sisters and my Mum in February at age twelve. Attended Westmount Public School.

1985 – Age twelve. Was sexually abused by a neighbourhood man.

1985 – Moved back with my Dad on the farm in June, at age twelve. Started back at Southwold Public School.

1985 – Sexual abuse started up again by same man, right around the time I was turning thirteen. It happened while I was visiting my Mum in London. I was still with my dad living at the farm.

1986 – At age thirteen, I had the neighbourhood man charged with minor offences to stop the abuse and get a restraining order in place.

1987 – Moved back to London with my Mum and sisters just before my 15th birthday. Attended Saunders Secondary School.

1988 – Started talking with my gym teacher regularly in February/early March. Age fifteen.

1988 – Suicide attempt. April 15th. Age fifteen.

1988 – Abuse with teacher starts Victoria Day weekend, May. Age fifteen.

1988 – In late June, I make new friends. Partying every weekend starts. Drug and alcohol abuse begins. Age fifteen.

1988 – Summer/early fall, I start counselling with a non-school counsellor.

1990 – I end the sexual relationship with the teacher when I turn eighteen.

1990 – I hook up with the man I will marry. Age eighteen.

1992 – I get married. Age nineteen.

1994 – I move to Toronto and drop out of University. Age twenty-one.

1994 – Begin experiencing extreme depression. First serious depression since age fifteen. Age twenty-one.

1995 – Have a meeting between me, the teacher, and both of our counsellors. Age twenty-two.

1996 – I move back to London, Ontario. Age twenty-four.

1999 – I experiment with a female friend. Age twenty-seven.

1999 – I attend my first 12-step meetings. I attend perhaps three meetings. Age twenty-seven.

2003 – I am prescribed Celexa. First relief I've had from depression for a decade. Age thirty.

2005 – In November of 2005, I have a massive breakdown. I'm hospitalized for five weeks. Age thirty-three.

2006 – September 11th. I walk away from everything. Age thirty-four.

2006 – I have an awakening in Rodney, Ontario on September 15th. I meet god. Age thirty-four.

2006 – I spend three weeks on the Oneida Reserve at the Oneida Family Healing Lodge. Late September into October. Age thirty-four.

2006 – I leave my ID, my name, and my life behind. I find myself homeless on the streets of Toronto. October and November. Age thirty-four.

2006 – November 11th. I get into Transitional Housing in Toronto for a bit more than a month. I go by the name Sam Robinson.
Age thirty-four.

2006 – I spend a week trying to hop a train illegally in Toronto.
December. Age thirty-four.

2006 – December 21st. I show up at my Mum's door in London. Age thirty-four.

2007 – January 11th. I set out on the Greyhound bus. I arrive in Los Angeles, California on January 17th. I stay at the LA Adventurers Hotel. Age thirty-four.

2007 – In February/early March, I move to Venice Beach, California, and live in a van. I go by the names Julie Nolke and Mary Auker while in California. Age thirty-four.

2007 – Cinco De Mayo Fiasco (May 5th). Age thirty-four.

2007 – June 21st. I arrive just outside of Payson Arizona – the Water Mill. I go by the name Mary Jane Seymore. Age thirty-four.

2007 – July 27th. I am baptized as a Mormon – Church of the Latter-Day Saints. I move to Payson and live with Bertha, and then with Roger not long after. Age thirty-four.

2008 – In November, I am stopped on the side of the road by unmarked sheriff's vehicles. I am voluntarily fingerprinted. My true name is revealed. Age thirty-five.

2009 – February 2nd. I am arrested after a smoking pot incident. Eventually I am taken into custody with Immigration officials. Age thirty-five.

2009 – May 25th. I arrive back in London, Ontario, Canada. Age thirty-five.

2011 – February 1st. I move to Windsor, Ontario, Canada. Age thirty-eight.

2011 – February 13th is the last time I ever use drugs or alcohol. February 14th becomes my sobriety birthdate. Age thirty-eight.

2012 – December 6th. I open the doors of White Feather Holistic Arts. Age forty.

2014 – In the fall, I initiate a lawsuit against my gym teacher and the school board. Age forty-two.

2017 – My Mum transitions in February. Age forty-four.
I love you Mum.

2017 – In November, my court case is dismissed under terms I am unable to discuss. Age forty-five.

2018 – I get my M1 motorcycle license. Age forty-five.

2019 – March 3rd. I marry my best friend on our 3rd anniversary at 3pm. Age forty-six.

2019 – In June, I participate in the Ripple Relays for the Women Riders World Relay. Age forty-six.

2019 – September 11th. I leave Windsor for a 12-day motorcycle adventure. I meet up with the WRWR in Thunder Bay, Ontario on September 19th and ride with them for three full days. Age forty-seven.

NOTES & WORKS CITED

Women Riders World Relay website: https://womenridersworldrelay.com/

Chez Monique info: https://www.westerlynews.ca/entertainment/short-documentary-showcases-chez-moniques-on-canadas-west-coast-trail/

Duca Chica website: https://ducachica.com/

Rider Waite Tarot Deck Images: The tarot images in this book do not belong to the author. The deck referred to is the Rider-Waite Tarot deck. Co-created by Arthur Edward Waite, a scholar, and William Rider, a publisher. They were hand-drawn by artist Pamela Colman Smith, who completed the commissioned seventy-eight paintings featured in the deck. Published in 1909 by the Rider Company, England.

The Addiction Solution: Unraveling the Mysteries of Addiction Through Cutting-Edge Brain Science, David Kipper MD, Rodale Books, 2010, Hardcover, 304 pgs.

You Can Heal Your Life, Louise Hay, Hay House Inc, 1984, Paperback, 272 pgs.

A Course In Miracles: Combined Volume Paperback, Foundation for Inner Peace, 1992 (orig. published in 1976), Paperback, 1249 pgs.

A New Earth: Awakening to Your Life's Purpose, Eckhart Tolle, Penguin Life, 2008 (orig. published in 2005), Paperback, 336 pgs.

Celestine Prophecy, James Redfield, Grand Central Publishing, 2018 (orig. published in 1993), Paperback, 288 pgs.

Whatever Arises Love That: A Love Revolution That Begins With You, Sounds True, 2016, Hardcover, 232 pgs.

The Law of Attraction: The Basic Teachings of Abraham, Esther Hicks and Jerry Hicks, Hay House Inc, 2006, Paperback, 224 pgs.

The Secret, Rhonda Byrne, Atria Books / Beyond Words, 2006, Hardcover, 216 pgs.

The Four Agreements: A Practical Guide to Personal Freedom, Don Miguel Ruiz, Amber-Allen Publishing, 1997, Paperback, 138 pgs.

Winnie the Pooh, A.A. Milne, Methuen & Co. Ltd., 1926

Birds of North America: A Guide to Field Identification, Chandler S. Robbins & Bertel Bruun & Herbert S. Zimm, Western Publishing Company Inc., 1966, Paperback, 340 pgs.

How The Grinch Stole Christmas, Dr. Seuss, Redbook / Random House, 1957, Hardcover 69 pages.

Bridge To Terabithia, Katherine Paterson, Thomas Crowell Co., 1977, Paperback, 208 pgs.

Be Here Now, Ram Dass, Harmony, Illustrated Edition, 1971, Paperback, 416 pgs.

The Tragedy of Hamlet, Prince of Denmark, William Shakespeare, New Folger's ed. New York: Washington Square Press/Pocket Books, 1992.

MUSIC CITED

AC/DC, *Back in Black,* Back in Black, Albert Productions and Atlantic Records, 1980, Vinyl EP.

Coldplay, *Adventure of a Lifetime*, A Head Full of Dreams, Parlophone / Atlantic Records, 2015, Vinyl LP.

Twenty One Pilots, *Stressed Out*, Blurryface, Fueled By Ramen, 2015, Vinyl LP.

Dobie Gray, *Drift Away*, Written by Mentor Williams, first recorded by Clarence Carter, MCA Records, 1970, Released by Dobie Gray, 1973.

Natasha Bedingfield, *Unwritten,* Unwritten, Phonogenic Records, 2004, Vinyl LP.

The Verve, *Bittersweet Symphony*, Urban Hymns, Hut Records, 1997, Vinyl LP.

The Eagles, *Hotel California,* Hotel California, Asylum, 1976, Vinyl LP.

Bruce Springsteen, *Born in the USA,* Born in the USA, Columbia Records, 1984, Vinyl LP.

Theory of a Deadman, *Santa Monica,* Gasoline, 604 Records, 2005, Vinyl LP.

Red Hot Chili Peppers, *Dani California,* Stadium Arcadium, Warner Bros., 2006, Vinyl LP.

Prince and the Revolution, *Let's Go Crazy,* Purple Rain, Warner Bros, 1984, Vinyl LP.

Elton John, *Your Song,* Elton John, Uni / DJM, 1970, Vinyl LP.

Chicago, *Feeling Stronger Everyday,* Chicago VI, Columbia Records, 1973, Vinyl LP.

Humble Pie, *Thirty Days in the Hole,* Smokin', A&M Records, 1972, Vinyl LP.

Avicii, *Wake Me Up,* True, PRMD & Island, 2013, Vinyl LP.

Nat King Cole Trio, *(Get Your Kick son) Route 66,* Capitol, 1946, Single..

Pink Floyd, *The Wall album*, Harvest /Columbia Records, 1979.

Metallica, *Fade To Black,* Ride the Lightening, Megaforce Records / Elektra, 1984, Vinyl LP.

The Grateful Dead, *Terrapin Station,* Terrapin Station, Arista, 1977, Vinyl LP. Lyrics written by Robert Hunter

Adele, *Hello,* 25, XL / Columbia, 2015, Vinyl LP.

Pearl Jam, *Alive,* Ten, Epic Records, 1991, Vinyl LP.

Supertramp, *Goodbye Stranger*, Breakfast in America, A&M Records, 1979, Vinyl LP.

Red Rider, *Lunatic Fringe,* As Far As Siam, Capitol, 1981 Vinyl LP.

Bill Withers, *Lean on Me,* Still Bill, Sussex, 1972, Vinyl LP.

Leonard Cohen, *Hallelujah,* Various Positions, Columbia Records, 1984, Vinyl LP.

One Republic, *Good Life,* Waking Up, Mosley / Interscope, 2008, Vinyl LP.

Eminem, *Not Afraid,* Recovery, Aftermath / InterScope / Shady, 2010, Vinyl LP.

Flo Rida, *Good Feeling,* Good Feeling, Sony Music Australia, 2012, Vinyl EP.

Kenny Rogers, *The Gambler,* The Gambler, United Artists Group, 1978, Vinyl LP.

Great Big Sea, *It's the End of the World,* Play, Warner Music Canada, 1997, Vinyl LP.

R.E.M, (original release), *It's the End of the World,* Document, I.R.S., 1987, Vinyl LP.

Snatum Kaur, *By Thy Grace,* Grace, Spirit Voyage Records, Vinyl LP.

Katy Perry, *Roar,* Prism, Capitol, 2013, Vinyl LP.

One Republic, *Counting Stars*, Native, Mosley / Interscope, 2013, Vinyl LP.

Sinead O'Connor, *Take Me To Church,* I'm Not Bossy, I'm The Boss, Nettwerk, 2014, Vinyl LP.

Alanis Morissette, *Head Over Feet,* Jagged Little Pill, Maverick, 1996, Vinyl LP.

Nickelback, *If Everyone Cared*, All the Right Reasons, Roadrunner / EMI, 2006, Vinyl LP.

A Tribe Called Red, *Electric Pow Wow,* A Tribe Called Red, Self-Produced, Released Online, 2012.

Imagine Dragons, *I Bet My Life,* Smoke + Mirrors, KIDinaKORNER / Interscope, 2014, Vinyl LP. Lyrics written by: Ben McKee, Daniel Platzman, Dan Reynolds, Wayne Sermon.

Love Inc., *You're a Superstar,* Love Inc, RCA Records, 1998, Vinyl LP.

The Revivalists, *All My Friends,* Take Good Care, Loma Vista Recordings, 2018, Vinyl LP.

Boston, *More Than a Feeling,* Boston, Epic, 1976, Vinyl LP.

Imagine Dragons, *Whatever it Takes,* Evolve, KIDinaKORNER / Interscope, 2017, Vinyl LP.

Arlo Guthrie, *The Motorcycle Song*, Greatest Hits by Arlo Guthrie, Reprise (LP) Warner Bros. (CD), 1977.

Rush, *Tom Sawyer*, Moving Pictures, Mercury, 1981, Vinyl, LP.

Trooper, *We're Here for a Good Time,* Knock 'Em Dead, Kid, MCA, 1977, Vinyl LP.

Lynyrd Skynyrd, *Freebird,* Pronounced 'Leh-nerd-Skin-nerd', MCA, 1973, Vinyl LP.

Papa Roach, *Who Do You Trust,* Who Do You Trust, Eleven Seven, 2018, Vinyl LP.

Tragically Hip, *Ahead by a Century,* MCA, 1996, Vinyl, LP.

Joan Jett, Crimson and Clover, *I Love Rock 'N Roll,* Boardwalk 1981, Vinyl LP, originally written and sung by Tommy James and the Shondells.

Tommy James and the Shondells, *Crimson and Clover,* Crimson and Clover, Roulette, 1968, Vinyl LP.

SELF LOVE AFFIRMATIONS

I invite you, the reader, to write any affirmations you would like to remind yourself of, here on this page.

Example:

I am worthy of happiness

____

____

____

____

____

____

____

____

____

____

____

____

GRATITUDE LIST

I invite you, the reader, to create your own gratitude list here. But please after writing what you are grateful for, write why you are grateful for it!

Example: I am grateful for my living room because it is a clear expression of who I am, and it makes me feel comfortable and cozy to be surrounded by my favourite things.

____

____

____

____

____

____

____

____

____

____

____

____

____

PERSONAL NOTES AND REFLECTIONS

I invite you the reader, to write down any reflections or notes you would like to jot down about the book here. It can be notes about something you read, or a few lines of a poem that you came up with while reading, or perhaps a song you were reminded of during my story. Anything you like, write away!

____

____

____

____

____

____

____

____

____

____

____

____

____

PHOTOS

Me, ready to roll on September 11, 2019,
heading out on my big adventure.

West Coast Trail, 2016.
Chatting with Monique, at Chez Monique's

Myself, Jess and Richard and his family on the West Coast Trail, 2016

The farmhouse I grew up in and visited on September 11, 2019

My brother Bob and I, September 11, 2019, Port Dover

Stella parked by the water in Gravenhurst. September 12th, 2019

Mckenzie, Amanda and I. North Bay, September 14, 2019

Tracey, aka, Mary Jane, Payson Arizona, Spring 2008

Drawn in Payson, Arizona, 2008:
"Blind Sacrifice."

Drawn in 2011,
in honour of the Leo.

"Sacred Feminine," drawn in 2012.
Serenity, my cat, modelled for this.

"Wise Patience," drawn in 2012.

"Bursting in Colour," drawn in 2012.

"Osiris," drawn in 2012.

"The New Earth," 2012.

"Rising Again," 2012.

"Peace," 2012.

"Building Anew," 2012

"Goddess," 2012.

Me trying not to tumble into Lake Superior,
at the Agawa Pictographs, September 16, 2019.

Me and Winnie the Pooh in White River Ontario, September 17, 2019.

Top left: Me, Helen and Kendra. Terrace Bay, September 17, 2019
Top right: Me and the hugest goose you've ever seen, Wawa, September 17, 2019
Bottom: The moose, Young's General Store, Wawa, September 17, 2019

Photos at Mount McKay, Thunder Bay, September 18, 2019.
Monique in top photo with me.

Photo of an eagle I took at Kakabeka Falls, Thunder Bay, September 18, 2019

Tracey hosting a White Feather drum circle, Summer Solstice June 2016.
Photo Credit: Conni Ma'iingan

Terry Fox Memorial, Thunder Bay. September 19, 2019.
A photo of the riders I would start my legs of the relay with.

Top: Joanne and I (at left), Terry Fox Memorial Thunder Bay, September 19, 2019.
Top Right: Janice handing me the baton at Drifter's in Terrace Bay, September 19, 2019.
Bottom: Medicine Wheel Stones painted for the WRWR by Marlene (Diesel) Brajak

Myself, the baton and Colette Tindall Edeling, Terrace Bay. September 19, 2019

Left: Ashley with the baton. September 20, 2019
Right: Donna with the baton. September 20.2019

Top: Joanne, myself and Ashley. Somewhere in Ontario, September 20, 2019
Left: Kelly about to put on the baton in Mildmay, September 21, 2019

Kelli (top); Maria holding baton (bottom).

Photos by the amazing Tim Butcher, Grand Bend Motorplex, September 21, 2019.

Top: A group of us outside The Checkered Flag, Mount Hope Ontario at the end of Day 207 of the WRWR.

Left: Me ready to go with the group around the track at the Grand bend Motorplex, September 21, 2019. Credit to the amazing photographer Tim Butcher!

The artwork I did for Vanessa Shields back in 2014.
This spider wove a beautiful web that brought our talents
and gifts together for the project of this book.

Tracey Rogers and Stella.
Open for New Adventures.

TRACEY ROGERS & STELLA

Photo by Petry Sijtsma-Poll, WawaNews.com
September 19th, 2019

Tracey Rogers is a business owner, writer, poet and artist. She self-published a book of healing poetry in 2011 entitled, *Becoming the Rainbow.*

Tracey graduated with her BA in English Language and Literature from the University of Western Ontario in 2012.

In 2013, Tracey appeared on an episode of *Life Story Project* on the Oprah Network, sharing her story of change, recovery and gratitude.

Tracey is active in the holistic community in Windsor, Ontario, Canada, where she resides with her husband.

A motorcycle enthusiast, a lover of cats, and always open to new adventures, you will most often find Tracey hanging out in her bubble of peace at her business, White Feather Holistic Arts.

Visit us on the web:

WhiteFeatherArts.com